JEFFREY STEINGARTEN

It Must've Been Something I Ate

Jeffrey Steingarten is *Vogue*'s food critic and the author of *The Man Who Ate Everything*. He trained to be a food writer at Harvard Law School and on the *Harvard Lampoon*. On Bastille Day, 1994, the French Republic made Mr. Steingarten a Chevalier in the Order of Merit for his writings on French gastronomy. Chevalier Steingarten discloses that his preferred eating destinations are Memphis, Paris, Bangkok, Alba, and Chengdu—and his loft in New York City, where he has recently created well over a firkin of cultured butter.

Essays in this collection have won a National Magazine Award and several prizes from the James Beard Foundation and the International Association of Culinary Professionals. *The Man Who Ate Everything* was a *New York Times* bestseller and the winner of the Julia Child Cookbook Award and the Guild of British Food Writers' Prize for the year's best book about food.

ALSO BY JEFFREY STEINGARTEN

The Man Who Ate Everything

It Must've Been Something I Ate

Jeffrey Steingarten

It Must've Been Something I Ate

The return of **THE MAN WHO ATE EVERYTHING**

VINTAGE BOOKS

A Division of Random House, Inc.

NEW YORK

FIRST VINTAGE BOOKS EDITION, OCTOBER 2003

The Library of Congress has cataloged the Knopf edition as follows:
It must've been something I ate : the return of the man who ate everything /
by Jeffrey Steingarten.
p. cm.
Includes index.
ISBN 0-375-41280-8
1. Gastronomy—humor. 2. Food—humor. I. Title.
TX631 .S72 2002
641'.01'30207—dc21   2002024676

Vintage ISBN: 0-375-72712-4

Author photograph © Hiro

www.vintagebooks.com

Printed in the United States of America
10 9 8 7 6 5 4 3 2 1

For Anna, Judith, and Sonny

Contents

It Must've Been Something I Ate

Introduction:

THE WAY WE EAT NOW

Technically, it is known as the Calamari Index, or C.I., and it measures precisely how far we've come as a nation of eaters over the past 30 years. In the sixties and for most of the seventies, calamari consumption in this country was among the lowest in the world. (They were most popular in Cyprus, Japan, Korea, Spain, Greece, and Italy.) Very few Americans would go near a cuttlefish. Everything about them was repulsive. My own Personal Calamari Index, or P.C.I., was truly pitiful as well.

And then, in the mid-eighties, the C.I. totally took off. Calamari began cropping up on every street corner in America. Raw fish would quickly follow. Today there is hardly a restaurant anywhere that doesn't offer fried, flavored, crispy calamari as an appetizer, paired with a themed dipping sauce. We love to munch on the multitude of crunchy little tentacles. We are amused to watch the curled rows of tiny suckers slide into our mouths. I have recently been eating bugs, as well. We'll get to that in a minute.

Thus, by graphing the weight of calamari the average American man, woman, and child consumes each year, we obtain an exact yet simple indicator of how completely we have overcome our inbred revulsion toward certain foods and, whether yielding to social pressure or truly opening up and evolving as human beings, have learned to love them. In the interests of accuracy, we should call it the Cephalopod Index, or C.I., because official statistics from the Food and Agriculture Organization (FAO) of the United Nations combine cuttlefish with squid and octopus under the overarching category of cephalopods. According to the FAO, between the early sixties and today, U.S. cephalopod intake soared by 184 times!

What better example can one imagine of the universal truth that no food is inherently revolting? Infants are not repulsed by the sight or smell of rotten meat crawling with maggots. Forty-two cultures around the world eat rats. And now, the creature that once inspired only nightmares to disrupt the Anglo-American sleep cycle has become commonplace.

What divine or cosmic force has wrought such a change? I would venture that at least half the credit is owed to the present author and his relentless international campaign to coax and, if necessary, humiliate people who hold on to phony allergies, bogus intolerances, nutritional nonsense, and provincial preferences. Once you master the chapter entitled "Fear of *Formaggio*," you will surely understand. Sadly, I nearly meet my comeuppance in "Taro, Taro, Taro."

As I related in the introduction to my first book, *The Man Who Ate Everything*, when I became *Vogue*'s food critic, I felt an ethical responsibility to rid myself of every psychological and cultural prejudice and inhibition preventing me from becoming the perfect omnivore, the ideally neutral critic. Six heroic months later, I had reached my goal, with two exceptions. First, I had failed to shed my distaste for desserts in Indian restaurants. But as I feel I completely opened my heart to them, I refuse to blame myself for what others might perceive a monumental personal failure. And second, under the press of time, I had temporarily recused myself in the matter of bugs.

Though insects are crunchy, nutritious, high in protein, inexpensive, and easy to cook, most people I know in northern Europe and North America (excluding Mexico) avoid them. Elsewhere, people are especially fond of locusts, grasshoppers, crickets, termites, butterflies, beetles, and the larvae and pupae of large moths. In *Presencia de la comida prehispánica*, Teresa Yturbide reports that when the Spanish conquerors arrived in America, they found the Maya and Aztecs enjoying roasted corn worms, tacos stuffed with grilled toritos (avocado bugs), and the red and white worms that breed and live in the maguey plant. (To retain their fat, the red ones were first roasted over low heat, then crushed with roasted tomatillos and chiles, and eaten with blue-corn tortillas.) Plus, they ate jumil bugs, wood larvae, green worms, the pupae and eggs of the big-shoed wasp, honey ants, vine ants, ant eggs, sage worms, and sun-dried chia worms, which are as long as your hand and have tentacles on their heads.

I will admit to an anguished ambivalence about bugs. My progress toward becoming a perfect omnivore in this area has been slow yet steady. I began in Tijuana, at the famed restaurant Cien Años. Mosquito caviar and most other Mexican insect specialties were out of season, but we were able to order fried crickets, which came with a bowl of green salsa and a basket of soft, warm, blue-corn tortillas in the style of Puebla. We formed tacos by wrapping the tortillas around the salsa and the crickets, and they were delicious. The little critters were sweet and nutty, and, as with other bugs I've tried, deep-frying had eliminated their squishy bodily fluids and rendered them so light and crisp that you might have thought they were delightful pepitas, salted roasted pumpkin seeds.

Yet I could not forget I was eating bug tacos. I kept imagining that the crickets would come back to life and walk out of the tortilla, onto the red carpet that is my tongue, and down my throat. I did much better at an amazing covered market in Chiang Mai, Thailand. Sure, I turned down the king-size batter-fried flying cockroaches, but I relished the deep-fried, inch-long, spindle-shaped yellow bamboo worms. They lacked both legs and faces, an advantage for the novice eater. For a baht or two, I bought a bag and ate them like Fritos. I love nearly everything deep-fried, but I especially love Fritos. My second trip to Chiang Mai witnessed a quantum leap forward. In the chapter simply yet eloquently entitled "Thailand," I share the happy news that my bug phobia has nearly been extinguished.

But all this talk about bugs is off the point. Most people who write about eating insects do so for the shock value, and although I am the last person in the world to eschew sensationalism, it does distract us from the fundamental lessons we must draw from our lives as omnivores and our responsibilities as mammals.

In all of Nature's kingdom, only mammals, female mammals, nourish their young by giving up part of their own bodies. For us, food is not just dinner. Our attitudes toward food mirror our feelings about mothers and nurturing, about giving and sharing, about tradition and community—and about whether the natural world seems inherently benign or hostile. Some people have good attitude and others have bad attitude. Which describes you? Just take this simple test. Read the two statements below and choose which one, in all honesty, you would be more likely to utter.

1. "I feel awful this morning, my skin is covered with bumps, and I can hardly see straight. It must've been something I ate."

2. "I feel light as a feather this morning, my mind is clear as a bell, and I've got a smile on my face for the whole human race. It must've been something I ate."

If you favor sentiments like the first, I'm afraid that you probably have a paranoid bias against the universe and a very long way to go. But it is not entirely your fault. So much of the world around us is still organized to frighten us about food. You would think from reading the newspapers that eating is the leading cause of death. It is not.

Nobody would recommend a nonchalant attitude toward germs. I have eaten raw chicken only twice, and that was in Japan, with peanut sauce, because everybody else was doing it. But the fact remains that food-borne illness barely makes it into the top 20 causes of death. There are 3 times the number of homicides, 6 times the number of suicides, and 20 times the number of fatal accidents.

I knew something was out of joint two years ago when several major papers reported the breaking news that Americans suffer 76 million food-borne illnesses a year, including 325,000 hospitalizations, and 5,000 deaths! The Chinese news service Xinhua sent out a dispatch. "5,000 Americans Die," they chortled. Okay, maybe they weren't chortling. But the American media had surely given aid and comfort to the enemy.

Are these numbers bogus? Not at all. But they were already more than a year old when the newspapers published them. (I recognized them instantly from my research on raw-milk cheese in the chapter "Cheese *Crise.*") They had been published in the fall of 1999 in *Emerging Infectious Diseases,* a widely available peer-reviewed journal of the federal Centers for Disease Control and Prevention. Old numbers do not belong in front-page headlines. One might call them news-borne illnesses. Why did the newspapers and the FDA want to frighten us? *Cui bono?*

The real news was that the number of food-linked fatalities was only half what had previously been thought. The headlines should have read, "Only Half of Americans Previously Feared Food-Dead Truly Are." Another CDC publication issued at about the same time was entitled, "Achievements in Public Health, 1990–1999: Safer and Healthier Foods." Let Xinhua put a spin on that one.

As the current craze for the class Cephalopoda demonstrates, acting fussy about your food is less and less in vogue. We've learned to be skeptical about most nutritional warnings. Now we know that salt is harmful to only 8 percent (or less) of the population. Much of what the government told us in the 1988 *Surgeon General's Report on Nutrition and Health* has been discredited, along with the nutritionists who believed it. We also know that eating lots of nonanimal fat does you no harm (and is probably better for you than a high-carbohydrate diet), that consuming bushels of fruits and vegetables does not lessen the risk of colon cancer, that drinking alcohol does prevent heart attacks, that nobody is so lactose intolerant that he or she can't drink a glass of milk, that no more than 2 percent of us truly have food allergies, that chocolate may even have protective powers. (Or maybe not. This tangled web is unraveled in "Chocolate Dreams," here-inbelow.) The eating public has dramatically relaxed, according to both National Restaurant Association surveys and the plummeting S.I. This is the SnackWell's Index, which measures our per capita consumption of SnackWell's cookies (fat-free but still very fattening) and thus the tendency of Americans to become and remain nutritional nincompoops. The SnackWell bubble burst several years before the stock market did. Until then, we were a nation obsessed with a ridiculous cure.

Thus, the forces of food phobia and prejudice continue to lurk. Here is my current theory. There is no society that encourages gluttony, and there never has been. Until recently, few people had enough money to be gluttons. And those who did were held back by law, religion, custom, or scarcity. None of these hinder us today. We are all in grave danger of running amok. We desperately need something to restrain us. That's why we invented the nutrition fads and fears of the past 20 years. Can it be coincidence that 1982 witnessed both the astounding tripling of cephalopod consumption in the United States and the first front-page nutritional scare story I can remember: *Time* magazine's infamous (with me) cover story, "Salt: A New Villain?" Of course not. There are no coincidences.

One can only pray that this insight will truly set us free.

A girl I met at a party said, "I know you. You're the man who writes about food for fun." I had forgotten there was any other way. That's truly what this book is about. It is about cooking old roosters in red wine; about making blood sausage in southwest France, lobster rolls in Greenwich Village, and bread in Rome; about growing vegetables in California and enjoying vegetables in Paris; about eating a wide swath through Thailand and sacrificing everything to make the perfect pizza. It's about the taste of salt and the taste of steak. It's about the mind-body problem. And about the elemental, primordial glee we feel every time we are called to dinner.

Who Is Having All the Fun?

For now, with nearly every bite I take, in the back of my mind there looms the same nagging question: Who is having all the fun? Is it my brain, or is it really me?

Toro, Toro, Toro

Brain Storm

As the Spit Turns

Cast Party

Taro, Taro, Taro

TORO, TORO, TORO

A ft here, drive 'em aft," I shouted. "Call all hands! Man the capstan! Blood and thunder! Lower away . . . and after him!"

I stood before the mirror in my bedroom, admiring my new outfit and rehearsing the handful of nautical phrases I had collected from my dog-eared copy of *Moby-Dick*. Soon I would be jetting toward Ensenada on the Pacific coast of Baja California, where I would set out upon an epic hunt for . . . the giant bluefin!

Why the bluefin? Simply because the raw meat from its belly is one of the most delicious things on Earth. Isn't that enough?

Bluefin are tuna, one of about 13 species, depending on who is doing the counting. They are among nature's most perfectly designed creatures, one of the largest fish in the sea (1,800 pounds appears to be the record) and among the fastest (capable of bursts as high as 56 miles an hour). Bluefin are able to navigate from Japan to California and back, from the Caribbean to Norway—they have binocular vision, acute hearing, sensors in their skin for pressure and temperature, and magnetic particles in their body that are thought to act as compasses. They are astonishingly streamlined, with hollows into which their fins retract and flatten at high speeds. Their bodies are 75 percent muscle. From birth until death, bluefin can never stop moving forward. If they did, they would die of suffocation. They are voracious predators, consuming up to 25 percent of their weight each day in sardines, squid, herring, and other living treats. They hunt like wolves, in deadly packs, which we call "schools," to make them seem cuter.

Bluefin are also the most valuable wild animals on Earth.

I have read that the world record for one giant bluefin is $83,500, set in 1992 at Tsukiji in Tokyo, the world's largest fish market. This comes to nearly $120 a pound. More typical auction prices these days at Tsukiji (pronounced "skee gee") range from $15 to $40 a pound, a weakness ascribed to Japan's current economic problems. The daily auctions at Tsukiji set the world prices for bluefin, because the Japanese are prepared to pay more than anybody else for their flesh. Whenever you're curious, go to fis.com, click on Market Prices, select Tokyo-Chuo under Far East Prices, and scroll down to Bluefin. I am always curious.

(*Ahi* tuna, a name you see printed with pride on most American menus these days, is yellowfin tuna, which the Japanese consider inferior not only to bluefin but also to southern bluefin, bigeye, and albacore, and just ahead of skipjack. "*Ahi*" is the Hawaiian name for yellowfin. Things Hawaiian have a special cachet in California, which they lack in the rest of the country. California is home of most American tuna canneries, and restaurants there were initially fearful that customers were avoiding the dish listed as "grilled tuna." The name *ahi* was a godsend. On the East Coast, it sounded vaguely Japanese. Boasting of *ahi* on a menu is like featuring USDA Commercial grade beef at a steak house.)

The price of a bluefin depends on its size, freshness, and shape (it should be roughly football-shaped, with a swelling underside). Most important is the quality of its flesh, especially the amount and grade of *toro*—the pink meat from its tender, fatty belly. Bluefin experts at Tsukiji carry a *sashibo*, a long, thin, hollow metal rod that can be plunged under the gills and right through the fish to extract a sample of its meat, layer by layer, like a geological core.

The upper half of a bluefin's body consists of rich, shiny red meat called *akami,* of which the middle section, the *naka,* is of the highest quality. Between the upper body and the belly is a dark, bloody muscle called the *chiai,* which many people will not eat, though my dog, Sky King, has no compunctions. Nearly all the *toro* is found in the belly, which gets fattier, more delicate, and more sought after the nearer it is to the head. The middle and tail sections of the belly are medium-grade *toro, chu-toro.* Toward the head lies the *o-toro,* great *toro,* the most delectable and expensive fish in the world. Right behind the gills is the *kama,* perhaps the choicest cut on the entire bluefin, although, among some connoisseurs, just the masticatory muscle is an object of profound gastronomic worship. I had some the other day and found it a bit sinewy. Some bigeye tuna have a rare and valuable form of *toro* near the bones on their dorsal side, the upper body, called *se-toro.* I may have tasted *se-toro* at a little dump of a sushi place in Santa Monica, but I'm not sure.

Two thin little rectangles of *o-toro* (great *toro*) at a top sushi place in this country will cost you $20, much more in Tokyo. That is why I have never been able to eat enough *toro* for complete satisfaction. Well, maybe I have, just once. Sometimes, I feel like a giant bluefin, my powerful musculature propelling me about the world in search of food. Like the bluefin, if I stop, I die. Isn't this astounding? So much for the idea that taste is subjective and mutable.

The Japanese are not alone in their love of tuna belly. I own an anatomical diagram of a bluefin published in Italy in 1919. It shows the *ventresca* or *sorra bianca,* the fatty belly, and above it, where the Japanese *chu-toro* lies, is the Italian *tarantello.* The part of the belly just behind the head—the fattiest and most valuable—appears to be called *pendini* or *spuntatore.* Things have not changed much since Pliny the Elder wrote in his *Natural History,* in the first century A.D.: "The choicest parts are the neck and the white flesh of the belly, and the throat, provided they are fresh. . . . The poorest parts are near the tail, because they have no fat; the parts from near the jaw are the most sought after."

Where were you when you first tasted *o-toro*? Me, I was in Los Angeles, ten years ago, sitting at the counter at Ginza Sushiko, a very fine sushi restaurant then in a little strip mall on Wilshire. The chef, Masa Takayama, placed two smooth pink rectangles of fish on my plate, and I took one, unaware that this, at last, was *toro.* At first it was like having a second tongue in my mouth, a cooler one, and then the taste asserted itself, rich and delicately meaty, not fishy at all. The texture is easier to describe—so meltingly tender as to be nearly insubstantial, moist and cool, not buttery or velvety as people sometimes say. Have you ever tasted a piece of velvet?

I knew this was one of those peak gastronomic moments you never forget, like the last time you ate a perfect peach, or the first time you tasted a ripe, raw-milk Camembert or sautéed foie gras, or every time you have white truffles or *pizza bianca*. I immediately formulated a theory that moments like these draw on the collective genetic memory of the human race, reaching across national and racial lines, superseding all questions of taste, culture, habit, or custom.

I can vaguely appreciate the romance of fishing. As a boy, I was able to read the first half of Ernest Hemingway's *The Old Man and the Sea* before losing interest. I have shared a charter or two out of Montauk, at the far tip of Long Island, to catch striped bass and bluefish (no relation to bluefin). And one of my oldest friends, usually well balanced, has become a fanatical fly fisherman. He flies to Tierra del Fuego (no joke) to catch river trout. Then, he throws them back. He does not like the taste of trout or any other fish, for that matter. His aim is to outwit these fantastically clever creatures—and, more profoundly, to subdue the primordial forces of Nature itself.

But that is not my goal. My goal is not to subdue Nature. My goal is to eat Nature.

And, let's face it. The bluefin tuna may be the most perfect creature in all the seven seas, but it is a fish nonetheless. For a human to trick a bluefin or a trout is really no contest. Sure, I enjoy vanquishing the primordial, elemental forces of the universe as much as the next guy. But for me, and for humankind since time beyond memory, the purpose of fishing is dinner.

Preparations for my trip to Ensenada had gone smoothly. The only snag was finding the right outfit. It was December. The weather could be balmy and dry, balmy and wet, cold yet dry, or cold and wet. I knew what I needed: a light but not flimsy shell crafted from a space-age fabric that is breathable yet water-proof. My closet was littered with 20 years' worth of allegedly breathable-yet-waterproof shells that in actuality either admitted water like cheesecloth, or hermetically held in one's body heat and moisture like a terrarium. At last, I found the ideal balance in a way-overpriced shell from Patagonia in chic and slimming black. This is not the perfect color if you need to be rescued from an angry sea, but since when was high fashion meant to be prac-tical? My friend Gloria Steinem, paraphrasing Thoreau, once told me that she avoids any occasion for which you have to buy new clothes. That's where we part ways. I feel that her view is at sharp variance with the ethos and mission of my principal employer. For the right to pursue and eat the giant bluefin, I would gladly buy any number of superfluous new outfits, while Ms. Steinem's scruples will leave her languishing on the dock.

My plan was to drive down to Ensenada and visit one of a handful of bluefin farms in the world, and probably the only one on the North American coast. Afterward, I would go in search of a tuna boat—a commercial or sports vessel—that would take me out in search of the wild giant bluefin. Ensenada is an hour and a half down the coast of Baja California from the U.S.-Mexico border crossing. The last half hour of coastline is spectacularly beautiful in any weather, and that day the air and ocean were crystalline and pure. I was driven down by Philippe Charat, a principal owner of Maricultura del Norte and its blue-fin farm off the coast. (Philippe was born 60 years ago, in Paris, to a Russian father and a French mother, who took refuge in Mexico before World War II. Later, he studied at Harvard and now lives in Rancho Santa Fe, north of San Diego, as a Mexican citizen with permanent U.S. residency.) Philippe had offered to show me his operation and then help me find a tuna fishing boat. Somewhere in between, we would have a lunch of abalone and perhaps a little raw bluefin. Only the thought of lunch could alle-viate my mild depression, brought on by the perfect weather, which was too warm and clear for my brand-new outfit.

We reached a rocky beach conveniently opposite Philippe's

floating bluefin farm, but the water was too choppy for us to use the small company boat. And so we traveled farther down the coast, clambered into a company truck, and drove for a nause-ating eternity on one of the most perilous dirt-and-rock roads I have ever known. High above the ocean, we occasionally glimpsed a magical sight—eight delicate, perfect circles on the glittering sea. These were the bluefin holding pens, in fact, not small at all, at 130 feet in diameter. At long last, we reached another beach. Disoriented and, I feared, permanently damaged, I clumsily boarded a small motorboat, and we threaded our way among the tiny pastel boats of Mexican sea-urchin divers and out onto the open water. Although these divers collect an exceptionally fine harvest, the Japanese auctioneers at Tsukiji refuse to take them; 20 minutes on this hellish road destroys their value.

The international trade in fresh bluefin developed in the 1970s, when methods of refrigeration and air-cargo handling became sophisticated enough that a giant bluefin could be caught or har-pooned off the coast of New England on a Monday, and be auc-tioned fresh in Tokyo on Wednesday. Until then, bluefin were primarily a popular game fish, attracting celebrity sportsmen such as Hemingway, Franklin Roosevelt, Amelia Earhart, and a competitive team from Harvard to the coasts of Maine and Nova Scotia. Bluefin were a complete nuisance to commercial fisher-men in the Northeast, getting tangled in their nets and yielding pennies a pound—and then only when the cat-food business was brisk. Americans did not enjoy eating oily, dark bluefin. Tuna here was a light sandwich spread canned on the Pacific coast. James Beard once wrote that tuna is the only food better canned than fresh (see page 24).

Once the heady prices at Tsukiji became available to nearly every bluefin boat in the world, a fishing frenzy followed. Purse-seine technology, involving vast nets that can be drawn closed around entire schools of giant bluefin, meant that more fish could be caught by one boat in one year than by all the traditional fishermen in the world combined! By the 1990s, the world bluefin population had been reduced by 80 to 90 percent. Quotas have been enacted and poorly enforced.

These issues are the subject of bloody battles among conservationists, commercial fishermen, and sport fishermen. Satellite-tagging studies may help us to understand the life cycle and migration patterns of the bluefin, about which we know next to nothing. Bluefin farms—established years ago in Japan and later developed with Japanese help in Port Lincoln, Australia; Spain; Ensenada; and elsewhere—may someday help alleviate this potential disaster.

In ten minutes, we arrived at the busy farming operation and its eight pens, each one a huge ring of pipes and floats from which hung a cylindrical net stretching 30 feet deep and anchored to the ocean floor another 20 feet below. Six months earlier, thousands of young bluefin had been caught in the open sea using the purse-seine method, towed back here very slowly, and distributed among the eight holding pens. All these operations, and the "harvesting" as well, are carried out by a large team of divers dressed entirely in black, except for bright yellow hoses connected to compressors on the surface, through which they breathe.

In all bluefin farms, the fish are kept for no more than six months, just long enough to fatten them and increase the quality of their *toro*. These are less like farms and more like ranching operations or feedlots—or the fattening of ducks for foie gras. Here they are fed freshly caught sardines, which Philippe and his partners believe gives them a better taste than the frozen sardines used in Australia. One reason for locating the operation in Ensenada was the active fishery here for sardines and anchovies.

We climbed onto a thankfully stable, flat-bottomed barge tied up to one of the holding pens, were briefly amused by sea lions and pelicans, then turned our attention to the bloody business taking place on the barge next to ours. It was harvesting time. By a manipulation of nets within one of the circular pens, 200 bluefin were confined to one small section. They were all about four feet long, and weighed between 50 and 60 pounds. (Only bluefin farms in the waters off Spain produce 300- to 400-pound fish, just large enough to qualify as giants.)

Divers swam among the bluefin and took hold of them, one at a time, thrusting a gloved hand and forearm into its gills and lifting it onto the open edge of the barge, which was completely padded with what looked like a gigantic sky-blue mattress puddled with bright blood. (Without the padding, and maybe even with it, the side of the bluefin that lies against the deck, called *shitami* in Japanese, will bring a lower price at the Tsukiji market than the upper side, *uwami*.) As each bluefin was slid onto the barge, one of several workers wearing blood-splashed yellow slickers and pants killed it nearly instantly, in the Japanese manner, with a spike to the head and a wire down the spinal column, which not only is humane, but prevents continuing muscle spasms that can damage the meat, "burning" it with the lactic acid released when a bluefin struggles for too long in a net or at the end of a sportsman's line. A good judge of tuna at Tsukiji, they say, can taste how a fish died.

Now, the bluefin was immediately bled, gutted, hosed down, and dropped into a slurry of water and ice to lower its body temperature and prevent spoilage. (Tuna are warm-blooded.) Tomorrow, it would be cleaned again, packed for shipment, and driven to the Los Angeles airport for its last run—probably to Tokyo but possibly to New York City, the largest sushi market outside Japan.

By now, I had concluded that I was not going to find my deep-sea tuna-fishing boat in Ensenada. The season was over. There were no sportfishermen in sight. Bluefin were being caught, but only as an incidental catch, by very large commercial fishing vessels that stay hundreds of miles out for three weeks or more, at least 20 times the number of days I had allocated for my boat ride, *o-toro* or no *o-toro*.

Though I was internally inconsolable, I kept it bottled up. I was even able to simulate voracious hunger at our very late abalone lunch. Then I gathered up my new outfit, still unused. Philippe and I bade goodbye to our companions and crossed the gestapolike U.S. border just after dark.

The next day, Philippe generously brought me a quarter of one of the harvested bluefin, about ten pounds of solid muscle in one long filet. It was a lower quarter, the part with the *toro*. I immediately got out my Japanese diagrams and began slicing and eating, eating and slicing. I was intoxicated by the huge pieces of *o-toro* and delicious pink *chu-toro* that made up half of my bluefin quarter. The highly prized *kama* behind the gills seemed to be composed of equal parts of fat and gristle, and I grilled it delectably over a charcoal fire. But my joy was tinged with foreboding. For I knew that my fated meeting with a wild giant bluefin still lay ahead.

My mouth still full of *toro,* I got on the phone, searched the Internet, and, after several hours, ascertained that the only bluefin fishing season in the entire world had just begun off Cape Hatteras on the Outer Banks of North Carolina. I bought a practical book about fishing for giant bluefin. It was called *Fish the Chair If You Dare.* (This refers to the revolving chair bolted to the deck, into which the angler is strapped to keep him or her from being dragged off the boat by his or her prey.) It soon became obvious that the last thing I wanted to do was go fishing in the open sea in the middle of winter. What arbitrary and destructive force was pulling me ineluctably toward my star-crossed encounter with this monstrous ruler of the frozen deep? I believe it was the editor in chief of *Vogue.*

In the absence of a landlubbers support group, I turned to my friend Joe. It was Joe, an avid game fisherman and Manhattan restaurateur, who two years earlier had unsuccessfully tried to interest me in going out after bluefin with him. Unsurprisingly, he jumped at the idea. His fishing friends knew very little about captains and boats available in Hatteras. We chose Captain Jeffrey Ross and his 55-foot boat, *The Obsession,* on the basis of very little information; chartered the boat for $1,000 (plus a 20 percent tip for the mate); figured out how to get to Hatteras, a town at the remote southern end of Cape Hatteras; and counted the days. My new outfit and I were ready for anything.

Joe and I met at Kennedy Airport in the early evening for our flight to Norfolk, Virginia. Airports closer to Cape Hatteras were closed for the winter. I knew that something was up when a gust of wind outside the terminal sent me sprawling as I got out of the taxi, and another prevented me from getting up. We soon learned that our flight would be delayed for at least three hours—a storm was approaching Hatteras from the south. We telephoned Captain Jeffrey Ross. He estimated that we had only a 50 percent chance of going out the next day. This is your captain's way of saying 25 percent—captains don't get seasick, and they have, after all, a financial interest in optimism. Joe and I headed back home.

Two weeks later, I flew alone to Norfolk—Joe's wife had just given birth—and drove nearly three hours in the dark to an oceanfront motel in Nags Head, North Carolina, near the northern end of Cape Hatteras. On the way I had two dinners, both at 7-Elevens. I booked a wake-up call for 4:45 a.m., the last time, I hope, that this will ever be necessary. I had arranged to share tomorrow's charter with five anglers from Richmond, Virginia. They had kindly volunteered to pick me up at 5:30 for the 75-minute drive to Hatteras, to a marina named Teach's Lair, to *The Obsession*.

We arrived as the sun was rising, quickly boarded *The Obsession*, and were soon speeding past the harbor buoys and into the open sea. The air was warming—my new outfit was perfect—and the sky was clear. But the water was painfully choppy. One of us became very sick and spent most of the rest of a long day facedown on the floor of the cabin. Three of us drank coffee and polished off several party-size boxes of Donettes. Two others, including me (wearing a scopolamine patch behind one ear), barely held our own until we reached the place where the bluefin were supposed to be, 34 miles out, an hour and a half from land, where the ocean was suddenly calm.

The bluefin fishery off Hatteras was discovered by chance in December 1992, in the waters over a shipwreck 14 miles from shore. Cape Hatteras vaguely parallels the coast of North Carolina in a sweeping arc, where a cold stream from the north and a warm stream from the south meet, a confluence that, for some reason, attracts migrating bluefin. Only sportfishing is allowed here. The National Marine Fisheries Service allows you to keep one bluefin per boat per day, and if you catch any at all, you are not allowed to sell it. If Neptune smiled on us that day, we would have to consume the *kama*, the *o-toro*, and the *chu-toro* all by ourselves.

Here is how you catch a bluefin: The mate plants three or four short, thick fishing rods in receptacles on both sides of the deck. Then he takes three or four dead fish from a cooler and baits the hooks with them. He pulls out several yards of line from each reel—big, brass reels—and throws the baited hooks into the water. Meanwhile the boat is moving slowly forward. The mate cuts up fish from another cooler and throws the pieces into the water, which is called "chumming," and is intended to attract a school of bluefin. Which is exactly what it did.

First one reel and then another started whizzing and whirring as bluefin went for the bait, were hooked in the sides of their mouths, and sped away from the boat, drawing out yards and yards of line. You sit in the fighting chair; a rod is thrust between your legs into a gimbal attached to the seat; another man stands behind the chair to turn it as the direction of the fish changes. You begin reeling in the bluefin, sometimes allowing it to make another run and pull out more line. Turning the reel against the pull of a bluefin is impossible. Instead, you repeatedly pull the rod back toward you by pushing off with your feet and then, as you lower it again, you furiously wind the reel to take up the slack.

Neptune did smile on us that morning. One bluefin after another hooked itself onto our rods. Each time, as soon as the bluefin was pulled to the side of the boat, the mate cut the line and set it free. We caught 15, I think, and kept one, which later, on the docks, clocked in at 145 pounds and 65 inches. It was just about my size, after a successful diet.

After watching nearly all morning, I took the fighting chair and caught an 18-pound blackfin tuna, not very good eating. I could not decide whether to be gratified or embarrassed. Then, in the afternoon, there was a 180-pound bluefin on the other end of my line, the largest catch of the day. Several times in our struggle, I had to let it run free before reeling in the line once again. Getting it alongside the boat took two of us. And then we cut it free. Girls and other friends have been extremely impressed by the photos. I was told that an unscrupulous fisherman would have thrown back the 145-pounder, even though it had died hours before, and kept the 180-pound specimen.

We returned to shore just before dusk. The sky was beyond spectacular. For 30 cents a pound, $40 in all, a man on the dock butchered our bluefin on one of several long, rough wooden tables. As my fishing mates ascribed to me some expertise in the edible anatomy of the bluefin, I was put in charge of guiding the butcher's knife. Good thing, too. Not only is it customary in this part of the world not to separate the *o-toro* and the *chu-toro* from the loin, but the fattiest part of the belly, five pounds of priceless *kama,* two thick triangles joined along one edge, is—strap yourself in for this one—thrown into the trash! They used to toss it to the dogs that prowl the marina, but the wooden deck got stained by the fat—defaced by *o-toro*!

I washed the blood and cut off ten slices of sashimi. After eating two myself to make sure they were truly top *toro,* I ate another two and offered the rest to my shipmates. They refused even the tiniest taste. They never eat raw fish and consider the fatty belly of the bluefin too greasy to grill. "Keep it all," they said, to a man. And so I did. If I lived near Hatteras, I would be in *o-toro* heaven every day of the week.

I examined those two triangles of fatty *kama* by the next morning's light. The flesh itself was pale pink, shot throughout with the finest veins of white, arranged in an infinitely branching pattern—close to the ultimate bluefin experience. I cannot describe how delicious it was.

Yet, I felt only small satisfaction in having landed a large, handsome, dumb, pitiable bluefin. Now that I have done it once, I would derive zero satisfaction from doing it again. I do not feel stronger or nobler for having triumphed over a fish. If I can do it, how hard can it be? I did feel physically, spiritually, and intellectually gratified at finding and landing, then sharing and consuming—nearly to the point of surfeit, but not quite—vast quantities of a food of which I had previously only dreamed.

My theory about the universal DNA of human gastronomic pleasure soon came crashing down. My friend Nafumi Tamura translated for me parts of several Japanese books about sushi. It came as a shock to learn that, though the Japanese have eaten tuna for a thousand years or more, in recent centuries it has been considered a poor man's food, and became popular only during the food shortages following World War II. Even then, the fatty belly of the bluefin was rarely eaten—it was considered too oily! Until the 1960s, the Japanese people appreciated *toro* no more than did my fishing partners from Virginia.

Here is what Ernest Hemingway wrote to Bernard Berenson the year he published *The Old Man and the Sea*: "There isn't any symbolism. The sea is the sea. The old man is an old man. The boy is a boy and the fish is a fish. The sharks are all sharks no better and no worse. All the symbolism that people say is shit. What goes beyond is what you see beyond when you know."

Now I know. Now I see beyond the symbolism of the primordial bluefin. Fatty tuna belly is fatty tuna belly, and I can't get enough of it.

APRIL 2000

"This is a fish that I think is better canned than fresh" appears on page 229 of *James Beard's Fish Cookery* (Little, Brown, 1954). Before laughing, one should reflect on one's own tuna awareness in 1954. "The albacore, which has the true white meat," Beard continues, "is the one used for the finest pack tuna fish and for the most delicate dishes." Tuna meant Bumblebee back then, and those small, expensive Mediterranean cans of darker tuna flesh poached in olive oil were next to unknown here. A generous reader, Paula Fromme, who fittingly lives on Marine Avenue in Brooklyn, supplied the source of that James Beard quotation, along with a gift of her own copy of the book.

BRAIN STORM

I was making fast work of a crisp roast duck and a bottle of red Bandol when my friend Michele called to inform me that profound interest in good food may be caused by a lesion in the anterior portion of the right cerebral hemisphere of one's brain. *My* brain!

Michele's source was a study in a recent issue of the respected journal *Neurology,* and she delivered the news without tears of condolence or sympathy. It was her latest foray in a war that has raged between us for 10 or 15 years. Michele relentlessly attacks what she regards as my obsession with good food. And I respond that it is only the weakness of her own sensory equipment that prevents her from making sensitive distinctions among the things she eats. Now, her muzzle to the wind, Michele sniffed victory.

Not for the last time in this sad and tangled tale, my appetite virtually disappeared. I pushed myself away from the table, washed my hands, looked up the word lesion (LEE-zhen), and learned that my brain may accordingly be afflicted with a wound, injury, or localized, pathological change in a bodily organ or tissue. I gently touched my scalp directly over where I imagined the anterior portion of my right cerebral hemisphere to be located.

I wasted no time in getting to the medical library and finding a copy of " 'Gourmand Syndrome': Eating Passion Associated with Right Anterior Lesions," by Marianne Regard, Ph.D., of Zurich, and Theodor Landis, M.D., of Geneva. And there, though not as stark and simple as I had first understood it, was the awful, possible truth about my brain.

The authors had hit upon their new syndrome with a case

eerily similar to my own. A successful Swiss political journalist suffered a stroke. Though he had once been indifferent to food, happy enough with his wife's cooking, and weighing only slightly more than he should, suddenly everything changed. As he lay in the hospital, recovering from his stroke, he could think only of food, of "good sausage with hash browns, or some spaghetti bolognese, or risotto and a breaded cutlet, nicely decorated, or a scallop of game in cream sauce. . . ." After four months he was able to return to work, but instead of covering politics, he persuaded his newspaper to let him write about food, which he did with great success. Drs. Landis and Regard fail to point out that there is no such dish as spaghetti bolognese, as spaghetti comes from the south of Italy and the pasta in Bologna is made with soft wheat and eggs. But otherwise, the case is a persuasive one.

Me, I had been a lawyer before taking the giant leap up to food writing nine years ago. In my case, there was no stroke or brain injury. Or was there? Just the thought of it all made me agitated. Should I telephone Switzerland? As always, my wife was the source of deepest consolation. "Better not," she chortled. "They'll probably find a lesion the size of a white truffle!"

Drs. Regard and Landis list a whole range of eating disorders that spring from brain injuries. Some cases of both anorexia and hyperphagia (your doctor's name for overeating) have been linked with tumors affecting the ventromedial hypothalamus, which certainly sounds to me like a part of the brain, and to a lesser extent with the temporal cortex. Even when eating problems such as anorexia and bulimia appear to have purely psychological causes, physical changes in the brain can also be present, especially changes in the neurotransmitter systems and the levels of serotonin and noradrenalin. And brain lesions affecting the neurotransmitter systems have also been linked with addictive and obsessive-compulsive behaviors, pathological gambling, kleptomania, and so forth. And then there's Pica's disease, in which patients display a "morbid craving for unusual or unsuitable food, such as the ingestion of ice, clay, laundry starch, lettuce, or cigarette ashes." Even in the midst of an impending personal tragedy,

I was gladdened to find, at last, hard scientific evidence that lettuce is an unsuitable food and that a craving for lettuce is evidence of a diseased brain.

But, until Drs. Regard and Landis came along, nobody had
connected excessive gourmandism with a disturbance in the old
gray matter. After they discovered the Swiss political journalist
and a similar case, they decided to test every patient diagnosed
with a cerebral lesion who was referred over a three-year period
to the neuropsychology unit at University Hospital in Zurich,
where both of them then worked. Of 723 patients, 36 exhibited
the gourmand syndrome, which the doctors defined as a newly
acquired persistent craving for, and passionate eating of, high-
quality food, having an onset at about the time the patient had
sustained an injury or tumor or hemorrhage. In all but one of
these patients, the lesion was located in the right front area of the
brain. Most of them also showed poor learning and recall of
simple visual figures, a deficit typically associated with right-brain
injury. The authors took this as powerful evidence that they had
found the site of a whole range of addictive behaviors.

I was puzzled by at least two things. First of all, Regard and
Landis insist upon referring to gourmandism as an "impulse-
control problem." But I see it precisely as the reverse. A person
who eats ten bags of potato chips or SnackWell's cookies in an
afternoon has an impulse-control problem. But a person like me,
who spends the afternoon—or a week of afternoons—planning
the perfect dinner of barbecued ribs or braised foie gras, has
clearly mastered his impulses. We passionate eaters elevate, we
ennoble the bestial impulse to feed into a sublime activity, into an
art, into the art of eating. And some of us create what might even
be called literature while we're at it. We transmute what animals
do into what the angels would do if angels ate food, which I don't
think they do, at least not in their official capacity. This is what
Freud called sublimation, the highest form of impulse control.
Yes, Doctor, I plead guilty to an obsession with beauty, edible or
otherwise. I am guilty as charged!

And, once we have turned eating into an art, and we see that it is good, then we practice this art as often as possible. And if, on occasion, an observer sees what appears to be nothing nobler than me wrestling with the wrapper on a giant package of miniature Fun Size Milky Way bars, this too is the art of eating. For isn't art nothing more nor less than whatever an artist does?

My second problem: Do all dedicated food lovers have something wrong with their noodle? Half of us? Ten percent? Drs. Regard and Landis are silent on this subject. And is a gourmand more likely than anybody else to have a brain lesion? The authors go no further than to say that "passionate eating has diagnostic significance when it occurs in previously 'normal' eaters and is associated with other organic behavioral alterations." The implication is that if I have been an abnormal, obsessed, extreme eater all my life, then there is nothing wrong with my brain and never was. But, if I had once ignored food and now spend hours and days in flights of gourmandism, I must be in real trouble. I tried to remember if I had ever been a normal eater.

The thick fog of confusion was oozing into every convolution of my poor brain. Nothing less than a complete workup by Drs. Regard and Landis could put my mind to rest. I settled down next to the telephone with several pounds of ripe summer fruit and a plate of French cheeses, and started dialing Switzerland. Within 15 minutes, I had found Regard's phone number in Zurich and Landis's in Geneva. I called Landis first, because I was not in the mood for Swiss-German hospital food. The news was bad. Landis, professor and head of the highly regarded neurological service at the Hôpital Cantonal, Universitaires de Genève, was on his August vacation and not expected back for more than two weeks! Regard was also away, but her summer holiday was nearly through, and three days later, I reached her at University Hospital in Zurich. It required an additional seven days of obsessive and perseverating telephone calls on my part before Regard was willing to interrupt the last week of Landis's vacation, which he was spending at home while learning to hang glide near Geneva.

Landis tried to persuade me to have my MRI—magnetic resonance imaging—done in New York or Boston. But I had a better plan: I would fly to Paris, catch up on some important eating, wait for him to call me to say that everything had been arranged, take the TGV to Geneva, treat Dr. Landis to dinner at one of the greatest restaurants of France, Marc Veyrat's Auberge de l'Eridan, close to the Swiss border—and then subject myself to his tests. Landis agreed, aided in his decision, I am sure, by my offer of a grand feast. There was no need for me to languish in Paris. He would handle everything. In a few days, when his hanggliding lessons were finished, I would fly directly to Geneva and jump the long queue for their most advanced MRI machine, as though I were an Arabian prince in a medical crisis.

And then, right there on the telephone, he began the neurological interview, taking a history, I guess it's called, inquiring in detail about the events in my life that might have given rise to a brain lesion, and about shifts in my eating behavior. Our mood grew quite serious and intense, broken only when I asked Landis whether he had ever studied the syndrome that afflicts 52-year-old neurologists who believe they can fly.

A week later, my taxi pulled up to the Hôpital Cantonal, Universitaires de Genève, where I was whisked upstairs to Theodor Landis's suite. Landis was every inch my picture of the Swiss neurologist—tall, good-looking, balding, and thin, with sharp, intelligent features and a calm, empathetic manner. It was already afternoon, and as the MRI machine would not be available until 8:15 the next morning, Landis went through all the other steps required for his diagnosis. After reviewing my history, he administered a portion of his standard neuropsychological examination—the full exam can take two and a half hours. I was asked to memorize and repeat a list of ten words, first immediately after Landis read them to me and then twice again later. I had to memorize and draw a complex figure made up of many straight lines and maybe a curve or two. And call out all the words I could think of in three minutes that begin with "S." Things like that.

My performance was, quite frankly, superlative, until we came to the learning and recall of a series of visual figures. Landis

showed me ten cards; on each was printed a simple drawing—
a pair of short parallel lines or a triangle with either a large dot
or a small circle drawn inside, I can't remember which. Then, I
had to draw them all from memory. After I had gotten four of
them, my mind went blank. I sat there, staring down at the
paper. Landis encouraged me. Nothing came. Uh-oh, I said to
myself, remembering what he and Regard had written about the
gourmand syndrome: "The most prominent cognitive symptoms
were visual-spatial dysfunctions." Uh-oh, Landis must have said
to himself, in French. And then we talked about it for a minute or
two. I think he used the word deficit or impairment, I can't
remember which.

After a cup of what Landis considers the best hospital coffee in
Switzerland—a judgment with which I have no basis to disagree—
we walked to the EEG (electroencephalograph) rooms. A tight,
red, elastic cloth cap was drawn over my hair, and 21 electrical
needles covered with sticky goop were painfully slid through
white holes in the cap and into my scalp. Soon, 21 little pens were
dancing to and fro as a long sheet of graph paper rolled beneath
them, recording my brain waves. Everything was perfectly normal, except that I ended up with a head of hair covered with
sticky goop. And I had washed it just two hours before!

Then, back to Landis's office for a long and very extensive
examination of my neurological signs, reflexes, and responses—
everything from the familiar knee-jerk reaction to weird ones like
the appearance of a faint quiver in my chin when Landis scraped
my palm. Nothing to worry about, he said, despite an occasional
borderline response on my part. It was nearly seven in the evening when Landis and I finished up. I could not stop thinking
about how poorly I had done at remembering those triangles, circles, and squares.

An hour later, Landis picked me up in his old white BMW for
the 40-kilometer drive through idyllic sub-Alpine hills and valleys
to the Auberge de l'Eridan on Lake Annecy, where chef Marc
Veyrat runs one of the most original kitchens in France. The six
hours that followed were proof, as if one needed proof, of the
transformative and bewitching power of great food.

Every bite of Veyrat's cooking is a celebration of the region—
Haute-Savoie and the Jura. There were 60 local cheeses, and a long
list of delicious local wines (and an extraordinary young sommelier named Bruno), and a huge wooden cart of fine traditional
and modern breads from local bakers. And every dish, whether
fish from the lake or fowl from nearby farms—everything from
the foie gras to the sorbets—was flavored with the wild herbs,
spices, roots, and mushrooms of the region. Bruno and other
young members of the staff get up at six in the morning and
climb into the hills to forage for the wild plants the chef will need
that day. For years I had avoided the Auberge de l'Eridan, fearing
that the food would be precious and tricky. It was the opposite.
Veyrat's achievement is that, while all his tastes and aromas are
unusual and provocative, his food is at the same time strong,
simple, and deeply satisfying.

Landis told me that he had never eaten on this level before, and
I admitted that I rarely eat so interestingly and so well. Could it
be that Landis was finally catching on to the heady upside of the
gourmand syndrome? Would he now admit that his phrase,
"excessive interest in fine food," was an oxymoron, a troubling
symptom of his own reluctance to wallow in pleasure?

We finished feasting at 2:30 a.m., and arrived back in Geneva
more than an hour later. My MRI was a little more than four
hours away.

Precisely on schedule, I lay supine and fully clothed on a sliding table as the MRI technician fitted an open cylinder over my
head, adjusted two pads over my ears, and inserted me into a
large circular opening in the wall. Over the next half hour, there
were four periods of imaging—or acquisitions, I think they're
called—each lasting between four and eight minutes, and each
marked by a series of crashing, clanging sounds at high volume.
My least favorite acquisition was the one that sounded like a New
York City garbage truck parked next to me on the table.

Before flying to Geneva, I had read a little about MRIs. The
machine beams a combination of electromagnetic and radio
energy at some part of your body. This causes the hydrogen
nuclei in the watery part to flip back and forth, which, in turn,

generate radio waves of their own. These are picked up by an antenna, fed into a computer, and turned into a picture. "The procedure is considered to be without risk to the patient," I read. They don't sound totally confident, do they? So, I lay there for half an hour, trying to feel my nuclei flipping back and forth and back and forth and back again, wondering whether I would ever be the same.

Then it was over, and they slid me and my table out of the machine, pulled the ear pads off, lifted the cylinder from my head, and led me next door into a darkened room filled with computer monitors and people sitting at them. There were Landis and Dr. Jacqueline Delavelle, an expert in imaging, waiting for the data from my MRI to thread its way through a central computer and reach their screen. Landis and I were in a merry mood. We joked about whether the computer could spot a hangover and about the advantages of being afflicted with the gourmand syndrome if you happened to live near Lake Annecy. And then the sections—visual slices—through my brain began to appear, 152 in all. There were three sets. One started at the top of my head and moved downward, a millimeter at a time, to my chin; the second started at one ear and progressed by five-millimeter slices—each less than a quarter-inch thick—through the midpoint of my brain and out to the other ear; and the third started at the back of my head and moved forward, slice by slice, toward my nose. The joking stopped as we all concentrated on the screen.

"There," said Landis, pointing. "Ah," agreed Delavelle. In one slice, my right brain seemed to have shrunk a bit from the skull, possibly leaving a curve of scar tissue. And in another, the ventricles—the interconnected, water-filled cavities of the brain— seemed a bit larger than you would expect them to be, mainly on the right side. "Gourmand syndrome?" Landis wondered aloud.

My legs were shaky as we walked back to Landis's office. I tried to smile amiably, to joke about our grand dinner. Then I admitted to Landis how anxious I suddenly felt about the whole thing. What I really meant to say was that I felt doomed and damaged, defective, disabled, and depressed. I think he understood.

"Forget all about it," Landis advised.

"But could you cure me if I asked you to?"

"You're not sick," he replied. "If the lesion occurred at your birth or soon after [I was a premature baby], then it cannot have resulted in the gourmand syndrome, because your brain would have compensated for it. If it occurred in that automobile accident when you were 20, that might be the cause. Old lesions are stable, unless they are connected with epilepsy; they don't get worse. And remember—the gourmand syndrome is perfectly benign. It has no negative implications for your life."

And yet, of course it does, or I mean it could have, theoretically at least. Let's assume that Dr. Landis is right—that my decision to stop being a lawyer and take up food writing was caused by an old injury to my brain. Landis seemed to be saying two contradictory things, one that there is nothing he or I could do about it, and the other that we would not *want* to do anything about it. But this is not true. If becoming an impecunious professional gourmand were merely a symptom with neurological causes, doesn't Landis have a duty to turn me back into a prosperous lawyer, or at least try to convince me that my decision was irrational?

Landis shrugged. "This is why I have never done my own MRI. And your case is fuzzy. Your eating habits did not change suddenly. The strongest indication we found was neuropsychological. If you're still interested, you might want to have a complete neuropsych exam done when you get home."

Instead, I flew to Paris and tried unsuccessfully to resume the normal life of a gourmand. For several days I ate only listlessly, barely able to consume more than three meals a day. One evening, I had dinner with my friend Hervé and his wife, Pascale, a physician, and their friend, the lawyer for one of the paparazzi accused of pursuing Princess Diana, who had died in Paris two days earlier. Someday I will tell you what the lawyer said. But I was far more concerned about myself.

"Radiologists will always find something," they told me. "You must get a second opinion." And, with their help, I was able to arrange a 4:00 p.m. appointment the next day—even though it

was Friday afternoon at the beginning of the Rentrée, the frenzied return of Parisians from their summer vacations. Two radiologists in the prosperous 16th arrondissement, Drs. Patrick
Sterin and Frederic Zeitoun, had agreed to read my MRI films
aveugle, blind—without knowing anything about me or why I was
there. I arrived with a heavy stack of 152 images under my arm.
Sterin and Zeitoun were impressed and a little overwhelmed
by the sheer number—they are usually shown just a half dozen
pictures of somebody's brain. We moved to a room with an illuminated wall, and the doctors spent a while sorting and viewing the pictures. And then, almost immediately, they identified
pretty much what Landis and Delavelle had seen in Geneva, a little scarring at the edges of the right brain and slightly enlarged
ventricles.

"But it is all entirely banal," they said, which, in a Parisian doctor's office, also means, according to my thickest French dictionary, "innocuous." The pictures were typical, they thought, of a
man of my wisdom, a kindly French euphemism for age. And, as
for the potentially ominous differences between my left and right
sides, they guessed that my head had been slightly tilted during
the MRI, causing the features on the right side to appear somewhat sooner and larger than those on the left. After all, they
pointed out, the section that should have sliced evenly through
the center of my eyeballs also showed the right one larger than
the left, which it is not. As they saw it, my brain fits quite harmo-
niously within my skull. Only then did I explain why I had come,
handing them a copy of the article in *Neurology.* They retired to a
corner and read it.

"Forget about your so-called lesion," Sterin advised. "Forget
about your syndrome."

Somehow, his advice had a beneficial effect, for that very evening I was able to resume my eating with renewed intensity and
fascination. I was, after all, in Paris—and wide though my travels
may range in their incessant and panoramic sweep from nation to
nation and continent to continent, it is still and always Paris that
claims the core of my culinary soul. There was a new cheese

shop to be discovered on the rue de Sèvres, and a boulangerie on the rue Monge. There were three models of croissant to be compared and contrasted at Ladurée on the rue Royale, and 20 books to be shipped home from La Librairie Gourmande, and two butchers with whom to explore the farthest reaches of bovine anatomy. And there were important new edible *objets d'art* that begged to be incorporated into my body: Alain Ducasse's creamed and truffled macaroni with sweetbreads and coxcombs, and Pierre Gagnaire's cappuccino of frogs.

And yet, I wonder if I will ever again be able to surrender to experiences such as these with the same naïve wonder and childlike euphoria of which I was capable—no, for which I lived—before my friend Michele stumbled over the gourmand syndrome. For now, with nearly every bite I take, in the back of my mind there looms the same nagging question: Who is having all the fun? Is it my brain, or is it really me?

NOVEMBER 1997

AS THE SPIT TURNS

Whenever I have nothing better to do, I roast a chicken. On average, I have nothing better to do about twice a week. That comes to a thousand chickens since 1990, over two million calories in all. I'll roast a chicken in the afternoon even when I am not hungry and have plenty of food in the fridge and a reservation for dinner. It's like a hobby.

I go through phases. By now I must have tried every conceivable variation, every pairing of temperature and time, trussing the chicken or leaving it loose, basting or not—with water, broth, or butter, hot or cold. For months, I will lay the little birds on their sides, then abruptly shift to the breast-up or breast-down school of thought. I have rubbed them first with herbs, spices, oil, or butter, or left them plain, and slid truffles under the skin. I have browned them first on top of the stove before popping them in the oven, or used a rack, or a little wire tower. I have tried free-range, organic, Amish, kosher, and supermarket birds, one pound, three pounds, or five pounds each. I have stuffed them with two lemons. You name it.

The great Brillat-Savarin declared, "We can learn to be cooks, but we must be born knowing how to roast." I often lie awake nights worrying about whether I was born to roast. It can be total agony.

It is not difficult to tell if you've got it right. Dark and crispy skin, intensely savory, covering every square millimeter of the bird with no unsightly white patches. Crunchy wings. Juicy breast meat, about 160° F on the instant-read thermometer. Succulent thighs, about 170 degrees. All the flesh firm and full of chicken flavor. But, for me, the skin's the thing. Some people roast a chicken and then peel off and discard the skin. What is the point? If you can't stand the skin, stay out of the chicken.

I won't give you the details of my all-time favorite way to roast the perfect chicken, because, by the time you read this, it will have changed, as it does every month or so. In fact, it already has. One method, often said to be the best, had eluded me for a lifetime, aggravating my nightly turmoil. And yet my straitened material circumstances have never made it possible. Until now.

Memories come flooding back. It was late October, a dozen years ago, in the microscopic Italian hill town of Albaretto della Torre. We had driven for miles in snow and sleet as the road wound ever upward through the gloom. At long last, we arrived— cold, wet, late, and disheveled—on the doorstep of Da Cesare, where we had reserved a table for dinner. Inside, we found a warm and rustic room of stone and wood and stucco, 12 tables of happy, thankful diners, and a large fireplace in which the forequarter of a baby goat was turning on a spit over red-hot coals and smoldering branches. We were served innumerable courses in which white truffles played a leading role, and then a chunk of kid. On the outside, its crust was intensely savory, crisp, and aromatic from the oak fire; within, the flesh was rich and tender and nearly falling apart. It was the best piece of meat I had ever eaten.

I returned the next morning to measure every dimension of Cesare's fireplace. He told me the spit must be 16 inches above the coals and that flames must just lick the back of the meat as they pass up the flue. He promised to teach me more when I was ready. I vowed then and there that, within a year, I would have a kitchen fireplace of my own, ready to be retrofitted with an iron spit and electric motor.

So I lied. Two years later, I started searching for substitutes. I remembered a ubiquitous countertop appliance from my suburban childhood called the Roto-Broil '400,' a streamlined glass-and-chrome cabinet with a powerful electrical coil under the hood and a smoothly spinning electric motor. I scoured the Chelsea flea markets and came up dry. The world is divided into two types of people. My type are the ones who couldn't spot a pink 1955 Thunderbird at a flea market unless it rolled over their foot. My friend Arthur Schwartz, host of one of the great radio food shows, allowed me to issue a moving appeal for a Roto-Broil '400' on the air. While waiting for a response, I resorted to the modern Farberware FSR200, an unenclosed electric tabletop grill with a rotisserie that can be raised and lowered in eight increments over an electric heating element. And it's spatter-free! I set to work roasting chickens, ducks, and legs of lamb.

Anything cooked over or near a wood fire (even a hardwood charcoal fire) will pick up the flavors of the wood and smoke. This is difficult to achieve with an indoor electric model. But my thoughts were now concentrated on the very concept of the rotisserie, on the inherent superiority of spinning an entire animal (or a substantial section of one) over, under, or alongside a good, strong source of heat. I remembered what Mrs. Randolph wrote in *The Virginia Housewife,* published in 1824 and still among the greatest of American cookbooks: "No meat can be well roasted except on a spit, and before a steady clear fire—other methods are no better than baking." Cooks in the nineteenth century also used the vertical method, still perfectly practicable today, of hanging a roast—say, a leg of lamb—from a string hooked to the roof of a fireplace just inside the opening. You twist it round and round, and let it go. The roast turns back and forth before the hot fire for five or ten minutes; then you twist the string again. A pan is set below the roast to collect its priceless juices.

The Farberware FSR200 excelled at roasting ducks. I became an expert at trussing—tying string around the bird to keep its shape compact, both for even cooking and so that I could bring the spit down near the heating element without singeing any stray or bulging parts, its wing tips, or its knees. Trussing birds has lost favor in the world of oven roasting, thanks in part to the canny observation of Barbara Kafka (in *Roasting: A Simple Art*) that tying the creature's legs against its body prevents the heat from reaching its meaty inner thigh, lengthening overall cooking time and producing dried-out breast meat. But the heating element of the Farberware FSR200 is so weak that raising a duck more than two inches above it makes for pallid skin and gray flesh; trussing is a necessity. I rub the bird with lots of salt and pepper. Then, to render out nearly every molecule of subdermal fat from a Pekin or Long Island duckling, I pierce the skin in a hundred places with the point of a sharp little knife, held nearly flat to the surface to avoid stabbing the bloody flesh. After an hour and a half of spit-roasting, more than a cup of fat has dripped into the pan, and the skin has become paper thin and delicious beyond my meager verbal powers to describe.

While enjoying my Farberware FSR200, I devised four hypotheses about why spinning a bird or a roast is far superior to what Mrs. Randolph disparaged as "baking," which is what most of us do to our birds and roasts in the modern household oven.

1. Meat turning on a horizontal spit is self-basting, as its surface juices and melted fats, torn between gravity and revolution, keep flowing over the exterior. But what are the true advantages of basting? Some now feel that basting is a wasted effort and does nothing to slow the loss of moisture. Harold McGee (author of *On Food and Cooking*) thinks basting with oil accelerates cooking, while basting with water slows it.

2. As meat spins toward and away from the fiery heat, it warms and cools several times a minute, preventing scorching, as we wait for conduction to transfer warmth to the center.

3. Spinning may swirl the internal juices about, making for faster, moister, and more even cooking. Or does circular motion draw the juices outward by centrifugal force?

4. In conventional ovens, heat is inefficiently carried to the surface of a roast; convection ovens cook more quickly by moving around hot air with a fan. Isn't twirling a roast in the hot air the same as swirling the air around a roast?

One morning, the telephone's ring roused my mind from these theoretical ruminations. It was radio personality Arthur Schwartz with news that my ship had come in. A listener had called to offer a Roto-Broil '400' in mint condition, with its original box and literature! The date on the side of the carton said 1956, but it worked as perfectly as if it had been sucked through a time warp. The electrical coils that wove back and forth above the inaugural chicken and initiatory duck were infernally hot, creating heavenly skin and nicely cooked flesh in just half the time of the Farberware, even though the distance between the meat and the heat in the Roto-Broil '400' cannot be adjusted. It was a day I will not soon forget.

But my Roto-Broil '400' would not live forever. I knew that. In search of a successor, I briefly turned my attention to three table-top vertical rotisseries on the market today, the Regal K7830, the Farberware FSR150, and the Oster Designer Carousel Rotisserie. You place a chicken or duck over a vertical shaft or tower—in some models legs up, in others legs down.

None brought peals of appreciative laughter to the *Vogue* test kitchen. The Farberware's heating element is too weak, even at the 560-degree setting, to brown and crisp the skin before the bird is done, and its construction makes removal of the bird, tower, and drip pan perilous. The Regal has a subsidiary heating element in the shaft that runs though the center of the bird, so the chicken flesh was done in just over a half hour, before the skin had crisped; this is a powerful appliance but ill designed, as the outer cabinet becomes unreasonably hot. The Oster takes an hour, gives you a fine view through a Plexiglas semicylinder, but leaves the wings soft and pallid. All three devices are closed tightly during roasting, which steams the meat. Vertical operation limits the amount of self-basting.

To test one of my four hypotheses, I compared the expensive DeLonghi countertop convection oven–rotisserie in its rotisserie mode (a feeble broiling element on the roof of the oven over a relatively short horizontal revolving spit, and no fan) and in convection mode (the spit does not turn, and the broiling element is off, but the fan circulates air with a maximum temperature of 450 degrees). Both convection chicken and rotisserie chicken were quite good, demonstrating that part of the advantage of spinning a bird or chunk of meat is to bring it into contact with hotter air. This test would have been more telling if the DeLonghi broiling element were more powerful.

Have you ever eaten *méchoui* in Morocco, a young lamb roasted for four hours on a spit over a bed of hot coals? I have, several times. *Méchoui* is like a foretaste of paradise, the tenderest and most delicious meat surrounded by the crispest, lambiest skin imaginable. You sit around a low table with friends and eat it with your hands, pulling pieces of flesh and crackling and dipping them into salt and spice. Never before or after have I been blessed with more skin than I could conceivably eat, acres and acres of it.

How can anybody call himself a roaster until he has made *méchoui*? I needed to get past my Roto-Broil '400' and back into flaming, snapping, glowing wood. I spent ten days in Southern California at my very own Casa Pacifica laying plans, and after numberless trips to Barbeques Galore at a minimall near San Diego, returned home with a Bar-B-Chef, a very heavy, large, simple black steel grill suitable for charcoal or wood. It has a 31-inch spit, and a crank to raise and lower the fuel beneath the cooking grate. Contrary to the salesman's assurances, it took an hour to remove from the car and four hours to assemble in a light rain. It never, ever rains in San Diego.

On its maiden voyage, my new grill and I spit-roasted one chicken over small wood logs and another over lump hardwood charcoal. Roasting experts nearly always tell you to build the fire next to the meat, not under it. Otherwise, the fire flares up as the fat drips down, charring the meat and coating it with soot from the burned, vaporized fat. But they have not eaten Cesare's kid. His fire is underneath, and his roasting long and slow, and I am determined to do as he does. Both chickens were edible only when I washed off the thick coating of soot, which left the skin smeared and dank. Sky King, our golden retriever, barely consented to consume the unfavorable evidence. I must return to Albaretto della Torre soon.

Then I tried the indirect method, tall volcanoes of charcoal piled up on both sides of the chicken with the hood closed tight. The temperature rose to over 500 degrees, probably voiding the Bar-B-Chef's very limited warranty. But the chicken was perfect, deeply burnished and succulent within, as was the duck that followed. With the hood down, just a few dry wood chips on charcoal were enough to lend the birds all the bosky flavor one would want.

Back in New York City, my assistant, Kathryn, defied my express and forceful edict and bought a Weber kettle for her Greenwich Village backyard. I have long hated all Weber grills because the company insists upon designing them so that the distance between the food and the fuel is never adjustable, which I consider completely indispensable to grilling. I counsel everybody I meet against buying them. But, as I had found success in San Diego with the indirect, covered method of spit-roasting (for which the height of the spit is not critical), I agreed to buy for Kathryn the Weber rotisserie attachment, a curved black sheet of metal that raises the walls of their 22-inch kettles to accommodate a nicely made stainless-steel spit and a barely adequate electric motor. At the start we used the little side baskets to hold the charcoal away from the center, under the chicken, and never attained a properly high temperature. The first chicken was only very good. Throwing caution to the winds, we dumped ten pounds of charcoal into the Weber, ignited it all, and 15 minutes later shoveled most of it away from the center. With the cover on, the temperature around the chicken soared beyond 500 degrees, and in 50 minutes, we had a perfect bird, with dark and crispy aromatic skin and the most succulent flesh imaginable, brimming with savory juice. Next step: spit-roasting three chickens at once on the long Weber spit.

The grilling season has barely begun. I would advise all of you who had once followed my advice and mothballed your 22-inch Weber kettles to buy the rotisserie attachment and join me for a summer of intense and frantic experimentation. Make sure you use free-range chickens and the kind of lump hardwood charcoal that comes in large, loglike chunks. Just remember that the Weber is still not a patch on Cesare's wood-burning fireplace in Albaretto della Torre.

AUGUST 1999

CAST PARTY

The edges of my bed are strewn with bottles of Advil, a gallon of springwater, four huge bars of dark Valrhona chocolate, an envelope of Tylenol with codeine, a two-pound bag of rabbit-shaped licorice from La Brea Bakery in Los Angeles, a bottle of good Scotch, and a pile of things to read. At the center of the bed, alternately writhing in excruciating pain and testing the theory that licorice can cure an ankle swollen to the size of a cantaloupe, is little me.

The day had dawned in bright expectation. I had spent the morning tinkering with my plans for a well-deserved trip to Paris, Sicily, Rome, and Crete. I was set to embark in only 36 hours. Then it was off to lunch at Wu Liang Ye on West 48th Street, my last Chinese meal for at least three weeks. Afterward, as I complacently walked along a tree-lined Manhattan street, my right shoe was suddenly gripped by a gaping crack in the sidewalk, my body twisted in the opposite direction, and I fell to the concrete. Getting into a taxi was tricky because whenever my right foot touched the ground, the pain made me gasp. The driver and six drivers behind him leaned on their horns, undoubtedly to distract me from my anguish. Once home, I hopped over to my desk and then the pantry, shoved some supplies and reading material into a shopping bag, and crawled to bed, dragging the bag behind me.

And here I lie. Yesterday, my wife flew to Beijing for a conference, and I am completely alone. Over the telephone, my doctor has prescribed RICE, not the cereal grass native to Asia and cultivated for its seed, but Rest, Ice, Compression, and Elevation. Rest and Elevation, the two principal talents with which nature has endowed me, are a breeze. Compression, I discover after one gentle squeeze, is out of the question. And, instead of Ice, I use four packs of frozen blue gel that had arrived with a recent delivery of designer sausages. Tomorrow, a set of X rays will determine whether my spring gastronomic adventure ends before it begins.

I sample the marvels in my shopping bag. The proofs of Molly O'Neill's new book have arrived, *The Pleasure of Your Company* (subtitled "How to Give a Dinner Party Without Losing Your Mind"), and I read them with great enjoyment. Then, I pore over a list, faxed by a Parisian friend, of the ten winners of the 1997 Grand Prix de la Baguette, awarded by the mayor of Paris. If I don't get to Paris soon, the Grand Prix de la Baguette will have gone stale.

I turn to the most recent food section from the *Los Angeles Times,* these days probably the best in the country. The entire front page and two excellent articles inside are devoted to Claudia Roden's spectacular and panoramic *The Book of Jewish Food: An Odyssey from Samarkand to New York* (Knopf). If my ankle is not broken and I can travel to Europe, I will spend time with Claudia in Herakleion on Crete. I glare at my ankle as though it were somebody else's.

Then the pills and whiskey have their intended effect, and I fall into a dark and dreamless sleep.

Day Two: The news is bad. There is a break in my fibula, above the ankle. I will have to wear a cast for at least five weeks and use crutches for three. So, I will spend the next 21 days at home, seated, supine, or prone. I begin scratching the passing days into my refrigerator door with a rusty whisk.

I spend the rest of Day Two e-mailing, telephoning, and faxing airlines, hotels, restaurants, and people in Europe to cancel my plans. I also discover that it is impossible to carry anything—say, a plate of crisp roast duck from the Chinese takeout place or even a cup of coffee—while both arms are dealing with crutches. On my first and only try, I drop the duck and its thick maroon sauce all over my nice new cast. So, I switch to a white terry bathrobe with huge pockets that can accommodate most fruits and baked goods, a mug holding any liquid hot or cold (though these do slosh over the rim), or an order of roast duck carefully dropped into a Baggie.

On **Day Three,** the mail is filled with fascination. Plus, it is the only thing I can get done in bed. A new food magazine is about to be launched; it's called *Cuisine.* One article will show how to use apple jelly to glue edible flowers onto a Brie; I hope it also tells you that it's impossible to find decent Brie in this country because of the FDA's rules against importing cheeses made from unpasteurized milk and aged for less than 60 days. South Florida's "first international charity wine event" wants me to save April 11 through 13 for them and the United Way. The third annual convention of Women Chefs & Restaurateurs will be held in New York City on May 4. All the heavyweights will be there. Just kidding. I know the founders and, to a woman, they are svelte and talented. The San Francisco Symphony will perform at the grand finale of the Sonoma County wine auction on July 26.

The Times Literary Supplement reviews two British books on food and ethics. One, *The Price of Meat,* is about the morality of raising and eating animals for food; it does not appear to say anything that Peter Singer, in his now classic *Animal Liberation,* did not cover years ago. The other is *Food Ethics,* a collection of essays that, in true British fashion, gives a host of other reasons to be nervous about eating. One chapter fondly recalls World War II and urges the current government to ration the food supply again so that people will be forced to eat in a more healthful way. Remind me please, did the British win the war or did the Nazis?

"Have you dreamed of supping in a spice market?" asks the Mauna Lani Bay Hotel in Hawaii. Can't say as I have. The excellent Home restaurant in Greenwich Village will open Drovers Tap Room at 9 Jones Street with a party. I am also invited to join Bill Cosby to celebrate the hundredth anniversary of Jell-O at Cooper Union. Six days later, Halcyon restaurant will re-create the last dinner served on the *Titanic,* whose many courses will include Consommé Olga, whoever she was, Filet Mignon Lili on a bed of Pommes Anna with a medallion of foie gras, and

CAST PARTY 47

peaches with Chartreuse liqueur gelée. Le Gigot has earned two
stars out of four in the *New York Observer.* CNN feels that Carolyn
O'Neil, its food and health correspondent, "would make an excellent profile for *Vogue.*" They have even sent me a videotape. I love
Carolyn, but I disagree with nearly all her views on nutrition and
fat. Plus, I'm right.

The Weber company announces that its (800) Grill Line barbecue hotline will reopen on April 1. I will not tell you the number
unless you promise to flood them with calls asking how any self-
respecting corporation can manufacture a grill that does not
allow you to raise and lower either the grid or the coals; Weber's
design has been my bête noir for years.*

The Florida Citrus Growers invite me to a dinner of Florida
cuisine at the James Beard House in Greenwich Village. *Appellation* magazine arrives from Napa Valley—after a slow start, it's
more opulent and interesting with every issue. But the recipe for
flammenkuche, which stands little chance of reproducing the
famed tart of Kientzheim in Alsace, makes me wonder about the
magazine's other recipes. The Regency Hotel wants me to drink
lots of single-malt scotches in their restaurant, The Library. Free.
The New York chapter of the American Institute of Wine & Food
wants me to taste more than 80 microbrews paired with the food
of 21 New York restaurants. Not free.

At last, I sustain a paper cut and retire to bed for two serious
hours of RICE. On the way, I try to enter the bathroom, which
is one step up. I stand there for five minutes, frozen, staring at
the step, afraid of falling. My excellent orthopedic surgeon at the
Hospital for Special Surgery, who also repairs the New York Mets,
has given me a mnemonic, but I cannot remember whether it is
"Up with the good [leg], down with the bad [leg]" or "Up with
the bad," et cetera. I telephone his office. When the answer
comes it is obvious. "Up with the good!"

*Although I have expressed the same sentiments whenever anyone would listen,
Weber's electric rotisserie attachment halfway redeems the company. See "As the
Spit Turns," page 36.

My wife phones from Beijing. She has squandered her first lunch on the Chinese mainland at a McDonald's. She informs me that Chicken McNuggets are far more popular than Big Macs. Who can doubt that she did this as an act of cheap defiance, knowing that if I were with her, our first meal would have been planned six months ago?

The twice-weekly delivery of mail from *Vogue* arrives in two shopping bags and a large cardboard box. My paper cut still smarts, and I am sick of mail. "Sufficient unto the day is the evil thereof," as the Utah branch of my wife's family likes to say. I will open the shopping bags tomorrow. On the other hand, there may be free food inside.

Dinner is enough vegetarian Indian takeout to feed half the adult population of Mumbai, the new name for Bombay. The Indians say it is really the ancient name. Why don't the French change Paris back to Lutèce? I e-mail my personal alternative physician, Dr. Andrew Weil, whose *Eight Weeks to Optimum Health* has just reached number one on the *New York Times* best-seller list. Soon he will be impossible to deal with; for now he is just my old college roommate Andy. Instantly, his answer arrives. First of all, he has just had an awful meal in Minneapolis, to which his triumphal book tour has taken him. Second, to speed healing I should try bromelain, 400 milligrams, three times a day on an empty stomach. Ha, ha. When was the last time either of us had an empty stomach? I will take Andy's advice.

Day Four: The *Vogue* mail will wait no longer, and neither will the telephone. I have never read my mail so closely or returned so many phone calls. Before, it was maybe 10 percent of my job. Now I'm good for little else.

The Memphis in May World Championship Barbecue has asked me to serve as a judge, for the second time. I am honored. I love Southern barbecue more than almost anything, and this is the contest referred to as "The Big One." I earned official certification several years ago after a grueling course on pork shoulder, pork ribs, and whole hog. My other favorite piece of mail is from Philippe Viron and his family's flour mills in Chartres. Their mission is the preservation and recovery of the traditional baguette made in France only from flour, water, salt, and, sometimes, yeast. Philippe has sent me a list of the additives now permitted by the evil European Commission in any bread labeled "French": acetic, lactic, and ascorbic acids; potassium, sodium, and calcium acetates and lactates; sodium and calcium ascorbate; lecithin; mono- and diglycerides; and various esters. Finding real food in Europe is fast becoming an uphill battle.

This is a fine day for books. Three classics of food writing have been reprinted by Lyons & Burford: Patience Gray's *Honey from a Weed*, Elizabeth David's *An Omelette and a Glass of Wine*, and Jim Villas's *American Taste*. The long-awaited *Steak Lover's Cookbook* (Workman) from William Rice is just out, a wonderfully written guide for reproducing at home the food you would eat at the epitomic steak house—if one existed, which it doesn't. The Orchid at Mauna Lani, which I believe is a hotel on the Big Island and not a flower, has invited me to experience the "Big Island Bounty" culinary festival in Hawai'i (as they spell it), at the end of May. Now they follow up with two phone calls a day. This is a "hosted invitation," as they put it, meaning, I believe, free. I would love to go, but I've made a rule against free trips. "Soothe your mind, body and soul during an oceanside massage at The Centre for Well Being," they promise. There are many intriguing seminars, including "Cognacs, Cigars and Confections," a trio I have never associated with either Hawai'i, as they spell it, or oceanside massage. The brochure stresses the Orchid's Beach Boys, always capitalized. Is this a crass appeal to female or gay food-writers? Do I sound ungrateful?

My wife telephones from Beijing. In another tawdry act of spite, she has avoided the grand banquet at her Chinese conference. She did, though, find some wonderful sesame buns griddled over charcoal on the street.

The *New York Times* Living section has a long article about how famed flautist Jean-Pierre Rampal is wild about sushi, without saying anything interesting about sushi. They have also run yet another article assuring you that your guests will really be more grateful if you feed them less food. Such sentiments are the product of a diseased mind. But there's a huge, fun-loving, food-loving cover story on new Los Angeles restaurants by Ruth Reichl. Three days from now I am scheduled to have lunch with her and our friend Marion Cunningham (*Fannie Farmer Cookbook, Fannie Farmer Baking Book,* et cetera) in Paris at Taillevent. I telephone them both with the tragic news. Later, Ruth and Marion torment me with these sadistic words: asparagus with truffles and brown butter sauce, sea urchin mousse, warm oysters with a light sabayon, frozen cream of salted caramel. I consider defenestration.

In the late afternoon, I attempt my first foray out of the bathrobe and out of the house. I am unable to cross Fifth Avenue between lights and cancel my foray. Endurance on crutches is all about upper-body strength and aerobic fitness. Why didn't somebody warn me years ago?

I RICE until evening, then realize I have bought nothing for dinner. I try various free food samples I have stored in the freezer. The Gardenburgers are quite poor, especially when thawed. The low-fat chocolate brownies and cookies are little better. Things look up slightly with frozen shrimp fajitas, then turn ugly with a pair of Zone shakes. Fifteen minutes of trivial kitchen work has taken me two hours.

Dropping things is the worst part. Picking them up is a complicated maneuver, and if they have splattered all about, there is no alternative to kneeling and crawling around on the floor with a roll of paper towels between my teeth. Most of the pain disappeared yesterday, and now my tribulations are limited to minor inconveniences and immobility. I have a tiny, temporary inkling of what it's like to be physically handicapped. (I can't remember the politically correct term.) If I had more character, I would pledge never again to complain for the rest of my life. But complaining is too much fun. I go to bed hungry and exhausted.

Day Five is Good Friday, the day the Italian army killed Jesus and blamed it on the Jews. Why do they call it Good Friday? It wasn't good for them, and it wasn't good for us.

I must bake today or I am doomed. Alfred A. Knopf, publishers, have unwisely decided to publish a collection of my articles, and their famed jacket designer, Chip Kidd, urgently requires one large loaf of my own very best freshly baked bread. To free my hands, I stand on one foot and lean against the table while weighing a kilogram of the finest organic bread flour from Giusto's in South San Francisco. The table slides away, the bowl overturns, and flour covers the floor. I cannot face cleaning it up, so standing amid the mess, I start all over again. Fourteen hours later the bread is edible but heavy and dense. I will give it another stab in a few days, after I have recovered from this humiliation.

Day Six: The mail brings my *Vogue* contract for 1997–1998. I peek inside to see if they have also included food stamps. At least the University of Nevada in Las Vegas has sent me a real $2 bill, thanking me in advance for filling out a survey for its hotel school. Famed food writer Barbara Kafka calls and offers to make me chicken soup. I ask her how one goes about baking bread on crutches. Put everything on the floor including the mixer and yourself. Barbara is brilliant.

The UPS man brings the ten-pound galleys of the Herculean rewrite of *Joy of Cooking*, expected in November from Scribners. My wife has nearly redeemed herself by having dinner at the 200-year-old China Beijing Wangfujing Quanjude Roast Duck Restaurant: pot-stewed duck gizzards served cold, duck web with mustard, stewed duck liver, duck tongues in mushrooms, duck wings in red jelly, deep-fried duck hearts with broccoli, and, at last, crispy duck skin rolled in pancakes. I think I have left out one of the courses.

The Culinary Historians of Southern California, headed by Charles Perry, has published a nice booklet of recipes from the century 1796–1896. Did you know that something called the *Pan Pacific Cookbook* was published in 1915? The excellent food-radio personality Arthur Schwartz is about to publish his magnum opus on Campania. Yum!

My appetite is nearly back to normal. A friend and I reserve a table at Mirezi, the Korean-fusion restaurant five blocks away. I give up after two and take a cab for the other three. The driver is livid. Inside, there is a slick stone staircase. Up with the good, down with the bad. I refuse to let the waiter take my crutches. Leaving the house is a mixed proposition at the best of times. I won't try it again for at least a week.

Day Seven is Easter, and people come to visit. Baker-owner Jim Lahey of the Sullivan Street Bakery brings a shopping bag overflowing with his artistry, including a Colomba Pasquale, the sweet Italian Easter bread based on a natural starter and flavored with candied orange rind. It is the perfect food—chewy and stretchy, tangy, sugary, and bitter. Reluctantly and politely, Jim critiques my bread. Tell me something I didn't know.

Days Eight through Fourteen begin with flowers from the editor of *Vogue*, 48 white double tulips in a crystal cylinder. Every day for the next week they open a little more, finally becoming a huge white cloudlike sphere over my desk.

Radcliffe College, whose Schlesinger Library has the finest culinary collection in the country, announces that Barbara Ketcham Wheaton will do a reprise of her wonderful seminars, "Reading Cookbooks as Social History," starting May 19. I would love to attend. A pile of magazines has come—the latest issues of *Food Arts*, with an excellent roundup by Eileen Yin-Fei Lo of Hong Kong eating places on the verge of reversion; *Flavor & Fortune*, a magazine about Chinese cuisine published in Suffolk County; the *Radcliffe Culinary Times*; and *New York* magazine, which has anointed Sullivan Street Bakery in its Best of New York issue. Welcome aboard, *New York* magazine.

Starbucks sends over several of their new coffee ice creams. Some of them are delicious, refreshing yet full of flavor. They've included gift certificates for all their other coffee flavors. Thanks, Starbucks. I telephone Le Cirque 2000 to inquire about access for the handicapped. Trefethen Vineyards sends me a bag of dirt with an April Fool's note: "Fruit to Follow." My beautiful friend Susana, a doctor of rehabilitative medicine, pays a late-night visit with her dachshund. He urinates on the couch. I sulk and read my media kit from the National Watermelon Promotion Board.

Or is it the National Pasta Association's ideas for summer pasta dishes?

Of the 10,000 or so PR people who specialize in food, five or ten are always welcome because they read what I write and bring me only products and events that will amuse or fascinate. The rest are totally clueless. Sarah Powers of Nike Communications is one of the five or ten, and today she makes a sick call bearing a bottle of Krug Grande Cuvée, her client and my choice for the finest champagne in the world. I invite over the California Milk Advisory Board, which will bring 10 or 12 California cow cheeses a week from now for a tasting; I've heard of only a few of them. *Cook's Illustrated* arrives, my favorite food magazine. Ben & Jerry's messengers over four pints of its new low-fat ice cream. Nothing can make me like xanthan gum or baked goods mashed into my frozen dessert. Still, the Sweet Cream & Cookies isn't bad.

Belson Porta-Grill has sent me their latest brochure, complete with testimonials from American Legion Post #10 in Barre, Vermont. These are big, serious outdoor grills, nothing portable about them. A Pig Roast Instructional Video and Booklet are available separately. I would order a Belson in two seconds if only I owned a patch of ground. Bulletin! The April 3 *New England Journal of Medicine* will be long remembered for the Harvard study by Ridker, Cushman, and others demonstrating that heart attacks are triggered by a systemic inflammation of the arteries! A blood test for a liver enzyme marker is at least as predictive as a cholesterol test. Now we understand why half of all heart attacks afflict people with normal cholesterol, and vice versa. The fat theory of heart disease has sustained another mortal blow. How many mortal blows will it take?

Balthazar Bakery has just opened at 80 Spring Street; the restaurant side is still a shambles, with no ETA. Talented baker Paula Oland is said to be in charge of the ovens, and if this is true, Balthazar's bread will rank with the best in the city. A reader tells my answering machine how much she hates me for referring to pre-1960s SoHo as "a post-Industrial nightmare of narrow, filthy streets and tenements." She seems to think I was referring to Little Italy, where she apparently grew up. Another reader who had an awful, costly dinner at L'Ami Lui in Paris wants me to tell everybody about it. Done. I never recommended L'Ami Lui in *Vogue,* though I have had some memorable meals there. Fran's Chocolates in Seattle sends me a press release. I love Fran's, but they forgot the chocolates. Senator Alfonse D'Amato's mother, Antoinette, has a new cookbook: *Cooking and Canning with Mamma D'Amato.* I swear not to hold her son against her.

AT&T offers me $40 in gift certificates for fruit from Harry and David if I switch to the One Rate Plan. I think I am going crazy.

And then, at last, my wife returns from China, bent low with culinary gifts: three bags of very fine tea; a liter of Suntory Pure Malt Whisky from the Narita duty-free shop; and a little Chinese thermos, perfect for carrying cold springwater in my bathrobe pocket from refrigerator to desk. I gulp down nearly a gallon a day, 16 round-trips.

Overcome with joy, I order a celebratory dinner from the 2nd Avenue Deli: hot pastrami, tongue, salami, chopped liver, pickles, rye bread. When our meal arrives, my wife turns up her nose, insists on walking to Union Square, and brings back a seaweed salad and some kind of Thai noodle thing—while my hot pastrami becomes cold pastrami. Can it be that life is returning to normal?

JUNE 1997

Author's note: A few weeks later, still wearing my cast, I traveled with my wife to Sichuan Province. On the way home, we were seriously assaulted by toxic airline food. For the full story, see the next page.

TARO, TARO, TARO

A rosette of Black Forest ham was all that remained of my business-class luncheon appetizer as we hurtled from the coast of China toward the islands of Japan. Beneath us, glinting as though it were a silver tray dotted with puffs of meringue, stretched the East China Sea. With some difficulty, I managed to saw through the ham, took a delicate sip of Diet Coke, and chewed ruminatively on the pink, smoky meat. Had it truly originated in the Black Forest of southern Germany and journeyed untold kilometers to Shanghai and onto a Northwest Airlines jet in time for lunch? With all the famous hams of China, why would a rational airline have expended such backbreaking effort?

I was getting all het up. Had they done a survey showing that an airline's business booms threefold when true and authentic Black Forest ham is fed to its passengers? I thought fondly of the giant packets of M&M's, both peanut and regular, that I had bought at the Shanghai airport, manufactured in China, but somehow capable of making me feel nearly home again. Perhaps the plane was crammed with German tourists, starving for a comparable foretaste of the Fatherland. Or had the ham been counterfeited in some squalid back alley in that boundless land of a billion souls? It bore no resemblance to its namesake, one of the world's finest porcine achievements. (The thinly sliced meat should be edged with white fat, and progress inward from a dry and crusty rose to a pinky softness. Ours was pale and mealy throughout.) Nonetheless, I raised another forkful toward my mouth—on an airplane, you never know which mouthful will be your last.

Just then, I felt an odd burning sensation on my tongue and lips. It spread slowly along the sides of my mouth, toward the opening of my throat, and underneath the tongue, where it began to cause quite a bit of pain. I stifled a wavelet of panic and whirled around to the passenger next to me. As luck would have it, that very passenger was my wife.

As my throat began to swell, I issued a series of amazingly coherent and penetrating instructions to her. The cause of my distress, I explained, was probably the food I had just eaten—*we* had just eaten. She should, for a while at least, eat nothing more. My malady was either a localized irritation of the oral cavity or a full-blown allergy. As everybody else in business class had eaten more or less the same food, a mere irritation could have been caused only by something particularly wrong with my portion— a dollop of preservative, a splash of disinfectant, some airline air-conditioning fluid that had gotten into nobody else's meal. These seemed only remotely possible.

The alternative was frightening. Everybody in America these days claims to be suffering from one food allergy or another, but the fact is that very few adults—no more than 1 or 2 percent—are afflicted with true food allergies. Being allergic means that your immune system has developed antibodies against a particular food (most often peanuts, tree nuts, milk, eggs, wheat, soy, fish, and shellfish). Eating the food causes—often within 20 minutes— a histamine reaction that brings on itching or irritation of the lips, face, and throat; hives; and, in severe cases, extreme swelling of these tissues, closing of the throat and air passages, and, finally— I could hardly say the word—*death* from what is known as ana-phylactic shock.

Though previously certain that I was free from all food aller-gies, now I was gripped by doubt. Could it be the peanuts in the giant bag of M&M's I had eaten at the Shanghai airport? I could have continued on this logical journey. But, not for the first time in my life, I was torn between the thirst for pure knowledge and the desire to stay alive. My wife's reaction was unexpected. "Bet you're really sorry you've spent half your life making fun of people with food allergies—including yours truly!" she chortled as a pink, half-chewed chunk of ham fell from her lips and rolled down the front of her blouse.

I refused to take her bait. "Listen. If this is a real food allergy, I will need a shot of epinephrine within about 15 minutes. So, we have ten minutes before we need to inform the stewardess of my condition. If we tell her before we are sure, we will make fools of ourselves—like all the hypochondriacs I write about. But any longer than that . . ." Here I stopped for fear that unaccustomed tears would well up in my wife's eyes, melting her mascara.

They remained bone dry, and I continued, "That gives us 10 minutes to figure it out. I will describe my symptoms every 30 seconds or so. Right now, the pain under my tongue is becoming more than just an irritation and the back of my throat feels as though it is blistering, but my breathing passages do not seem to be closing."

We continued our mental police work. Assuming the problem was not a food allergy, the cause was probably something I had eaten that my wife had not. She had indeed consumed some M&M's, though being a layperson, she could not remember which flavor; as the plain M&M's package remained unopened, they must have been the same peanut flavor I had enjoyed. Then, just before takeoff, we had shared one tiny dish of warm, business-class, roasted mixed nuts. It was possible that I had hastily finished off, say, all the Brazil nuts before she had gotten to them, but unlikely—given my wife's highly competitive nature at table.

The rosette of ham had been served on a round plastic plate lined with some kind of dark green leaf on which were also several thin slices of melon and a halved quail's egg with a little black caviar. Both of us had finished the quail's eggs, some of the melon, and some ham. My throat was beginning to close, and though my breathing was still pretty easy, I had started to wheeze. The discomfort under my tongue was becoming unbearable. Five minutes remained before we would need to call the flight attendant and her syringe of epinephrine.

And then, as we hastily examined our plates, I saw it! In the violent sawing that my ham had required, I had cut through the round leaf underneath. I had consumed the merest sliver, but my wife's leaf was entirely intact.

Breathing with slightly more difficulty, I shared my discovery. She would not listen, preferring to accuse me of hypochondria and malingering, saying that I was probably having an excessive negative-aesthetic response to the poor quality of the ham, to its numbing saltiness. To prove her point, she demanded that I cut a wedge from my leaf and let her eat it.

I went along, giving her no more than an eighth of the entire thing. She popped it into her mouth and happily chewed away. "Either you have the most unlikely food allergy ever recorded," she giggled, "or you are the biggest phony in and around the East China Sea. . . ." At that very moment, she emitted a noise that the "aaaaarrrrrggggghhhhh" of the comic books can only weakly suggest. Her hands flew to her throat, her body arched backward, her eyes bulged, and her throat emitted three or so additional "aaaaarrrrrggggghhhhh"s.

As if by magic, my own pain had begun to subside. My throat still felt rough, but my wheeze had disappeared; the fire under my tongue had gotten no worse, and the burning on the sides of my mouth was nearly gone. As my suppressed panic over death by anaphylactic shock disappeared, I became almost giddy, which my writhing wife misinterpreted as joy at her own misfortune. I lifted a glass of Diet Coke to her lips and explained that she had just consumed 20 times more of that mysterious green leaf as I had. Either the leaf itself, or something on it, had poisoned us both.

Our fine flight attendant, nicknamed Jinx, was skeptical for a half minute—after all, nobody else on the plane had complained, and the identical appetizer had been served on at least half of Northwest's weekly flights from Shanghai to Tokyo for the past year or more. But after I gave her my business card, she blanched, and soon became my partner in detection. As I sliced the leaf in half, she located two Ziploc bags, so that Northwest could have the leaf analyzed chemically and biologically, while I could retain my share of the evidence. She assured me that, whatever the attitude of her employers, I would receive a copy of the report. The plant itself was difficult to identify just from the appearance of its leaf—which had apparently been cut into a perfect circle to fit the plate.

We three parted at Narita Airport, Jinx to her Seattle home, my wife to Tokyo for three days of business—the nature of which, as she was still suffering from severe dysphonia and dysphagia (words I later learned from a book on plant toxicology), I never did grasp—and me, now feeling only the slightest tickle at the back of my throat, back to New York City. As if by magic, a Mr. Noriyuki Okuzaki materialized, the manager of in-flight service in Japan, who, probably fearing bad publicity, pledged that by the time I reached home, the identity of the offending plant would be discovered. As we talked, my wife slowly passed out of sight on the moving sidewalk. She looked back with an expression I took to be bitterness that Northwest Airlines was so solicitous of her husband while she was still nearly incapacitated.

The airline official assigned to meet me at Kennedy Airport had the answer: *Colocasia esculenta,* more commonly known as taro, whose large starchy subterranean tuber, probably native to India, is crucial to the diets of most Pacific Islanders (including native Hawaiians, who mash it up and call it *poi*). It is also eaten enthusiastically throughout Southeast Asia, Africa, and the Caribbean. But the leaves require very careful handling. He promised that the taro-leaf decoration would immediately be removed from all Northwest flights. I would be kept informed.

I was soon put in touch with Peter Wilander, the airline's managing director for onboard services, who, over the next three months, proved always resourceful and good-humored. From his remote post in Minneapolis, which I believe is in Minnesota, Peter has to worry about caterers in 90 cities, who prepare the 350 main courses and 80 appetizers that Northwest is currently serving. Peter and I set out to find the answers to three essential questions: What harm can eating a raw taro leaf cause? Why were we the only passengers attacked by it? And how did it get into a Northwest Airlines meal?

Peter started on the Internet, and I telephoned the federal

Centers for Disease Control and Prevention in Atlanta. Peter learned that, like spinach, uncooked taro leaves contain oxalic acid, which can sometimes irritate our mucous membranes. I learned that the CDC knows nothing at all about taro and very little about oxalate poisoning. As for the possibility that some pesticide or other was the problem, an expert at the Environmental Protection Agency assured me that contact with pesticides has little effect on the human mouth or throat. When I searched for information about taro at the library of the New York Botanical Garden, everything became clear—up to a point.

Oxalic acid, found in several bitter green vegetables, can harm us in two awful ways. A huge amount of it in our diet causes crystals to form in our kidneys and irritates the lining of our stomach so badly that it can kill us. Humans hardly ever eat that much oxalic acid, though I found one report of a death caused by too much sorrel soup. In some plants, such as taro, the oxalic acid combines with calcium to form calcium oxalate, which sometimes takes the form of raphides—long, needlelike, microscopic crystals that can easily pierce our mucous membranes. They are insidiously constructed with long grooves that channel another poison in taro—not yet identified—into the wound. In short, uncooked taro leaves are little more than hideous, microscopic, poison-creation-and-delivery systems!

Young taro leaves are eaten in lots of places, but they are always cooked first, and this removes their acrid, burning qualities. I consulted my Filipino friend Romy Dorotan of Cendrillon restaurant in New York City, where he serves *laing*—dried taro leaves that he first simmers in coconut milk until they resemble creamed spinach, then wraps in fresh taro leaves and simmers again. Romy buys his fresh taro leaves in the Flatbush section of Brooklyn, where Korean grocers cater to the taro-hungry Caribbean population, who call them *callaloo*.

It was astonishing and incomprehensible that my wife and I would be the only passengers to have complained. Most passengers on Northwest's weekly Shanghai-to-Narita run are Japanese, Chinese, and American. Neither the Japanese nor the Chinese share the American tendency to put everything green and raw into their mouths. But surely at least one American passenger must have tried to eat his or her taro leaf? Peter and I were stumped.

And how had this insidious garnish found its way onto the Northwest menu? Meals in and out of Japan are pretty much "designed" and tested in Japan, and then reviewed by Peter and his department—meaning that micromanagement from Minneapolis is less exacting than with meals on flights in and out of the United States. And meals on infrequent flights like Northwest's weekly Shanghai-Tokyo run are subject to even less control. Northwest offices in Tokyo or Minneapolis come up with the general outlines of each dish, the caterer in Shanghai produces samples, and a final recipe is settled on—though the caterer may keep control of decoration and even some garnishes, such as the toxic taro leaf. Peter Wilander never seemed to be engaging in spin control, but his account did aim me in the direction of casting most of the blame for my wife's dysphonia—now no more than a joyous memory—on the local caterer in Shanghai, or, at worst, on the Japanese office.

I pressed Peter to launch a witch-hunt and comb Northwest's records in Minneapolis and Tokyo to discover where the idea of a taro-leaf decoration had come from and who had approved it. Just this once, Peter seemed evasive, finally conceding that he was unwilling to turn the Japanese operation upside down—with all the loss of face that would result—just to pin the blame on some individual, for my sake. I can't decide whether Peter was being reasonable. Northwest was acting so little like an airline and Peter so little like a company man that any complaint on my part seems ungrateful. Still, there is somebody somewhere in their Japanese operation who walks the earth, unpunished.

Tarogate came to something of a resolution when, after ten attempts, I was finally able to speak with Mr. Wilson Lee, deputy general manager of the Shanghai Eastern Air Catering Co. Ltd. Yes, he had been working there when the Black Forest ham appetizer was invented, and he was willing to take responsibility for any mistakes he had made. His chef apologized for my distress but had never imagined that anybody would actually eat a decorative, poisonous taro leaf, especially since the Chinese never eat anything raw except fresh fruit.

Later I discovered in a roundabout way that United Airlines, which also employed Shanghai Eastern Air Catering, had several years earlier received complaints from customers about uncooked taro leaves. United substituted another garnish—I believe it was lemon leaves—but never warned its competitors. It did, however, warn Shanghai Eastern Air Catering. Did Shanghai Eastern inform Northwest?

As for the authenticity and travels of the Black Forest ham: In 1996, China outlawed the import of all pork products from Europe, giving real or purported health concerns as its justification. Shanghai Eastern Air Catering shifted to *prosciutto crudo di Parma,* manufactured, of course, in Australia. How it came to be known as Black Forest ham on the Northwest menu is a mystery that, I fear, will never be solved.

FEBRUARY 1998

A Deep and Blinding Insight

Just as we were polishing off a full and happy lunch . . . I sensed that somewhere inside me was taking shape a deep and blinding insight.

SALT CHIC

My first step was to buy a pocket-sized electronic scale capable of weighing one-thousandth of a gram, the kind of scale you might find at a major drug deal in, say, the Everglades. Next, I took 13 different kinds of salt from my pantry, packaged them up, and sent them off to the AmTest laboratory near Seattle for the most minute analysis. And then, I reserved a seat on the next day's flight to Palermo, Sicily. Within days I was installed in the exquisite medieval mountaintop city of Erice, feasting on hillocks of freshly made sheep's-milk ricotta and broad platters of hand-rolled couscous moistened with rich fish broth. But that wasn't the point of my visit. Far from it. The point was pure science. Before I was through, I would solve the riddles and enigmas concerning the taste of salt.

Nothing in the food world today is chicer than salt, and despite an excess of God-given modesty, I must admit that I got there very, very early. Now, every gourmet store sells costly varieties of salt in a rainbow of colors from the world over. Food fans who once brought back unusual olive oils to their friends back home now come bearing bags of exotic salt. Chefs plan special dinners in which each course is paired with a particular type of salt. Food writers compete to demonstrate their intimacy with salts from the ends of the Earth and their disdain for Diamond Crystal and Morton's. Confided the owner of one Manhattan gourmet shop to the *New York Times,* "I don't even use regular salt anymore. It's like cooking with sour wine." I've just read a recipe that has us pour a certain $25-a-pound salt into our pasta water.

It is a rare day when I feel that I stand at the very forefront of fashion, at the cutting edge of chic, but this is one of them. Just look at my countertop. There is a jar of Sicilian sea salt from the vast salt flats at Trapani, and pouches of powder-fine Indian black salt, which is really a beautiful, indescribable lavender, and Thai salt, which is simply white. There's regular table salt and kosher salt (which should be called "koshering salt," as it was originally, and still is, used to prepare meat in accordance with Jewish dietary laws). My British Maldon sea salt comes in lovely square flakes; there is Korean salt roasted in vessels of bamboo; one type of Hawaiian salt is coral-colored because of the red *alae* clay lining the salt pools, and the other is black from a lining of lava rock. I am not sure how the rose-tinted salt from Maras, Peru, got that way. Please remind me to place a call to Maras, Peru. And, as you'd expect, there are bags of *fleur de sel,* the most delightful type of sea salt because, after evaporation by the sun, it is collected by hand from the fluffy and ephemeral top layer of the salt pools, almost like snowflakes; mine are from Guérande and from the Île de Ré in Poitou-Charentes and from the Camargue in southern France. Each crystal of *fleur de sel* is said to form around a single *alga* (the singular form of *algae*), giving it what some sniffers perceive as the aroma of violets. Maybe someday I'll smell the violets, too.

And to think that only 10 or 12 years ago I was as benighted as the rest of America, believing that salt is salt, totally sodium chloride—the NaCl we first met in high school. I still remember the day in Paris when the scales were lifted from my eyes. I was having dinner with two friends in whose palates I had learned to place great trust. When the food arrived, each brought out a small, square wooden box of polished walnut. They slid the lids to one side, exposing a cache of airy white crystals. It was *fleur de sel* from Guérande, their favorite everyday, multipurpose salt.

Just taste it, my friends urged. And so I did, first dropping a little pinch onto my tongue and rubbing it around the inside of my mouth, then tasting the restaurant's salt in the same way, and back again to the *fleur de sel.* The difference was obvious on the first try. The regular table salt was bitter, unpleasant in the back of the tongue and mouth; the *fleur de sel* was simply salty—a pure, pristine, and very pleasurable saltiness.

And so I, too, acquired a little walnut box and filled it with *fleur de sel*. I bring it out only in Europe. I tried it once here, but the derision was even more painful than sprinkling my food with regular American table salt.

My salt sophistication has only soared since then. Let me tell you about Oshima Island Blue Label Salt, one of the rarest in the world and among the most expensive. It is evaporated from the primordially crystalline seawater around Oshima Island, in the middle of the vast and empty ocean, 45 minutes by plane from Tokyo. It is available for purchase in small amounts only by members of a club called the Salt Road Club. And I am a card-carrying member—without doubt the only member with whom you are acquainted and, I have been told, the only American granted admission. Our membership card is a lovely shiny plastic ocean blue, and I carry it always in my wallet, next to my heart. My friend Nafumi Tamura, who had helped me last year by translating some Japanese materials on the history of sashimi, arranged for my membership through her mother's home address in Osaka. In a remarkable twist of fate, Nafumi now works in the kitchen of a hot new restaurant in Manhattan named Fleur de Sel.

There is about a half pound of Oshima Island Blue Label Salt in a bag on my counter, and it is currently my favorite salt of all—only in part because of its rarity and dizzyingly high status—but I use it infrequently, so as not to squander it all before next year's harvest. In fact, I don't use it at all. How chic is that?

Now somebody has thrown a stink bomb into our midst. He is Robert L. Wolke, a retired chemistry professor who has written a series of three articles in the *Washington Post* claiming that all salt tastes the same! If two salts seem to differ, he says, it is only because their crystals differ in shape and size—even though their chemical composition is essentially identical. When texture is not a factor—when, as in cooking, the salts are dissolved in liquids—their tastes are completely indistinguishable. No salt is chemically saltier than any other. Wolke makes lots of clumsy fun of people who think otherwise. His series of articles won two important awards for newspaper food journalism.

The food world was in an uproar. If Wolke is right, then all of the money, time, and pride we have devoted to exotic salts has been completely wasted, and we are now exposed as pretentious frauds. My single claim to chic would be washed down the drain. Somebody has to prove Wolke wrong!

I was surprised that his articles won those journalism awards. To make the argument that all salts taste alike because their chemical composition is nearly the same, Wolke needs two crucial pieces of evidence—a chemical analysis of various types of salt, and a scientifically conducted, comparative taste test of them. He has neither. He doesn't mention any of the tests that others have already conducted (I know of two, both unpublished), or make plans to conduct one himself. He simply asserts that the amounts of other minerals mixed in with the sodium chloride are too small to taste. Wolke may be right, but he surely doesn't prove it.

We can all certainly agree on some basic facts about salt. All salt comes from the sea, including inland salt deposits left by prehistoric seas. Evaporate water from the open ocean, and you will end up with a sludge containing about 75 percent sodium chloride and the rest a wide variety of minerals, dominated by magnesium and calcium. Refine the sludge further and you will get edible white table salt, mainly sodium chloride, plus about 1 percent other minerals. Different refining methods produce salt crystals that look entirely different from each other—some are like snowflakes; others are dense cubes. Kosher salt is shaped in hollow, stepped pyramids. That's why different salts melt at different rates on the tongue and why a teaspoon of one type may weigh half again as much as another. (Shirley Corriher, food scientist and author of *CookWise: The Hows and Whys of Successful Cooking* [William Morrow Cookbooks], tells me that some salts dissolve *nine times* faster than others.) Fluffy crystals of *fleur de sel* or thin flakes of Maldon salt sprinkled on dry food will melt immediately on the tongue, delivering a powerful hit of saltiness. The compact cubes of Diamond Crystal and Morton's melt slowly, reluctantly releasing their salty taste over a longer span of time, to which one writer attributes the bitterness of common table salt. Sprinkled on moist dishes like tuna tartare, *fleur de sel* will dissolve quickly, whereas Diamond Crystal may remain in crunchy form for some time, possibly an advantage. But used on dry, grilled meat, *fleur de sel* will still give your tongue a salt rush.

These are the taste effects of texture, which Wolke and the other salt skeptics acknowledge, at least in principle. But texture disappears when salt is dissolved in water—or in a sauce or a stock. There, it becomes 99 percent sodium chloride and 1 percent a bouquet of other minerals. Can we taste them? If so, would this help explain and justify the different tastes of various salts? Wolke says no, the other minerals are too dilute to taste. But nearly everybody can taste the difference between bottled mineral water and tap water. Yet mineral water contains only one-twentieth of 1 percent of dissolved minerals, versus a full 1 percent of other minerals in salt.

So, I figured, the salt skeptics are probably wrong. But could I prove it? I made elaborate plans to give it a try, which is one reason I traveled to Erice.

In Erice is the Majorana Centre, which hosts scientific conferences. There were two of them in early May, one concerned with gravity and black holes, which are not my specialties, and the other with molecular gastronomy, which is, sort of. The biennial workshops in molecular gastronomy were begun eight years ago by my friends Hervé This, Ph.D., now at the Collège de France; the late Nicholas Kurti, former professor of physics at Oxford University and secretary of the Royal Society; and Harold McGee, whom we will meet later. The meetings attract scientists, chefs, and some journalists, from England, France, Italy, and, to a lesser extent, the United States.

This year, the topic was the texture of food. Do you realize that a slice of bread is a fractal, just as much as ferns and coastlines are? This means that if you enlarge a photograph of a slice of bread to double or quadruple its original size, the pattern of holes and bubbles will look the same as in the original photo. The developing mathematics of fractals may soon become the scientific way of describing the texture of bread.

Despite the official subject, Hervé gave me a green light to conduct a salt tasting. Two scientists were corralled into helping me—David Kilcast and Alan Parker. David Kilcast, Ph.D., is the head of Sensory and Consumer Science at the Leatherhead Food Research Association (a leading food-research center) in England. Alan Parker, Ph.D., is a scientist who specializes in food texture at Firmenich, S.A. (among the world's largest flavor and perfume companies), in Geneva.

We three met for lunch at the restaurant Monte San Giuliano (the only good place to eat in Erice), which you reach through a flowered courtyard and up an old stone stairway, all with views of the salty Mediterranean. When I brought out my 13 Ziploc bags of white crystals and my gram scale, we sensed a gathering momentum among management, staff, and a neighboring table of diners to throw us back down the antique stairway. But, after flashing our badges from the Majorana Centre, we were reluctantly allowed to proceed with our power lunch.

The idea was that we would compare pairs of salts using what is known as the duo-trio method. David and Alan sketched out the general procedure. We would dissolve each type of salt in water, to eliminate the influence of texture—and, therefore, Wolke's major claim. In each trial, a subject would be given three little plastic cups holding salt solutions. He would sip from the first cup, a reference sample containing American table salt. Next, he would sip from the other two cups, one containing the same table salt and the other containing one of the chic, expensive, and exotic salts I had brought from America. Then, the subject would try to pair the two samples of table salt—or identify the chic salt, the one that didn't match the other two. If he succeeded, this would be a sign that American table salt tastes different from its upscale cousins. If the overall outcome was random, with just as many wrong pairings as correct ones, then we would have failed to prove that different salts taste different.

To my bitter disappointment, David and Alan decided that four salts were the maximum we could compare, considering the available time. I chose the four: *fleur de sel* from Guérande and from the Île de Ré, because these two are so prized among gastronomes; the famous Sicilian sea salt from Trapani, a city on the plain directly below Erice; and Oshima Island Blue Label salt because of its price, rarity, and the major role it has come to play in my shaky self-esteem. We dissolved the American table salt to various concentrations and tasted them; for some reason, we all arbitrarily agreed that the amount of salt in seawater, about 3 percent, was the ideal standard.

David and Alan organized everything, with the help of a charming young French taste scientist named Christine Fayard. The experiment would be conducted in double-blind fashion, meaning that the scientist conducting each tasting would be ignorant of which cups contained the chic-salt solution and which salt had come from the supermarket. They would conscript eight or ten subjects, and each would taste all four pairings.

The next day, everything went as planned, except that nearly everybody wanted to be a subject and the atmosphere in the tasting room tilted toward chaos. The scientists withdrew to tabulate the outcome, which they announced at the group's next session. *The results were random!* Only one taster got them all right, the identity of whom modesty prevents me from disclosing. (This outcome will randomly occur an average of one in every 16 trials, about 6 percent of the time, a rare event but, sadly, not rare enough to justify hubris on my part.) We had failed to disprove the salt skeptics!

Noticing that I had climbed up on a low stone wall and was teetering over a sheer drop down to the salt flats of Trapani, and understanding my desolation at the outcome of our tasting, David Kilcast generously volunteered the taste laboratories at Leatherhead to repeat the experiment soon after he returned to England. He would use trained (though not specifically salt-sensitive) subjects and the same five salts, plus two others I slipped in. I suggested that we decrease the concentration of salt. Seawater overwhelms the palate, I argued, preventing one from tasting the other minerals. Aren't we humans genetically programmed to gag when we swallow seawater? David did not react to the evolutionary argument, but his staff in England discussed the issue and favored a 2 percent concentration.

Back in Manhattan after a few days of very fine eating in Palermo (including the best pasta with sea urchins I've tasted* and the famous Palermitan sandwich of sliced cow's spleen and lung stewed in lard and nestled, dripping, in a crisp roll between a slab of fresh ricotta and shreds of cacciocavallo cheese, at the Focacceria San Francesco), I played around with salt solutions and voted for 1 percent. They ignored me.

While I nervously awaited news from England, the chemical analysis from AmTest arrived. I had given them a list of all the minerals in seawater, and this is what I had asked AmTest to measure in my salt samples. I had high hopes for my lovely Hawaiian red salt and black salt—until I read the labels. The colors are supposed to come from the red clay or lava rock lining the ponds where the Hawaiian seawater is evaporated; now the labels concede it's regular sea salt mixed with clay or lava. Please! This is little different from garlic salt or seasoning salt or that fancy salt from Venice that's mixed with herbs and spices. It is not really salt. I eliminated Hawaii from the competition.

All 13 salts turned out to be about 99 percent sodium chloride and 1 percent other things. AmTest reported that the amount of several of the elements in seawater was too small for their instruments to measure. But they found relatively large amounts of other minerals. Overall, the weightiest impurities were sulfate, followed by nearly equal parts of calcium and magnesium, plus smaller amounts of potassium, silicon (what sand is made of), iron, phosphorus, strontium, and aluminum.

Can these be tasted? I retired with my calculator for some serious figuring. The average chicken soup contains about 1 percent salt, or 10,000 parts per million. Averaging the numbers from AmTest for all 13 salts, I estimated that the average chicken soup

*You'll find the pasta in "Prickly Pleasures," page 435.

seasoned with the average salt contains 224 parts per million of bitter minerals and metals. Can we taste an amount as small as this? If the minerals were on their own, the answer is obviously yes; it's the difference between distilled water and mildly mineralized bottled water. Or, just dissolve a scant quarter teaspoon of salt in a quart of water. Anybody who can't distinguish this weak salt solution from ordinary water should see a doctor. Plus, bitter tastes are said to be even more obvious than salty ones. The salt skeptics must be wrong. But, would we be able to prove it? On one hand, the ample sodium chloride in salt may mask the much weaker taste of trace minerals. On the other hand, some table salts contain a much higher percentage of minerals than the average.

Among the 13 salts, Diamond Crystal salt contains the least amount of nearly everything other than sodium chloride; *fleur de sel* de Guérande is very high in magnesium. The roasting of Korean salt seems to have no effect on its chemical composition and, therefore, on its taste. Two Japanese salts, including the treasured Oshima Island Blue Label Salt, were the highest in calcium and sulfates. The only advantage Blue Label has over its much more common and inexpensive relation, Red Label Salt, is double the calcium—and a texture like *fleur de sel*. A third salt from Japan showed the highest percentage of total minerals among all 13 salts, by a wide margin. Powdery, lavender-colored Black Indian salt has the most iron and aluminum. (Could it possibly be adulterated with sodium silicoaluminate, the most common additive in commercial salt, used to keep it free flowing, the way Morton's is? Diamond Crystal contains no additives.)

Two days later, my fertile musings were interrupted by an e-mail from David Kilcast with his results. This time there were 20 tasters, or "panelists," sitting in individual booths at a constant room temperature of 72°F, all under Northlight illumination. Panelists who correctly distinguished the chic salt from Diamond Crystal were asked if they liked it and why.

As it turned out, some chic salts were indistinguishable in taste from ordinary table salt and others were quite distinct. This means that the salt skeptics are wrong in principle, though it is obvious that some quite plain-tasting salts are promoted with unfounded enthusiasm. The Sicilian sea salt could not be distinguished by anybody. (Of the many available types of salt from Trappani, ours was, unfortunately, excessively white and refined.) Otherwise, a majority of panelists identified the chic salt in every case, but a bare majority is not enough to be statistically significant. To my chagrin, the *fleur de sel* from the Île de Ré fell into this category. Still, I'll leave it in my polished walnut box for its texture.

Two chic salts were marginal, distinguished by 13 out of 20 panelists, which would happen by chance 13 percent of the time, certainly a rare event but not rare enough for statistical significance. (Statisticians consider an event significant—nonrandom—if it would occur by chance only 5 percent of the time.) These were Oshima Island Blue Label Salt (oops!) and the *fleur de sel* from Guérande. The panelists generally preferred Oshima Island over table salt, finding it milder but not less salty. They did not prefer the salt from Guérande, which some found sulfurous.

The roasted Korean salt was detected 14 out of 20 times, which is nearly significant, but panelists were particularly unsure, and some used words like *astringent, fizzy,* and *strange* to describe what must result from the bamboo-roasting technique.

The winner and clear champion was a sea salt from Okinawa, which a friend named Kathryn had brought back from Japan, and which I decided to slip in at the last minute, as its feeling on the tongue seemed so much like that of *fleur de sel.* Sixteen out of 20 panelists could tell it from Diamond Crystal, which would happen by chance only 1 percent of the time. And panelists were unusually certain about their decision. The bad news is that a strong majority of those expressing a preference liked the Diamond Crystal better, describing the Okinawa salt as bitter, astringent, or acidic.

Whew! What have we accomplished? The salt skeptics have been sort of defeated, I feel, but ours is a Pyrrhic victory. As we knew beforehand, the textures of various chic salts have a powerful effect on their taste—but mainly when they reach the tongue with their crystals intact. Now we know that most of the chic salts could be distinguished just by their taste, but not always with a high level of statistical significance and not always to the detriment of Diamond Crystal. I wonder what a 1 percent dilution of the salts would have turned up.

Nafumi Tamura had reported from the kitchen at Fleur de Sel that different salts seem to act differently in tuna tartare, and probably in other foods as well. Even if the minerals in some salts are difficult to distinguish when dissolved in water, can they still change in other ways the taste or texture of things we eat? That is the question. I have begun looking into this, which means I have e-mailed Harold McGee for help. (Harold is probably the leading authority on food science in this country and author of the classic *On Food and Cooking: The Science and Lore of the Kitchen* [Scribners]. It was he who forced that spleen, lung, and lard sandwich on me in Palermo.) Harold's immediate guess was yes, that, even at low levels, minerals can affect the taste and texture of food. Sulfates might contribute an unpleasant smell; iron can split fatty acids into smaller, more volatile (and aromatic?) molecules. Then Harold actually looked it up and quickly discovered two more examples. Magnesium and calcium can free up some of the sodium that is bound to other food molecules, *making the salt taste saltier.* And they can prevent valuable aroma molecules from getting stuck in thickeners—things like the pectin in jams—keeping them available for our sensual pleasure.

I looked back at the 13 chemical analyses from AmTest. Common American table salt has the smallest amounts of both calcium and magnesium. Oshima Island Blue Label is highest in calcium (by quite a margin), trailed by the French *fleurs de sel.* *Fleur de sel de Guérande* and Thai salt have the most magnesium, trailed by all three salts from Japan and then the other *fleurs de sel.* Can this explain why my French friends still prefer *fleur de sel de Guérande*? Can it help us discover the trapped and hidden perfumes in our dinner?

Well, that's just a start. But I think we've got them on the run.

MAY 2001

Author's note: When Harold McGee discovered even more about the taste of salt and its effect on salt cod, he generously sent me this paragraph:

"The quality of the salt used influences the quality of the salt fish. Unrefined sea salts in particular are the home of hardy bacteria (species of *Bacillus, Micrococcus, Corynebacterium, Halobacterium, Sarcina*) and molds *(Wallemia)*, which contribute desirable flavors during curing and drying, but can get out of hand in warm, humid conditions and cause discoloration, sliminess, softness, and off-flavors. (The pink, salt-loving bacteria can grow between 60 and 180°F/15 and 80°C!) Unrefined sea and rock salts are also likely to contain significant traces of calcium and magnesium (in chloride and sulfate compounds), which prevent the slight yellowing that pure sodium chloride produces in white fish (perhaps by binding to fatty acids and blocking their participation in browning reactions); but at levels above about 0.5 percent they slow salt penetration, toughen the muscle fibers, and impart a bitter taste."

FEAR OF *FORMAGGIO*

Cheese is probably the best of all foods, as wine is the best of all beverages.   PATIENCE GRAY

The stunning woman seated next to me at the vast banquet table plucked the golden curls of Parmesan cheese from her salad, piled them up on the tablecloth, and stuffed the slimy greens into her perfect mouth. Once again, Fate had thrown me together with a serious food phobic—this time, a pitiful cheese-avoider—and, once again, I felt a responsibility to attempt a cure. The Mother Teresa deep within me is always grateful for opportunities like this.

When I requested an explanation for her behavior, she could only say that cheese is bad for your heart—and, anyway, that it makes her sick. She was, temporarily I am sure, unable to remember the phrase "lactose intolerance," which is what I think she was driving at.

Where to begin? I examined my new patient. Her bare shoulders were beautifully muscled and lightly tanned. A thin gold chain fell across her deeply sculpted collarbone, and from it was suspended, below her provocative supersternal notch, a large onyx cross. I decided to begin with the religious approach.

I pointed out that God tells us in the Book of Genesis to eat everything under the sun, which is why He designed humans as omnivores and equipped us with all-purpose dentition and digestive systems. Here I expected my companion to touch her cross in pious agreement and pop a sliver of Parmesan into her mouth. Instead, she seemed completely distracted by her own reflection in a silver water pitcher. I decided to bring out the big guns. Food phobics like her, I insisted, are at least as troubled as people who avoid sex, except that the latter will probably seek psychiatric help while food phobics justify their mental aberration in the name of allergies, genetics, vegetarianism, nutritional theories, food safety, obesity, or a particularly sensitive nature. And, didn't she realize that food paranoia has nearly destroyed both the genial dinner party and the warm family meal, and, with them, our sense of festivity and exchange, of community and sacrament?

I was just warming to the subject, getting to the psychopathology of cheese avoidance itself, when my dinner companion violently pushed away from the table, said something about needing to phone her personal body sculptor, and left the table. The telephone must have been some distance away, because even by the time we finished dessert, she had not returned.

For the balance of the meal, I reflected on how irrational my former dinner companion had been. Like her, most people who avoid cheese give one of two excuses, or both of them at once—lactose intolerance and fear of heart disease. Cheese has very little to do with either.

Fear of lactose seems to be the fashionable phobia of the 1990s. Half the people you meet these days are almost proud to tell you that drinking milk makes them sick, bloated, and gassy, gives them cramps and even worse. This has led many of them to avoid cheese, one of life's great pleasures. *The truth is that very few people are lactose intolerant and that, anyway, most cheeses contain no lactose.*

Lactose is the natural sugar that makes up about 5 percent of a glass of milk. People who are lactose intolerant cannot digest lactose because their small intestines do not produce enough lactase. This is the enzyme that breaks lactose down into glucose and galactose, which can then be absorbed into the bloodstream. Unabsorbed lactose can cause problems as it continues down the digestive tract, although other enzymes in the milk itself, like

those that turn milk into yogurt, can often ferment away the rest
of the problem.

Many people who believe they are lactose intolerant really
aren't, and most people who truly are can easily tolerate the
amount of lactose in a glass of milk before they get sick. This was
proved in a study conducted at Massachusetts General Hospital
and published last year in the *New England Journal of Medicine.*
Subjects had been recruited who felt sure they had a severe problem with lactose—severe enough that they avoided the amount
of milk you would put in coffee or on breakfast cereal. All 30 were
given the objective hydrogen breath test: If they were truly lactose intolerant—if they really could not digest milk sugar—
excess hydrogen would be found in their breath. As it turned
out, 9 of the 30 did not suffer from the condition, despite their
certainty.

For the next two weeks, all the subjects were given a glass of
milk to drink with breakfast every day. In one week, the milk was
treated with lactase, the enzyme that would allow anybody to
digest the lactose in their milk; in the other week, the milk was
untreated. Each day they were asked to rate their discomfort on a
scale of 0 to 5. Not only was the average discomfort score very
low—between 0 and 1—but both types of milk were given the
same ratings, even though the milk treated with lactase could not
possibly have caused discomfort even to the most severely lactose
intolerant. The study concluded that it takes a full quart of milk
to give cramps and gas to everyone whom the hydrogen breath
test shows really is unable to digest lactose.

My suspicion is that people are inclined to blame milk for all
their digestive aches and pains because lactose intolerance is so
much in the news, and dairy products are under such attack by
nutritionists and the media that blaming milk usually goes
unchallenged. But not at my table.

As for the idea that cheese can trigger symptoms of lactose
intolerance, *the happy secret is that fresh cheeses contain very little lactose, and that fermented, ripened cheeses contain no lactose at all!*

You make cheese by coagulating the casein in milk (its main

protein) by adding rennet or a starter or both. This causes the casein to form clumps, called curds. Then, you drain off the thin liquid that remains, which is called whey. Finally, you gather the curds and either eat them fresh in ricotta or cottage cheese, or pack them together and let them age and dry and ferment.

When you drain the whey, 98 percent of the lactose drains away with it. All the rest is consumed in the early stages of fermentation and ripening, as lactic acid bacteria convert this sugar into tangy lactic acid and the carbon dioxide responsible for the holes in Swiss cheese. That's why the American Dietetic Association used to recommend cheese for those who could not tolerate milk. Cheese is out of favor these days because it is high in saturated fat, which is thought to put cholesterol into your bloodstream, clog your arteries, and cause heart attacks.

So, I was surprised to hear Dr. Serge Renaud, a leading French nutritionist and former director of the Lyon office of INSERM, the French equivalent of our National Institutes of Health, give a lecture several years ago showing that countries with large amounts of cheese in their diets do not seem to have higher rates of heart disease. There certainly is a strong association around the world between the consumption of dairy products generally and the rate of coronary heart disease. But, when you compare national cheese consumption with heart disease, the correlation entirely disappears. After all, the French and the Greeks eat more cheese than anybody and have among the fewest heart attacks. For most American nutritionists, the presence of saturated fat in cheese is enough to make them condemn it, despite all evidence to the contrary. But it appears that *fermented* dairy products (including cheese, yogurt, and cultured butter) do not lead to heart disease.

I have recently searched the medical literature from the past 30 years. I was amazed at how little serious work had been done on the subject. Most often, cheese is simply lumped together with other dairy products. The one large-scale survey that did look at cheese itself was reported in the *American Journal of Clinical Nutrition* in 1988; it was based on a study of 27,529 Seventh-

Day Adventists in California, many of whom are vegetarian. Consumption of meat and eggs *was* associated with heart disease (and some other causes of death), but cheese did not show an association with any of them. More recently, Jeffrey Segall, a London epidemiologist, reviewed in the *International Journal of Cardiology* every relevant study since the 1960s, and found no connection between cheese and heart disease (and an ambiguous connection with eggs).

Dr. Renaud's theory is that the calcium in cheese combines with dairy fat and carries some of it out of the body. He has done some experiments with rats and gotten statistically significant results, but the amount of saturated fat eliminated seems to me too small to matter. Segall thinks that the lactose found in milk (but, as we have learned, not in cheese) is the real culprit, not only because it apparently increases the absorption of both saturated fat and cholesterol into our bloodstreams, but also because, in theory, the galactose into which lactose is broken down can theoretically make the walls of our arteries more susceptible to attack from fatty lipoprotein particles. Segall's reasoning has been widely criticized, but nobody has proposed a better explanation. Why eating cheese does not seem to lead to cardiac disease will remain a puzzle until lots more work has been done, but the fact is that nothing in the medical literature directly connects cheese and heart attacks.

I would have told my dinner companion all these things—and set her free from her crippling cheese phobia—if only her personal body sculptor had not kept her on the telephone so long. Her absence did give me the chance to enjoy the shavings of savory Parmesan she had left strewn around her plate, and to reflect upon this most perfect of cheeses.

MARCH 1997

THE MAN WHO COOKED FOR HIS DOG

A fat bitch," I announced, licking the juice of a wood-grilled lamb sausage from my fingers, "is never an easy whelper." I was reading from the breeding section of a book called *The Golden Retriever: 47 Exciting Full-Color Photos.* Sky King listened intently but said nothing, and not simply because he had not yet learned to talk. I have found that young males of all species have a limited attention span when it comes to discussions of whelping and obesity.

But, as always, Sky King's gaze was eloquent—as it had been earlier that evening when I dumped a plastic cupful of upscale dry-dog-food pellets into his bowl and turned away to take care of my own dinner, a half-dozen fat little sausages crackling over a smoldering fire of oak and mesquite on the grill just outside the kitchen door. "I know that you are a fair-minded human," he seemed to be saying, "and that you have only my best interests at heart. But are you absolutely sure that I should be eating this pile of dead and desiccated pellets while you experience the feral delights of flesh? Who's the carnivore here, anyway?"

I glanced back at Sky as if to say, "Cats are carnivores, dogs are not." But I had gotten his message. Dogs did not evolve eating dry dog food, and they do not prefer it now. Sky likes a good tomato, a hunk of raw steak, a hunk of grilled steak, pitted cherries, peaches, pizza, overcooked lamb sausages, running shoes, and Fudgsicles. He is ambivalent on the subject of sweet corn and has little use for Good & Plentys. Sky loves to eat in bed.

Once we had finished our respective dinners, Sky and I watched the sun setting over San Diego, where he lives, and to which I was paying one of my frequent visits. We went back inside and together began to formulate a plan for answering the critical question: What on Earth is a growing dog supposed to eat? We ordered a dozen books via the Internet, settled into a comfortable chair, and began reading the relevant sections of *The Golden Retriever: 47 Exciting Full-Color Photos,* the only resource immediately at hand. Apart from that caution concerning obese females, its culinary advice was sketchy: Dry dog food is the easiest, served four times a day and moistened with hot water for the youngest puppies, less often and with less water as the puppy matures, and dry as a bone for adults. (The benefits: nutritional balance, total convenience, and minuscule stools.) This was the advice we had followed thus far with Sky King, whom my wife had named after a popular serial hero of radio and black-and-white TV in the forties and fifties, a fictional and fearless rancher-pilot who performed daring rescue and law-enforcement missions in his small private propeller plane. "Out of the clear blue of the Western sky comes Skyyyy Kiiiing!" each episode began. Sky's name is not yet among the ten most popular for North American dogs, which are currently Sam, Max, Lady, Bear, Maggie, Buddy, Tasha, Chelsea, Holly, and Shasta. Tasha?

I was forced to admit that Sky had a point about dry dog food. I myself rarely eat food in pellet form, and if a nutritionally perfect human food pellet existed, as it does in science fiction, I doubt that many of us would enjoy it. I never eat canned food except for tuna, foie gras, and that superb *boudin noir* from the tiny town of Urt in southwest France, preserved in metal at its sanguinary peak.* I rarely eat processed or factory-made food, and I never eat chicken by-product meal, fish meal, or chicken digest, three prominent ingredients in the highly recommended, super-premium, super-costly large-breed-puppy formula called Eukanuba, chosen for Sky by my wife and our veterinarian, who sells the stuff for more than twice the price of Purina Dog Chow

*The remarkable *boudin noir* of Urt is celebrated in "It Takes a Village to Kill a Pig," page 237.

in the supermarket. Even though I rarely chew on rubber toys, I do not feel that I am a radically different creature from a large-breed puppy. Why shouldn't Sky eat pretty much what I do?

Dogs love monotony. Dogs love stability. Change disturbs their digestion. Dogs have a weak sense of taste and do not care about flavor. These are some of the excuses dog owners use to justify their sloth and assuage their guilt over serving the same tedious dry dog food month in and month out. But if, as one always reads, a dog's sense of smell is an inconceivable million times more finely tuned than ours, they can surely teach humans a thing or two about flavor.

According to the Pet Food Institute, the first commercial dog food was created in 1860 by an American named James Spratt, who traveled to England to sell lightning rods and stayed to manufacture dog biscuits. Canned and dry dog food did not become a ubiquitous convenience until after World War II, when it took its place alongside such other labor-saving inventions as pop-up toasters. Before then, people regularly cooked for their dogs. And yet America had not become a nation of sick and crippled canines.

Most arguments about what humans or dogs or even pandas in the zoo should eat wind up in a discussion of evolution: What did we eat in prehistory, when our genes were being hatched? What did we eat in the wild before civilization twisted and perverted our native instincts?

Sky King and I certainly do have different family trees. I, presumably, descended from the apes. Sky's and every other dog's remotest ancestor was a weasel-like Eurasian mammal called a miacis. Over the course of 60 million years, the miacis evolved into jackals, wolves, and foxes. Then, a mere 12,000 years ago, one of these, a small gray wolf from India, gave rise to every dog that has come thereafter, except for some African breeds that may have descended from the jackal.

But if I am an ape and Sky is a weasel, why do we both love pizza? And why do we both go wild over roasted beef bones? Maybe evolution is irrelevant at dinnertime. Somehow, man and dog became fast friends almost immediately. There is a grave in Israel, 10,000 years old, containing a human skeleton with its arm around the skeleton of a puppy! And, ever since then, dogs have eaten human food, at least part of the time.

It seemed incredible to me that, at the age of eight months, already at 80 percent of his ultimate weight of 85 pounds, Sky had never been allowed to gnaw on a real animal bone. He had been restricted to rubber and nylon facsimiles of bones, purchased on the cockeyed contemporary theory that even the heaviest and most solid of bones can splinter and, if swallowed, cause internal damage—a prime example of the denaturalization, medicalization, and alienation of pet care in America. And my wife naively wondered why Sky had mortally wounded two of her Manolo Blahnik treasures. Bones would be my first project.

The next morning Sky and I drove to the supermarket and discovered that California food stores are not puppy friendly. Slumped uneasily in the backseat, Sky was inconsolable until I returned with ten pounds of marrow bones from the freezer case in the meat department, precut into two-inch sections—heavy and nearly indestructible calcium-rich rings sliced from a cow's thick legs and bursting with the most sumptuous treat that nature has to offer: rich and fatty marrow. I may be an ape and Sky a weasel, but 12,000 years of earthly cohabitation with canines enabled me to prepare, at home, with absolute perfection, on the very first try,

---

SKY KING'S ROASTED MARROW BONES

2 lbs. frozen marrow bones, cut into 2-inch lengths

1 tsp. salt

Preheat the oven to 400°F.

Rub a little salt into the ends of the marrow-bone segments. Lay them on their sides in a broad, flat, shallow bowl. Microwave at full power for 10 minutes.

Transfer the bones to a baking dish or small roasting pan. Pour the juices and fat in the bowl over them. Roast in the preheated oven until nicely browned, about 20 minutes. Let cool to the body temperature of a rabbit.

The body temperature of a rabbit is 101°F, as is Sky's. Food that is any warmer may burn his little mouth. Wait until the bones are cooler, and Sky's joyous, impatient barking will cause hearing loss in his chef-owner. Sky may have evolved from a weasel or a wolf, but the golden retriever is not an ancient breed. Sky is a gun dog, a sporting dog, a hunting dog. As we had learned in our reading the night before, goldens were created in the middle of the nineteenth century by a man called Lord Tweedmouth (not a joke) on his estate in Scotland, when he crossed a yellow wavy-coated retriever formerly owned by a cobbler in Brighton and a Tweed water spaniel. (I am amazed by this account. What, besides price, then, distinguishes a purebred golden retriever from a mongrel?) Sky has never come across a rabbit in San Diego, except in the shape of a biscuit, but when he does, he will find the little creature's body temperature just about ideal for dining. Or so I am told by an expert at the Iams Company (maker of Eukanuba), which runs a fine scientific research program on dogs and their cuisine.

With Sky deeply lost in the pleasures of his very first animal bone, I planned another trip to the supermarket. But first, I placed calls to New York City to speak with two of the leading French chefs in America for ideas about what to cook for Sky. Most French chefs become great experts at canine cuisine early in their careers because the only cooking they are permitted as 16-

year-old apprentices is for customers' dogs. Even today, dogs are welcomed at most of the finest restaurants of France. By contrast, the restaurants of Southern California are surprisingly inhospitable. Not long ago, Sky was unfeelingly ejected from the outdoor terrace of a taco place in Solana Beach. In New York City, dogs were banned from the insides of restaurants by a 1972 law, but as a recent survey by Molly O'Neill in the *New York Times* has reported, restaurants in New York welcome dogs to their outdoor areas with open arms—plus ceramic water bowls and tempting doggy menus. New York's Pierre hotel and Boston's Four Seasons positively worship your dog—the Pierre with a basket lined with Frette linen cradling a biscuit on which the dog's name is written, and the Four Seasons with a Pet Menu of Shepherd's Pie, Rin Tin Tin tartare, and you can guess the rest. After the Solana Beach affair, Sky agreed to stay at home when in San Diego, if we would devote a reasonable percentage of the money saved to buying him either a new set of toys or a live rabbit. We chose the former.

Jean-Georges Vongerichten (Jo Jo, Vong, Lipstick Café, Jean Georges, the Mercer Kitchen, Prime in Las Vegas, and several others) grew up in Strasbourg in Alsace, and as a teenage apprentice at the great Auberge de l'Ill, he lived above the restaurant with the other boys and worked at menial tasks from eight in the morning until midnight, except when he was allowed to cook for the customers' dogs. Sunday was family day at the Auberge de l'Ill, and as many French families cannot conceive of a festive dinner without their dogs, 20 animals would appear each Sunday. Some dogs returned nearly every week, and their preferences were well known. Some owners telephoned ahead. For the others, young apprentices would cook rice and green beans with braised beef, veal, or rabbit, particularly the bony front legs that are rarely served to humans. Jean-Georges remembers that the pressure was intense, because a dog's dinner had to be ready exactly when its owners' main courses were served. After the meal, the waiters were responsible for walking the dogs.

At his next job, working for Paul Bocuse, Jean-Georges had the honor of cooking for the great chef's three huge and ravenous hunting dogs. Jean-Georges himself grew up with canines under the dining-room table. His parents' dog Bizou ("Kiss") recently died after 14 happy years sharing all the Strasbourgeoise specialities the family ate—*choucroute garnie à l'alsacienne,* roast pork with pureed carrots, knackwursts, *backeoffe,* and *flammenkuche.* Bizou's coat was always shiny and her health an inspiration to all those around her.

Daniel Boulud (Café Boulud, Restaurant Daniel) grew up on his parents' farm near Lyon, where their dogs were mixed-breed shepherds who ate together from a vast three-gallon communal bowl. The family would cook a rich, nutritious soup or stew for their midday meal, and what was left became the foundation for their animals' repast. Bones were added—plus pasta, beans, potatoes, or rice, and milk from the cows in the barn, and cheese rinds and meaty table scraps. The meat was always cooked, Daniel remembers—raw meat would have inspired the dogs to chase after the family's chickens.

I told Daniel that I was about to leave for the supermarket and needed advice about what to prepare for Sky's very first home-cooked meal. His response was instantaneous—a thick soup of root vegetables with beef short ribs and milk. I asked Sky what he thought and, hearing no objection, whipped up a giant batch of French Country Soup for Dogs and Their Owners, which Sky King enjoyed even more than I.

For Sky, it was as though a veil had been lifted, as though the scales had fallen from his eyes, as though he were tasting food for the first time. In the days that followed, I cooked thick soups of white beans with carrots and fennel and large pieces of boned stewing fowl. And a huge gratin of macaroni with tomatoes and ground turkey. And a massive rice pilaf with hearty chunks of beef stew. The only way to tell if I had gotten the dish right was to taste it, which led me to the conclusion that I should not feed Sky anything I would not enjoy eating myself. After a few days of this, and noticing that when I ate Sky's food my own diet was far better balanced than when I cooked for myself, I concluded that in an ideal world, man and dog would eat the very same food every day—though with less salt and fewer spices in the canine version, because dogs seem to prefer their food a bit blander than we do.

The 12 books arrived, most of them excruciatingly cute recipe collections for biscuits and other treats. *The ASPCA's Complete Dog Care Manual* assured us that Sky's needs for vitamins and minerals were pretty much the same as mine. Most vets and dog-food companies want you to believe that only commercial products can be "balanced and complete." Feed a dog too little fat or a bit of extra protein and you will have a mangy, sickly, complaining pet on your hands. The problem with these claims is that the experts also tell you that every environment and every breed of dog requires a different balance, and that there is no way that the heterogenous race of canines—prehistoric predators, foragers, and scavengers—could have evolved to require precisely one elaborate menu of nutrients, any more than the race of humans has.

Feeding a dog cannot be an indecipherable mystery. The authorities at the National Research Council and the experts at Eukanuba (who, while opposed to home cooking for dogs, were willing to share their wisdom) call for about the same balance of nutrients—25 to 30 percent calories from protein, mostly animal protein, 25 to 40 percent fat calories, and the rest carbohydrates (about the same as for humans)—though the NRC notes that some dogs thrive on fat levels as high as 76 percent. Dogs do not have a problem with cholesterol. The charts say that Sky needs about 2,000 calories a day overall, though this can differ with the weather, the breed, the heaviness of his coat, how much exercise he gets, and so forth. The only real test is his health, his waistline, and the shine of his coat.

There *are* some differences between Sky and me. Chocolate is simply deadly for some breeds; a pound of milk chocolate can kill a 20-pound pet. But evidence that onions cause anemia applies only to cats. Some adult dogs appear to be lactose intolerant, but the expert who sounded most sensible to me explained that dogs grow to have difficulty digesting milk only when they are deprived of it; feed them a little milk and their enzymes return. Only dry dog food, you may have heard, properly cleans a dog's teeth of unattractive plaque buildup. Researchers have compared soft dog food with dry, but nobody has bothered scientifically to compare eating dry dog food with gnawing on sturdy bones, which appears to work just as well. For the health of a dog's intestines, 3 percent of his diet should be in "moderately fermentable fiber," which can easily be gotten from fruit and vegetables. Not for the first time in recent history, it looks as though the traditional French diet exactly fills the bill.

Sky has lost all interest in premium dry-dog-food pellets and, despite the inconceivably tedious character of air travel for grown dogs, is contemplating a trip to New York City for a week or two of home cooking. The folks at Eukanuba claim that Sky's attraction to real food is explained by the time we spend together in the kitchen and the amusing rituals of cooking, which Sky enjoys watching as he stands next to me on his hind legs with his paws on the countertop. Dogs do love novel foods, they say. This means that in a month or two, when Sky has completely forgotten his dry dog pellets, he will approach them with the same excitement he now reserves for the *cassoulet de Castelnaudary*. Any bets?

DECEMBER 1998

WHY DOESN'T EVERYBODY IN CHINA
HAVE A HEADACHE?

J ust as we were polishing off a full and happy lunch at the famous old Mei Long Zhen restaurant in the city of Shanghai, I sensed that somewhere inside me was taking shape a deep and blinding insight. We visited the kitchen. Each chef stood before a wide black wok set into a ceramic counter over a fierce fire. Next to each was a table holding a dozen or so bowls of condiments and flavorings into which he dipped the edge of a broad, shallow ladle as he prepared each dish: light and dark soy, salt and sugar, hot chili oil and ground dried red pepper, broth and cooking oil, white and black pepper, finely chopped garlic and ginger and scallions, cornstarch, and, finally, a bowl of white Gourmet Powder—the Chinese name for MSG, monosodium glutamate. There was not a restaurant kitchen we saw in all of China that lacked an ample supply of Gourmet Powder.

And then, as we left the Mei Long Zhen and melted into the crowds on Nanjing Xi Lu, their name for West Nanjing Road, it fully and finally struck me: *Nobody in China has a headache!*

About a third of the American population believes that MSG in their food gives them headaches, a burning sensation in their skin, facial pressure, and chest pain—or worse. Could it be that these 90 million souls are nothing but crybabies and hypochondriacs? Could it be that what Americans have for the past 30 years referred to as the Chinese-Restaurant Syndrome does not exist in China, a nation long noted for its large number of Chinese restaurants? Could it be that Americans love to fear their food?

Thus began an investigation that would require several months of slavish effort. But first I needed to eliminate the most obvious possibility: *Maybe everybody in China does have a headache!*

After a stroll to our swanky modern hotel proved longer and dustier than the Shanghai street map had promised, I embarked upon a series of interviews that was to consume upward of a half hour. My six subjects were nearly everybody at the hotel who could speak English—the concierge, the reservations manager, the young woman in the business center who controlled the fax machine, a waitress in the cocktail lounge, and so forth. First, I asked each of them whether he or she had eaten lunch. Then, I asked if he or she had a headache. As soon as my first subject, the concierge, answered yes and no, respectively, I had certain proof that not everybody in China had an MSG headache. Then, after conducting the remaining five interviews and boldly extrapolating, I was able to conclude that nobody in the entire city of Shanghai, the largest Chinese settlement in the world, had a headache, despite the profusion of Gourmet Powder on practically every street corner.

These results made me glad. When it comes to phony food allergies and intolerances, I am not an unbiased observer. No, I am a fiend at rooting them out. And the fear of MSG strikes me as particularly odd because the same chemical in its natural form has been used as a flavor enhancer since at least the eighth century.

In 1908, a professor at the University of Tokyo, Kikunae Ikeda, became interested in the delicious flavor that the traditional Japanese seaweed broth lent to anything cooked or flavored with it. The seaweed was *kombu,* known in English as giant kelp or sea tangle, a massive plant that grows up to 30 feet long off the northern islands of Japan. At least since first recorded in A.D. 797, and probably much longer, *kombu* has been harvested and dried on the islands' beaches and shipped to the rest of the country.

Ikeda discovered that the active taste ingredient in *kombu* is glutamic acid. This is the most common amino acid in the human body, where it is linked with other amino acids to form various proteins, including our muscles. In its separate, free form, glutamic acid lends foods a richly savory taste, a perception of thickness and "mouthfulness," a harmonizing of flavors. Ikeda named this taste *"umami,"* the Japanese word for "deliciousness," and, in the years that followed, scientists in Japan would prove to their satisfaction—and to that of many Western researchers—that *umami* is an independent, basic taste alongside the quartet of sweet, sour, salty, and bitter that had been widely accepted for over a century.* While giant kelp may have the strongest concentration of free glutamate—the naturally occurring form of MSG—I was amazed to discover that the second highest is found in Parmesan cheese! And right behind are sun-dried tomatoes and tomato paste! Two or three ounces of Parmesan cheese contain enough free glutamate to give a headache to anybody who claims to be sensitive to MSG, and yet I have never heard of a Parmesan Headache or Tomato-Paste Syndrome. This is what makes me so suspicious of people who say they are sensitive to MSG.

A few years after Ikeda's discovery in 1908, a young associate at the University of Tokyo discovered another *umami* substance—inosinate, or IMP for short—that explained the taste of savory Japanese broths made with dried bonito flakes. And in 1960, a third source of *umami* was identified—guanylate, or GMP, found in high concentrations in shiitake mushrooms.

The three *umami* chemicals were once thought of as flavor enhancers or potentiators. But years of testing have not shown that any of them intensifies the four other basic tastes. Synergy seems to be the key. When you add free glutamate or inosinate (or *kombu* broth or a sprinkling of Parmesan) to other foods, the small quantities of natural *umami* substances already present in the food itself are greatly enhanced and intensified. And when tiny amounts of glutamate and IMP are mixed together, their flavoring power is increased 16 times.

This all explains an endless number of gastronomic pheno-

*Some prominent taste scientists no longer believe in the idea of discrete basic tastes, whether 4 or 14, but for those who do, *umami* qualifies: Foods with high *umami* ratings stimulate a separate set of receptors and nerves in the mouth. And the *umami* taste cannot be duplicated by mixing together sweet, sour, salty, and bitter tastes.

mena, puzzles, and mysteries, both East and West. *Umami,* and especially glutamic acid, are why we love pizza and sprinkle Parmesan on pasta, and why we find French fries and hamburgers so much more savory with ketchup. And why the tomato has become the most popular vegetable in the world. (As Raymond Sokolov describes it in *Why We Eat What We Eat,* "The tomato focuses and improves recipes that were appealing before the tomato was available but that became extraordinarily attractive after it was added.")

It also explains why *dashi*—the heady Japanese broth used to prepare nearly all boiled dishes and to flavor sauces and rice—is made simply and at the last minute from both dried bonito flakes (for their IMP) in combination with dried *kombu* (for its free glutamate), and sometimes has a few slices of shiitake floating on top. In a country that raised very little meat until well into this century, the deeply, almost mystically, savory *dashi* was fundamental to the preparation of nearly all food. Connoisseurs are said to judge a Japanese restaurant by the quality of its *dashi.*

And why fermented fish sauces and intense extracts of meat and vegetables have been valued for at least 2,000 years: The Roman *garum,* the *nam pla* of Thailand and *nuoc mam* of Vietnam, British beef tea, Bovril, Vegemite, and Marmite—not to mention Worcestershire sauce—all contain huge amounts of free glutamate. Soy sauce has nearly as much as Parmesan cheese. In studies, broth flavored with a little MSG was judged more palatable than plain broth by both newborn babies and the elderly. Human milk contains lots of glutamate, cow's milk almost none.

Young peas contain more free glutamate than the mature vegetable, but ripe tomatoes contain much more than pale pink ones, which may explain why we love young peas and old tomatoes. And, like tomatoes, young cheeses contain less far less glutamate—and far less flavor—than fully ripened specimens. Oysters have the highest glutamate level in February and March, and the lowest in August, when we are not supposed to eat them. As Iberian ham, the most splendid in the world, undergoes its 18-month cure, the amino acid that increases most is glutamate.

Remove the free glutamate from crab, and it loses its crabby taste entirely.

Free glutamate is most commonly found in vegetables, inosinic acid in food derived from animals. So, there is a synergistic effect when we cook or eat meat and vegetables together, intensifying the savory *umami* character of both. Mother Nature or God, whichever you prefer, designed our taste buds to find a balanced diet more delicious than a lopsided one.

MSG went into commercial production soon after Ikeda's discovery, first as an extract of *kombu* itself, now by fermenting substances such as molasses or wheat. It is used in great quantities in the American food-processing industry, in soups and stews and nearly everything else, to make up for a lack of true flavor from chicken or meat. Sometimes it is adequately labeled, but usually not. (If MSG is added in its pure form, the FDA requires that it be included in the ingredients list; but MSG may be concealed within "hydrolyzed protein" or "autolyzed yeast extract," and, in some circumstances, the FDA requires nothing on the label at all.) For consumers, MSG is sold in our supermarkets as Ac'cent.

"For several years since I have been in this country, I have experienced a strange syndrome whenever I have eaten out in a Chinese restaurant, especially one that served northern Chinese food." So began a seismal letter sent to the *New England Journal of Medicine* in 1968 from Robert Ho Man Kwok, M.D., a medical researcher from Silver Springs, Maryland. The editors printed the letter, adding the somewhat facetious title "Chinese-Restaurant Syndrome," and a wonderful new disease was born.

Kwok's symptoms were a numbness at the back of his neck that radiated to his arms and back, general weakness, and palpitations—a milder version, he wrote, of his own hypersensitivity to aspirin. Kwok proposed several possible causes: an allergenic ingredient in soy sauce, the generous use of cooking wine, monosodium glutamate, or the high sodium content of Chinese food—in salt, soy sauce, and MSG. His letter brought a flood of replies from other doctors. Some of the letters were whimsical; other doctors expressed relief that they were not alone in their physical reactions to Chinese food. A medical acronym emerged—CRS, for Chinese-Restaurant Syndrome. And, without much scientific reason, the attention of the medical community soon focused nearly exclusively on MSG as a profusion of case reports was published—essentially anecdotes in medical clothing. One investigator even blamed MSG for his 38-year-old wife's two-week bout with depression, her doubt-ridden and gloomy fantasies, and unprecipitated outbursts of rage. If only wives like his could be cured by simply taking away their MSG.

It was not until 1993 that a scientifically controlled, double-blind study was performed, in research by Tarasoff and Kelly. The authors examined 19 previous studies and found that only six were statistically rigorous; three tested MSG mixed with food and three tested MSG on fasting subjects in the absence of food. Only large doses of MSG on fasting subjects provoked anything resembling the Chinese-Restaurant Syndrome. When MSG was mixed with food, reactions pretty much vanished. (MSG in food raises the level of glutamate in our bloodstreams no more than a high-protein meal does.) In the authors' own research, MSG was given in capsule form, 20 minutes before breakfast, as much as three grams at a time, equal to the total average daily intake of MSG in Taiwan, which boasts the largest per capita consumption in the world. There were no differences in the reactions of subjects given MSG and those given a harmless placebo. The only one who was sure he had experienced Chinese-Restaurant Syndrome reacted only to the placebo.

Tarasoff and Kelly identified ingredients in Chinese food besides MSG that might cause the problem: peanuts, shellfish, and eggs, to which as many as 1 percent of us may truly be allergic; histamines in some Asian ingredients that can cause headache, flushing, and palpitations; and high levels of sodium, which can cause flushing and facial tightness in some people. As far as I can tell, nobody has tried to test any of these hypotheses by feeding subjects Chinese food with and without MSG, an experiment I try to perform at least twice a week.

The most recent research took a different approach. Rather

than look for reactions to MSG in the general population, William H. Yang, M.D., and his associates tested only people who had already identified themselves as sensitive to MSG. Yang began with a huge, five-gram dose and considered anybody who responded with even two symptoms from a long list of possibilities to be sensitive to MSG. Of 61 subjects, 18 did react to MSG while showing no false responses to the placebo. The reasonable conclusion was that a small subgroup within the general population really does respond to MSG dissolved in a liquid and drunk on an empty stomach—which, short of an injection, is the fastest way to raise your blood levels of free glutamate.

The fact that fewer than one-third of Yang's subjects actually did respond to MSG should be no surprise to fans, like me, of double-blind oral provocation or oral challenge studies such as these. What I love about them is that they always demonstrate that most people who feel they are somehow allergic or intolerant to one food or another really aren't. Typical is a 1994 British study in which the members of 15,000 households were asked whether they experienced any of a long list of symptoms when they ate milk, eggs, wheat, soy sauce, citrus, shellfish, nuts, or chocolate. A full 20 percent of the respondents said yes. When a portion of them were tested in a double-blind challenge, fewer than a fifth actually reacted to the feared food. The other 80 percent were seeing, or feeling, things that weren't there.

Does this mean they were psychologically troubled? I vote yes. While there is an endless amount of psychiatric literature about people who see things that don't exist, I have found only two or three papers about the psychology of people who experience symptoms that cannot possibly be caused by their food.

Dr. Yang's results were more or less consistent with those of a report commissioned by the FDA from the Federation of American Societies for Experimental Biology (FASEB) and completed in 1995. The FDA found no evidence for the life-threatening consequences that some enemies of MSG have claimed for years, but it did accept reports that asthmatics may be more sensitive to MSG than the general population.

FASEB neither tested the other proposed culprits in Chinese food nor considered the presence of large natural amounts of glutamates in many savory foods. But it concluded that there is a tiny subgroup within the general population—most estimates put the number at around 1 percent—who show signs of Chinese Restaurant Syndrome after consuming an oral dose of at least *three grams in the absence of food*. Three grams is more than all but 5 percent of the U.S. population consume on average in an entire day. But what does this have to do with Chinese-Restaurant Syndrome? It is obviously impossible to consume a Chinese meal in the absence of food. Or is it?

Are you part of that tiny little 1 percent? Or are you an MSG crybaby? If you are among that hapless 1 percent, you may still be the one to blame. My favorite MSG research came from Karl Folkers and his associates at the University of Texas. In two papers written in the early eighties, they showed that people who react to MSG may be suffering from a vitamin B6 deficiency. After treatment with vitamin B6 supplements, MSG reactions in all but one subject disappeared. Those not given vitamin B6 continued to be sensitive to MSG. The implication is that people who complain of Chinese-Restaurant Syndrome are not eating right, not consuming enough peanuts, walnuts, wheat germ, chicken, fish, eggs, or vitamin pills. It is, as I have long felt, all their fault. Folkers's findings have never been contradicted, but they have not been picked up by anyone else in the field.

The 1995 report to the FDA decided that Chinese-Restaurant Syndrome was an "inappropriate" term, and recommended changing the name to MSG Symptom Complex, or MSC. This concern for political correctness blinded the researchers to the ultimate truth. As you will see, they should have changed the name to Chinese-*American* Restaurant Syndrome.

I am sure you have noticed that we are within inches of solving the mystery of the Chinese-Restaurant Syndrome. Some of the earliest reports of CRS involved meals that began with won-ton soup, a ubiquitous first course back in those culinarily primitive days of the late sixties. And we now know that people are unlikely to react to MSG unless they consume large doses dissolved in a liquid on an empty stomach. So, the culprit is obviously the Chinese-American restaurant of 1968. CRS should become CARS.

Thus, the only way to get an MSG headache at a meal is by starting off with a large order of second-rate wonton soup. This is a gastronomic offense so unlikely in these sophisticated times that we can confidently announce that, like smallpox, this scourge has been wiped off the face of the Earth.

MARCH 1999

CHEESE *CRISE*

You're the top, you're a Waldorf salad
You're the top, you're a Berlin ballad
You're the nimble tread of the feet of Fred Astaire
You're an O'Neill drama, you're Whistler's mama
You're Camembert!
                                                    COLE PORTER

Early that morning in Paris, in a tiny shop tucked away on an untrafficked stretch of the rue de Grenelle, a man wrapped my package in several layers of plastic, and then in a sheet of crisp gray paper, which he taped carefully at both ends.

"Not even the dogs at Kennedy Airport will smell through this," he boasted. I forced a smile, paid what he asked, hurried from the shop, and headed for Orly. His roll of plastic did not impress me. For three years ago, I had discovered a safer way of bringing dangerous contraband into the United States. My secret method is called *declaring everything*.

Once the plane took off, I ordered several miniature bottles of red wine and a knife with which to open up my package. Inside were twelve pounds of the greatest cheeses known to humankind, Reblochon and Pont l'Evêque, Alsatian Munster and Époisses, Langres and Livarot, Brie de Meaux and Brie de Melun, and, on top of everything, two versions of Camembert which, along with Torta del Casar from Spain, represents the pinnacle of human achievement in the field of soft and semisoft cheese.

Soon I was deep into one of the Camemberts. The rind was a velvety white, flecked here and there with red, and it gave off a faint odor of mold. Underneath was the creamy, golden "pâte," supple and ripe through and through, properly salty, succulent but not excessively runny, rich with an incomparable aroma that has been identified scientifically as S-methyl thiopropionate, and poetically as *les pieds de Dieu*. Locals are said to prefer their Camembert with an unripened stripe of chalky white at the center; they call it the *âme*, the soul of the cheese.

Camembert is one of 26 cow's-milk cheeses granted an Appellation d'Origine Controlée designation (or AOC) by the French government, which allows the name to be used only by cheese makers who follow precise specifications. (Camembert's AOC was awarded in 1983, though it has been produced in its present form since the French Revolution.) It must be made in the Camembert area of Normandy from unpasteurized local milk, neither fortified by whey proteins nor tarted up with coloring. The milk must never be heated above human body temperature, the mold must be filled at least four separate times with a ladle whose diameter is precisely that of the mold, the cheese must be 4½ inches in diameter and 1¼ inches high, and it must be salted with dry salt, not brine, dried at a precise temperature, and aged for three weeks in specified areas of Normandy. And it is completely illegal in the United States.

All the cheeses in my package are illegal in the United States because they are made with unpasteurized milk and aged for a relatively short time. The Food and Drug Administration (FDA) is quite clear about this in the Code of Federal Regulations, Title 7, section 58.439: "Cheese made from unpasteurized milk shall be cured [aged] for a period of 60 days at a temperature not less than 35 deg. F." This standard, which applies to both imported and domestic cheeses, has been in effect for 50 years. Typically, it bans young, briefly aged unpasteurized cheeses— either imported or made domestically. But it does allow cheeses prepared from unpasteurized milk that have been aged for 60 days or more, such as Parmesan, the great British cheddars, most Italian pecorinos, Cantal, Laguiole, and many other lactic treasures.

Not only does the FDA show absolutely no inclination to relax its ban on young, soft cheeses made from unpasteurized milk, but it has tried to impose its pasteurization rules on the rest of the world. And now it is planning to crack down on long-aged cheeses as well. This alone has the world of cheese lovers, including me, in a panic. The FDA assures me that any further tightening of the 60-day rule would somehow spare Parmesan, pretty unanimously considered one of the world's greatest cheeses by cheese lovers. But the FDA won't explain how.

Red wine and Camembert make for a narcotic compound, and soon the depredations of the federal government drifted from my mind as I fell into the peaceful sleep of the just. I had already filled out my customs form, and yes, I had declared everything. To Question 11 ("I am [We are] bringing fruits, plants, meats, food, soil, birds, soils, or other live animals, wildlife products, farm products; or, have been on a farm or ranch outside the U.S."), I had put a check in the yes square. My cheeses were surely food and, being handmade and unpasteurized, were also, I figured, farm products. In the margin I wrote, in clear block letters, "See other side," where I explained, "Raw-milk cheeses (i.e., unpasteurized) aged or cured for fewer than 60 days." Nobody could accuse me of the slightest deception. I was completely at peace.

A few hours later, when I handed my form to the customs inspector, he carefully read both sides, and as always happens, he waved me through with a broad smile, never mentioning my contraband cheese, which, as it had in the past, gave my friends and me enormous pleasure during the week that followed. My golden retriever Sky King and his friend Henry have become connoisseurs of the rinds of raw-milk cheeses, which they wolfed down enthusiastically to celebrate my return from Paris. Give Sky King a large Parmesan rind, and he'll work on it for days, as though it were a bone possessing endless perfume.

The experience left me bursting with vexing questions and

warring emotions. First of all, if there's a law against bringing young raw-milk cheeses into this country; if they are so haz-
ardous, why have I repeatedly been allowed to bring them in?
Was I being rewarded by some unseen Hand for unimpeachable
honesty?

Second, am I justified in feeling that, by and large, raw-milk
cheeses are far more succulent and delicious than their pasteurized versions, which often taste like gummy plastic?

Third, is the FDA justified in feeling that these fantastic raw-
milk cheeses younger than 60 days are dangerous? And, if so, why
is everybody in France busy consuming them at the rate of nearly
a pound a week for every man, woman, and child? Are cheese
lovers just as suicidal as those Japanese fans of the poisonous
puffer fish, known to them as *fugu*?

Fourth, why is the FDA suddenly concerned about raw-milk
cheeses that have been aged for 60 days or more? Have these
recently (or ever) made people ill?

And fifth, if the FDA is wrong about raw-milk cheeses, as I
hope it is, how can we citizens mobilize against the government,
rising up and crushing the totalitarian and fascistic forces that
threaten our eating pleasure in the name of hygienic sterility?

Answering the first question should have been a total breeze. It
wasn't. I telephoned two cheese experts. One was certain that the
government had recently issued an exception for tourists who
bring in five pounds or less of raw-milk cheese for their own
enjoyment. The theory, she guessed, was that if you want to kill
yourself, even the FDA will let you. The other cheese expert confirmed this five-pound exception, citing the first cheese expert as
her authority.

I have not been in a law library for at least five years now, and
was reluctant to return. By a great stroke of luck, I discovered an
astonishing Web site where, in the comfort of my own home, I
could find nearly every federal law and regulation, plus the laws
of every state and Canada, including court decisions. In a day of
searching, I could find no exception to the strict FDA rule, five
pounds or otherwise. I telephoned the USDA, which has inspec-

tors, an army of them, at every port of entry. They revealed that they have no jurisdiction to enforce the FDA's rules, and are chiefly concerned with the health of animals, not of humans. The USDA has several inspectors in every airport customs hall; if they catch you with the smallest scrap of raw or cured meat, they practically read you your rights. The FDA has many fewer inspectors than the USDA, and I have never encountered one as I passed through customs. Instead, the FDA relies on the Customs Service, on the cheerful men who always wave me through, ignoring my humiliating confessions, clearly written in block letters on the reverse side of the customs form.

Could it be that the Customs Service has an unspoken policy of benign neglect in the matter of cheese? Their officials in Washington, New Jersey, and New York City tried to persuade me that they do not. They are expected to enforce 440 laws and regulations from 40 federal agencies, I was told, and they can't do everything at once. When I telephoned the FDA, they first claimed to be unaware of the sloppy enforcement of their cheese rules at America's borders, then shifted to blaming the problem on the pitiful number of FDA inspectors compared with the ubiquitous hordes of agents from the USDA.

I didn't know what to think, except that it is impossible to get a straight story from the government, even in a matter as crucial as cheese. And that I would order a thousand Waco bumper stickers if I owned a car.

Then again, maybe I wouldn't. What could be more pleasant than the loose enforcement of an oppressive law? Two weeks ago, a leading producer of water buffalo milk from Salerno, southeast of Naples, Italy, carried with her into the United States a large white Styrofoam cooler filled with *mozzarella di bufala* made only a day earlier from her own raw milk, so that her friends in New York City could have a good taste of the real stuff. Though she declared the cheese on her customs form, she and her bulky cooler passed through unchallenged. The mozzarella was fantastic.

The four best cheese shops in New York City carry raw-milk

French cheeses aged for fewer than 60 days—Camembert, Époisses, Pont l'Evêque, Livarot. These are, of course, contraband. Somebody smuggles them in. (The only other American city where I've found young raw-milk French cheeses is Los Angeles, though at very limited times of the year and in limited varieties.) I buy them all the time, though they are often disappointing. After all, it is hard enough to find a perfect Camembert even in Paris unless you know precisely where to shop. Is the FDA somehow not serious about its ban? Not a bit. It has shut down cheese shops and cheese departments with plastic quarantine tape and confiscated entire container loads.

Incidentally, in telephoning around to the FDA, USDA, and Customs Service, I discovered a yawning cultural divide. Officials stationed in Washington, D.C., were for the most part shocked that New Yorkers would go to such lengths to get their hands on raw-milk French cheeses. Officials of the same agencies in New York City, on the other hand, took our obsession for granted—maybe even shared it—suspecting that FDA inspectors here must be looking the other way. Highly placed officers at two leading public-interest organizations in Washington acted as though nothing could be more frivolous than concern over what one referred to as "those gourmet cheeses." I can't imagine why we let people in Washington tell us what to eat.

What is so special about raw-milk cheese? they ask. The answer is pretty clear. Most of the world's great cheeses are made from raw milk. There *are* a few exceptions—the finest of which is probably Colston Bassett Stilton from Britain, which suffered only slightly when, in the midst of a listeriosis outbreak about ten years ago, caused in fact by pasteurized-milk cheese, the cheese maker went over to pasteurization. But it is rare—probably impossible—to find a soft, young cheese made from pasteurized milk that has the strength and complexity of flavor and the succulence of any of the raw-milk cheeses in my contraband package on the airplane. Real cheese was one of humankind's major innovations and is still one of its greatest sources of pleasure.

When you pasteurize milk, you heat it in order to destroy any dangerous microorganisms that may live in it—mainly bacteria—which can cause a host of illnesses, with symptoms ranging from mild stomachache to, yes, death. The problem is that at the same time you prevent the development of the complex flavors we love in great cheese. I've collected a pile of scientific papers on the subject. (Very little of the research is American, by the way.) In one famous study, eight scientists from France, Belgium, and England discovered the one sulfur compound responsible for the ineffable perfume of true, raw-milk Camembert—the S-methyl thiopropionate I mentioned earlier. Very little of it survives if milk is pasteurized before it is turned into Camembert. Another paper showed that various harmless lactic-acid bacteria found in unpasteurized milk are specific to the land where the cows graze and contribute to the aroma and ripening of the cheese made from it. This confirms the gastronomic motive behind the AOC system, which specifies for each protected cheese the places where the cows may graze, the location of the cheese-making facilities, and the ripening caves.

For further enlightenment, I e-mailed two authors of the Camembert paper. Both are experts in the chemical basis of cheese flavor. Dr. Sophie Sable (of the Laboratoire de Genie Proteique et Cellulaire at the University of La Rochelle) replied, "Pasteurization acts on two levels. It can modify the structure of caseins, triglycerides, and other components of the milk. Some of the natural milk enzymes (lipases, proteases . . .) are also destroyed by heat treatment. The formation of flavor compounds and the texture and appearance of the cheeses will be affected. Secondly, the most important effect of pasteurization is to destroy all the microorganisms acting during the maturation of the raw-milk cheese—the most imortant factor in the development of cheese flavor. It is not the volatile flavor compounds which are destroyed by pasteurization but the precursors of these compounds and also the enzymes involved in biosynthesis metabolisms of aromatic compounds. I think it's very important to protect raw-milk cheese."

Professor Eric Spinnler (Institut National Agronomique Paris-

Grignon) explained that lots of work is being done, mainly in France, to identify which of the harmless bacteria and chemical compounds in milk contribute to cheese flavor. The idea is that these could be added back to pasteurized milk before the cheese is made. In 40 years, his laboratory has collected 1,300 bacterial strains from milk. The problem is in screening these bacteria and discovering what each contributes to flavor. Identifying one or two characteristic aroma compounds in each cheese is not enough. "Very often the quality of flavor is related to its complexity," he writes. When eating a cheese with just a few flavor compounds, the consumer will tire easily. "The complexity of flavor is a token of durable appreciation. Each time you taste it, each time it's a different story, but each time it's not so different." This last sentence comes from a poem by Paul Verlaine (1844–1896) about the ideal lover, which Professor Spinnler attached to his e-mail. I am thinking of sending it to the FDA's poetry library.

If I have left even a shred of doubt about the sensory, hedonic, aesthetic, cultural, and spiritual advantages of raw-milk cheese, then I give up. If you don't agree, I suggest that you stop here and go out and buy yourself a nice package of Kraft slices.

Does raw-milk cheese make us sick? According to the federal Centers for Disease Control and Prevention (CDC) in Atlanta, 200 known diseases are transmitted through food. (As an overall cause of death, food-borne illness barely makes it into the top twenty. There are two dozen times the number of accidental deaths, six times the number of suicides, and over three times the number of homicides.) The carriers include viruses, bacteria, parasites, toxins, metals, and prions, if you believe in prions. Each year, these cause an estimated 76 million illnesses in the United States (ranging from stomachaches to much more serious maladies), 325,000 hospitalizations, and 5,000 deaths. In a surveillance report covering the years from 1988 to 1992, the CDC traced most food-borne illnesses to restaurants and cafeterias, and to salads, fruits, vegetables, seafood, and Mexican food. Dairy products were among the safest foods, blamed for only 2.7 percent of food-related illnesses, with contaminated cheese responsible for only a fraction of these. (Of course, as most cheese eaten in America is made from *pasteurized* milk, this fact in itself does not say anything about the safety of raw-milk cheeses.)

The most dangerous food-borne illness is listeriosis. Once you contract it, your chances of being hospitalized are 90 percent; although the disease can be treated with antibiotics, your chances of death are still 20 percent. You do not want to get listeriosis. Fortunately, listeriosis is extremely rare. While the listeria bacteria can be found in many types of raw food, and sometimes in raw milk and cheese, fewer than 1 percent of all food-borne illnesses in the United States are due to listeria. For reasons not entirely obvious, listeriosis is often associated in people's minds with cheese. The last major outbreak of listeriosis in this country was in 1998. It was caused by hot dogs.

According to a journal article written by scientists from the FDA and the CDC, "Cheese-associated Outbreaks of Human Illness in the United States, 1973 to 1992," 58 deaths over the course of that 20-year period were traced to eating contaminated cheese. Two of these were caused by a bad batch of New York City mozzarella containing salmonella, and the other 56 by *queso fresco*, usually referred to as "Mexican-style soft cheese," a notorious source of listeriosis. Of these 56 deaths, 48 occurred in just one outbreak of listeriosis in Los Angeles in 1985. An analysis in the *New England Journal of Medicine* in 1988 traced this outbreak to just one manufacturer of *queso fresco*, and then to only one of its plants, which purchased raw milk and pasteurized it before turning it into cheese. The two likeliest explanations were either that this particular plant had bought infected raw milk and then failed to pasteurize it effectively, or that the milk or cheese had become infected in the factory after it left the pasteurizer. FDA inspectors found that the 27 dairy farms supplying the raw milk were modern and clean; that the herds showed no sign of infection; and that the plant's pasteurizer was working properly, although it had possibly been operating above its capacity.

Yet, somehow, the FDA, on the basis of no evidence, concluded that the dairy herds must have included sick animals that were secretly eliminated in the weeks that elapsed before its inspectors arrived, and that somehow the contaminated raw milk had been badly pasteurized. Swabs taken from around the factory—the walls, floors, and machinery—were full of listeria bacteria and particularly of strain 4b, which is often the cause of epidemics. Whether or not the infestation should have been discovered during earlier FDA inspections of the plant, the FDA went out of its way to blame the outbreak on raw milk from apparently healthy cows. But the evidence makes it at least equally likely that the contaminated factory, the cheese-making environment, had reinfected the pasteurized milk—that the raw milk had nothing to do with it at all. This would have been an unsatisfying conclusion to the sworn enemies of raw-milk cheese. A letter from an expert at the University of California at Davis to the *New England Journal of Medicine* raised these same questions.

Listeriosis is nearly entirely confined to pregnant women and their fetuses, the elderly, and persons with impaired immune systems. (Only one of the deaths in the 1985 *queso fresco* outbreak in Los Angeles was an exception.) On the telephone with the FDA, I helpfully suggested that, if they are still as worried about cheese as they are about hot dogs, a warning label aimed at the susceptible groups should do the trick. They replied that very few people read or respond to warning labels. But isn't every driver expected to read stop signs or face the consequences? And, I pointed out, pregnant women and people with HIV are nearly all under the watchful care of a doctor, who would certainly warn them against eating soft cheeses, as the FDA and CDC have instructed doctors to do. Maybe that would work, said the FDA, but what about salmonella and *E. coli* O157:H7, which do not attack one limited risk group?

In any case, by the FDA's own analysis, nearly all deaths from eating cheese in the past few decades were caused by listeria bacteria in the soft Mexican cheese called *queso fresco,* manufactured in Los Angeles. Eliminate these deaths and the fatality rate falls to two deaths in 20 years, which is next to nothing. Ban *queso fresco,* or clean up the plants in Los Angeles, and cheese will be considered harmless.

The possible danger from eating young, raw-milk cheeses would be most effectively demonstrated by statistics from countries where raw milk is common, especially France. But, to my knowledge, the FDA has never published data about the dangers from cheese-borne listeriosis, salmonella, or *E. coli* infection in any country where raw-milk cheeses are legal.

We do, however, have lots of local, American experience with the possible hazards in eating long-aged, raw-milk cheeses, because these are permitted by the FDA. Why is the FDA intending to stiffen its own 60-day rule? Are aged, raw-milk cheeses more dangerous than we had thought?

The idea behind the 60-day rule is that, as cheese ages, it loses moisture and becomes so much more acidic and salty that bacteria cannot live in it. The survival of some pathogens way past 60 days in raw-milk hard cheeses in the laboratory has been suggested by one or two studies, and the FDA has commissioned research "to confirm" this. But even if the finding is confirmed, its practical importance is doubtful. I have searched all publicly available data from the FDA and CDC and found, in all recorded U.S. history, only *one* outbreak of disease traced to aged, raw-milk cheese. The culprit was salmonella, and no deaths resulted. Many American cheese makers use raw milk to produce excellent hard and semihard cheeses. A warning label instead of a ban would at least give us the right to choose what we eat. Come to think of it, let's forget the warning label. To repeat, practically nobody in the United States has ever gotten sick after eating a raw-milk cheese that was aged for more than 60 days.

The FDA has told me that, if mandatory pasteurization would save just one life a year, the agency would have no choice but to require it. The FDA says it has no authority to balance the risk from eating a certain food against the benefit or pleasure we might derive from it. (This is what the agency does on a daily basis when considering drugs and medicines and their side effects.) But you and I perform this kind of balancing act every day, whenever we cross the street or get into a taxi. Your lifetime chances of being electrocuted are one in 3,000. This means that, of all the Americans alive today, 100,000 of them will die of electrocution. But, somehow, we have decided not to junk our entire electrical system. We apparently value hair dryers and e-mail (and heat and light) more than we value 100,000 of our fellow citizens. Society as a whole balances risks against benefits all the time. The FDA should let us consumers choose whether we want to take on the tiny risk in eating raw-milk cheese.

Meanwhile, the FDA has also been at the center of an international struggle over cheese. The Codex Alimentarius Commission, or Codex for short, is an international body (165 countries belong) that has been writing standards for food hygiene, safety, pesticides, additives, packaging, labeling, and so forth. Our delegates (from the FDA, USDA, and EPA) had been urging mandatory pasteurization for all cheeses, and we lost. Instead, the provisional Codex document mentions pasteurization as just one example of the measures a country might require to control food-borne illnesses. It was a standoff: We could not impose pasteurization on the Europeans, and they could not impose raw milk on us. I have been told that though our delegates put a brave face on the matter, they were deeply unhappy with this result and not, astoundingly, for gastronomic reasons. The issue is trade. There is a remote chance that if France can prove that an alternative to pasteurization is just as safe (as the Codex implies), the World Trade Organization will rule that our pasteurization requirements are *artificial trade barriers* and must be struck down, both internationally and domestically, as happened recently when we successfully sued to make the Europeans swallow our hormonal beef. O happy day!

But I am a realist. As I write this, there is a rainy Paris afternoon outside my hotel window. The French will not be able to conquer our import barriers before I fly back home, or even in the coming year. I know that. And so, on the way to the airport, I will buy 10 or 15 pounds of aromatic, creamy, yielding cheese.

And when I arrive at JFK, I will be sure to declare absolutely everything.

JUNE 2000

Author's note: The FDA's study failed to "confirm" that raw-milk cheese aged for more than 60 days can be dangerous. This—and public criticism—appears to have made the agency back off. At the same time, almost without notice, a long-term listeria risk assessment conducted by the CDC and the FDA concluded that even soft, young raw-milk cheese is many times less likely to give you the disease than, for example, smoked fish! Soon, however, our borders were tightened, as the mad-cow scare and hoof-and-mouth disease in Europe led the ubiquitous and militant USDA inspectors at airports to worry about cheese nearly as much as they do raw cured meats. Slowly, things are returning to normal, i.e., the muddled and irrational state in which they wallowed when this chapter was written.

The Impossible Dream

This is the story of an impossible dream, a dream of bread, a dream come true.

THE LOAF THAT NEARLY DIED

This is the story of an impossible dream, a dream of bread, a dream come true.

But first let me fill you in on the background. Whenever my professional duties force me to travel to Paris, I like to hit the ground eating. I make a deal with the airport taxi driver, and we whiz around Paris collecting the breads or other foodstuffs by which I am particularly compelled that year. Once it was fifteen croissants, another year, twenty kilos of *pain de campagne*. Most often it is baguettes. Bursting with anticipation, I come prepared with a map of the city, on which I have placed a little red dot at the site of each boulangerie, fromagerie, or epicerie, and draw a line between them that wiggles its way from the 15th, where I triumphally enter the city, to the far-off 20th, where my journey ends with a baguette from La Flute Gana and a brief visit to Oscar Wilde's tomb. After three or four stops, when the driver grows nervous about all the crumbs in the backseat, I calm him with some free bread. After six or seven stops, I calm him with extra francs. Not all French taxi drivers share my fixation on the ideal baguette. Few can even recognize one.

Both bakers and laypersons who are unlucky enough to be younger than I have no memory of the true French baguette, which began to disappear around 1960. I will always be grateful that my parents first took their infant son to Paris that year, where an indelible memory of the true baguette was impressed forever upon his tiny yet fertile brain. After 1960, economic pressures (and the government's benign rules replacing piecework with hourly wages) brought high-speed mixers, machines for dividing dough and forming loaves, and the strong, high-gluten American and Canadian flours needed to stand up to them. As one French expert explained it to me, instead of designing machines to work with the old recipes and the soft, creamy French flours, the industry changed the bread to fit the machines. The traditional French baguette began to disappear. In its place emerged a tasteless, fluffy, pale and bleached impostor.

The true baguette is thin, between about 24 to 28 inches long, slightly flattened, weighs nine to ten ounces, and has five or seven oblique slashes along the top surface, made just before baking, to allow the dough to expand before the crust has set. The crust itself is toasty, tight, and crackling, and the insides (known as the "crumb" in English or the "*mie*" in French) are creamy—nearly golden—never bone white, and marked by an irregular profusion of glossy bubbles and holes, some as large as olives.

The true baguette is made only from flour, water, and salt—and, usually, yeast for leavening. Countless French techniques exist for arriving at the same goal, but the classic recipes call for a brief, slow kneading and a fermentation of several hours with only a little yeast. A true baguette must be baked directly on the hearth; its underside never shows the telltale curve and waffle pattern of a metal pan. Its most elusive qualities are the strong, simple sweetness of the crumb, though absolutely no sugar can be added, and a nearly paradoxical quartet of textures—around the air bubbles, the crumb is dense, moist, stretchy, and extremely tender, all at the same time, with no hint of rubberiness, no dry, tough sheets or filaments of gluten.

In the 1980s, M. Poilâne on the rue du Cherche-Midi became everybody's ideal of a baker. His wood-burning oven produced huge, dark, round, delicious, grainy, acidic *pains au levain*—loaves that at their best defined the ancient handmade country bread. Baguettes were lightweight city loaves—perishable, white, usually risen with manufactured yeast instead of wild sourdough cultures, and of relatively recent origin. (As the writer Edward Behr tells it, today's baguette originated in the last decades of the 1800s but did not come into its own until the 1930s.) French bakers who remembered how to make true baguettes had become rare and celebrated. Old M. Ganachaud in the 20th arrondissement knew how, as did Professor Raymond Calvel, and a young teacher whose class I visited at Ferrandi, the trade school in Paris for aspiring young cooks. But fashionable young bakers such as Poujauran in the 7th or Kamir in the 14th did not have a clue. There were times when I grew so desperate that I wondered whether real baguettes existed outside my—call it Proustian if you must—imagination.

Yet my own search continued unabated. Every trip to Paris included an inconvenient excursion to M. Ganachaud's remote bakery and an occasional lunch with him at the Auvergnat bistro around the corner. Once, when his workers had badly underbaked his wonderful, trademarked, extra-slim *flutes,* the restaurant's very large proprietress greeted us by beating the frail M. Ganachaud about the head and shoulders with two pale and flaccid *flutes.* She was not kidding.

And then, as the 1990s gathered speed, the true baguette began to make a powerful comeback, first in Paris, then all over France. The French government issued guidelines for *"pain de tradition française."* Several flour companies started milling old-fashioned flour. And the mayor of Paris launched the Grand Prix de la Baguette de la Ville de Paris, the prestigious annual competition for the best baguette in the city.

As the day for the 1998 competition drew near, I made plans to attend. And then the most preposterous error occurred. Instead of appointing the usual jury of 15 extremely distinguished experts and *"personnalités remarquables,"* the mayor of Paris appointed 14 of them and one of me! I was totally on cloud nine. Not only would I be forced to eat more than 100 baguettes in the brief space of a morning, but I would be doing my part in saving the magnificent loaf that nearly died.

I arrived early at the Chambre de Métiers in the 12th arrondissement to watch the bakers bring in their bread. All the 1,400 professional *boulangers* in the City of Paris are eligible to enter the contest, simply by showing up between 8:30 and

10:00 a.m. on the morning of January 30 with a baguette in one hand and an unmarked envelope containing his or her name and address in the other. There is no written application. Some baguettes were carried in paper bags and some were wrapped around the middle with waxed paper, but most were bare. None of the bakers wore sterilized plastic gloves. Several had brought their dogs. Yet somehow none of us judges was afraid of contracting a fatal bread-borne infection. We were, after all, in Paris.

My fellow judges drifted in. They included Alain Ducasse, perhaps the greatest chef in France; Ghislaine Arabian, the highest-ranking woman chef; the gastronomic correspondent for *Le Monde*; the editor of France's premier baking journal; Hélène Macé de Lepinay, the deputy mayor for culture; last year's laureate, René-Gérard Saint-Ouen, whose bread I have enjoyed for years at 111 boulevard Haussmann in the 8th; and Philippe Faure-Brac, who won the title of Best Sommelier in the World in 1992. President of the jury was Gérard Leban, deputy mayor for commerce, industry, and craftsmen. Come to think of it, I've never met the deputy mayor of New York City in charge of craftsmen.

By 10:00 a.m., all the judges and 104 baguettes had been logged in. Eight baguettes were eliminated on technical grounds, mainly because they fell outside the 60-to-70-centimeter and 250-to-300-gram guidelines. The 15 judges were then seated at a vast U-shaped table that reminded one of the League of Nations. In the first round, each of us tasted and scored 32 of the baguettes, awarding each one a score from 0 to 4 on each of five criteria, for a possible total of 20, which seems to be the perfect score in nearly all French contests. The five criteria were aroma, taste, appearance, *cuisson* (how well it was baked), and *alvéolage*, the internal structure of holes and bubbles. At least a quarter of the baguettes I tasted were as fine as anything I can remember. Can you picture my mental and spiritual ecstasy?

It took us about 45 minutes to get through 32 baguettes apiece, and another 10 minutes for the staff to total up the scores and select the five winners from each group. Then, we all tasted the 15 highest scorers, and graded them anew. The judges groaned and gagged softly as the last few baguettes were passed around, but we persevered with great discipline, so as to be fair to the final candidates. I would never have thought it possible to reach satiety eating the greatest baguettes in all of Paris. I doubt that I will ever again suffer from that heavenly affliction. Most of those baguettes were nearly perfect.

And then the president of the jury, M. Leban, opened the identifying envelope of the greatest baguette in Paris and possibly the world. The winner would be awarded 20,000 francs, about $3,333 on that day, and become the official supplier of baguettes to the Elysée Palace, residence of the president of the French Republic!

M. Leban paused and blinked. He conferred with an aide. A huddle ensued. And then an announcement was made. The winning baker, instead of putting his name and address in the envelope, had written: "Anonymous. The baker cares only for his customers." He had thumbed his nose at the contest, at the mayor and his deputies—and at us, his anointed judges! And yet, stuffed full of the finest bread, fat and happy, none of us was disturbed for more than a second or two. The other winners were simply promoted one notch apiece, and number eleven was brought into the top ten. The new number one was announced: Antonio Teixeira, baker-owner of Aux Délices du Palais, 60 boulevard Brune, 75014, Paris—the baker of the best baguette in the City of Light, official supplier to the Elysée Palace.

Over the next few days, I visited all ten winning bakeries, starting with M. Teixeira's. Aux Délices du Palais is in a working-class section of the 14th, where Teixeira also sells pastry, inexpensive candy (including Mars bars), and two less expensive baguettes—a *baguette normale* and a *banette*. At 32, Teixeira is trim, dark, and nice-looking, and, on that day at least, wore a permanent smile. He was born in Portugal—his parents immigrated to France when he was seven—and he has been a professional baker for the past 15 years.

From a hallway behind the shop, we descended a narrow flight of wooden stairs into the basement, where Teixeira resumed his baking—slashing and loading the risen baguettes into his oven so that they would be ready for the dinnertime rush. Between batches, we polished off a bottle of Bordeaux and munched on sandwiches of salami and his perfect championship baguettes—crisp, tender, aromatic, golden, and sweet, with a wonderfully chaotic pattern of holes and bubbles—and glanced from time to time at an excellent pneumatic pinup taped to the front of his oven just under the buttons and controls.

Unlike the other winning baguettes, which take only five or six hours from start to finish, Teixeira's are made with a natural starter that takes two days to concoct—yet his final product is sweet and without perceptible acidity, a technique he learned at baking school.

The sun was setting over Paris, and dinnertime was drawing near, and when I climbed up to the shop again, not at all unsteady from my half of the bottle of Bordeaux, a long line of customers, mostly women, stretched out into the street. As they reached the counter, nearly all of them said, *"Une baguette normale, s'il vous plâit, mais pas trop cuit"*—a regular baguette, please, but not too well done—a request once reserved for old people or children without all their teeth. Only one in 20 asked for Teixeira's championship *baguette à l'ancienne,* for which he charges seven francs, just over a dollar, instead of the usual two francs seventy for a mediocre loaf, hardly worth eating. Why do they insist that their baguette not be too well done? How many charred baguettes are lurking in the back alleys of Paris, ready to spring?

I wanted to pummel them all with a bundle of underbaked *baguettes normales.* These customers are why the French baguette almost died out, and why its revival sometimes seems such a Sisyphean project. But visiting the birthplaces of baguettes two through five brought a happy song to my heart. In an astounding commercial coup, all four were Rétrodors, the brand name for baguettes produced by neighborhood bakeries using the flour, recipe, and other specifications of one of France's finest flour mills, the Minoteries Viron in Chartres.

I can think of no marketing scheme that has the potential to bring more gladness to humankind than this, or at least to that vital subgroup residing in France. Other millers had the idea of a branded baguette even before Viron. In 1996, the winner of the Grand Prix de la Baguette was a Baguépi, baked by M. Gosselin at 123-5 rue de Saint-Honoré with a flour very similar to Viron's. I tried Gosselin's baguette a few months ago: It was still terrific.

There are French food lovers who fear that these branded baguettes may bring standardization to the world of handmade bread. Having wandered in a harsh and barren Parisian baguette wilderness for 20 years, I will feel that I've reached the promised land if Rétrodor and Baguépi set a *minimum* standard that innovators can strive to exceed. Besides which, when you pop in on five or six Rétrodor boulangeries in a row, you find that the final product varies from very good to banal, depending on the attention and skill of the baker.

The Rétrodor recipe is simplicity itself. No natural starter, no pre-fermented dough. The flour is only 10 percent protein. Water is a hefty 70 percent of the weight of the flour, the yeast is 1.05 percent, and salt 1.75 percent. Everything is mixed for eight minutes, at a slow 40 turns a minute. The dough rises for three hours. During the first hour it is turned every 20 minutes. And that's it.

There is no American baker—no American child, in fact—who could not follow these instructions. And American artisan bakers are just as adept as their French counterparts. Yet I had never tasted an American baguette with the sweetness and tenderness of the French paragon. The great American bread revolution started around 1980 in Berkeley, California, with naturally leavened sourdough breads baked at the Cheese Board and the Acme Bread Company. For the next decade, most young artisan bakers concentrated on working with natural starters, known in French as *chefs*—pieces of dough in which wild yeast and lactic acid bacteria live happily in symbiosis, generating the gases, alcohols, and acids that give this bread its complex taste and chewy texture. Their models were the *pains au levain* produced by Poilâne in Paris and by Acme. Compared with such a primitive and primordial adventure, the baking of white, yeasted breads did not interest them. Their baguettes were, for the most part, perfunctory.

At the beginning of the 1990s, I became convinced that the real challenge for American bakers was to put aside their sourdough and work on creating truly great baguettes. Whenever a new artisan bakery opened in America, I would order a half dozen. Inevitably, I recycled them as bread crumbs the next day. A few years ago, at a conference in New York City on bread, I showed a slide I had made from a photograph of the perfect baguette in Philippe Viron's little book, *Vive la Baguette*, and announced that there was no baker in America who could replicate this bread. The outcry against me was quick and merciless. This is how tough love and true compassion are repaid. As time in all its fullness would reveal, I was wrong.

In 1996, at the international baking contest in Paris known as the Coupe du Monde—the World Cup—the American team (fielded by the Bread Bakers Guild of America, the league of artisan bakers) astounded the baking universe by trouncing every other nation—even France itself—in the main event, traditional breads, including the baguette. Your correspondent just happened to be at the Coupe du Monde to witness our national triumph.

What goes wrong when the same breads are baked here?

I have spoken with a good number of artisan bakers—and with Maggie Glezer, who is hard at work on a book on handmade bread in America—and the consensus is that French flour holds the secret. Both industrial and small-scale American bakers have favored high-protein flour that produces, when kneaded with water, strong sheets and ropes of stretchy, elastic gluten. Gluten enables dough to rise dramatically; as the thousands of air bubbles in the dough expand with increasing volumes of carbon dioxide and water vapor, the gluten helps the bubbles grow without breaking. But the gluten in "strong" American flour makes dough that is typically elastic, springy, and resistant to stretching. European bread flour of the type produced especially for baguettes by Rétrodor and Baguépi measures much lower in protein than ours, but produces dough that is remarkably extensible; with only a little force, the dough can be stretched into long strands and ropes that neither break nor snap back like a rubber band. In a baguette, the result is a network of large and irregular bubbles with tender, relatively dense bread in between. Baguette flour has a creamy, nearly golden color, and many writers, including Elizabeth David, believe that low-gluten flour has much more taste. Alexander Viron advises American millers not to discard the aleuron layer between the bran and the heart of the wheat berry, which contains lots of flavor and color.

Of the four principal types of protein in flour, the two that combine to form gluten when mixed with water are the glutenin and gliadin. Researchers had thought that the ratio of these two proteins might determine whether the gluten in a particular flour would prove to be especially elastic or extensible when kneaded. Nothing seems to have come from this hypothesis, or from the idea that the molecular weight of a subfraction of glutenin might tell the story. One scientist who has devoted a lifetime to understanding the protein in wheat thinks that typical American bread flour is simply too high in total protein to bake a proper baguette.

Craig Ponsford of Artisan Bakers in Sonoma, California—a lead baker on the 1996 American team—has been experimenting with unusually soft, creamy domestic flours that resemble the French varieties. The other day, I telephoned him with the Rétrodor recipe, and two days later, the man from FedEx brought a bundle of four baguettes, crisp and sweet, creamy, and full of holes in a dense and moist and tender crumb. If my current job had not reduced me to penury, I might be looking for a second home in downtown Sonoma.

JULY 1998

BREAD IN PARIS, UP-TO-THE-MINUTE

The most interesting boulangerie in Paris these days is owned by Eric Kayser, with two shops just a few numbers apart on the rue Monge in the 5th arrondissement. Kayser is a former baking teacher and an acknowledged master at the age of 36. He bakes an incredible variety of breads, and uses a liquid sourdough starter to leaven nearly all of them, including the croissants.

The best croissants are made by Poujauran in the 7th, a baker unjustly popular for his bread, which is often mediocre. But his croissants are everything they should be—extremely flaky on the outside; very light in the hand; possessing a perfect balance in flavor between the sweet, the salty, and the acidic from cultured (lightly fermented) butter; easy to break in half cleanly, without destroying the croissant; moist inside, yet with all the internal layers visible; and preternaturally delectable. Considering all the ersatz and inferior croissants around, it is crucial to eat the real thing every so often.

The true baguette continues its firm recovery from near extinction in the sixties and seventies, thanks in good part to the annual Grand Prix de la Baguette. As long as you ask for *"baguette de tradition"* or *"à l'ancienne,"* you won't go wrong with any of the boulangeries on my list.

THE BEST CROISSANTS

POUJAURAN, 20 RUE JEAN-NICOT, 75007

KAYSER, 8 RUE MONGE, 75005

THE BEST BAGUETTES (ALPHABETICALLY)

AUX DÉLICES DU PALAIS, 60 BLVD. BRUNE, 75014

GOSSELIN, 125 RUE SAINT-HONORÉ, 75001

LE GRENIER À PAIN, 52 AV. D'ITALIE, 75013

JULIEN, 75 RUE SAINT-HONORÉ, 75001

RAOUL MAEDER, 158 BLVD. BERTHIER, 75017

ROLLET PRADIER, 6 RUE BOURGOGNE, 75007

(RENÉ) SAINT-OUEN, 111 BLVD. HAUSSMANN, 75008

THE BEST CHAIN OF BOULANGERIES

PAUL, SEVERAL LOCATIONS,

INCLUDING 63 RUE MONTORGUEIL, 75002,

AND THE RUE DE BUCI, 75006.

ADDICTED TO LOSING

Guns will make us powerful; butter will only make us fat.

AIR MARSHAL HERMANN GOERING, 1936

Late on the morning of September 15, 1997, the awful news trickled in. The FDA (the federal Food and Drug Administration) had just pulled fen/phen from the market. Barely controlling the waves of panic that surged through my lean and athletic body, I sprang out of my chair, threw off the bathrobe in which I sometimes work until the approach of lunchtime, pulled on a pair of jeans, and bounded out the door. If I could reach the pharmacist before word reached his ears, I would be able to get my last refill. It would possibly be the last fen/phen refill in America!

I had been taking fen/phen, the most fabulously successful and effective diet drug known to man, for just over two and a half years and, despite my heavy responsibilities as a food critic and my enviable talent for gaining ceaseless pleasure from eating, I had lost 30 pounds. And it was perfectly legal, dispensed only with a doctor's prescription. Twelve pounds more and my weight would be down to chubby again, for the first time in seven years—for the first time since I had entered my current profession. Not only were my cholesterol, blood pressure, and triglycerides down, but I was nearly able to fit again into the largest of several costly, beautiful, handmade Savile Row suits that still hung in my closet, purchased before the practice of food writing put such exquisite garments beyond my financial reach. There was a new spring in my step, a taut smile on my face.

Why was the FDA trying to take away my fen/phen? The previous July, doctors at the prestigious Mayo Clinic had announced that 24 women taking fen/phen had suffered damage to the valves of their hearts. Five had needed surgery to repair the problem. So, the FDA sent out 700,000 warning letters to doctors around the country, requesting any further reports of heart-valve problems. When it finished analyzing the data, the FDA found that 32 percent of 291 patients taking fen/phen had exhibited heart-valve abnormalities. And, this morning, the FDA struck.

Me, I didn't believe a word of it. Fen/phen is really a combination of two FDA-approved medications, fenfluramine and phentermine. Fenfluramine, marketed as Pondimin, a bright little round orange pill, had been in approved use since 1973; phentermine since 1959. A closely related chemical, dexfenfluramine, sold as Redux, though authorized by the FDA only a year before, had been used in Europe for more than a decade. Eighteen million prescriptions had been written for these drugs in the United States in the previous year. And now, out of the blue, all of a sudden, some doctors somewhere were claiming that one-third of their diet-pill patients had suffered damage to their hearts. And nobody had noticed? If they had said one out of ten, I might have believed it and gone into a suitable panic. But one out of three? Please.

I arrived at the drugstore. I had nearly three weeks' supply of Pondimin in my medicine cabinet, and one refill left on my prescription. With luck, I would soon have nearly two months' worth and lose another five pounds. And, by then, the FDA might get over what I suspected to be an excessive concern over other people's heart valves. (To be perfectly accurate, the FDA had not itself banned Pondimin or Redux; it had persuaded the manufacturers to withdraw the drugs. Phentermine, sold as Adipex or Ionamin, was left untouched by the FDA action.) Besides, a new diet drug, known as Meridia, was on the horizon.

I forced myself to slow down and take a deep breath as I entered the shop and sauntered back to the prescription counter—feigning interest in the shelves of hair-care products as though my greatest worry in the world were split ends. "Hi, there," I said casually. "Just passin' by. Thought I'd pick up a cou-

pla things." And before you knew it, I was cantering home with a
month's supply of Pondimin, a bottle of shampoo, and a celebratory pint of Häagen-Dazs Chocolate Chocolate Chip. I could feel
the happy little orange pills jingling against their amber plastic
vial.

Two and a half years earlier, my weight had been approaching
dangerous levels. My BMI, body-mass index, had been 31, high
enough to qualify officially for obesity. Your BMI is a measure of
your weight compared with your height, just like those Metropolitan Life height-and-weight charts, but calculated as your
weight in kilograms divided by the square of your height in
meters. In case you have been spending too much time in the
gym to master your metric conversions, you can use this formula: Take your weight in pounds, multiply it by 703, divide the
result by your height in inches, and then divide again by your
height in inches. It's easier than it sounds, especially if, as I do,
you recalculate your BMI several times a day. Or you can go to
nhlbisupport.com/bmi/bmicalc.htm on the Internet and type in
your numbers.

You have read the same statistics I have—a BMI over 28 triples
the risk of death by stroke, heart disease, and diabetes. And
300,000 Americans die prematurely every year because they are
fat. We spend $68 billion extra a year on health care because of
obesity. Plus $30 billion for weight reduction programs and diet
foods. That comes to an annual $392 for every man, woman, and
child in the entire country. The average American got eight
pounds fatter over the past 15 years. I had gained four times more
than this in only half as long.

You can imagine, then, the joy and hope that had filled my
heart when I observed several friends shed their excess weight
with complete and total ease. Their secret was fen/phen, and
soon it would become mine as well. Fenfluramine is an anorexic
agent—it allows you to eat less and still feel full. One problem
with conventional diets is that as you cut down your eating, your
body reduces the rate at which it burns energy. The phentermine
half of the partnership, the Ionamin or Adipex, is an amphetaminelike drug, though apparently without the addictive potential

of amphetamines. It keeps your entire system going at a nice fast clip.

My primary-care physician, after delivering the warnings found in the *Physicians' Desk Reference* (and the package inserts), had been glad to help out. He required me to come in for a checkup every few months, though the dangers seemed either minor or rare. The only really scary medical warning concerned Pondimin: it was estimated that 18 out of a million users contracted a disease called primary pulmonary hypertension, or PPH—considerably more than the one or two per million among the general population and maybe two to four per million among the obese. PPH is no laughing matter. The artery leading from the heart to the lungs becomes mysteriously narrowed and, after a period of increasing shortness of breath and disability, the right ventricle of the heart can fail. Half of those afflicted with PPH will die within four years. On the other hand, 18 out of a million Pondimin or Redux users translates to only one in every 55,556. That seemed like an acceptable risk. Now, the estimates of danger have doubled. This is getting closer to home. But as an editorial in the *New England Journal of Medicine* pointed out, diet drugs can save 280 obese people for every 14 who would die from primary pulmonary hypertension. Hard to beat those odds.

My earliest days on fen/phen were not carefree. A day or two after I opened my first bottles of Pondimin and Ionamin, I came down with a case of intermittent fever and violent shivering. Now, I have heard of a transient drug reaction known as serotinergic syndrome, a central nervous system response to an increase in serotonin, which is what Pondimin apparently causes. Maybe that's what I had.

A few days later, I settled into a brief period of such atrophied appetite that I worried I might have to switch professions again. But soon my interest in food returned—with the difference that although my enjoyment had been fully restored, I could feel completely satisfied after eating only two or three bites. And as soon as one meal was done, I did not start thinking of the next for at least a half hour. This was a breakthrough in itself. Fen/phen was a miracle!

The side effects were annoying: irritability, quickness to anger, long periods in which I would have nothing to say, loss of short-term memory, diminished sense of humor, and, when I tried to write, the inability to find the words. Plus, the amphetaminelike qualities of phentermine made me obsess about details, which led to some tiny difficulty with deadlines. I should also mention that there were occasional moments when my customary amorousness and priapism completely deserted me. But, I was losing weight—quickly at first, then more slowly as time wore on.

In the six months before the FDA's action, I was able to do no better than maintain my new weight, but I had no plans to stop taking the pills. The medical journals agreed that most people who do so gain back the pounds they have lost.

And that is the key to all of this. Most people do not take harmful or disturbing drugs unnecessarily. If they could lose weight by cutting down on the French fries and taking the stairs, they would. But masses of evidence show that the tendency to obesity is heavily influenced by one's genes. (Identical twins reared apart weigh the same, some people overeat and stay slim, et cetera, et cetera.) And so, two-thirds of all people who lose a substantial amount of weight regain it within a year. Nearly all will regain it within five years. Even if you believe that those of us with an inborn tendency to gain weight can counteract it through severe and permanent restrictions on our diets and exhausting exercise regimes that squander several hours a day, why should we wreck our lives when we can take a pill instead? Only a masochist would think otherwise. For most people, obesity is not a moral failure. It is a medical problem. At least I think it is.

After two and a half years on fen/phen, my BMI was down to 26.5, well out of the danger zone but still above the optimum, which is 21, though I feel that some girls can be awfully attractive at a BMI of 19, which translates as five feet four inches and 110 pounds, or six feet and 140, both of which are still presumably above Kate Moss levels.

As my Pondimin supply dwindled, a debate raged among

researchers about the true frequency of heart-valve leaks; whether the problem reverses itself when patients stop taking diet pills; and how common the problem is among the general population. The *Wall Street Journal* surveyed doctors at 21 clinics and medical centers across the country at the end of October 1997, and reported that, of 746 patients who had taken Redux or Pondimin, only 57 had valve problems. That came to 8 percent. Some doctors reported only one troubled patient, or none at all. This was good news but not good enough. An 8 percent risk may be acceptable for really fat people. But what about me?

The last fen/phen refill in America—my 50-day supply—lasted longer than 50 days, what with recesses for writing and those lapses in short-term memory that sometimes tricked me into thinking I had taken a pill when I had not—and dumped me off the diet train just as we were approaching the carnal temptations of Thanksgiving, Christmas, Twelfth Night, and Epiphany. In the three months that followed, I gained a pound a week. My BMI was inching up into the obesity zone, 20 percent above my ideal weight. Eight pounds later, and the buttons began to strain on two expensive shirts I had ordered from a famous shop on Jermyn Street in London. I weighed more than I had in over a year.

One morning, I fled the United States and drove around northern Mexico, begging pharmacists in Tijuana and Ensenada for fen/phen. They offered me Prozac without a prescription, for a dollar a pill, but refused to sell me either Pondimin or Adipex—even though Adipex is still a legal and approved medication! My Spanish was not good enough to figure out the problem, but it struck me as sad that drugstores in northern Mexico are so terrified by the Drug Enforcement Administration that they don't even follow their own laws. In Rosarito, on the coast, after failing to find a rational pharmacist, I ate several delicious and juicy tacos filled with wood-grilled beef and returned to the United States for dinner.* I could have bought heroin more easily.

And then, at the end of March, the first carefully controlled

---

*Read all about these glorious tacos in "Crossing the Line," page 263.

study of Redux's effects on heart valves was reported. One thousand seventy-two overweight men and women took Redux for 77 days, and then were given echocardiograms (the expensive but definitive sound-wave imaging of the heart). None showed significant heart-valve leakage. None! Was 77 days long enough to tell anything? Redux is intended only for short-term use by the truly obese, and is not to be taken for several years by people who want to look better in their bathing suits. Or so the reasoning goes.

What monumental hypocrisy! Of what conceivable use is a diet drug that may help a poor 350-pound man or woman lose ten pounds once in a lifetime? Everybody knows that diet drugs will inevitably and predominantly be taken over extended periods by the borderline obese, whose genes cause them to gain weight much more easily than they can take it off. Nice, normal, average people like me.

Dr. Janet Woodcock of the FDA would not be budged by the Redux study, telling the *New York Times,* "We believe there is a significant rate of valvular abnormalities. The data suggest it is related to the duration of exposure." Yet, even as she spoke, the federal Centers for Disease Control and Prevention found that the size of your diet-pill dose may matter more than the length of time you took it. Things were getting very confused.

It is early March. Stripped to the waist, I am reclining on an examining table in my new cardiologist's office. He has listened to my heart and detected a very slight murmur, which can be either a resonance in my chest cavity, known as a physiological murmur, or the turbulence of my blood as it swishes back and forth through a malfunctioning valve, known as a pathological murmur. Now he is pressing a transducer hard against my chest and moving it around, and there on the TV screen is a vague black-and-white picture of the diaphanous valves within my heart, opening and closing, opening and closing like clockwork. But, are they closing tight enough? Or are they thickened and sluggish and leaky? Leaky valves allow some of the blood the heart has pumped to flow back, decreasing the heart's efficiency, making it work harder, causing it to enlarge, even causing it eventually to fail. The doctor throws a switch and the system goes into Doppler mode, and suddenly the image of my valves is overlaid with intense primary colors showing the direction of blood flow, the areas of turbulence. I am getting nervous. My heartbeat quickens.

But there is no backflow of blood, no sign of turbulence. My heart valves are perfectly healthy, showing just a little of the calcification, stiffening, that inevitably comes with age. The murmur is physiological, not pathological, an echo in my strapping chest. Thank God. The doctor mentions that he has seen only one case of heart problems that can be explained solely by the ingestion of fen/phen, plus a few ambiguous cases.

I telephone my primary-care physician, the doctor who gave me the prescription in the first place. He shows what I consider to be irrational signs of resistance. I give him three choices. One, he can renew my Adipex (the utterly blameless phentermine), which, after all, has been shown in some of the medical literature to be just as effective alone as when taken with fenfluramine. Two, he can write me a prescription for Meridia—just approved by the FDA—which appears not to damage people's heart valves, although it can dangerously raise their blood pressure. Or, three, he can sit there, as passive and comatose as a reptile in the sun, and refuse to do anything—while his patient's BMI inexorably climbs toward stroke, heart attack, diabetes mellitus, and cosmetic embarrassment.

He ponders for a week, then declines to write me a new prescription. He is probably afraid of a potential lawsuit, despite the FDA's approval of both Adipex and Meridia. I offer to sign anything. He refuses. Now he is my former primary-care physician.

I do not want to gain another pound. I must get my hands on a bottle of Meridia. But how? I telephone the American Society of Bariatric Physicians at (303) 770-2526. The word "bariatric" was made up around 1970, comes from the ancient Greek word for weight, and is intended to increase the respectability of this medical specialty. I follow the recorded instructions, and soon my fax machine produces a list of diet doctors. Two have offices in swank neighborhoods, and one of these is a woman on Central Park South. She is my choice.

Her office does not look like what the newspapers refer to as a "pill mill," a vast suite of rooms crammed with doctors who see patients for five minutes and write a hundred prescriptions a day. We chat for 40 minutes, but she does not examine me. She feels I am a good candidate, though she is a little worried about my blood pressure, which is just on the high side of normal. Many of her patients have been gaining weight like crazy since fen/phen was withdrawn. She herself has followed 700 patients and found no sign of heart-valve damage. It's all politics, she says. She does not fill out a prescription blank. Her cashier sells me the capsules—and they are expensive. Maybe she *is* a pill mill.

At home, I already possess two sphygmomanometers for measuring my blood pressure: the standard kind, with a stethoscope, arm cuff, pressure gauge, and inflation bulb, all in black; and a pretty reliable electronic model that automatically inflates a wrist cuff and gives you a reading within 30 seconds. I have always loved weighing and measuring things, especially my own mind and body, and so it is fun keeping an eye on my physical reaction to Meridia, which I do several times a day.

A week later, Meridia seems to have halted my weight gain, though I am not losing any. In the medical literature, I read that Meridia does not, as claimed, help you burn stored fat as it reduces your eating. If it works at all, it is by controlling your appetite. Like every diet drug sold thus far, Meridia tinkers with just one small aspect of our weight-maintenance system. Fifteen genes and hormones regulate all the body's activities affecting weight. What some of us are waiting for is a way of controlling all of these at once, of resetting our thermostat, of making us like normal people. For a while, it looked as if the key was a hormone named leptin, produced in high concentrations by our fat-storage cells when they have logged in enough fat to keep us going in the cold months; this is precisely what all our systems controlling appetite and metabolism need to know; leptin spreads the news. But now, leptin is the subject of controversy and potential disappointment. I was kind of banking on leptin.

One day I can think of nothing but food, especially carbohydrates. Every ten minutes I find myself in the kitchen, leaning into the open refrigerator, looking for something sweet, toasting five slices of delicious handmade bread, opening a bag of potato chips. For half the day I teeter on the edge of a binge. I read over the Meridia package insert. One possible side effect of this new diet drug is "increased appetite." Wait just one minute! My blood pressure, usually 120 over 85 or 90, is now regularly 135 over 95. I telephone my new crack cardiologist, who says not to worry about these numbers yet. My BMI of 28.5 is simply too high.

I read an article criticizing BMI as a criterion for overweight. Comparing your height to your weight does not make allowances for the size of your bones, your lean muscle mass. A huge football player or boxer with nearly no fat on his or her body but lots of muscle will have a soaring BMI and absolutely nothing to worry about. Somehow, I do not feel that I belong in that category, though I do practice a bit of weight training daily. I was never one for aerobics.

The point is that body composition—how much of your body is made of fat—is more important than your weight. The only absolutely accurate way to determine your body-fat percentage is autopsy, which I have decided to postpone. Nearly as accurate are experimental and very expensive techniques that resemble undergoing an MRI of your entire body. But there is a little machine that looks like a bathroom scale and sends a weak current through the soles of your feet, said to be as accurate as the caliper method and the one where they dunk you in a swimming pool. The prospect of a whole new way of measuring myself is absolutely intoxicating, and I immediately obtain the latest model from the Tanita company. I am 28.4 percent fat. Men over 30 years old should be between 17 and 23 percent fat. Women over 30, who have more curves than men, are expected to be a little fatter, 20 to 27 percent.

Meanwhile, the medical world has been hotly debating the

true dangers of obesity. On January 1, the *New England Journal of Medicine* published a paper in which the link between BMI and mortality was compared for different age groups. The risks of being fat decrease as you get older, so that by the time you are 65, your chances of dying from the major chronic diseases such as cancer and heart disease are nearly the same no matter what you weigh. And then we learn that the statistic everybody throws around—that 300,000 die prematurely every year because they are fat—turns out to be baseless. It comes from a 1993 article in the *Journal of the American Medical Association,* where 300,000 deaths are attributed to "diet and activity patterns," not to obesity itself. We all know skinny overeaters and skinny couch potatoes. Are they less healthy than fat people who do three hours of aerobics a day? Some experts say yes.

Me, I'll obsess about my weight until I look right and feel right, which may take forever. It's interesting to debate whether obesity makes us die a few years earlier, or whether fitness is more important than fatness, but let's face it: The real reason most of us go on diets is cosmetic. And you cannot blame magazines like *Vogue* for infecting us with an exaggerated concern about looking too chubby. Men have it worse than women. Over the past 3,000 years, women with a BMI way above 21 have been celebrated in painting and sculpture. But I cannot think of one statue honoring a naked fat man—except maybe the Buddha. By my calculations, Michelangelo's *David* had a body-fat percentage of about 16 percent, and I am still about 12 percent away.

WHAT DID THE FIRST OLYMPIANS EAT?

What more perfect diet can there be? According to Diogenes Laertius (d. A.D. 222), the early Greeks fed their runners and discus throwers dried figs, fresh cheese, and wheat—in between bouts of wrestling with animals. Later, the famed Pythagoras or somebody else of the same name introduced meat, and lots of it—oxen, bulls, goats, and deer, all of which were said to free athletes (who were also warned against desserts, cold water, and too much wine) from sickness and to prolong their youth. Galen sensibly counseled against running as a way of slimming. Philostratos complained that "fancy Sicilian food" was creeping into the athletes' diet, which now included white bread made of ground meal sprinkled with poppy seeds; fish, which had once been explicitly barred; and pork, delicious pork. I am happy to follow Galen's advice against running. But which Greek training diet should we choose—cheese and figs, massive doses of animal protein, or tasty fish and pork?

With thanks to Grivetti and Applegate in the May 1997 *Journal of Nutrition* (Supplement).

HAUTE CHOCOLATE

Lost in a haze of carnal pleasure, I lounged in Jean-Paul Hévin's sleek shop on the rue Saint-Honoré in Paris, sipping from a cup of his sumptuous hot chocolate and meditating upon the Olmecs. For it was the Olmec people of southern Mexico who, while building the first major civilization in the Americas more than 3,000 years ago, discovered a method for turning cocoa beans into chocolate, a tricky process at the best of times. They were also the ones who carved those huge nine-foot, stone male heads. Across the vast gulf of time, the Olmecs are calling to us. "Chocolate equals civilization," they are saying, "and vice versa."

After the Olmecs came the Mayans and the Aztecs and their rich variety of hot and cold cocoa drinks, plus porridges, gruels, and solid chocolate snacks, all probably unsweetened but flavored with native flowers and chili peppers. Columbus almost didn't discover chocolate. Then, just in the nick of time, on his fourth and final voyage in 1502, he captured a 150-foot-long Mayan trading canoe off the island of Guanaja, near Honduras. Among its many treasures was a stash of cocoa beans, which Columbus called almonds, and which the Mayans also used as money. Columbus knew none of this because he lacked a translator that day; he brought the cocoa beans back to Spain, where he died four years later, never realizing what these almonds were.

In 1528, the first chocolate recipe reached the Old World with Hernando Cortés. With cocoa beans from the huge shipload he had brought, he mixed up some hot chocolate and served it to the

Holy Roman Emperor Charles V in Toledo, and the Spanish frenzy for chocolate broke out, even though another 50 years passed before a regular trade in cocoa beans developed. Today, some of the finest dark chocolate (from the Valrhona company) is named Guanaja, after the place where Christopher Columbus discovered chocolate without knowing it.

The first Frenchman to drink chocolate is said to have been Cardinal Richelieu's older brother, who took it for vapors of the spleen, a cause of melancholia. Soon afterward, in 1691, the first French hot-chocolate recipe was published. The Europeans preferred simple sweetened cocoa drinks made with vanilla and sugar, minus the Aztec chilis. By this time, Spanish and Portuguese Marrano Jews had become masters in working with cacao. (Marrano, from the Spanish for "pig," refers to Jews who pretended to convert to Catholicism in order to remain in Spain after the expulsion of unrepentant Jews in 1492.) Large numbers of Marranos had settled in the French city of Bayonne, which then became a world capital of chocolate-making.

Another 50 years, and chocolate ice cream was discovered. But the world was forced to wait endlessly for dipped chocolates to be created. Although the Aztecs did prepare solid chocolate treats, for the most part chocolate was consumed in liquid form—as a medicine, a recreational drug, and a gastronomic pleasure—until the nineteenth century.

When Carolus Linnaeus, the great Swedish botanist who, in the 1700s, classified all living things according to a system we still use today, came to the cacao tree, he totally lost his scientific reserve and named it *Theobroma cacao*, "food of the gods." I have long wondered whether Linnaeus was moved more by chocolate as a recreational drug or as a supremely delicious beverage.* Whenever I take chocolate ice cream for medicinal reasons, I can hear the advice of the great French lawyer and gastronomic author Jean-Anthelme Brillat-Savarin, who wrote in 1825, "People who habitually drink chocolate enjoy unvarying health,

---

*Is chocolate one drug, or many? Please turn to "Chocolate Dreams," page 177.

and are least attacked by a host of little illnesses which can destroy the true joy of living." He recommended hot chocolate with ambergris for obsessional thoughts and dullness of spirits. Though I never suffer from either of these, I frequently follow Brillat-Savarin's prescription (minus the ambergris) as a prophylactic.

Today, the French have become the greatest chocolatiers in the world, miles ahead of the Belgians and the Swiss. Nobody makes finer bonbons and bars of chocolate, milk or dark, than La Maison du Chocolat, Jean-Paul Hévin, or Michel Chaudun in Paris; Belin in Albi; or Le Roux in Brittany, also famous for his salted-butter caramels. And nearly every esteemed chocolatier and pastry shop in Paris offers its own vision of the ideal *chocolat chaud*.

It was this thought that roused me from my reveries. As I sat and sipped in Jean-Paul Hévin's shop, I was neglecting the wide world of chocolate out there on the streets of Paris. The wintry drizzle was in my favor, because really cold and unpleasant weather can justify, as I see it, what would ordinarily be considered a nauseating display of gluttony. In the immediate area were three other major hot-chocolate destinations: Fauchon, near the Madeleine; the old Ladurée tea room on the rue Royale; and Angelina in the arcade along the rue de Rivoli. Later, I would take a cab to the nearest Maison du Chocolat and walk to two pastry shops on the Left Bank, near my hotel.

Nearly every cup I drank that afternoon was just what the lawyer ordered. The ideal hot chocolate is made with the finest cocoa powder or solid chocolate or both. The resulting beverage should be neither too thin for serious satisfaction nor too thick to refresh; neither too bitter to produce the childlike enjoyment we seek, nor so sweet and simple as to insult the intellect. The harsh flavor and gritty texture of cocoa powder and the soft fattiness of solid chocolate should be blended so that neither can be distinguished. As a general rule, one's first swallow should induce a long interlude of silence. If I had to rank the six cups I drank that day, Ladurée's and Hévin's might be on top and Angelina's on the bottom—dragged down by the rough bitterness of raw cocoa powder.

I was less depressed than usual to leave Paris a few days later because the acclaimed French pastry chef Pierre Hermé, author of both Fauchon's and Ladurée's recipes, had e-mailed both to me, and I could hardly wait to try them at home. When I arrived, however, a whiff of political scandal hung in the air. It all started when a top *Vogue* editor, perhaps hoping to gain favor in Washington if the unthinkable should befall us, wrote that Mrs. George W. (Laura) Bush is "famous for her hot-chocolate recipe" (and listed its Web page). The Bush presidential juggernaut was clearly eager to position Mrs. Bush as dedicated equally to the kitchen and to literacy or whatever (weren't literacy and chocolate-chip cookies Barbara Bush's thing?), hardly imagining that anybody would actually try her formula. But somebody did—the staff at *Vogue*'s vast and rigorous off-premises test kitchen. The unanimous verdict was that Mrs. George W. Bush's "famous" recipe reliably produces the poorest cacao beverage that anybody has created in the three millennia since the Olmecs created this drink of the gods—runny, pale, and nearly flavorless, bearing only the tastes of hot water, undissolved cocoa powder, a miniature-marshmallow garnish, and in a pitiful attempt to challenge Martha Stewart's lifestyle leadership, the Christmas candy canes with which she recommends you stir it.

News of this hot-chocolate imposture spread across the land like warm cocoa butter. If a woman can't manage her kitchen, people were saying, how can she handle a literacy program, or whatever. Her husband's handlers soon shifted into damage-control mode: Mrs. Bush's Web pages are now buried deep within his site, and any trace of hot chocolate is now exceedingly difficult to find.

While George W. and Laura were warding off their own political extinction, successfully as it turns out, my assistant and I happily busied ourselves with an extensive experimental program, perhaps more extensive than if we had been testing methods for, say, steaming kale. First, in a frank *homage* to fellow lawyer and food writer Brillat-Savarin, my assistant Kathryn and I replicated the recipe he gives in *La Physiologie du Goût*.*

Then, we tried ten other hot chocolates, including Pierre Hermé's. Pierre's won. Now we had our provisional best method, which we prepared with various combinations of cocoa and chocolate. The pairing of Valrhona cocoa and Scharffen Berger dark chocolate (70 percent cocoa) won. We took a break and had a whirl with Angelina's packaged hot chocolate (available from Chocolat, in Bellevue, Washington, 888-826-4354). It is the best prepared mix I've tasted, but nowhere close to several of the recipes and ingredient combos we had already tried.

Pierre's recipe uses cocoa powder and chopped chocolate in perfect balance, so that the cocoa powder deepens and lengthens the taste of the chocolate without turning the mixture harsh and gritty. Pierre feels that the addition of cream makes hot chocolate heavy and masks the cacao flavor, so he begins with diluted milk. Yet the texture of his hot chocolate is silky beyond compare.

*Brillat-Savarin recommends dissolving chocolate, presumably semisweet, in water as it heats (1½ ounces of chocolate for each cup of water) and letting it "boil" for 15 minutes. Both Brillat-Savarin and M.F.K. Fisher prefer their chocolate made a day ahead, then reheated and refrothed just before consumption.

CHOCOLAT CHAUD

(adapted from Pierre Hermé)

2¼ cups whole milk

¼ cup bottled still water

¼ cup (generous) superfine granulated sugar

1 100-gm bar (3½ ounces) dark bittersweet chocolate,
Scharffen Berger, Valrhona, or Lindt (see note, below),
finely sliced with a serrated bread knife

¼ cup cocoa powder, loosely packed (1 oz. or 28 gm),
preferably Valrhona

In a 2-quart saucepan, stir together the milk, water, and sugar. Bring to a boil over medium heat. Add the chopped chocolate and the cocoa and bring to a boil again, whisking until the chocolate and cocoa are dissolved and the mixture has thickened. Reduce the heat to very low.

Blend for 5 minutes with an immersion mixer or whirl the hot chocolate in a standard blender for half a minute, until thick and foamy. Yield: Four 6-ounce cups of hot chocolate.

Note: I use a dark chocolate containing close to 70 percent cocoa, though Lindt bittersweet also works just fine. The Mayans and the Aztecs considered the froth the best part. Today, five minutes with an immersion mixer or a blender accomplishes what a half hour of beating did long ago.

TIERS AND LAUGHTER

"Why a cake?" I demanded. "Why not a meatloaf? Hand in hand we'll clutch a ribboned carving knife and solemnly slice a meatloaf. Or a pâté de porc, pâté de grives, or pâté de perdreau—all with woodcock jelly."

Our wedding was only two panic-packed weeks away. The place would be a disintegrating Manhattan loft in which we had lived together for seven years. The music would be two friends, a cellist and a harpsichordist, playing the slow—call it tragic—movement of a cello sonata by Vivaldi. (It was the late 1970s and, in keeping with the times, I had built the harpsichord myself.) We had found a judge and procured the marriage license, and my three-minute fainting spell at City Hall had already become, completely unjustly, a source of general amusement and ridicule. The guest list was small, fewer than 20; a month later, we would have a large party with dancing. The bride would wear pale pink and white and spend an absolute fortune on a haircut. The groom chose navy and cream. The most convenient date was April 1, but when none of our friends took the idea seriously, we switched to April 2. Against my better instincts, there was to be no dowry.

The menu was easy: plenty of Russian caviar and French smoked salmon with toast and blinis and bottles of icy vodka. Plus champagne for those who believed either that champagne goes with caviar, which is false, or that champagne goes with weddings, which is obvious. The dessert was still completely open to question.

Despite our supernal feelings for each other, neither of us was entirely clear about why we were getting married, except to make our two remaining parents happy, one parent each. In that era of grand and petty rebellions, this monumental act of filial piety totally exhausted our capacity for adherence to traditional values, of which a wedding cake was a central example. I was simply not a cake kind of person, and a standard three-tiered, basic white, gummy, and distasteful wedding cake seemed unthinkable. So we chose what was then, incredibly, a state-of-the-art dessert: hard, gigantic, out-of-season strawberries dipped into dark chocolate the night before by the groom's own trembling hand. Even back then, some major malcontents did not allow their politics to interfere with their cakes; when counter-culture personality Jerry Rubin got married in 1978, his fellow Yippie Abbie Hoffman briefly emerged from hiding—he was wanted on a cocaine charge—to deliver a wedding cake he had baked himself.

Today, at last, I understand what I had failed to grasp in those days so long ago and far away: *An ornamental cake is absolutely and totally essential to every wedding and to the years of marriage that follow.* Even the modern Japanese have adopted the custom. Their cakes are just like the white three-tiered Anglo-American model, except that they are inedible, made of white wax (with a small zone of real cake to allow for the ceremonial cutting) and can be used again and again by the company from which they are rented.

For the Japanese, white is not the color of purity or virginity as it is for us. White is the color of death and mourning. Virginity is not crucial to the Japanese idea of marriage (as it is, against incredible odds, with us), and this works quite well with other elements of the Japanese wedding, which is full of deathly imagery that symbolizes the end of the bride's ties to her family. For both Japanese and Westerners, the cake itself stands for fertility because it, or at least the edible part of it, is made from grain, a nearly universal symbol. That's why we throw rice as the joyous couple leaves the wedding celebration and heads toward the marriage bed, and one reason a special bread or cake and not a special meatloaf has been central to our wedding rituals at least since the Greeks and Romans.

The bride in ancient Greece spent several days preparing the wedding bread with her own hands, then gave it to the groom. Today's brides are less clever, but their mania for wedding cakes still grips the land, with the richest families and most public personalities vying for the largest, most elaborate, and most ornamental cake that money can buy. The great wedding bakers of America are besieged at least a year in advance for June nuptials (get married in January and you can choose from among the best), and stories abound of private jets ferrying prefabricated cake layers to the remotest parts of the world, including Nigeria and Oklahoma, along with the artists who will assemble and decorate the cake on the spot. Top baker-decorators charge between $8 and $20 per serving, plus transport. The hotel or banquet hall adds an extra $2 to $3 for cutting and serving an unfamiliar cake.

Why should such passion surround a simple and ancient fertility symbol that could take the form of a large loaf of good, honest bread, I wondered. To discover the reasons, I bought every wedding magazine at my local newsstand—11 in all; took a short course in suburban Connecticut in baking and decorating wedding cakes; visited one of the most famous practitioners in the country and interviewed several others; paid a visit to one of the grand wedding palaces in New York's Chinatown; spent several hours lurking around the nearby New York Cake and Bake Supply, which carries everything from premade sugar flowers to edible spray paint; read Simon R. Charsley's *Wedding Cakes and Cultural History* (the authoritative history of the British wedding cake) several times; and dipped into a few dozen other anthropological and historical treatises. Visiting Chinatown was the most fun, because we got to see cakes that had built-in, circulating electric fountains, and taste cakes filled with mashed taro root, and because we ate lots of dumplings afterward.

My exhaustive survey of wedding magazines reveals that only the semiannual *Martha Stewart Living Weddings* is suitably serious about both wedding cakes and all the other food—most of it lovely to look at, and recipes are included. Where Stewart's train jumps the tracks is in her mistreatment of the groom. Get this: "Through the tie he chooses, the groom reveals his vision of the world."

Bridal comes from the Old English "bride-ale," which refers to the drinking of ale at the wedding feast. At Anglo-Saxon weddings, small cakes were distributed, but these were more like flat, grainy breads or oatcakes. The Anglo-Saxons had no sugar. Their cakes and those of the ancient Romans were more like biscuits, and were broken above the bride's head in a shower of crumbs and morsels that suggested fecundity. These were the first bride cakes. In medieval England, bakers flavored them first with spices and then with "plumbs," a term for dried fruits, which explains why the plumb or plum pudding of the English Christmas need not contain any plums at all, either fresh or dried. Then came nuts, another hint at fertility, and, when it became available, sugar. Eggs were soon substituted for yeast, and by the seventeenth century, at least among those who could afford sugar and spice, the dark English fruitcake had been born. By the time the first recipe for what was now called Banbury Cake was published in 1655, it had become the obligatory wedding confection. Cavalier poet Robert Herrick coined the expression "wedding cake" in 1648, but nobody followed him until the nineteenth century.

British cakes were not covered in icing, white or otherwise, until a hundred years later, when Mrs. Elizabeth Raffald first published her famous and eternal cookbook in 1769. It is not that icing was unknown—*glace royale*, or royal icing (at its simplest, a mixture of powdered sugar and egg whites that dries to a rock-hard finish), had been imported from France at least a hundred years before. But the British simply did not care to ice their fruitcakes before Mrs. Raffald, who added ground almonds to the standard formula and spread it on. Thus, the white wedding cake was born.

The Victorians contributed their fondness for height, creating the modern three-tiered cake, often with an elaborate sugar superstructure. (The technique for piping sugar icing through a paper cone may have been invented in Bordeaux long before, but it did not reach England until the 1880s. Thus, Queen Victoria's own daughters married too early to have true white, ornate Victorian wedding cakes.) Middle-class families with enough money to buy only one tier satisfied their longing for altitude by placing the cake on a tall stand and planting a vase of flowers on top. Only when the Victorian taste for virginal whiteness yielded to Edwardian license did British wedding cakes take on color in their decoration. Inside, they remained the same dark, fruity cake created two centuries earlier.

Modern-day American wedding cakes descend directly from these British (and Australian) ancestors. They fall into three broad categories. Rarest is the incredibly elaborate, all-white Victorian cake decorated with flowers, urns, arches, vases, and trellises of *glace royale,* with an artistry and skill that would have made the queen herself proud. The leading practitioner is probably Cile Bellefleur Burbidge of Danvers, Massachusetts, and casting your eyes upon any of her cakes will take your breath away. I have never tasted one.

Equally elaborate but more up-to-date are cakes covered with a newer material known as "rolled fondant," apparently pioneered in Australia and England. Rolled fondant has the consistency of stiff Play-Doh, and is composed of sugar, gelatin, corn syrup, and glycerin—all cooked together, then kneaded like bread, and cooled. You can make it at home. I have. It can be rolled into sheets less than a quarter-inch thick, cut with any knife or scissors, then draped and pressed over any cake, producing, without great skill or talent, a porcelainlike surface.

You can spot rolled fondant a mile away: Most routine cakes made with it have rounded edges and look a little like tea cozies. But the most witty and extravagant wedding cakes today are first paved with fondant and then modeled, dyed, sprayed, and adorned with delicious buttercream ornaments, barely edible gum-paste flowers, or rock-hard *glace royale.*

The problem is that, like hardened sugar icing, fondant may be edible in theory, but it is never appetizing. The cake cannot be refrigerated once the fondant is applied, so its insides must be extremely durable. Except for very young children, nobody eats the layer of fondant—it is simply one of the rules of the art form that every bit of the cake be technically edible—and wedding guests are somehow expected to know that it is permissible to peel off the outer layer. I have always felt that picking apart the wedding cake is a sign of disrespect for an object of such momentous historical and symbolic meaning. And so, I spend the final hour of every wedding banquet that ends with a fondant-enrobed cake gripped by a sense of guilt. The good news is that in the hands of an artist like Colette Peters of New York City, the results can be staggering. In her most famous design, the layers are separate and of different sizes and colors, each made to look like a beautifully wrapped wedding present, and arranged in the form of a pile or stack.

More delicate but less elaborate are the cakes of bakers like Sylvia Weinstock. The tiers are made of rich, tender cake, and the fillings can be soft and moist because the overall creation is assembled and decorated quickly. The icing is a smooth, light, and scrumptious buttercream. The gum-paste flowers (always botanically correct) are made long in advance but applied at the last minute, their leaves piped on with green buttercream. On an even more ethereal gustatory plane, Markus Färbinger at the Culinary Institute of America fashions his flowers (on his rare floral cakes) only out of pure, pulled sugar—featherlight, translucent, and good to eat or dissolve in your coffee.

Which version you prefer depends on how important you think it is actually to eat the wedding cake. From Roman and Anglo-Saxon bridal biscuits and spiced medieval breads to the white Victorian sugar palaces, wedding guests were rarely expected to taste and swallow the bride cake, which was more often meant to be broken, or distributed as good luck charms among the guests. Early in this century, in a rite of sexual magic, the bride was expected to pass small pieces of cake through her wedding ring and distribute them among the female guests, who would tuck them in their left stocking and, once safely home, put the pieces under their pillows to inspire dreams of prospective husbands. Even today, it is not uncommon for the cake to be wheeled out upon the dance floor to the accompaniment of a brass fanfare, cut by bride and groom, then distributed in little boxes, while another dessert is served. For the Japanese, eating the cake is completely beside the point; its purpose is entirely symbolic—the fecundity of grain, the deathly whiteness, and something else as well.

This something else is key to understanding the wedding cake, and yet its meaning eluded me, until I read about an old Scottish custom. It was once the practice to pin a multitude of favors made from fancy ribbons to the bride's skirt; at some point during the wedding banquet, these were plucked off by the guests. In the more modern and less raucous version, the favors were attached to the wedding cake. And now it is clear: The wedding cake is a symbol for the bride herself, and the cutting of the cake is the loss of her virginity—however many years earlier this may actually have occurred. Throughout the last century, as the wedding cake grew taller and whiter, more tapered at the top and more delicately decorated, it truly began to look like a bride. Now we understand the wedding-cake mania, the reason why, for many brides, the cake and its decoration are nearly as momentous as her dress. From a gastronomic point of view, the modern wedding cake is a bride you can put into your mouth.

JUNE 1998

IS PARIS LEARNING?

Where were you when you first heard the news? I was in somebody's backyard in Paris, in the suburb of Asnières. We were boiling the head of a huge 400-pound pig over an outdoor gas burner, the first step in transmuting it into the most delicious *boudin noir*, blood sausage, you've ever tasted. Didn't I tell you that story a year ago?*

Our good friend François Simon, distinguished food critic at *Le Figaro*, was late. It seemed obvious to me that, after carefully avoiding our eight hours of hard labor, François would innocently swan in for the feast. How could I have been so unjust? The phone rang. It was François, who bore some astounding news. Philippe Legendre, the youngish chef at Taillevent, long one of Paris's greatest restaurants, was leaving to head the kitchen at the newly renovated George V! Michel Del Burgo, who had only recently arrived at the Bristol Hotel with two Michelin stars from Carcassonne, in the south, would now leave the Bristol to replace him! And Eric Fréchon, who had left the haute cuisine restaurant at the Crillon a few years earlier to open what was soon to become the best new bistro in Paris—first called La Verrière and then Le Restaurant d'Eric Fréchon—would give up his own restaurant to take over at the Bristol. Oh, and somewhere along the way, Michel Roth was moving from L'Espadon at the Ritz Hotel to revive the once towering but now tottering two-star Lasserre, where, in my late teens, I ate my first three-star meal without my parents. I would describe every bite, every sip, every moment if there were room.

*Yes, on page 237, "It Takes a Village to Kill a Pig."

We tore our attention away from the poaching pig long enough to gasp. This is not how developments in the grand cuisine are supposed to unfold. Taillevent's last chef, the distinguished Claude Deligne, had worked there for more than 35 years. Nobody, not even the window washer, would dare to leave Taillevent.

Yes, there had been early warning signs of turmoil in the haute cuisine. First came news that Mme. Ghislaine Arabian, the highest-ranking woman chef in France, had been forced to leave her ill-starred two-star kitchen at Ledoyen in the park of the Champs-Élysées after she angrily fired one of her young cooks on camera during the making of a television documentary.

And the tsunami of mid-1999 is not yet over. Before we had even finished eating all of our *boudin noir,* we read in the press that Alain Ducasse was denying rumors that his three-star restaurant was losing money, and that the Accor Group, which had bought the restaurant when it purchased the Hôtel Le Parc, wanted him to move out or shift his cooking downmarket. The rumors proved true, and shortly after Ducasse's lavish New York City restaurant opened, he returned to Paris on Bastille Day to make plans to open again in the fall at the Plaza Athénée hotel. Meanwhile, Ducasse's influence could be felt all around Paris at the many restaurants whose kitchens he supervises or advises, or whose chefs he has trained: Il Cortile, Le Relais du Parc, La Grande Cascade, Hédiard, Ledoyen, Opéra, Royal Monceau, and now even Le Voltaire.

Sure, I will return again and again to Taillevant, to the cutting-edge Pierre Gagnaire, the peerless Ducasse, and the very lovely Le Grand Vefour. I have long rated French haute cuisine, at its most polished, as one of the great achievements of humankind. But I nonetheless devote much of my time in Paris to finding the most wonderful and inexpensive new bistros and brasseries.

My gastronomic friends there are growing impatient with me. It is as if I am consigning France to the role of theme park, a Francoland of glorious boulevards and monuments, where men wear berets, women wear Chanel, and everybody follows recipes that are 100 years old. In a new twist on cultural imperialism, Americans expect the French to remain nineteenth-century noble savages, and want the French to want this for themselves. While the rest of the world is busy developing a global cuisine, global design, and global music, we believe that France still resists (and should resist) all forms of globalism and, holding on to its charming though antiquated political and agricultural systems, sink further into cultural irrelevance and economic insignificance.

We could not be more wrong. France has the *fourth-largest economy in the world*, though it is just twenty-first in population. And, despite those pictures of angry French farmers we see on television, France is also *the second-largest exporter of food in the world*. Aren't you astonished? It was a French economist, after all, who first campaigned for a unified Europe, and although France was a little slow to embrace the Internet, it is now modernizing at least as fast as the rest of us.

What they can't figure out is how to modernize their food. (The Italians seem to waste little energy on this subject. They have by and large been content with traditional cooking; you can probably count the stems of lemongrass in the entire country on the fingers of one hand.) All over Paris, since the end of the recession, a new kind of French restaurant has been springing up, neither bistro nor haute cuisine nor anything in between. There we were at Bon, the hottest eating place in Paris—at least it was that June—and the most recent in a series that began four years ago with Buddha Bar and now includes Le Télégraphe, Lo Sushi, Alcazar, Asian, Man Ray, and Spoon. All of them are elegant and delightful spaces. (Bon was beautifully designed by Philippe Starck, who is one of the owners; I would pay an hour's rent, without food, just to gaze at the tentlike dining room, the lovely garden, and the exquisite shop selling overpriced ingredients. I would certainly ask them to turn the lights up. It took us hours to decipher Bon's menu in the dark.) All attract a chic crowd, the same sort of youngish urban professionals wearing black turtlenecks who in most World Cities flock behind a smaller, elite group of artists, musicians, the extremely beautiful, and hip celebrities who can make or break this kind of restaurant, at least at the start. The idea is that people these days want much more than food when they go out to dinner. They want to be entertained.

The food may be okay or mediocre, but it is never wonderful and rarely generous, the way it can be at any of my favorite bistros. And it usually has a gimmick: Lo Sushi's raw-fish conveyor belt, Spoon's impossible mix-and-match menu featuring American junk food, and the organic ingredients at Bon, where the foldout menu tells you which items are *"diététique," "biologique"* (organic), *"végétarien,"* or any combination of the three. And next to each item is a health claim. Clear bouillon favors the elimination of toxins; steamed duck favors intellectual activity, endurance, and libido. Tongue in cheek? One can only hope. And how does it all taste? Second-rate sushi, tasty California rolls with real crab, soggy and leaden *"galettes aux 5 cereales"* (grainburgers), mushy quinoa, very nice shrimp, fine duck (who would have thought it?), and some acceptable desserts catered by Ladurée, full of scrumptious butter, cream, and sugar, and all noted on the menu as *"bon pour le moral."* On the other hand, have you ever had a good meal at an American health-food restaurant?

An entertaining new place to eat, with architecture that is both stunning and amusing, and what one might call Franco-Italian Lite cuisine, is **Georges**, on the roof of the Centre Georges Pompidou. The views are terrific, especially at dusk. The staff is harried but quite agreeable. The food, catered elsewhere in the Costes brothers' empire, has no pretensions to seriousness and, as a result, succeeds admirably. So, you can start with mushrooms in olive oil, carrot juice, two tartares, or guacamole, which, surprisingly, appears on the menu as *"Fouetté d'avocat (légèrement épicé)."* (Don't they know the word guacamole?) Then, you're on to salads, sandwiches, and pasta, or for the lustier eaters, such as your present guide, grilled filet mignon with Béarnaise or an acceptable sole meunière, one of the world's great dishes. The cheese comes from Marie-Anne Cantin, one of Paris's serious affineurs, and the desserts from Stéphane Secco, a newly fashionable pâtissier in the 20th arrondissement, much of whose work is, sadly, overrated. Prices are a bit high, but then again, how often do you have a really good time at a museum restaurant?

Yes, Franco-Italian Lite is certainly one of the currently popular new World Cuisines, but the dominant theme in most of these sleek new restaurants is Asian fusion. This is easy to do in a city like Paris, where there are so few good Asian restaurants for comparison. But it is also harder to do, because Asian ingredients are hard to find here and Asian cooking techniques not widely known or knowable. One raw-material problem is raw fish, a ubiquitous treat at the high end of new World Food, used in tartares, ceviches, carpaccios, barely seared fillets and slabs, sushi, and sashimi, preparations requiring the freshest and most pristine fish, a level of quality available to very few (if any) restaurants in Paris. Plus, many of the Chinese here, at least those who cook in public, are ethnic Chinese from Southeast Asia. Their restaurants, mainly in the area called Belleville in the 20th arrondissement, promiscuously mix Cambodian, Thai, and Vietnamese cooking with the various cuisines of China, and none of them survives the ordeal. Paris did not benefit from the exodus of chefs and money from Hong Kong in the eighties. As Hong Kong Chinese with command of a second language speak English, they imigrated to Australia, Canada, and the United States, where they could be understood.

A happy exception is **La Mer de Chine**, again near the place d'Italie in the 13th arrondissement. The chef and staff are from China itself, from the area around Jiu Zhou (which the French spell Téochew), famous for its hearty and flavorful version of Cantonese cooking, its many goose and fish specialties, and a native population of brigands and pirates. Everything we ate at La Mer de Chine was memorable—a dome of poached chicken and greens, glazed with a savory crystal sauce; tiny soft-shell crabs imported (frozen) from Vietnam; a wonderful omelet stuffed with shredded greens and a kind of rice paste; and a heaping plate of salt-cooked duck tongues (English ducks, we were told, not the French variety). Dessert was a scrumptious plate of tiny fried dumplings with sweetened taro inside. This is the place to which other Chinese chefs come late at night, often on their motorcycles, and La Mer de Chine has become my favorite Chinese restaurant in Paris, even counting the much more elegant Chen, the only Asian restaurant in France ever to receive a Michelin star. Dinner will cost about $30 per person before wine or beer. Someday, I will figure out where all but the most expensive Chinese restaurants in the world buy the same fluorescent lights, the same sooty ceiling tiles, the same square, battered gray air-conditioning vents.

Like Molière's Bourgeois Gentilhomme, who was happily surprised to learn he had been speaking prose all his life, the French have always excelled at a mild form of fusion. Diderot, in his famous *Encyclopédie*, recommends Japanese soy sauce over the Chinese version, and advocates long aging (volume 15, 1765). Curry powder appears in recipes written 100 years ago by Escoffier. Blinis with caviar or smoked salmon and even couscous seem today as much French dishes as they are Russian or Moroccan. Spring rolls, called by their Vietnamese name, *nem*, were unavoidable in French haute cuisine throughout the eighties. The first time I ate (or even thought of) Asian-French fusion was the famous lobster with Thai herbs at the celebrated three-star L'Oasis in La Napoule on the Riviera, in the late seventies (the restaurant at which Jean-Georges Vongerichten, who is now renowned for his blending of Thai and French cooking, apprenticed when he left his native Alsace).

The French have been content to ransack foreign cuisines for novel flavors, without much understanding of them. The Thai herbs at L'Oasis were used to flavor a traditional pink French cream sauce in which the lobster lay, shell and all. It was Alain Ducasse who, through his cookbooks and his grand restaurant in Monaco, nearly single-handedly taught the French to be serious about Italian olive oils, wines, rice, and white truffles, which the *Larousse Gastronomique* had long considered inferior to the black. Just five years ago, it was possible to order risotto at a fine Paris restaurant and receive a bowl of basmati rice floating in a tasty broth, or to see a top French chef cooking fresh pasta in boiling milk for ten minutes straight. Paris is about to get its very own restaurant Nobu. We'll see how his brand of fusion is received.

Meanwhile, Ducasse marches ahead toward his own vision of a French future. At his grand restaurants in Paris and New York City, his aim is to create a modern version of *la grande cuisine française*—rich, elaborate, delicious, technically complex, and very expensive. Ducasse believes that modern cooking technology (precise regulation of very low cooking temperatures, for example) and the ultimate in raw ingredients allow him to push French haute cuisine into new territory. At one late-winter dinner in Paris, my most recent, the January asparagus were the thickest and most delicious I had ever tasted—bright green, wider than your thumb, perfectly cooked, with the barest crunch throughout, and unusually sweet. They had been grown under cold frames north of Avignon, then carried directly to Ducasse at about $4 apiece. Next to them was a rich, warm zabayone, barely lightened for the times, with a pool in its center of pureed black truffles that had simply been rubbed through a sieve. Ducasse himself appeared at our table to stir the black into the yellow in the pattern of a marble cake, and pour it over our asparagus. Nobody could forget this dish, or several others we ate that night—and, somehow, paying $66 for an asparagus appetizer did not feel outrageous.

That meal made Spoon Food & Wine all the more puzzling. Spoon is Ducasse's gesture to the next millennium. The two main themes are freedom of choice and the blurring of international boundaries, with a stress on American popular classics. The menu requires you to mix and match—main ingredients, garnishes, and sauces—though likely as not, when you try, the waiter will warn you that the combination you have chosen will simply not work. A prominent theme is what we can call American vernacular food. Some ingredients have been very ill chosen (gummy Philadelphia Cream Cheese in the cheese course, and Ben & Jerry's ice cream laden with stabilizers [including Chunky Monkey and New York Super Fudge Chunk]). But some of the desserts are better than their American models; the New York cheesecake is light, tender, and full of tangy flavor, and Spoon's Special Doughnuts are eggy, buttery, rich, and light, all at the same time, and I managed to snag the recipe.

I left Spoon Food & Wine wondering what this all means for the future of French cuisine. Ducasse is trying to provoke, explained a longtime intimate of the chef. He is trying to remove all boundaries between cuisines, another friend guessed. Are the French bored with their own food? Are they so desperate to modernize that they will try anything? Have they lost all confidence in their history? The answer to that must be no. Ducasse's haute cuisine is full of assurance as it carries on where the nineteenth-century lawyer Lucien Tendret and Ducasse's master Alain Chapel left off.

One day I invited François Simon to join me for lunch. I was curious about the most-talked-about sandwich in Paris, *Le Sandwich Tiède à la Truffe Fraîche au Pain de Campagne Grillé et Beurre Salé* at Michel Rostang's somewhat old-fashioned two-star restaurant, at which I have taken several happy meals over the years. As you'll see in the recipe that follows, lavish quantities of butter and sliced black truffles are allowed to infuse for a night or two in the refrigerator between two slices of country bread (from a bakery named Bigot, across the street), which is then grilled on both sides so that the perfumed butter oozes into every pore and bubble. We dined luxuriously and happily (I much more than he) and discussed the current culinary situation in France.

Everything is in a state of confusion now, François said, but now, in the new millennium, everything will become crystal clear. Soon, most restaurants in France will fall into one of three categories. First are the museumlike establishments where food is taken very seriously, where chefs replicate the important dishes of the past and treat the creation of new dishes as a fine art. Then come the bistros and brasseries serving good food at low prices, predominantly hearty traditional dishes, sometimes lightened and modernized. Restaurants that fall between these two extremes will disappear. And, in their place will emerge what François calls leisure food, Disneyland food, food for fun, ethnic places, and restaurants like Spoon Food & Wine, which he seems to like. Spoon is a very serious joke, he explained.

Now I understand it all.

And I am glad that the bistro will survive in François's future. My current number-one favorite is **L'Avant-Goût**. The dish that first drew me and my Parisian friends to the 13th arrondissement, a few blocks' walk from the Place d'Italie, was the *pot-au-feu* of pork, a dish that young chef Christophe Beaufront may have invented and always posts on his blackboard menu. You get a broad bowl with tender hunks from every part of the pig (bright pink because they're demi-sel, lightly cured), from meaty jowls to curly tail; plus fennel bulbs and sweet potatoes, all in a wonderfully spiced broth, aromatic with cloves, juniper, cinnamon, saffron, garlic, and leeks. As with a conventional *pot-au-feu*, your first course is a cup of the same broth with croutons, here dotted with ground fennel seed and chopped tomatoes. This is easily enough for an entire meal and costs 95 francs ($13 at mid-2002 exchange rates).

On my fourth visit, I was finally able to bypass the pork, and everything we tried was new. Beaufront had modestly redecorated the place in sunny yellows and piglet pinks, and there could not have been a more pleasant room to dine in. Vulturously, we ordered three appetizers for the two of us, including a nicely roasted, mild young goat cheese served with a wonderful tomato sorbet and a miniature salad of presumptuous little peppery greens, later identified as *cresson d'Alenois*. Hard put to decide among the main-course candidates, we ruefully passed up the *quail en cocotte* and chose the most perfect *onglet* (hanger steak) I can remember, this specimen beefy, juicy, and tender at the same time (a small miracle), on a light sauce of pan juices and wine lees; and a delectable fillet of rascasse, served with an eggplant compote made slightly exotic and Levantine with coriander seed. The price for all this, plus dessert, was $20 per person, not counting the wine. If we had arrived in an even more wolfish state, we could have had the six-course tasting menu for $26.

Beaufront started out in the haute cuisine, trained first by Michel Guérard and then by Guy Savoy, for whom he ran the well-regarded modern bistro on Avenue Niel, before opening his own place in 1997. His background is like that of the other young chefs I have been tirelessly pounding the Parisian pavement in search of, and writing about, for six years now. They were nearly all sous-chefs at the grand establishments of Paris—most of them talented and rigorously trained—who became pessimistic about their economic prospects in the haute cuisine during the recession that gripped France during most of the nineties. They decided to strike out on their own and open bistros in the storefronts around Paris that had been emptied in those hard economic times.

The best of them are dedicated to preserving the deep flavors of regional French food, to innovation when it is called for, and to low prices, always from 160 to 190 francs ($22 to $26). It started with the pioneering **La Régalade**, opened by Yves Camdeborde when he resigned as sous-chef at the Crillon. This, and eight or ten of the 30 bistros that followed are among my favorite casual restaurants in Paris: L'Avant-Goût, of course; **L'Épi Dupin**; **L'Os à Moëlle,** and the more expensive **L'Affriolé**. (You will find addresses and phone numbers later on.)

Two relative newcomers are **La Cave de l'Os à Moëlle** and **Le Pamphlet**. The first, across the street from its older brother (*L'Os à Moëlle* is masculine and means "marrow bone"), has a little wine shop in front and two large tables in the back, one round and one long. Dining is communal, unless you reserve for six or ten, and it's like a large family dinner cooked by the French grandmother you never had. (The cook and owner is Thierry Faucher, another sous-chef from the Crillon who broke away when he saw La Régalade thrive.) For starters, there were bowls of cold asparagus soup, then charcuterie—terrines of country pâté and of blood sausage, a bowl with rillettes of guinea hen, plus pots of mustard and cornichons—and finally, a platter of cold snails. The main course was a brandade—commonly salt cod whipped with potatoes and flavored with garlic and oil, but here made with haddock—in a pool of sweet, strong langoustine sauce. Second helpings of everything are kept on a sideboard or, in winter, on the coal stove in back. Then, the sideboard is covered with desserts—an apple compote, cups of custard flavored with vanilla and orange, bowls of rhubarb and rice pudding, a pear tart with almond pastry cream, conserves of mango and of red fruit. Lunch cost us 120 francs apiece (about $16.50), plus 117 francs for the excellent Médoc, which we bought on the way in, paying a wine-shop price.

At Le Pamphlet, Alain Carrère displays his proud origins in Béarn in southwest France by updating familiar recipes and presenting them attractively but without pretense. Two of these were among the most delicious things I ate on my last trip to Paris: a veal shank braised for seven hours, until the meat could not have been more tender or deeply flavored, and an unusual rillettes of rabbit. Elsewhere, these are often dense, cold, and fatty, but here they are light, warm, and lean, though still full of flavor. Dessert was a financier baked just for the occasion. I returned to Le Pamphlet on the last day of my trip so that I would not be recommending a pig still halfway in its poke. Co-owner Fred Arniaud arranged a long menu *dégustation* that was far less distinguished than what we had eaten for our simple lunch.

Some older establishments seem to have given up. I revisited the Balzar recently, in the 5th arrondissement. As the putatively paradigmatic neighborhood brasserie, it attracts both neighborhood French and trendy Americans. (A writer for one of our most distinguished magazines dizzily named it the best restaurant in the world.) The forced bonhomie as we entered soon turned to rudeness as we grew tired of waiting for our table. Very little of the food would be worth revisiting. The huge bowl of gratinéed onion soup, for example, was two inches of burned and clotted cheese over two inches of sodden bread, with a tiny puddle of pallid pink liquid at the bottom, bereft of the deeply restorative beefy essence it should have had. Most dishes at the Balzar's near-namesake, Balthazar, in SoHo in New York City, are superior. I have read that habitués of the Balzar in Paris are relieved that, though it was bought by the Flo group nearly three years ago, nothing has changed. I am surprised that this would make anyone glad. But the young chefs are superbly qualified to keep French traditions alive, rendering the old dishes, with their great depth of flavor, as exciting as when you first tasted them, and renovating those whose charm has faded.

L'AFFRIOLÉ, 17 RUE MALAR, 75007, 01 44 18 31 33

L'AVANT-GOÛT, 26 RUE ROBILLOT, 75013, 01 53 80 24 00

LA CAVE DE L'OS À MOËLLE, 181 RUE DE LOURMEL, 75015, 01 45 57 28 28

L'ÉPI DUPIN, 11 RUE DUPIN, 75006, 01 42 22 64 56

GEORGES, TOP FLOOR OF THE CENTRE POMPIDOU, 01 55 35 36 85 OR 01 44 78 12 33

LA MER DE CHINE, 159 RUE DE CHÂTEAU DES RENTIERS, 75013, 01 45 84 22 49

L'OS À MOËLLE, 3 RUE VASCO-DE-GAMA, 75015, 01 45 57 27 27

LE PAMPHLET, 38 RUE DEBELLEYME, 75003, 01 42 72 39 24

LA RÉGALADE, 49 AV. JEAN-MOULIN, 75014, 01 45 45 68 58

LE SANDWICH TIÈDE À LA TRUFFE FRAÎCHE AU PAIN DE CAMPAGNE GRILLÉ ET BEURRE SALÉ
(from Michel Rostang)

1¼ oz. fresh very aromatic black truffle
2½ Tbs. salted butter, at room temperature
2 slices country bread
¼ tsp. salt, preferably French *fleur de sel*

Cut the truffle into slices, about 12 to the inch. Lavishly butter both sides of bread. Sprinkle with the *fleur de sel*. Pave one slice of bread with overlapping slices of truffle and cover with the other slice of bread. Wrap the sandwich in plastic wrap and refrigerate for at least 24 hours. When ready to eat, grill on both sides under the broiler or in a toaster oven, one side at a time. Rostang serves an entire sandwich to each person, with a little winter salad. You can slice it crosswise into 4 or 6 strips and serve as a little treat.

SPOON'S SPECIAL DOUGHNUTS
(from Alain Ducasse)

¾ cup whole milk

⅓ cup granulated sugar

4 extra large eggs

1 lb. all-purpose flour (3 cups measured
by the scoop-and-level method)

1 large pinch of salt

1¾ tsp. SAF-Instant yeast or 2 tsp. active dry yeast

¼ lb. (1 stick) unsalted butter cut into six chunks,
at room temperature

1 cup confectioner's sugar, loosely packed

3 Tbs. water

Oil for deep frying

The night before: In the bowl of a heavy-duty mixer designed for kneading bread, whisk together the milk, sugar, and eggs. Sift the flour into another bowl, and combine with the salt and yeast. Using a wooden spoon, gradually beat these dry ingredients into the liquid until a dough forms. Then, attach the bowl and dough hook to the mixer and knead at moderately low speed for 10 minutes, until the dough is smooth, scraping down as necessary. Cover with plastic wrap and leave at room temperature for 1½ hours.

Attach the dough hook again and knead the butter chunk by chunk. Then scrape down both the dough hook and the bowl, and resume kneading for 5 minutes. Scrape the dough into a 3- to 4-quart container, cover, and allow to double in volume (to about 7½ cups) at room temperature, about an hour and a half. Gently deflate the dough by turning it over with a rubber spatula. Cover and leave it in the refrigerator overnight.

The next day: Roll out the dough on a well-floured surface into a square of even thickness (about ⅜-inch thick) just over 12 inches on a side. With a 4-inch doughnut cutter, cut out 9 doughnuts. Place them on well-oiled sheets of parchment or waxed paper, and let them rise, covered, for about an hour until double in height, about ¾-inch thick. Meanwhile, knead the scrapes of dough into a ball, and let them rest, covered, for about 20 minutes, before rolling out again and making more doughnuts, for a total of 16 if you've done a perfect job. Mix the confectioner's sugar and water in a small bowl to make a glaze.

Pour 2 or 3 inches of oil into a wide pan and over medium heat bring to 360°F (on a frying thermometer). Fry the dough-nuts, turning frequently, until a light reddish brown, about 3 minutes. (The insides should be cooked but very moist and rich.) Remove to a rack and immediately brush with the glaze. Best when still warm.

OCTOBER 2000 AND MAY 2001

LINING UP

I am totally sick of New York's restaurant reservation rat race. In the latest tempest, somebody from the fashion department at *Vogue* brazenly published the secret, private, VIP phone number for Balthazar, the excellent SoHo brasserie that, nearly two years old to the day, is still the hottest reservation in the city. By my way of thinking, she and her colleagues are traitors to their class, for they're the ones who benefit most from VIP numbers at places like Balthazar. Oh sure, they apologized. They said they were sure the secret number had been published everywhere. The people at Balthazar found this an odd excuse, since at least one of the editors had used the number only the week before, believing it was secret.

In any event, the damage had been done. Balthazar telephoned 3,000 customers with a new secret number. I hope they didn't tell the girls at *Vogue*. But they did tell a *New York Times* staffer named Rick Marin (usually among the wittiest writers they have over there). Marin turned right around and published the new secret number!

Keith McNally, owner of Balthazar, had had enough of the feckless press. According to reliable reports, McNally told everybody who called the new number that it had been changed again, and gave out Marin's own home number. Asked to comment, McNally vehemently denied that he had done this, describing it as an act of extreme immaturity, but saying that if he did do it, he will never do it again, and if he does do it again, he apologizes in advance for any inconvenience that may result.

A week later, the Balthazar computer crashed, and a month of reservations—more than 6,000—vanished. The restaurant staff expected pandemonium, but there were very few problems, probably because all those people who can never get a table, even though they telephone under the name of Robert De Niro or call to reconfirm a reservation they haven't made, never found out about the disaster. At this writing, Bob De Niro is the most droppable name in New York City.

I have been reading lots of newspaper articles about restaurant reservations. Every year or so, reporters telephone the hottest restaurants, wait to be abused, and write about it. And every year they object to the same things: interminable busy signals, VIP phone numbers, rudeness and attitude on the part of the telephone staff, having to reserve weeks ahead, having to confirm the day before, having to give your credit-card number for reservations of six or more.

To me, only rudeness and attitude are unpardonable offenses. Busy signals may be annoying, but should a restaurant be expected to rent more than ten telephone lines, as places like Balthazar and Nobu (another of the hottest New York tickets) do? Anybody really serious about eating in a given restaurant should have no problem with advance reservations and with offering some kind of guarantee that he or she will show up. Three tables of no-shows at a small restaurant can erase an entire evening's profit. (As a friend has pointed out, you get charged for a facial if you don't show up, which was news to me, just as you may if you don't cancel a doctor's appointment in advance.) By the same token, restaurants that keep you waiting more than 15 minutes have probably overbooked way more than was necessary to compensate for cancellations and no-shows. They are either inexperienced or extremely greedy and should somehow pay for it. So should doctors.

Keeping a restaurant full without offending customers by making them wait is more an art than a science. There are many rules of thumb: Tables for two will average two hours at dinner, tables for four two and a half hours, and so forth. Diners who begin eating between 8:00 and 9:30 will spend a longer time than those who come much earlier and may have after-dinner plans, or those who arrive much later. A restaurant can stay full with a seating at 6:00 and a seating at 9:00; in New York City, few diners want to start eating at 6:00, but some will happily arrive at 10:00. One trick is to make very few reservations at 7:00 and 7:30, which can block a table for the rest of the night. But can you tell early diners that you need the table back by 8:30 or 9:00, as they do at Nobu, or go with the flow and trust that all the little decisions made by the reservation people and the maître d' will produce a smooth and prosperous evening?

It's time to simplify, I tell myself, to go back to basics. And so I make a resolution. For one entire week, I will not make one restaurant reservation. I will just show up.

My first mission is dinner at Super Sushi, a little place on one of those shabby streets just north of Houston in downtown Manhattan. (Super Sushi is not its real name.) There is always a line out front, and I have long wondered why. A friend and I are window-shopping in SoHo late on a Saturday afternoon. I telephone Super Sushi from a street corner to inquire into their rules.

"No reservations. You stand on line," says the Japanese-accented voice on the phone, volunteering that the wait is now about an hour.

"Yes, I understand. But, surely, it must be possible to leave one's name with you, walk down the street for a pitcher or two of margaritas, and return 45 minutes later in time for some of your fabled sushi."

"No, not possible," he replies. "You stand on line."

"Of course. But then it must be possible to have a little glass of something at your bar while we wait, perhaps some fantastically expensive and ancient sake."

"No bar, you stand on line."

My friend is sure that, insensitive to the nuances of Japanese custom, I have misinterpreted what the man said, and so we walk past Super Sushi. Sure enough, there is a line of 30 people.

I ask one of them, "You're just standing here, waiting? No snacks, no drinks?"

"That's right," he replies. "The food is *that* good."

My mouth begins to water, but, as I am not in the mood for an hour's wait in the early evening chill, I make plans to investigate further and, in the meanwhile, just show up somewhere else.

To my amazement, even in early spring, when New Yorkers love to stroll the streets, many of the most popular restaurants that take no reservations prove to be no problem at all. Maybe I have just been lucky. Lunch at Tabla's downstairs Bread Bar (baked in deep and fiery tandoors right before your eyes) and dim sum at Triple Eight Palace in Chinatown are a total breeze, as are dinners downtown at the relocated Korean noodle and barbecue place called Bop, and uptown at the singles and couples haunt once called Sofia and now renamed Serafina. At Bar Pitti, in Greenwich Village, you leave your name—not on a written list but in Massimo's brain—pick up a glass of wine, and wait on public benches along Sixth Avenue, in contravention of the New York City ordinance against possessing, "with intent to drink or consume, an open container containing an alcoholic beverage in any public place except at a block party, feast, or similar function for which a permit has been obtained." The bartender warns us that some customers have been ticketed, which does not improve the taste of a wine that needs all the help it can get. But a predicted half-hour wait becomes ten minutes when three girls peel off to eat at Da Silvano next door, and we are seated next to a fantastically beautiful model whose date looks like a complete dope, if you ask me.

I always run into long lines at Pearl Oyster Bar on Cornelia Street, but I eat there anyway because I love the food, and I have even learned to love the lines, at least a little. Pearl is a narrow little place decorated a bit like a shoreside diner in Maine, with a long counter at which most customers sit, plus two tiny tables in front and a shelf along the wall where some people start their appetizers while waiting for a place at the main counter. The cuisine is like the decoration, New England vernacular—steamed and fried clams, the most perfect lobster rolls imaginable,* fine

*For Pearl's lobster rolls in your very own home, please read "On a Roll," page 343, and do what it says.

French fries, salads, and an ever-changing range of baked and broiled fish. As soon as we enter, a waitress offers us a glass of wine. Nobody at the counter stays more than an hour, so we feel a continual sense of progress. The Village crowd is friendly and even fun. We are given a present of crisply fried oysters before dinner to compensate for a slightly excessive wait, and, eventually, the meal is as good as ever. This is the only line I will wait on with a jolly sense of humor.

And then there is Carmine's, a sprawling Italian-American place on the Upper West Side that benefits, I am certain, from its relative proximity to the George Washington Bridge. Although only nine years old, the place was constructed to look ancient and a little grimy, and it is only the great friendliness and charm of the bartenders, hostesses, and waiters that make the evening bearable. They hand us a pager as we enter—and an amazingly precise estimate of how long we will end up waiting. We stand near the bar, looking for two seats to come free, and then we sit at the bar and have too many double Scotches on an empty stomach, so that we slip off the bar stool too many times, but never facedown. Somebody passes us platters of fried zucchini and fried calamari. They are cold and soggy, but they do settle the stomach. We notice the bar menu and order stuffed mushrooms and spiedini. The former are edible. And then the pager buzzes, and we walk unsteadily up the stairs, ready to face a ten-pound lasagna.

Fortified and optimistic from a week of just showing up, I lay the groundwork for a visit to Super Sushi. I telephone in advance, and this is what I learn: The restaurant opens its doors for dinner at 5:00 p.m. There will be approximately 15 people on line. As the room holds about 35, everybody on line will be admitted at opening time, plus the next 20 who come along just after 5:00. Then, at 5:30 or so, a line will form again.

A friend and I arrive at a few minutes after 5:00, expecting to be feasting on ethereal sushi within minutes. But something is incredibly, grotesquely wrong. A line of hungry people, three rows deep, snakes back and forth in front of Super Sushi. We count 30 of them. Maybe the doors have not yet opened? We peer through the steamy storefront windows. Every seat has already been taken. It is a Friday afternoon, Good Friday, in fact. Do some people still have to eat fish on Good Friday for religious reasons?

I make a quick calculation. The entire restaurant will have to clear out before we, and the 30 people in front of us, can enter. Nonetheless, after a brief debate during which another couple gets ahead of us, we join the line. At 5:32, the first diners exit, and a mumbled cheer goes up. Four minutes later, another couple leaves. At this rate, we have an hour more to wait.

My friend and I temporarily run out of conversation. This must be the only boring street in all of New York City. It is lined with old, dark apartment buildings, plus a dry cleaner, a psychic, and an empty Italian restaurant. A woman walks past and tells all of us that there is fine sushi around the corner and lots of empty tables. Nobody budges.

Why are all these people wasting their time standing on line? Who wants to eat raw fish at five in the afternoon anyway? Don't they have anything better to do? The menu does not look particularly inexpensive. Why don't they work an hour overtime and stash away enough to make a reservation at one of the four or five truly excellent sushi places uptown? Maybe they don't have jobs. Maybe they're unemployable.

People like to wait because it enhances the value of their experience without increasing its cost, my friend announces, delphically.

A thin, nice-looking Japanese woman, probably the owner's wife, comes out to tidy up the line, which has spread onto the sidewalk in front of the adjoining building. They must have gotten complaints. The air is growing chilly and the gray sky threatens. Cars clatter down the crumbling street, trailing fumes. I want to walk over to the thin, nice-looking Japanese woman and violently shake her by the shoulders and demand to know why she and her husband work so hard to maximize the pain among their customers. Instead I take out my cell phone and begin calling in a Sarin gas scare, which will clear the place out. I lose my nerve and return to the more passive fantasy of poking the thin, nice-looking Japanese woman in the nose.

After an hour, we begin talking with the people around us. To

my surprise, at least half are first-timers who have come on a recommendation from a friend or a guidebook (one of which speaks
of "sushi heaven," and gives Super Sushi a food rating as high as
Lutèce). The couple ahead of us live in Colorado. I tell them that
real New Yorkers would not have to wait on line if tourists from
Colorado stayed at home, where they belong. I tell them that
people from Colorado are like cholesterol, blocking our city's
arteries. They have read about typical New Yorkers who insult
innocent tourists, but they have never experienced one, and they
seem truly appreciative. For them, it is like visiting the Statue of
Liberty. I am reminded that while New Yorkers say "standing on
line," the rest of the English-speaking world says "standing in
line."

As we crawl toward the storefront, we see a notice that Super
Sushi accepts only the American Express card, which the Colorado couple lack. Sensing their panic, we encourage them to
change their dinner plans, maybe go to the airport a day early.
But soon we relent, and direct the guy to the nearest ATM,
around the corner in an ill-smelling bodega. In Colorado, they
keep their ATMs in spotless malls.

After an hour and 40 minutes, we reach the last leg of the line,
which runs along the front window. There are many signs posted
there, mostly hand-lettered. Super Sushi allows no groups larger
than five. Super Sushi has four appetizer specials for April. There
are also several dusty plates of cheap plastic facsimile food, an
ominous sign. (In Japan, plastic food comes in many grades.)
With four people ahead of us, the line comes to a complete halt.
I press my nose against the glass and look intently for signs that
somebody is getting ready to finish, to pay, to leave, to die. A
woman pushes back her chair and stands—but then disappears
into the bathroom. Another puts on her jacket, but only, it seems,
because she is cold. Every time I see someone put down his chopsticks, I pray he has eaten his last.

We consider cutting our losses and surrendering our investment of 115 minutes. My friend disagrees, pointing out that many
of the people on line are native Japanese, and that this is a positive

omen of a good dinner. I point out that very few Japanese can afford really good sushi back home and so have no standard of comparison. And then, nearly two hours from the minute we arrived, eight people leave at once, and we are shown to our table in a cramped corner near the door to the kitchen. Nothing has been spent on decoration.

We order four appetizers, both the raw and the cooked, plus sushi for my friend and sashimi for me. The food arrives quickly. I take a tentative nibble, next a larger bite, then two bites at a time. Suddenly I stop, in a state of shock. This is the worst Japanese food I have eaten all year—giant, ragged, floppy pieces of less than pristine fish. Don't you just hate raw fish when it is slightly above room temperature and really, really mushy? When it separates and gaps along the muscle fibers? By standing on or in line for an hour or two, my fellow customers have subjectively transformed this awful food into the best sushi in New York City. Can I be totally wrong about this?

Maybe I was hasty in condemning the reservation rat race.

Every popular restaurant has its version of a VIP list and regularly holds back 10 or 20 percent of its tables for people who are important to the restaurant or "friends" of the restaurant. The only valid question is who the owner considers important. A regular who comes in twice a week is more important to most restaurants than a tourist who phones a month ahead of time and is unlikely to return, especially after the buzz has died. A high school friend or a visiting chef may be more important than a stranger from Central Park South or Beverly Hills. And a sprinkling of celebrities is important to restaurants like Balthazar that attract customers partly by their glamour. If everybody who wanted reservations at the hottest 20 restaurants in New York for the hottest hours of the week could get them simply by calling early enough, the restaurants would no longer be hot. "People's sense of who they are is affected by who is sitting next to them," André Balazs, an owner of the Mercer Hotel in SoHo, told the *New York Times*, "and that is the full explanation of why a restaurant is perceived as hot or not hot."

I care much more about food than about fashion, and have made reservations in France three months in advance for places like Joël Robuchon and Alain Chapel. I always use a pseudonym when reviewing restaurants in New York. Even when eating for pleasure, I do not use VIP numbers, except at five favorite restaurants where even my unmemorable face would be recognized anyway. I will never, of course, be able to review any of these five.

I spent a morning with the reservationists at Balthazar and Nobu, listening to endlessly ringing telephones and generally diplomatic responses. Balthazar's computer maintains a VIP list and a super VIP list, named the Green Phone, a reference to the telephone at one of Keith McNally's earlier restaurants reachable only through a super VIP number. But McNally assures me that he holds back from his reservation system a hundred seats a day for walk-ins, for people who just show up with a friendly attitude and are willing to wait for an hour or so at the bar. I am extremely eager to test this idea. But when the people at Balthazar finally get around to telephoning me with their new secret number, I will certainly take the call.

JUNE 1999

There is a God in Heaven

But as luck would have it, there is a God in Heaven. Medical researchers now know that not all saturated fats are the same, and that cocoa butter does not raise our cholesterol.

Chocolate Dreams

Scraping By

Caviar Emptor

Cream of the Crop

CHOCOLATE DREAMS

I t was the merriest Christmas present one could ever hope to receive. The gift had arrived early, in the middle of December, two years ago. It was an article in the prestigious *British Medical Journal* showing that men who eat candy live longer than men who don't.

As a man who eats candy, I reacted with both comfort and joy. The researchers were two epidemiologists from the Harvard School of Public Health, who had followed the fortunes of 7,841 older men for five years. The outcome was amazing. During that time, the candy eaters were 30 percent less likely to die than the candy haters. This works out to nearly one additional year of life, just for eating candy.

As long as I can remember, male candy eaters have been ill-used, misunderstood, and denigrated, in films and on television, as weak, self-indulgent, soft, effeminate, undisciplined, and venal. Most of us have been driven underground. We eat our candy alone and on the sly. We never experience the intimacy of sharing candy with others—unless we have chosen our mates wisely. We empty boxes of Good & Plenty into our jacket pockets and sneak them one by one into our mouths during meetings and on buses. (I am forever discovering those little pink-and-white treasures in every article of clothing I own. The trick is to avoid candies that have been to the dry cleaner.) We eagerly await the extended isolation of transatlantic flights and buy a party pack of Milky Way miniatures before boarding. One of President Ronald Reagan's great achievements was putting a jar of jelly beans on his desk. It was like seeing the Marlboro Man holding a lollipop. But people's memories are short.

And then, in that week before Christmas two years ago, the *British Medical Journal* announced that it is we who have been stronger and smarter and better all along, and much more highly evolved. I was maliciously delighted to read that anti-candy men are older and more likely to smoke and drink. I picture them staggering arthritically into dark, smoky saloons, coughing helplessly into their nicotine-stained, candy-free hands.

The Harvard researchers had no firm explanation for candy's life-giving qualities. They did point to a growing pile of research suggesting that eating chocolate is good for us, and they guessed that the men who ate candy must have included chocolate in their candy dishes.

Over the years we have heard many claims about chocolate—that it gives us migraines and acne; that it contains the same chemical that floods our brains when we fall in love; that it is full of saturated fat, which will clog our arteries; that women regularly treat their PMS with chocolate; that eating chocolate kills dogs and horses; that chocolate is the Prozac of candy. More recently, the positive claims have escalated. Now chocolate is supposed to be good for our hearts; it is even said to decrease the risk of cancer.

I hate it when this happens. *60 Minutes* incorrectly explains that the French have fewer heart attacks because they drink red wine, and sales of red wine in the United States double the next day. Some researcher who enjoys appearing on television tells us that broccoli prevents cancer, and suddenly everybody treats broccoli as a magic bullet. Wait a month, and oatmeal replaces broccoli. Wait long enough, and every menu item in God's creation will have its moment in the sun. And then we can go back to eating a little of everything, the only sensible plan in the first place.

I have been an avid lover of good chocolate since early infancy. It has long been my favorite vegetable product. On all business and recreational trips that take me away from home for longer than two or three hours, I carry a supply of Valrhona Noir Gastronomie, my favorite all-purpose dark chocolate, right there in my computer bag. I even carry Valrhona on trips to France for fear that the shops will be closed when I arrive, perhaps as a result of one of their countless holidays. I do not need some Harvard epidemiologist to give me permission to eat chocolate. Chocolate is its own reward. But still . . .

After a meticulous search, I have discovered that there is hardly a newspaper or magazine in America (from *The Nation* to *Forbes,* from the *New York Times* to the *Sacramento Bee*) that has not run a story in the past year or two about the supposedly scientific claims that eating chocolate can improve one's health. The idea itself so amuses journalists and their editors that most of the articles are brief, remind us of the famous health-food joke in Woody Allen's *Sleeper,* and leave it at that.

And so I decided it was time to look deeply into chocolate, to separate fact from fiction, the sheep from the goats. I read widely and telephoned around. The easiest part was dealing with acne, migraines, and allergies—all of which have, over the years, been blamed on chocolate. After much intense investigation, we now know the real answers. Eating chocolate is not connected with acne. It does not cause migraines or headaches. And allergies to chocolate are very rare. That's it. Until a rigorous study to the contrary appears, nobody is allowed to use acne, migraines, or allergies as an excuse for being hostile to chocolate. Nobody is allowed to mention them in the same breath.

Next, I drew up a list:

WHAT IS CHOCOLATE MADE OF?

sugar
caffeine
minerals
saturated fat
theobromine
flavanols (like the ones in red wine)
phenylethylamine (the amphetaminelike love compound)
anandamide (which mimics the active ingredient in marijuana)

And then I went to work.

Does chocolate contain vitally important minerals that are hard to get from other foods? Sure, copper and magnesium. But you can also take a pill every morning.

What about caffeine? A standard bar of milk chocolate contains the same amount of caffeine as a cup of *decaffeinated* coffee. You would have to be fantastically sensitive to caffeine to fear a feeble little chocolate bar.

Isn't chocolate chock-full of saturated fat, the kind that clogs our arteries, restricts the flow of blood to our hearts, and makes us die? Yes and no, mainly no. This is such a crucial issue that I feel it deserves at least 1,000 words below. Just kidding.

But it *is* important. Dark chocolate is approximately one-third fat. The native fat in chocolate is cocoa butter—unless you buy a really cheap and repulsive brand that substitutes inexpensive and dangerous hydrogenated vegetable oil or even lard or beef tallow for the more valuable cocoa butter (which is then sold at a premium to cosmetics makers). And cocoa butter is, by its chemical structure, a saturated fat. So, it's been assumed that chocolate is bad for our hearts.

But, as luck would have it, there is a God in Heaven. Medical researchers now know that not all saturated fats are the same, and that cocoa butter does *not* raise our cholesterol. One study found that "exaggerated consumption" of cocoa butter actually lowers it. I will investigate further. And now I read that— are you sitting down?—much of the cocoa butter we eat just passes through our bodies unabsorbed—40 percent, by some measurements. This means that chocolate contains its own totally natural form of Olestra! It might also mean that a bar of chocolate with a 400-calorie rating on the nutrition label effectively contains only 300.

Now we move on to the spiritual aspects of chocolate. Put another way, does chocolate truly lift one's mood in the manner of an illegal, psychoactive drug? Let's glance back at our list of ingredients. Four of them have the potential to meddle with our minds. As we have already dispensed with caffeine, it is time for the second drug: theobromine. How did it get its name, and what does it do to us? Remember that when the great Swedish botanist and taxonomist Carolus Linnaeus named the cacao tree, he aptly called it *theobroma*, "food of the gods." So, many years later, when chemists first isolated one of the psychoactive chemical compounds in chocolate, they named it theobromine. It's defined as a bitter, volatile alkaloid resembling caffeine in its chemical structure. But, compared with caffeine, it has only a mild stimulant effect in human beings. Horses and some dogs react quite dramatically to theobromine, which is why you're warned never to feed chocolate to your dogs. Some people will tell you that their pet once ate an entire pound of M&M's without having a seizure or a heart attack. This appears to depend on the dog's species. As Sky King, my peerless golden retriever, often requests chocolate for dessert, I must soon get to the bottom of theobromine. Meanwhile, we humans can be confident that if chocolate has the potential to alter our mood, it's not because of theobromine.

Drug number three is phenylethylamine, pronounced fennel-ETHEL-uh-mean. Just learning how to say the word will make you feel much better. This is an amphetaminelike psychoactive drug whose effect is said to resemble, as is the case with Ecstasy, the feeling of being in love. Yes, there is a tiny amount of phenylethylamine in chocolate. But a salami sandwich has more, and I know of nobody besides me who reports feelings of love after eating a pound of salami.

Another interesting point: In the many psychological studies I've read, chocolate cravings are also far more common than salami cravings. So, it can't be the phenylethylamine that draws us to chocolate. Otherwise, salami would be a more popular gift on St. Valentine's Day.

The fourth and final drug in chocolate is anandamide or something close to it. Anandamide is a naturally occurring chemical in our brains that mimics the effects of eating or smoking marijuana or hashish. Plus, it appears to stretch out the mood-enhancing power of any marijuana that may already have entered our system through eating or smoking, inadvertent I'm sure. A very close relative of anandamide (*ananda* is Sanskrit for "bliss") can be found in chocolate. Is it possible that such kitchen classics as the hashish brownies in *The Alice B. Toklas Cookbook* rely on just this synergy? Can eating chocolate frugally extend and enhance the pleasurable effects of smoking marijuana, the price of which, I have read, has soared to astronomical heights? Do our chocolate cravings result from an addiction to anandamide? Doesn't anandamide also lower our blood pressure and pulse rate? Does all this mean that chocolate is a total wonder drug?

The tragic truth is that, even if these speculations were true, you would have to eat 20 to 30 pounds of chocolate at one sitting to experience the ananda of anandamide. Even I am not tempted. That's twice as much chocolate as the average American eats in a year.

If none of the mood-elevating drugs that bring glamour to chocolate has any effect on its eaters, why do so many people love chocolate in a nearly addictive way? We are not the first to ask such a question. Being a total stranger to chocolate addiction myself, I turned again to the psychology literature. I'll try to whiz through it here:

When men crave foods, they tend to crave savory foods. Women crave sweets. (Maybe this is why men who eat candy are so disrespected.) Chocolate is the most craved food among American women; half the women in North America crave chocolate. Women have more food cravings in the days before and just into menstruation, but the degree of their preference for chocolate over other sweets does not change.

A study of Spanish men and women showed that although Spanish women crave sweets more than Spanish men do, only a quarter of the women in the survey craved chocolate, about the same as for the men. The implication is that the preferential craving for chocolate among American women is cultural, not chemical. This has been confirmed in clinical tests in which American women reacted similarly after swallowing capsules of white or dark chocolate. White chocolate contains none of the mood-altering compounds we've been discussing.

Sweets and other carbohydrates increase the passage of tryptophan, an amino acid, from the bloodstream into the brain, at least in the rat's brain. The tryptophan stimulates the production of serotonin. The presence of serotonin in the synapses between nerve endings is thought to alleviate depression. So, women who eat lots of sweets during episodes of late-luteal-phase dysphoric disorder, your psychiatrist's name for PMS, may be medicating themselves for depression—while preferring chocolate sweets for cultural reasons. The problem with this theory is that the increase in serotonin would in the best of circumstances be small, and that in any event, carbohydrates eaten along with fats or proteins have even less effect on the availability of tryptophan. Chocolate contains about equal amounts of fat and sugar.

There is a growing consensus, I think, that most women eat sweets, and especially chocolate, when they feel blue because this makes them happy. It makes them happy because sweets taste so good, and for most women, chocolate tastes even better. Eating anything delicious stimulates the production in the brain of endorphins, a natural analogue to morphine. Put another way, people crave chocolate because it brings them intense doses of sensual and aesthetic pleasure. This cheers them up.

At last we have the answer. The secret chemical ingredient in chocolate is . . . chocolate! That's all it is.

Now we must leave the realm of mind-altering chemicals and venture into the murky world of flavonols. This is one of the families of chemical compounds thought to explain why people whose diets are richest in fruits and vegetables die least often from heart disease. Flavonols are most plentiful in tea, red wine, apples, blueberries, cranberries, and chocolate. (Among apples that have been tested, Red Delicious and Granny Smith have the most; Macintosh and Yellow Delicious have the least.) Flavonols can, at least in the test tube, prevent oxidative damage to our cells and our DNA. Before LDLs (the bad cholesterol) can turn into plaques that narrow and harden our arteries, the cholesterol must be damaged through oxidation, which antioxidants prevent.

There are many types of edible antioxidants, including the vitamin E pills I swallow every morning. Not only is chocolate much more pleasant going down, but the flavonols in it also reduce the clumping of platelets and the tendency of our blood to clot, and they help relax our artery walls. The Dutch are so convinced of the health benefits of eating foods rich in flavonols that they surveyed their country's eating habits to locate the sources of flavonols in people's diets—with an eye to making nutrition recommendations. Fifty-five percent of the flavonols in the Dutch diet come from tea and 20 percent from chocolate. Norman K. Hollenberg, M.D., Ph.D., professor at Harvard Medical School, has written, "The evidence for the health benefits of cocoa and chocolate at least matches, and probably exceeds, the evidence favoring green tea and red wine."

This sounds like a benediction for chocolate lovers. Unfortunately, the consensus among researchers is that if drinking red wine does prevent heart attacks, it is the alcohol, and not the flavonols, that does the trick. *There are simply not enough flavanols in either wine or chocolate to make much of a difference. That's really all we need to know.* Still, there has been no study like the Harvard candy project that has demonstrated one way or the other whether men who eat chocolate live longer. I've got my fingers crossed.

A good part of the recent pro-chocolate research has been sponsored by Mars, Inc. (maker of Snickers, Milky Ways, M&M's, and Dove chocolate bars), which has an interest in everybody's eating more chocolate, especially *Mars* chocolate. But it *has* been carried out by very reputable scientists at Pennsylvania State, the University of California at Davis and at Irvine, and elsewhere. Although I have long been an admirer of Mars, Inc. (founded by Fred and Ethel Mars in 1911 and still privately owned by members of the family) for its achievements in candy-bar excellence, especially in the area of Milky Ways, and now for the medical research it has sponsored, I was recently troubled to learn about its Cocoapro marketing program. In what looks like a move to appropriate the business benefits of chocolate's new healthy image, Mars announced that it has discovered top-secret ways to guarantee that none of those priceless flavonols are lost as their cocoa beans are processed into chocolate. This sounds like a typical marketing fantasy, but Harold Schmitz, Ph.D., director of science at Mars, convinced me I was wrong. Mars has, indeed, discovered that proper handling of cocoa beans during cultivation and at each stage of processing—fermentation, roasting, and alkali treatment—can drastically raise or lower the flavonol content of the resulting chocolate.

If chocolate has been optimally processed from bean to candy bar, it gets the Cocoapro seal of approval. Only Mars products are eligible. The company won't reveal how *my* favorite chocolates, or any other brand, perform in the tests because, Schmitz says, when a chocolate maker is oblivious to preserving flavonols, the level varies dramatically from one batch to another. But if the people at Mars are convinced that their methods are indeed vital to the continuing existence of sentient life on Earth, don't they feel horribly guilty about withholding the secrets from other chocolate companies?

Looking to cash in on all the good news about chocolate is Hawaiian Vintage Chocolate, which burst on the scene about ten years ago with the only cocoa beans grown in the United States. For a while, everybody was using their chocolate, but gradually, people came to realize that, patriotism aside, it simply did not taste as good as many other brands. Maybe that's why they introduced for Valentine's Day last year what they call "functional" chocolates. Their Love Truffles are claimed to have a Viagralike effect. And so forth. Whether the Hawaiian chocolate people add aphrodisiacal substances to their candies or possess proprietary chocolate-processing secrets is impossible to tell from their incoherent promotional literature.

Not even the desire to boost sales can explain Hershey's current folly. It has added The Spa at the Hotel Hershey, where the multitude of treatments include the Whipped Cocoa Bath, Cocoa Butter Scrub, and Chocolate Fondue Wrap. The fondue is an exclusive formula of warmed moor mud and essence of cocoa. And here is how the Whipped Cocoa Bath is redundantly presented in the brochure: "Settle into our foaming chocolate milk bath for a soothing and softening signature Hershey experience. Milk will soften and renew the skin while you indulge in this chocolate experience." Hershey's chocolate has finished either dead last or in the bottom quartile in every chocolate tasting I've attended in the past five years. If they worked a little harder on the taste, they might not need to mix their product with warmed moor mud.

Back at Mars, Inc., I had one last troublesome issue to get off my chest. I wondered why my beloved Milky Way bars lack Mars's own Cocoapro seal. Schmitz explained that the chocolate used in Milky Ways is not processed in an optimal fashion. If it were, he guessed, its "flavor profile" might change. Thereupon, Milky Way fans would grow disappointed and bitter and desert the brand.

I think Mars is right. Some things in life cannot be improved upon, and not everything we eat need make us live forever.

FEBRUARY 2001

SCRAPING BY

O nly the French have a word for those crispy and delectable
bits of food that stick to the inside of a baking dish, the
ones you scrape off and eat as crunchy tidbits. The word
is *"gratin,"* and comes from *"gratter,"* to scrape. Gratin later came
to mean the crispy, golden crust of an oven-browned casserole,
and now, by extension, it refers to the entire dish itself, from
upper crust to creamy insides, as in a zucchini gratin or a cardoon
gratin (one of the greats) or a potato gratin (the greatest), which
happens to be the point of today's lesson. It is conceivable that
the Norwegians or the Koreans have a single word for the
crunchy scraps that stick to baking dishes, though I seriously
doubt it, and in English it takes about a half dozen.

I have read in an authoritative source that Grenoble, a city in
southeast France in the area known as the Dauphiné, was named
"Gratin City" by the ancient Romans. This makes no sense to me,
though the Dauphiné is certainly gratin-crazy, and the greatest
potato gratins are those called *gratin dauphinois,* bubbling with
cream and butter, with hints of garlic and nutmeg, crisp and
browned on top and wonderfully rich inside. But the Romans
knew nothing of this dish, for the potato is a starchy tuber native
to South America and the potato gratin was not possible until the
Incas discovered the cow in about 1530, when the Spanish arrived
in Peru, dragging their cows behind them, those working founts
of butter, cream, and milk. Before 1530, the Incas had no cows and
the Europeans had no potatoes. The Incas' largest edible mammal was the guinea pig, not famous for its milk. In a profound
sense, then, you could give both Christopher Columbus and the
Incas a joint award for discovering the potato gratin.

To say that I am completely obsessed by potato gratins would be unfair and unjust, unless the fact that I have baked at least one of them every week for the past ten years is your idea of an obsession. There must be 200 potato gratin recipes on my bookshelves, some for *gratin dauphinois* (in which cheese and eggs are sometimes added to the cream and butter), some for *gratin savoyard* (in which broth or drippings from a roast substitute for the milk and cream), and some for unusual versions containing layers of onions or starchy root vegetables.

My lifetime favorite, perfected only recently, is so fantastically good that I have made it every day for the past few weeks. The potatoes are only one layer thick, so they become wonderfully crisp on top and bottom, and where the slices overlap hides a treasure trove of richly thickened cream possessing a wonderfully cheesy, peppery flavor. This is the miracle of the best *gratins dauphinois*—properly constructed, they acquire a rich and cheesy taste even when they contain no cheese at all! That's why I consider sprinkling Parmesan or Gruyère on or in a *gratin dauphinois* to be a gross and pitiful imposture, an admission of failure.

Where does the mystery cheese taste come from? Totally stumped, I e-mailed Harold McGee (author of *On Food and Cooking* [Macmillan]), on vacation in France, and telephoned Shirley Corriher (author of *CookWise* [Morrow]) at home in Atlanta, and received somewhat similar answers. This is how Harold put it: "The potatoes absorb water from the liquid, which also evaporates, so you get a concentration of the fat and protein and solubles, much as you would in fresh [cheese] curds. Then the heat will encourage rapid reactions, some products of which will resemble the products of slow ripening [in cheese]. They have found pyrazines (typical of Maillard browning reactions) in Gruyères, for example. A first approximation to an answer anyway." Now we know.

Here is how my perfect recipe came about. Last winter a friend in Paris, Mme. Frédérick Grasser, gave me a wonderful cookbook called *La Table au Pays de Brillat-Savarin (Food in the Land of Brillat-Savarin)* by Lucien Tendret, first published in 1892 (and now available in a paperback facsimile from Editions Horvath in Lyon). The great gastronomic writer Brillat-Savarin and Lucien Tendret were distant relatives and natives of Belley, though 75 years apart—in the culinary heartland of Burgundy, and were both lawyers, further proof, if any were needed, that lawyers make the finest cooks. ("Avocat à Belley" is how Tendret signs the title page.) Tendret's book is full of rich and luxurious ingredients—game, sweetbreads, foie gras, and truffles—and his recipes have been borrowed, with and without credit, by some of France's most celebrated chefs, among them the late Alain Chapel and through him, Alain Ducasse. Gertrude Stein or Alice B. Toklas claimed to have a manuscript copy of Tendret's unpublished recipes, and Toklas gives one of them, a composed salad, in her famous book. But there are humble dishes as well, simple soups, legs of lamb, gratins. I pored over this lawyer's cookbook with mounting admiration and excitement, and when I discovered Tendret's potato gratin, I knew that someday soon, I would be in heaven.

A year later, after the publication of my own book, *The Man Who Ate Everything,* a newspaper interviewer who accompanied me for a day asked me to cook something. As luck would have it, my pantry was bursting with the ingredients for making multiple loads of potato gratin, and I executed Tendret's version for the first time and entirely from memory, an exceedingly risky venture. Failure could have spelled public humiliation, the end of my culinary career, and a return to the practice of law. As with most old cookbooks, Tendret's recipes leave out the mundane details of temperature, times, and amounts, but my profound experience with potato gratins and my masculine intuition supplied the missing information. Still, I was filled with trepidation as I pulled the baking dish from the oven. The result was a resounding triumph, the most delicious gratin either my interviewer or I had ever hoped to taste. Her newspaper story ran for seven columns, including a lovely photograph. Yes, I was in heaven. I immediately recorded every ingredient, measurement, and sleight of hand.

The idea of a gratin is very simple. You slice or cut the featured ingredient, usually a vegetable or two, into small pieces that will cook easily and evenly. You may sometimes precook them on the stovetop to shorten their time in the oven. Then you butter a low, broad dish, add the main ingredient and any condiments and flavorings, such as pieces of cooked bacon or thin slices of cheese, pour in broth or milk or cream or white sauce, sprinkle the top with something that will crisp up in the oven such as bread crumbs or grated Parmesan or Gruyère, dot the top with butter, and bake for an hour or more. Part of the liquid will evaporate, part will be absorbed into the solid ingredients, and part—the more solid parts, the fats and proteins in the milk and broth—will coat the featured vegetable with an intensely flavorful concentrate. The cooking is finished when most of the liquid is gone and the rest has thickened, the vegetables are nicely cooked, any cream has just begun to break up into clear butterfat, and the surface, the gratin, is beautifully browned and crusty and delicious. If your gratin is truly brilliant, the bottom will become golden and crisp as well.

The trick is to have all four happen together. This depends on the oven temperature, the size of the vegetable pieces and how thickly they are layered, the size of the dish and its height and the material it is made of, and where you place the dish in the oven. For a potato gratin, you also have to worry about which variety of potato you choose—potatoes full of starch, baking potatoes for example, will thicken the milk and cream more quickly; the waxy varieties will require more time in the oven—and whether you rinse the potato slices and wash away the surface starch. A recipe that forgets to specify all of these things (most of them do) is a prescription for random, eccentric results, and probable disaster and dishonor, which is why the recipe given here is so detailed and exacting.

Not everybody would agree. "Gratins know neither exact science nor exact timing," Madeleine Kamman wrote in *Savoie* (Atheneum, 1989). "They bake as they please, in the time they feel like, and can be contrary if one is in a hurry. This is because no two ingredients entering a gratin are ever identical: Every cream and stock texture and heaviness will be different, and each vegetable will have its own speed of softening and of absorbing the cream. No recipe followed to the ¼ teaspoon will ever give you a civilized gratin."

You be the judge. The oddest thing happened two days ago. I opened one of my many copies of Lucien Tendret, turned to his potato gratin, and started translating his recipe. Something was horribly, embarrassingly wrong. Yes, as I had remembered it, he calls for starchy potatoes; he arranges the slices in one layer in the baking dish rather than piling them high; and, yes, he bakes the gratin for a while until all the liquid has been absorbed, then adds more liquid, and bakes it some more. But Tendret slices his potatoes very thick, adds cheese at every stage, and uses meat broth and drippings instead of milk and cream! His is not my potato gratin at all. It is a *gratin savoyard,* which is what Tendret calls it.

I reread *La Table Au Pays de Brillat-Savarin* from cover to cover, searching for even a hint of a recipe similar to mine. Nothing! Perhaps I had taken it from another cookbook? I flipped through a dozen of them published over the winter. Would I now be accused of stealing the recipe and claiming it for myself and for Lucien Tendret, Avocat à Belley? Would a special prosecutor be appointed?

Or is it possible that I have created the absolutely perfect potato gratin all by myself?

GRATIN DAUPHINOIS

4 Tbs. butter (½ stick)

1 cup (scant) milk

1 large garlic clove, peeled and lightly crushed

½ tsp. freshly ground white pepper

¾ tsp. salt

⅛ tsp. freshly grated nutmeg, about a dozen gratings

1½ lbs. *baking* potatoes

1½ cups heavy cream

Special equipment: A large, low baking dish made of enameled iron,
glass, or earthenware. The quantities in this recipe work out
perfectly when baked in a dish measuring about 120 square inches
on the inside bottom, where the slices of potato will lie. This translates into a rectangle 9-by-13 inches, or 10-by-12 inches; an 11-inch
square; a 12-inch circle; or an oval 10 by 15 inches. An enameled iron
baking dish is preferred—mine is made by Le Creuset—because it
produces a delectable crust underneath the potatoes.

A hand-slicing device, such as a traditional French stainless-steel
mandoline or a much less expensive but excellent plastic
Japanese-made device manufactured by Benriner.

Let the butter soften at room temperature for an hour or so.
Meanwhile, preheat your oven to 425°F.

Place the milk, garlic clove, white pepper, salt, and nutmeg
in a small saucepan, stir, bring to a boil, and remove from the
heat.

Meanwhile, liberally butter the bottom of the baking dish
using about half the butter. Peel the potatoes, rinse them, and
pat them dry. Then, slice them ⅛-inch thick, discarding the
smallest slices. (This is easier with a slicing machine, inexpensive or elaborate. The quantities and cooking times given here
work out best when the slices are even and close to ⅛ inch. Just
keep adjusting your slicing machine until a little pile of eight
slices measures an inch high.) Under no circumstances should

- - - - -

you wash the potatoes after they have been sliced—the surface starch is absolutely indispensable.

Evenly arrange the potatoes in the buttered dish in *one layer* of overlapping slices. (Begin by laying out a row of slices along one narrow end of the baking dish, overlapping each one about a third of the way over the slice that came before. Repeat with a second row, overlapping the entire row about a third of the way over the first row. Continue until the baking dish is neatly paved.) You will undoubtedly have some slices left over. Please do not try to cram them in.

Bring the milk to the boil again and pour it over the potatoes, removing the garlic. Cover the pan with a sheet of aluminum foil. Bake in the middle of the oven for about 15 minutes, until most of the milk has been absorbed. Meanwhile, bring the cream to a boil, and remove from the heat. When the potatoes are ready, remove and discard the aluminum foil. Bring the cream back to the boil and pour it over the potatoes, dotting the surface with the remaining butter.

Bake, uncovered, for another 20 to 25 minutes, until the potatoes have turned a golden brown, spotted with darker, crisp areas. (Rotate the baking dish halfway through if the gratin is browning unevenly.) The underside of the gratin will also be brown and crispy in spots. But do *not* wait until most of the cream has broken down into clear, foamy butterfat. The potatoes should be dotted with thickened, clotted cream, especially between the slices.

Let the gratin settle for 10 minutes. (This will allow the excess butterfat to drain to the bottom of the dish.) Then eat immediately—taste and texture suffer with each passing minute. Cut into 6 or 8 rectangles with a blunt knife and serve each one with a thin, wide metal slotted spatula.

Author's note: My Korean-American researcher, Mira Seo, informs me that there *is* a Korean word (or words) for the crusty scraps that stick to baking dishes: *noo roon bop.* This, however, covers only the crispy layer of browned rice that sticks to the bottom of the pot, which is not the same thing as gratin. Thus, though we should have learned in the early fifties not to get Koreans angry, I'll stand by my story: Only the French have a word for it.

Mira, who has hopes for a doctorate in classics from Princeton, also informs me that the ancient name for Grenoble is indeed Gratianopolis. This does not, however, mean "Gratin City." In A.D. 379, the city was named for the Emperor Gratian.

If you cook this potato gratin every day of the week, you may in time begin to welcome minute variations. Here's one of which I'm proud: Follow the first four paragraphs of the recipe above but mix in the cream with the milk and flavorings, and after the potatoes have been arranged in the baking dish, bring everything to the boil again, pour over the potatoes, dot with butter, and bake at 325°F in the lower third of your oven for about an hour and a half. No aluminum foil, no double baking. Near perfection!

CAVIAR EMPTOR

*There are caviar lovers who swear they can tell the identity of
the master [caviar-maker] by rolling a bit of caviar around
their tongue.*

SUSAN FRIEDLAND, *CAVIAR* (SCRIBNER'S, 1986)

I am as ardent a caviar lover as the next guy. I am surely as serious about caviar as Galileo, who used to send caviar to his daughter, a cloistered nun; just as zealous as the unlucky Pope Leo X (the Reformation started on his watch), who savored his caviar on slices of grilled bread with trout from Lake Garda; and surely as enthusiastic as Batu Khan, grandson of Genghis, who was enticed by caviar and candied apples at the Monastery of the Resurrection on the banks of the Volga River in the midst of his conquest of the entire Caspian basin, then and now the source of the world's best caviar. But could Galileo taste the identity of the master who made his caviar? Could Leo? Can I?

A frigid glass of vodka sat on the table before me next to six flat cans of caviar worth $500 in all, and a set of mother-of-pearl spoons. I scooped up a little pile of salted sturgeon eggs, brought them to my lips, and rolled them from right to left on my tongue, then rolled another little pile from front to back, and a third little pile around in a circle. I made a fist and plopped a hummock of caviar on the tender flesh between my thumb and forefinger, and tasted it from my hand as, I have read, real professionals do. I pressed each spoonful up against the roof of my mouth and made the little eggs pop, and they sprayed their pungent oil throughout my mouth.

Even if my life depended on it, I could not have identified the mastermind behind those little black obsidian beads of beluga, those ivory orbs of osetra, those subatomic spheroids of sevruga. I have never met a caviar master, the men who grade the eggs by color, size, touch, and smell, and decide how much special salt to add, and delicately mix in the salt with their hands. Their work has been compared with that of master winemakers. I can't even imagine what it would feel like to know which caviar master had made my caviar.

Besides, my caviar problems are really much simpler than this and much more serious. I have a rough enough time finding really good caviar of any kind without ascending to the more celestial realms of caviar appreciation. Now, I wonder whether we should be eating caviar at all, at least beluga caviar. And, most of the time, I can't even decide how caviar is supposed to taste. That's a big problem for caviar lovers like me and Batu Khan.

But now I feel I may have made a breakthrough. It was accomplished, to be perfectly frank, by throwing money at the problem, lots of money. I have purchased probably $3,000 worth of caviar over the past few months, and now it is gone. Maybe $4,000. I figured that if I kept on eating caviar, different types and grades, nationalities and ethnic origins, something would come, some notion of how to judge caviar. It's worked in the past on other foods, though with the sacrifice of far less money, and it may now have worked again.

But first, the facts. *Caviar* means salted sturgeon eggs. The salted eggs of other fish may be called caviar, too, but only when the word is preceded by the name of the fish, as in salmon caviar or whitefish caviar. The three main types of (sturgeon) caviar are beluga, osetra (also known as *osciotr, ocetra, oscetra, oscietra, asetra,* et cetera), and sevruga. These are not grades, colors, or sizes of caviar. They are simply Russian names for the three principal species of sturgeon that live in the Caspian Sea, the world's largest inland sea, and the source of 90 percent of the world's caviar. *Mal-*

ossol on the label means that the eggs have been only lightly salted. On the other hand, I can't remember a can labeled with the Russian words for "heavily salted."

Beluga sturgeon are gigantic, the largest fish found in fresh water, as heavy as 2,500 pounds and as long as 30 feet (though, as you would expect of any story about either fish or caviar, the most gigantic sturgeon ever caught has many shapes and sizes). Beluga eggs are dark gray, very large (just over one-eighth inch in diameter), thin-skinned, and slightly soft, and they generally bring the highest price, these days $100 or more an ounce, less than two level tablespoons, the most expensive food on earth. Osetra sturgeon come next. They are middle-size, both as fish and as eggs; their price is middle-size as well, about $80 an ounce; their eggs can be golden or tan or gray; firmer than beluga, they pop nicely against the roof of the mouth, and their taste seems the most varied, often with hints of butter or nuts and sometimes even fruit. Sevruga are the smallest and least prestigious; their eggs are black and have the basic, unadorned, assertive taste of caviar. Or so I had thought.

From the moment fine caviar leaves the master's hands, it must be kept under refrigeration, at or below the freezing point of water but higher than the freezing point of caviar, about 26°F, depending on its saltiness. The exception is pasteurized caviar, cooked in its jar until sterile. This can be an amusing little condiment, but pasteurization removes a good deal of the taste and texture we prize in fresh caviar. Whenever you see caviar in glass jars on unrefrigerated shelves, it has been pasteurized.

There is nothing exotic about eating fish eggs. The Egyptians salted and pickled them in 2500 B.C., not as a delicacy but for sustenance. Today we can enjoy the roe of the crab, trout, sea urchin, paddlefish, lumpfish, hackleback, shad, carp, and, I have read, snail. The salted, pressed, and dried eggs of gray mullet or tuna are the Italian *bottarga*, pungent and delicious when shaved over white beans or pasta. The Japanese artfully dye and flavor the neutral, crunchy roe of the flying fish and call it *tobikko*. Fresh and pristine salmon caviar can be as delicate as salted sturgeon roe, with the most diaphanous skin holding a light and subtle fluid, though most commercial salmon caviar is gluey, yolky, leaky or broken, desiccated, disgusting.

In the late 1800s, a center of world caviar production was . . . yes, the United States of America. They say that sturgeon ran so thick in the Hudson River that you could walk from Manhattan to New Jersey on their backs. Their roe was so cheap that it was given away in bars like pretzels and peanuts, in hopes of increasing the customers' thirst, or used as bait in lobster traps.

It is hard to believe that the caviar handed out in a thousand Manhattan saloons to be slathered on bread and washed down by beer was produced by a venerated master, meticulously and hygienically packed into jars or cans, and kept under strict refrigeration, as it would be today. The New York Public Library has a fine collection of restaurant and banquet menus, and if you glance through them, the earliest serving of caviar you find is in 1880, after which caviar was offered quite regularly among plebeian hors d'oeuvres such as olives, herring, celery, and radishes. A description of caviar in *The Epicurean* (1893), a cookbook written by Charles Ranhofer, chef at Delmonico's, the greatest American restaurant of its time, shows that caviar back then could not have been the object of worship that it has become. "[Caviar] is composed of sturgeon's roe, preserved in salt, pepper, and onions, and then left to ferment," Ranhofer wrote. "It is a very heavy article of food and very difficult to digest. When the caviar is too hard, it can be softened by working it with olive oil and lemon juice." Today we would not recognize this as caviar.

At the same time, an immigrant named Henry Schacht started a caviar business on the Delaware River, using "the finest German salt." He shipped most of his product to Germany for a then-lavish dollar a pound, where it was sold as Russian. Some was then imported back into the United States. According to a report of 1900, "fully nine-tenths of the Russian caviar sold in the American and European markets [comes from] sturgeon caught in the Delaware River." Soon afterward, the Delaware and the Hudson would become entirely fished out, and the domestic caviar business collapsed.

For the first half of the twentieth century, Russia controlled sturgeon fishing in the northern Caspian and bought rights from Iran for the rest. Ninety percent of the caviar coming into this country was Russian. Then, in the 1950s, under the shah and with American help, Iran developed its own fishing industry and its skill in processing caviar; 95 percent of the American market shifted to Iran. In 1979, soon after the Ayatollah Khomeini came to power, a state corporation called Shilat was formed to manage all Iranian caviar production. It operated with increasing efficiency and expertise in controlling fishing in the southern Caspian, managing sturgeon stocks, keeping the quality of caviar high and hygienic, and documenting the life history of each 1,800-gram can of caviar (nearly four pounds) as it moved from the shores of the Caspian through Tehran to Europe and America. Russia and Iran ran huge hatcheries to introduce millions of sturgeon fry into the Caspian every year. The world had become a paradise for caviar lovers.

And then, in 1987, the roof fell in. First, the U.S. government banned imports of all Iranian goods, including caviar, leaving us at the mercy of the Russians. Three years later, the Soviet Union came apart, and its sturgeon fishery became a free-for-all among the governments of Russia, Azerbaijan, Kazakhstan, and Turkmenistan, the four former Soviet republics that border the northern Caspian. Unemployment there was widespread, and anybody with a small boat could catch a sturgeon to feed his family. In the unlikely event that the fish was female, mature, and pregnant, her eggs would be a windfall. Soon, in each caviar port, this new chaos was organized by local elements of what we have come to call the Russian mafia. Poaching and overfishing were rampant, and the quality of caviar from the northern Caspian plummeted. Russian immigrants controlled the American markets from their new homes in Brooklyn.

At last, fortune smiled again when, in March 2000, then Secretary of State Madeleine K. Albright responded to Iran's democratic elections by relaxing the rules against the importation of carpets, pistachios, and caviar. Soon the caviar began flowing in, in four-pound cans packed at the Iranian shipping ports on the southern Caspian and closed with the seal of Shilat. Traditionally, Iranian caviar has been treated with a small amount of borax, which, because of its action as a preservative, permits the use of less salt and produces a sweeter and firmer product. The federal Food and Drug Administration has been hostile to other foods preserved with borax, but as the FDA has no formal regulations against the stuff, and as nobody eats enough caviar for it to matter, borax has not been a problem for importers. Iranian caviar is now the world's best.

Today, caviar is taken from a worldwide range of sturgeon: wild sturgeon in China, sturgeon farms on the Gironde River in France and in California, and paddlefish from the Tennessee and Ohio Rivers. Even sturgeon in the Hudson may be coming back—a few years ago, the Hansen Caviar Company claimed to be producing it. But several species of Caspian sturgeon are threatened with extinction.

The sturgeon is not exactly a picture-perfect poster fish for wildlife management, not like the sleek and puissant bluefin tuna, the cute and clever dolphin, the bookish whale. The sturgeon is a very large and very ugly fish—grotesque, really, especially its face. It is a bottom feeder living in a twilight world of silt and muck. Its beady, closely spaced eyes are nearly sightless. The sturgeon senses food—grubs, crayfish, worms, larvae, plant life—with thin strips of flesh that hang in front of its mouth like a scraggly mustache and are called "barbels," from the Latin word for beard. Barbels give the sturgeon a remote underwater sense of smell, and when food is at hand, the barbels taste the food before it enters the sturgeon's mouth, as the whiskers of a catfish do. (Don't you wish you could taste food before it enters your mouth?) Beneath and behind its huge snout, which is shaped like a monstrous shovel or a scary scythe, depending on the species, sits a vast recessed and toothless mouth whose thickened lips push out into a funnel that hoovers up its prey.

Man is the sturgeon's only predator. Some conservationists unjustly place all the blame on us caviar lovers. The truth is that the Caspian sturgeon population and the eggs gathered from it have been declining for decades. The Russians have built dams on the Volga for 60 years, increasingly preventing the sturgeon from spawning upstream; the Caspian has been evaporating for centuries; pollution has increasingly made it inhospitable. The worst may be yet to come. Geologists estimate that beneath the sea floor lies the largest untapped pool of oil in the world. Overfishing may soon become only a minor problem.

For nearly three years now, all 27 sturgeon species the world over have lived under the protection of the Convention on International Trade in Endangered Species of Wild Fauna and Flora, or CITES: Two sturgeon species are immediately threatened with extinction, trade in several others needs to be tightly controlled, and the rest must be monitored because their eggs can easily be confused with those of threatened species. Legally traded caviar must have a CITES permit from the country wishing to export it; the amount must fit within that country's quota. Recently, the U.S. Fish and Wildlife Service brought two dramatic prosecutions against caviar smugglers. The Iranians have been fastidious in their enforcement of the international rules, and comparatively little poaching goes on within their waters, except for some reported smuggling to Europe and the United States through Dubai.

Most caviar exported from the former Soviet Union, up to 90 percent of it by some estimates, is illegal. And the beluga sturgeon is in serious peril. It now yields less than 2 percent of the caviar taken from the Caspian. At a recent CITES meeting, a ban on beluga and on worldwide trade in its roe was proposed. But the Iranians and former Soviet republics successfully argued that the economic disruption to their Caspian fishing communities would be too great and that their restocking programs are likely to be successful. (Iran's hatcheries have already brought back one threatened species, the Karaburun, a type of osetra with brownish eggs and a fine flavor that now amounts to more than half the Iranian catch.) But it seems to me that until the former Soviet republics—Russia, Kazakhstan, Azerbaijan, and Turkmenistan (if it exports caviar at all)—can control fishing in their waters, the only way to prevent massive poaching of beluga sturgeon is to outlaw entirely non-Iranian beluga caviar. My own personal boycott has already begun.

For most people, buying caviar is a harrowing and humiliating experience. You are about to spend $100 or $1,000, and you have little idea about what you are supposed to prefer, what you really do prefer, and whether you are likely to get either. I have long found that many problems in the material realm of existence, such as those involving apartments or automobiles or clothing, are not really apartment problems or automobile problems or clothing problems. They are money problems. Rich people do not have apartment problems. Perhaps the same is true of caviar, I reasoned.

Yet the more I spent, the more confused and panicky I became—until a fateful meeting with a tin of fresh sevruga. Four times in recent months, I have conducted informal little caviar tastings, on each occasion sampling numerous types of caviar from various importers, resellers, and retailers, about a pound in all. In each tasting, though I included an ounce or two of beluga for the sake of comparison, most of the caviar was osetra (some of it labeled imperial, tsar, royal, or more than one of these), golden osetra, sevruga (some with fancy second names), American caviar from Stolt Sea Farm's white sturgeon in Elvarta, California (800-525-0333), and paddlefish or hackleback caviar from the tributaries of the Mississippi.

My expectations were regularly dashed. Beluga is the most expensive and often considered the best, but in most of my tastings it wasn't, especially when it had originated in the former Soviet Union. In California, I bought jars of Petrossian (800-828-9241) and Urbani osetra at the local Whole Foods market, and wished I had not. Beluga from Tsar Nicoulai (800-952-2842) in San Francisco was pretty perfect beluga; but I found I usually preferred osetra. Nothing from Caviar Russe in New York was impressive; nearly everything ordered from Paramount Caviar (800-99-CAVIAR) was of high quality, if not always the inspiration for a peak experience or religious moment. Pressed caviar (made from broken eggs of several species), which the Russians are said to love with blinis and cream for its strong flavor, was quite delicious in "demi-pressed" form from Caviarteria (800-422-8427), on Park Avenue, as was everything but the beluga from that shop. The level of variation has always surprised me. Nearly all Iranian caviar comes from Shilat, which sells to only 11 wholesalers. Most legal Russian caviar is brought into the United States by Petrossian, which has had a monopoly from time to time since the 1920s—especially in the years between 1979 and 1989, just when the Iranian supply was disrupted by an American boycott.

Golden osetra, preferred these days by the cognoscenti, once or twice had a taste and texture that gave me such intense pleasure as to justify the extinction of any species of fish, and even some mammals. Just kidding. The most memorable caviar in all the weeks of tasting was a golden osetra from Browne Trading Company (800-944-7848) labeled Daniel Boulud's Private Stock. (Daniel is one of this country's great French chefs.) It possessed all the fundamental qualities that one looks for at the start (I'll list them all later), plus its flavor was astounding—the most buttery, nutty, warm, and luxurious I can remember. When I ordered some again a month later, it was very nice but not transporting. On that occasion, their regular dark pearl-gray Iranian "asetra" won the day. Richard Hall, the very experienced taster at Browne Trading, told me that if 15 identical-looking 1,800-gram cans—unopened since they were sealed near the shores of the Caspian—arrive on the same day from Porimex in Lachen, Switzerland (the firm to which Shilat has allocated 25 percent of the total Iranian production), the caviar in every can would differ in color and taste.

The current-day fashion for golden osetra stems, I think, from legends surrounding the pale golden caviar said to have been reserved for the shah or the tsar, depending on who is telling the story. I have seen modern-day photographs of these eggs and read many accounts of their origins. In some, they come from the albino beluga, or from any albino sturgeon, or from the rare golden osetra sturgeon, or from the yellow-bellied sterlet, or from the clumps of pale eggs found behind the gills of some beluga and osetra sturgeon, or from sturgeon fished through the ice by Cossacks in early March. The idea of possessing and physically incorporating a food once reserved for the cruelest absolute rulers of the world must be a dizzying vision to a young investment banker or high-tech entrepreneur. But golden caviar can be bland, undistinguished, and very expensive. Like beluga, it can easily disappoint. The most delicious caviar in my fourth tasting was a sevruga from Petrossian. Buying beluga or golden osetra because it is expensive or because its name denotes luxury is base and venal.

Golden osetra was once my absolute favorite, but now I have learned not to play favorites with caviar. I think it comes down to this: Fine caviar has large, uniform eggs, spherical and unbroken, distinct from one another, and glistening with a light film of oil. The eggs are firm but not hard, and pop nicely against the palate. They have a fresh marine aroma but never smell or taste fishy. Their flavor is never bitter or overwhelmed by the taste of iodine.

Caviar is simply not worth paying good money for if the eggs are broken or leaky and swimming in oil. Or dry, or mushy. Or much smaller than you bargained for, or concave, or too soft to pop against the palate. Or bitter, muddy, or dusty tasting. This is defective caviar, which, if purchased at a great discount, can be successfully used in cooking or diluted with chopped egg, minced onions, and sour cream and served with melted butter on blinis. The Russians used these accompaniments with pressed caviar—a strong, jammy condiment made from broken or inferior eggs. To serve them with fine caviar is considered by Europeans an American gastronomic offense.

Once you've determined that yours is fine caviar, free from defects, then which caviar is best becomes a simple matter of your taste and your mood. The Petrossian sevruga we sampled near the end of those free-spending days was strongly flavored but not bitter. It had a clean oceanic taste, yet on top of this it yielded amazingly sweet and fruity flavors. The eggs were separate but didn't pop explosively; still, it was hard to stop eating it.

Sometimes, though, you are in the mood for the huge, dark, pearly eggs of Iranian beluga (remember, our boycott of the northern Caspian is still in full force and effect); the eggs will pop softly and opulently release their oils and juices; they will probably be more delicate, even more neutral, than any other caviar. Or you might prefer the chic and stylish appearance of golden osetra and the possibility that you may experience an epiphany. This happened to me only once in $4,000.

So. There is no one, ultimate caviar experience. There are many fine caviars in this world, but many more that lack freshness, physical integrity, or a clean, marine flavor. But unless you are buying a half pound of the stuff, in person, you will probably never get to taste it in advance. Yes, some importers and retailers are generally more reliable than others, but nobody's perfect. The solutions are either lavish spending or learning to be content with less expensive treats, such as delicate and diaphanous salmon and trout eggs.

And even then, your chances of guessing the identity of the caviar master are way less than zero.

MARCH 2001

CREAM OF THE CROP

As soon as I arrive at the Chinos', a 20-minute drive north of San Diego plus ten minutes to the east, I nearly always enter their farm stand through a door on the left, say hello to everybody on duty, and start eating. First I eat half a basket of the best strawberries in America, the smallish, irregular, incredibly sweet and perfumed *Mara des bois,* developed in France with a heady foretaste of the European wild strawberry. Nobody has them but the Chinos. Then I eat half a basket of the other best strawberries in America, the tiny conical Alpine variety, in your choice of red or white, hard to distinguish in aroma from French *fraises des bois.* Also only at the Chinos'. As long as I pretend to take notes, nobody gawks at my behavior.

Then I eat four orange cherry tomatoes. Most farmers grow the Sun Gold variety, which had been fine enough for me until I sampled what the Chinos grow, the Sweet Orange version from Japan, which they chose for its more complex flavor, just as they chose the Yellow Sweet Gold over the common Yellow Mini Candy type you see nearly everywhere, if you're lucky. Then I eat a white cherry tomato because it is fun to eat a white cherry tomato. Then I eat half a basket of the best boysenberries I have ever tasted—tender, very sweet, and full of boysenberry flavor, without all that acid to confuse you. And then I get down to work.

My work this morning is contemplating the meaning of the Chinos. Their farm is tiny by California standards, 45 vaguely triangular acres under extremely dense cultivation in the luxuriant San Dieguito River Valley, between the justly named Del Mar, on the Pacific Ocean, and ritzy Rancho Santa Fe, where, I have read, the average house is worth $1.5 million. The San Dieguito River Valley is filled with polo fields and polo ponies, country clubs and Republicans. But these are not your typically gruff, dismissive, anhedonic Republicans, for they line up every morning at the Chinos' farm stand, which is coyly labeled THE VEGETABLE SHOP in corny, balloonlike lettering reminiscent of Peter Max. I had thought that Republicans line up only at driving ranges and public executions. But no, these Republicans know their produce. They know what good is.

This is certainly one of the meanings of the Chinos. They are simply the best growers of vegetables and berries in the United States, and in food circles, they are very famous for it. Nearly everything they grow is sold directly to the public at this one farm stand, situated, in typical Chino fashion, on the second most inaccessible corner of their land, invisible from the busy Via de la Valle that runs along its western boundary. It is amazing to think that everything produced on these 45 acres is somehow funneled through this little structure of plywood and concrete, maybe 30 feet long. There is certainly a possibility that somebody in America grows a finer rutabaga than the Chinos, that somebody else does a slightly better job with bok choy, but there is nobody, anywhere, who grows so many things so perfectly. They grow 50 varieties of melon and 60 varieties of tender lettuce. Only here can you find red Japanese carrots, purple Chinese long beans, black and gold turnips, purple Okinawan sweet potatoes, and sweet multicolored Indian corn.

How the Chinos made themselves experts in everything they grow, I am just beginning to understand. This is not a job for standard humans. It is a job only for the inspired and the possessed. Take their tomatoes, grown in every color, size, and pattern. The Chinos grow Cherokee Purple tomatoes and Caspian Pink tomatoes, Mr. Stripey tomatoes and Pink Grapefruit tomatoes, Sweet Orange and Sweet Gold tomatoes, Mini Capri Pink tomatoes and Favorita. Plus Orange Paruche, Pepi, Red Ore, Israeli, Yellow Plum, Red Plum, Yellow Pear, Red Pear, Liberty Bell, Golden

Sunburst, Red Currant, Yellow Currant, Stokes Yellow Cherry, Mini Orange, Green Zebra, First Lady, Juliet, Early Cascade, Miracle Sweet, Red Peach, White Peach, Golden Peach, Red Gold, Yellow Ruffles, Yellow Stuffer, Green Pineapple, Evergreen, Great White, White Wonder, Large Brown, Brandywine Black, Pruden's Purple, Rose, Hillbilly, Big Rainbow, Persimmon, Amana Orange, Lemon Boy, Tangerine, Carolina Gold, Golden Girl, Mountain Gold, Ultra Pink, Grande Rose, Brandywine Red, Santiago, Tango, Richard's Secret, Enterprise, Big Beef, Ultra Girl, Ultra Boy, Emperator, Yellow Roma, Italian Gold, Super San Marzano, Green Grape, and Dixie Golden Giant tomatoes. They invented both the brown striped tomato and the red-gold striped tomato all by themselves.

The tricky part is seeing to it that all of these tomatoes taste terrific, their sweetness balanced with a good acidity and a full tomato flavor. The first time, customers buy with their eyes, one of the Chinos told me, but they come back for flavor. Or something like that. I have always assumed that every seed packet comes with a little instruction booklet, like a VCR or cellular phone. Plant on April 1, three inches deep. For greater sweetness, add some sun. For more assertive acidity, water at 11 in the morning. Apparently, I am incorrect. Learning how to grow a new vegetable requires technical knowledge plus lots of trial and error. Pioneers like the Chinos use test plots rather than cover several acres with what may turn out to be a difficult or repulsive plant. (They are now testing white nectarines, crosses between apricots and plums, varieties of sweet potato, and, for the University of California, weeds.) They once tried ten varieties of yellow seedless Japanese watermelon. Did you know that some melon seeds cost a dollar apiece?

As I lean against the wall of the farm stand, my meditations are briefly interrupted when somebody brings me a brown paper bag of just-picked apricots, and I absentmindedly eat half a dozen as I consider that a central chapter of the American food revolution started right here in 1969 when the Vegetable Shop was opened. Something was taking shape in the worldwide Zeitgeist. In France, the nouvelle cuisine was gathering force, waiting to

be officially discovered in 1972 in a famous article by journalists
Henri Gault and Christian Millau. This was not the degenerate
branch of the nouvelle cuisine that was to dominate 15 years later,
of precious plate arrangements, overhandled food, fear of flour,
and excessively reduced cream. This was a cuisine of hand-raised
foods, always local, never shipped, available only in season,
picked in the morning, and cooked the same day, right before
mealtime. In Berkeley, California, Alice Waters would open Chez
Panisse in 1971 and, with her extremely talented cooks—Jeremiah
Tower, Mark Miller, Jonathan Waxman, Paul Bertolli—change
our understanding of natural ingredients, how we grow them
and how we cook them. Alice met the Chinos in 1978, introduced
to them by an epochal green bean, and began buying as much of
their produce as she could, shipped the 500 miles to Berkeley by
Greyhound bus. Then Peter Allen, a longtime customer, introduced Wolfgang Puck to the Chinos when the original Spago
opened in 1982. Chino produce immediately became indispensable to the branch of California cuisine Wolfgang was inventing,
strewing Chino vegetables on his pizzas and chopping them into
his famous salad.

Nibbling on a raw ear or two of the Chinos' remarkable corn
(not only the sweetest I have tasted, but it also tastes like corn), I
watch two of San Diego's leading chefs arrive—Martin Woesle
from Mille Fleurs in Rancho Santa Fe, and newcomer Trey
Foshee, who has recently taken over as chef at George's at the
Cove in La Jolla. Along with two nearby country clubs and two
other restaurants, these are the only eating places in San Diego
County where customers can feast on Chino vegetables and
berries. I know this is hard to believe. If the Vegetable Shop were
located in New York City, it would take the city's riot squad to
keep order. Last year at the Union Square Greenmarket, down
the street from my house, I witnessed a near fistfight between
two top chefs over the last three pounds of fresh white cannellini
beans. Fresh white beans are a great delicacy in Tuscany, available
for a few weeks every summer. The Chinos have them for five
months a year, and sell them already shelled. They also have fresh
Appaloosa beans, Snow Cup beans, cranberry beans that look

like cranberries, deep red through and through, a bean called Money and one called Atlas, Rockwell beans, Squaw Yellow, Steuben Yellow Eye, Kilham Goose, Calypso, Taylor's Horticultural, Jacob Cattle, Flageolet, Aurora, and Blackeyed Peas—each with its own particular flavor, color, and pattern, selected by the Chinos from a universe of infinite possibilities after they had grown each candidate and cooked up a batch or two.

But how can even a Chino know what a rutabaga should taste like?

The Chinos' parents, Hatsuyo Noda and Junzo Chino, emigrated from Japan to California in the early 1920s, met at a produce market in Los Angeles in 1930 (as one story has it), got married, first sold and then grew vegetables, bought a house and three acres of greenhouses in Carlsbad, down the coast in San Diego County, raised vegetable seedlings and flowers (including prizewinning asters), and leased some land in the San Dieguito River Valley, where they grew peppers and along the way brought six children into the world. At the start of World War II, the entire family was sent for three years to a desolate internment camp in Poston, Arizona. Upon their release, now with seven children, they learned that the man to whom they had entrusted their property had sold it and squandered the proceeds. So they moved to the land they had once rented near Del Mar, worked out a sharecropping arrangement with the owner, and were able to buy all 55 acres in 1952. Two more children made nine. (If you are interested in all the dates and details, Mark Singer's article in the November 30, 1992, *New Yorker* is an excellent place to look.)

All the children attended college. The two oldest sons went to Stanford, became physicians, and settled in Orange County; the oldest daughter moved to Los Angeles and married; another son became estranged from his father. The five remaining children are the Chinos I met on my first visits to the farm, starting in 1990, shortly after I became a food writer, and these are the Chinos I see on nearly every visit. I regret that I never met their remarkable parents.

At first, the Chinos' income came from growing commercial crops such as broccoli, celery, and cauliflower, and some specialty crops, and selling them into the wholesale vegetable market in Los Angeles. As produce brokers had no interest in their more exotic fruits and vegetables, and as prices for standard vegetables deteriorated in the late sixties, the Chinos began selling directly to the public while keeping the wholesale side going. Corn, tomatoes, and strawberries were the staples. Then, as more customers were drawn to the Vegetable Shop, the Chinos expanded their production of unusual varieties. Within four years, their stand was earning as much as their traditional business, and by 1979 they had stopped selling wholesale entirely.

My ruminations are again interrupted when Tom Chino comes to fetch me. (Tom is the youngest Chino, 50 this year, and as president of Chino Nojo, Inc., is officially in charge of the farm. When Tom graduated from the University of California at Berkeley, he became a cancer researcher at the Scripps Clinic in La Jolla, but returned to the farm for good in the late seventies, after both of his parents suffered heart attacks. He and his wife, Nina Mac-Connel, have a nine-year-old son named Makoto, who just did extremely well on his first standardized tests. I have him slated for Harvard.) At the back of the stand, Tom has laid out four melons for me to sample, the first of the season—three French varieties and one Crenshaw. Some are sweet and luscious; one tastes like a pumpkin. I nearly always tell Tom the truth.

He shows me the professional way to test a melon. Fruit are generally sweeter around the flower end (the little button opposite the stem). Melons are also especially sweet around the rough, yellowish spot where they rested on the ground. So, to obtain an average sample, you cut a piece halfway between the stem and flower end and halfway between the yellow spot and the opposite side. Having mastered these principles, I wait until Tom gets distracted by something and quickly cut the sweetest part from every melon, and quickly eat it. As I see it, this is not actual cheating, for it demonstrates that I have understood the lesson well; besides, Tom himself eats only the sweet tips of his strawberries and tosses the rest, and Makoto takes after his father. Tom typically wears faded jeans and a plaid shirt and carries a walkie-talkie to speak with the workers in the fields, four interns from Japan and 13 workers from Oaxaca, in southern Mexico, all of them highly skilled.

The Chinos believe that produce should be consumed in season, near where it is grown. Tom blames the supermarkets and wholesale produce brokers, not the farmers, for the sad state of mainstream fruits and vegetables in America. "People have no conception of what's in season," he has said. "At the supermarket, everything is in season all the time. And everything tastes out of season all the time. Commercial buyers control what's available in the markets. Their buying power is so great that they can dictate what the grower can sell, how it is packaged, and how it is harvested. The grower is really at their mercy."

Whenever I return to San Diego for a visit to my wife and Sky King, our incomparable golden retriever, I drive up to the Chinos' at the first opportunity and spend most of the day. Sky loves Chino Farm, particularly the strawberries. Tom does not like Sky when Sky poops in his fields. The Chinos use chicken manure for fertilizer, never a chemical that would pollute the ground. They spray as little as possible—only to protect corn against worms and strawberries against mold when the weather has been rainy. And they use a soap spray against aphids.

This week, I drive up every day and leave Sky King at home. This is serious work, contemplating the Chinos. Today I arrive at the crack of dawn, 9:30 a.m., only five and a half hours after Tom arose and read the *New York Times*. He must be a morning person.

Tom's sister Kazumi (also known as Kay) comes to the farm stand to find me. She has agreed to teach me how she makes her famous apricot conserves. The apricots are halved and then cooked so that they remain plump and intact in their jars. Back in New York City, I once offered Kazumi's conserves to my friend Pierre Hermé, probably the greatest pastry chef in France. Pierre quickly and silently consumed half the jar, a really big jar, paused for breath, turned to me, and said, "This is perfect, *non?*"

Kazumi is the oldest Chino on the farm, though she looks far younger than her years—attractive, small, and endowed with an exhausting level of energy. Long ago she took on the role her mother had played, which on my first few visits I incorrectly assumed to be that of a housewife. But Hatsuyo, Mama Chino, was also in charge of the planting schedule and the hot-houses, where she started all the vegetables. Nowadays, most of the larger seeds are planted directly in the fields, and most of the smaller seeds are started by Kazumi in the hothouse. I watch her as she plants a seedbed, as it is called, the first step in creating life. After the seeds sprout, they are transplanted within the hot-house, and finally replanted in the fields.

Kazumi and I walk back to the simple modern building where she and Fred Chino live, another brother who, with brother Frank, is responsible for the early-morning tractor work, a job their father did. Fred is also in charge of the raspberries, boysen-berries, and Concord grapes, and is continually making fruit ices and ice creams. Already this morning he has brought a paper cup of his fine chocolate ice cream for me to taste. Tomorrow, he will show me how to make his delicious boysenberry ice, which is when I'll give you the recipe—if it works.

Frank is a master woodworker and the handsomest Chino, tall, thin, and graceful. He spends three months in Japan, near the family seat, every winter, when his work is not needed on the farm. He used to drive a biweekly vanload of vegetables to Spago and work for the evening as a pizza chef before returning to Del Mar in the early morning, and he loved exchanging Los Angeles restaurant gossip. Now he seems more contemplative, and spends part of every day building a beautiful wooden Japanese room next to his workshop.

Kazumi has everything ready for our jam-making lesson. It is a major success, and the mechanics are far simpler than I thought. (Dexterity is vital, which for me requires the assistance of a friend.) There is nothing like preserving for rescuing a mediocre apricot or immortalizing a perfect one. Kazumi shows me her federal and state canning licenses. Until recently, she sold her conserves at the Vegetable Shop. Now she gives them away to friends. Characteristically, Kazumi modestly attributes her method to Wolfgang Puck's mother. The Chinos are always giv-ing credit to somebody else. This is way too Japanese for me.

KAY CHINO'S APRICOT CONSERVES

(With thanks to Wolfgang Puck's mother)

4½ lbs. of firm but yielding apricots, neither rock hard
nor very soft; their flavor is the most important thing
4 cups granulated sugar
¼ cup water
2 Tbs. freshly squeezed lemon juice
Special equipment: a deep, heavy, broad sauté pan, at least
12 inches in diameter; 5 1-pint jam jars, with lids; a 4-inch-deep
roasting pan large enough to accommodate the 4 jam jars, laid on
their sides; a short wide funnel for filling the jars—not easy to find.

Wash the jam jars and lids in very hot water, preferably in your dishwasher. Fill the roasting pan with an inch and a half of water, lay the jars on their sides in the water, and bring to a simmer on the stove top. Every so often during the jam-making, turn the jars so that all their inner surfaces are immersed in simmering water at one time or another. Fill a small saucepan with water, add the lids (if they are the 1-piece type) or the inserts (if they are 2-piece), and bring to a simmer.

Halve and pit the apricots. You should have 4 pounds' or 8 cups' worth when you press them firmly into the measuring cup.

Put the broad sauté pan over high heat and add about ½ the sugar and all the water. Stir constantly until the sugar dissolves, then clears, and finally reaches the thread stage. (You can use one of two indicators, or both: The molten sugar will reach 230°F on a candy thermometer; when you let the sugar drip off a spoon, it will form a thin thread in the air.) Add about half the apricot halves. Cook, stirring constantly, until the fruit exudes its orange juices, tinting the molten sugar, and becomes limp and loses its hemispherical shape. Add the rest of the

- - - - -

sugar and stir until it dissolves and begins to bubble. Add the rest of the apricot halves and cook, stirring constantly—just until all the fruit has become limp. All the apricot halves should remain intact.

Remove from the heat. Stir in the lemon juice. Remove the jars from their water bath and fill (to the glass ring just below the threads) with the apricot halves and their syrup. Remove the lids (or inserts) from their water bath and seal the jars. Invert the jars until they cool, by which time the apricot halves will have begun reabsorbing juice and become plump again. If the juice around the fruit is clear rather than milky, you have cooked the apricots a bit too long. Makes 4½ pints.

Note: If you prefer the apricots to be less intact and more jam-like, cook them until they fall apart—after you add the second half of the fruit. Kazumi uses the same method with other solid fruits (excluding grapes but including strawberries). Her *Mara des bois* conserves are spectacular.

I drift back to the farm stand for the few minutes before lunch. Nina has brought me the menu from a much-talked-about vegetarian Indian restaurant in London. Nina loves to travel, but the four Chinos whose lives revolve almost completely around the farm, including husband Tom, rarely leave it. And yet they are impressively cosmopolitan. I have slowly learned to appreciate that the Vegetable Shop is one of the ganglia, the major nerve centers, for the exchange of food knowledge and food gossip in the entire Paris-Tokyo region.

At the stand, I am introduced to a San Diego couple with a house in Provence who give me a list of their favorite restaurants near Avignon; they never eat out in San Diego. Tomorrow, I will meet an owner of Chicken of the Sea, who privately cans, in the

Italian manner, the highest quality Pacific tuna, to give to friends; I will visit him in San Pedro as I glacially prepare for a *Vogue* piece about bluefin tuna (see page 11). And one of the Chinos' friends brings them the best piece of Texas barbecue I have tasted, a huge brisket cooked for 24 hours. Kazumi asks me to slice it with a sashimi knife. There is little they have not tasted, as I was reminded a month ago when I lugged a pound of bonbons from my current favorite among Paris chocolatiers, only to learn that somebody had brought them the same box last year. (I would have taken it back home, but I believe that would have been considered rude.) A few weeks ago, Wolfgang Puck drove down from Los Angeles just to pick up a load of Chino vegetables. He brought the amazingly thick, sweet white asparagus he imports from Austria to serve at Spago and a box of ravioli filled with the sweetest puree made with Chino peas, and after much urging, he cooked up everything for the Chinos. Wolfgang is a very fine cook.

Now it is time for lunch, which Kazumi prepares every day of the week for the entire family. She has somehow accomplished this during our laborious jam making. Today it will be a gratin of fresh cannellini beans (adapted from a recipe in *Marcella's Italian Kitchen*, by Marcella Hazan), sliced Japanese cucumbers (crisp, less bitter, and with fewer seeds, Tom explains, because they are parthenocarpic, my favorite new word), a sumptuous bowl of homemade Japanese pickled mackerel, a take-out roast chicken (none of the Chinos is a vegetarian), arugula sprouts (tiny little leaves, powerfully peppery), and corn cream. I love lunch at the Chinos'.

Tom and Nina cooked me some corn cream during my first visit, nine years ago, and it was a revelation. This dish is the essence of corn. It contains no cream, just the insides of the kernels, the pale milk and the yellow germ and none of the cellulose. If you cannot find extremely sweet and tasty corn, you should put off the project.

CHINOS' CORN CREAM

6 or 7 ears very sweet, flavorful corn
4 Tbs. very good unsalted butter (½ stick)

A corn creamer is an inexpensive device that cuts the kernels open and scrapes out their contents as you push the ear of corn along it. The Chinos' corn creamer is made by Lee Manufacturing and costs $5 or $10. Alternatively, hold each ear of corn in your hand and run a small, sharp knife down each row of kernels to slit open the top of each kernel. Then hold the ear vertically in a large bowl and use the back of the knife to scrape the contents of the kernels into the bowl. This is called "creaming" the corn.

Cream all the corn. You should have between 1½ and 3 cups. Put the butter in a 2-quart saucepan over medium heat, using between 2 and 4 Tbs., depending on the volume of the corn. When the butter is half melted, add the corn and stir constantly from the bottom of the pot to prevent the corn from burning. Cook until the corn cream thickens and has the texture of oatmeal. At the first sign that the corn is beginning to bubble and approaching the simmer, remove it from the heat. Serve immediately or keep warm over very low heat. You will probably not need salt and pepper. Makes 3 cups, enough for a side dish for 6.

The day after tomorrow, on the Fourth of July, Kazumi will serve hamburgers, hot dogs, fried chicken, and potato chips for lunch, with Fred manning the grill. Their mother loved the Fourth of July. I enrich their gastronomic knowledge by explaining in some detail why Nathan's hot dogs are superior to their usual choice, Hebrew National.

Tom takes me for a trip through the fields on a beat-up electric golf cart. We stop at the rows of corn, and he shows me how to tell when corn is ready for harvest: The silk begins to dry, and when you squeeze the tip of the ear through the husk, you can feel that it has broadened out. As corn is at its peak for only three days or so, the Chinos schedule 60 staggered plantings so that there will be excellent corn every day for nearly seven months!

We lurch on to the strawberries—huge, red, and picture perfect, the kind of California varieties such as Diamante and Chandler that I never buy in New York City, where they arrive hard, dry, and tasteless. I had assumed this to be a genetic flaw in all California strawberry varieties, which have been designed for shipping around the country, and I blamed it on an unhealthy alliance between strawberry breeders at various branches of the University of California and rapacious agribusiness. I am wrong again. These are fine varieties of strawberries when they ripen in the sun and are picked one by one. I guess it is not so easy to pick strawberries.

Or beans either. Last year, I asked Tom how he knows when to pick fresh shell beans such as cannellini or cranberry beans, which are hidden from view in their pods. He e-mailed me back: "There is a cascade of events that occur during the maturation of a bean. At what point the bean stops accumulating starch and starts losing water is a bit ill-defined. In summer, the whole process from being too green to being too dry (less than 20 percent moisture) may take only two days." Just as I had thought all along. Tom reads lots of technical books and journals, and Xeroxes the easiest parts for me.

We careen over to the cardoon patch. This is a vegetable popular in France and Italy but little known in America; the part you

eat resembles a gigantic branch of celery but is related to the artichoke. The French and I cook it with beef marrow, truffles, and
meat juice, or make a creamy gratin; the Italians require it for
bagna cauda. Tom has offered to cut some cardoon flowers for
me, which, it turns out, are spectacular-looking and resemble
artichokes gone to seed. I have eaten Italian cheeses made by
coagulating the milk proteins with dried cardoon flowers instead
of animal rennet to form curds. For breakfast, Tunisians thicken
milk with cardoon flowers, then flavor it with orange-flower
water and sugar. This is one of my fondest memories of Tunisia.
Several crucial experiments lie ahead.

As we bounce back to the farm stand, I ask Tom about some of
the other vegetables. The Nantes carrots are sweeter than typical
American carrots, he tells me, but too brittle for commercial
growers who harvest by machine. The yellow, white, and red carrots are grown just for the fun of it. Kohlrabi is just kohlrabi, as I
have always suspected. The unusual red Savoy cabbage is from
Denmark. The celery root is from Holland, and the white onions
are the same sweet, mild variety as Maui and Vidalia onions
(known officially as Yellow Granex) but improved here by restrict-
ing sulfur in the fertilizer, which further reduces the noxious sulfur compound that makes you cry.

What is really special about everything here, Tom points out,
is that everything they sell is picked that morning, and all the
work is organized to make that happen.

The sun is getting lower, and the air is filled with a golden
light. The fields are lovely, bordered by palm trees and a ridge of
hills in the distance. But Tom, who could find a dark side to winning the state lottery, is pessimistic. Last year, he said, sales of
peeled carrots in U.S. supermarkets exceeded for the first time
sales of whole carrots. The Chinos' revenue remains about the
same from year to year, while their expenses rise. Their own well
has become too salty and they must buy water at prices that have
risen to $60,000 a year; in the highly subsidized Central Valley, it
would be $2,400. As the USDA and the University of California
encourage family farms to shift to growing higher-priced spe-

cialty crops and support the creation of farmers' markets as an outlet for these crops, more small farmers are catching on to some of the vegetable varieties the Chinos pioneered.

It is clear to me that all this is defeatist and unnecessary. Marketing—that's the answer. I climb into the farm stand and speak with Linn, Barbara, Madlin, and Alex, who work there nearly every day. They all seem to have an almost religious reluctance to sell anything, to explain why a particular vegetable is special and delicious and available only here, and how to prepare it. I see one customer after another bewildered and intimidated by the unfamiliar bounty. People leave with $10 worth of tomatoes or corn when they would have been happy to take home $50 worth of all sorts of things if they only knew what they were. I propose that the Chinos print a sign for every variety, giving names, brief descriptions, advantageous qualities, why they are unique to the Chinos, and how to cook them. I am in the midst of my peroration when Kazumi comes up behind me and says firmly, "No signs." And that's it.

As she does every day, Kazumi has brought me gifts—a 35-pound jug of rice-bran oil; some of the apricot jam we made together; part of a good lemon pound cake, and part of a French cheese that somebody gave them this morning; beautifully wrapped coffee-flavored jelly-bean candies from Tokyo; my cardoon flowers; and lots of berries and vegetables to take home for dinner. For a while, my wife felt so guilty about accepting huge bags of produce without being allowed to pay for it that she curtailed her visits to the Chinos. Me, I am made of stronger stuff. I'll be back early tomorrow morning—or at least in time for lunch.

FRED CHINO'S BOYSENBERRY ICE

2¾ lbs. fresh, sweet boysenberries, about 9–10 cups
(I've also used blackberries)
1¾ cups granulated sugar
Juice of 1 lemon and 2 small oranges
2⅔ cups water
¼ cup Licor Cuarenta y Tres (a vanilla liqueur made in Spain and
imported by Wm. Grant & Sons, New York) or ¼ cup Grand Marnier
plus 1 tsp. vanilla extract

Roughly puree the berries in a food processor and pass them
through a strainer fine enough to hold back the seeds but open
enough to let through the fruit pulp. (Fred does this in one step
with a Champion Juicer.) You should have about 3⅓ cups of
pulp and juice. Mix well with the remaining ingredients. Chill.
Freeze in an ice-cream maker. Makes about 1 quart.

Climb Every Mountain

"Climb every mountain," I sang, my voice soaring on the triumphant last syllable as I struggled to lift a 23-pound turkey from the kitchen floor.

Birds of a Feather

It Takes a Village to Kill a Pig

Downtown and Far Away

Crossing the Line

Wilderness Enow!

Flat Out

Explaining Espresso

Thailand

BIRDS OF A FEATHER

"Climb every mountain," I sang, my voice soaring on the triumphant last syllable as I struggled to lift an immense 23-pound turkey from the kitchen floor, onto which it had tumbled after slipping from my greasy grasp. Yes, I had been climbing my own special mountain, and now the summit was in view. Would I reach it today, or ignominiously slide down the sharp and jagged scree to lie bloody and lifeless at my final resting place?

"Ford every stream," I continued, as I dusted off the turkey. The kitchen floor had been nearly hospital-level spotless, and so embedded in the turkey's padded skin were nothing more than a flip-top soda-can tab, a bamboo chopstick hand-carved in Kyoto, a star anise, and a red blessing cord from Wat Pho in Bangkok, where the huge golden Buddha reclines, propped up on his right elbow.

"Follow every rainbow," I crooned, my voice lofting again at the final syllable as I readied my short sharp knife for the critical first cut. " 'Til . . . you . . . find . . . your . . . dream." I savored every word, just as they did on the original cast album. Yes, this was a dream and a rainbow and a mountain all rolled in one, though not much of a stream. For on Christmas and Thanksgiving and on special occasions all the year through, when a turkey is called for, there are three summits that every true cook must scale, three rainbows that every true cook must follow, before she or he can say to her- or himself, "Today I have mastered the turkey. For once the turkey has not mastered me!"

In years gone by, I had successfully followed two of the three great turkey rainbows. First was the fabled Thompson's Turkey, rediscovered by the Utah branch of our family, a large bird stuffed with 29 ingredients, including crushed pineapple, water chestnuts, celery, bread crumbs, numerous spices, ground veal and pork, and lots of butter and fat; brushed with a paste of onion juice and flour; and roasted for five hours until the skin turns black and flaky and the flesh so tender and juicy that it can be carved with a spoon.*

Second came the Deep-Fried Turkey. It was in Charleston, South Carolina, in August 1993, long before the newspapers and food magazines had turned Deep-Fried Turkey into a fad, standing under a banana tree in John Martin Taylor's backyard that I first lowered a 15-pound, unstuffed fowl into 20 quarts of canola oil, bubbling in a giant stockpot set over a portable propane burner, then watched it for an hour as the subcutaneous fat rendered out and the skin became papery and perfect, which is the true purpose of any turkey.

And now, with the turn of the millenium close at hand, only one mountaintop remained to be conquered. Its name is Turducken, and it is a creation of the Cajun people of southern Louisiana, who take a chicken, a duck, and a turkey, remove most of the bones, and then stuff the chicken into the duck, and the duck into the turkey, and tuck savory stuffings in between. The entire thing is roasted for quite some time—as long as 13 hours. Then, being nearly boneless, it is simply sliced crosswise, each slice revealing six concentric rings of juicy goodness. Whatever it took, I would construct and roast a true Turducken before the year was out.

This was not an easy promise. My past attempts at deboning fowl had been catastrophic, producing chickens and ducks so pocked with holes and gashes that stuffing oozed in all directions. I sorely regretted that day 25 years ago when, learning to cook in the French manner from Julia Child's very first volume, I had

---

*Most readers will want to purchase *The Man Who Ate Everything* (Knopf, 1997) before Thanksgiving for the complete instructions.

skipped over the part about deboning turkeys. And now I could afford no mistakes.

Oddly, I had turned up only one printed recipe for Turducken, in *The Prudhomme Family Cookbook* (Morrow, 1987). Two versions on the Internet were nearly exact copies of it. Would the Prudhomme recipe produce a model Turducken? What is an authentic Turducken anyway? Who made the first Turducken and when did they do it? Putting together a Turducken from scratch is a huge commitment of time, money, labor, and energy. Without an authentic recipe, I was not willing to begin.

I will admit that I had already formulated a theory. The Cajuns descended from French settlers who in 1604 had immigrated to the maritime provinces of Canada, which they called Acadie, or Acadia in English. During and after the French and Indian Wars, the victorious British expelled the Acadians, many of whom were drawn to Louisiana, still largely French. (Many Cajuns are bilingual even today.) "Cajun" is short for Acadian and was a derogatory name until a generation ago. Now it is used by Cajuns themselves.

So, here was my theory: The French have many recipes in which fowl are boned or skinned, stuffed with their own meat or that of other creatures, and roasted or boiled. These are called *galantines* and *ballottines*. Are they the ancestors of the Turducken? Did the Cajuns bring the recipe for *galantines* from southern France to the New World? The etymological evidence is not encouraging. According to the *Oxford English Dictionary* (I lack the French equivalent), the word *galantine* entered the English language through Chaucer around 1400, though it meant a sauce for fish or fowl. Around 1725, it acquired today's meaning. This implies that if food news traveled quickly from France to England in those days, the *galantine* had to have been invented in France after the Acadians had settled in Canada.

I needed to taste a Turducken or two and study their construction, composition, taste, and texture. For this I turned to two well-known Louisiana butchers: Hebert's Specialty Meats in Maurice and the Gourmet Butcher Block in Gretna, just over the Mississippi bridge from New Orleans. The problem was that neither place qualifies for USDA approval, an extremely expensive and, in many ways, unnecessary ordeal. As a result, neither Hebert's (pronounced AY-bears, roughly in the French manner) nor Gourmet Butcher Block could legally ship its Turduckens across state lines. Both butchers were ready with makeshift solutions: You telephone their nearest Mail Boxes Etc. (or another shipper) and ask them to buy you a Turducken and send it overnight by FedEx or UPS. Everything will be charged to your credit card.

The two Turduckens arrived—frozen, rectangular blocks of near-solid protein. Each could serve 20 to 30 celebrants. The Hebert Turducken weighed 19 pounds, cost $55 (plus $90 for special packaging and shipping from nearby Allied Services), and was stuffed with pork sausage and corn bread; for an extra $5 we could have substituted rice, alligator, shrimp, broccoli and eggplant, or crawfish. The Gourmet Butcher Block Turducken weighed 17 pounds, cost $59 (plus $50 to their local Mail Boxes Etc.), and was also stuffed with the standard sausage and corn bread; various seafood stuffings would have cost $5 more. (They also sell a Turducken stuffed into a pig. It is 36 inches long, too large even for most restaurant ovens but perfect for a standard Southern barbecue pit made out of an oil drum.) Both Turduckens need to be thawed in the refrigerator, then roasted at 375°F for four hours covered and one hour uncovered. The Hebert Turducken was more artfully deboned, leaving half the leg bone in place, which helps maintain a bit of turkey shape; the other presented itself more as a rectangular solid.

Both Turduckens were excellent, full of taste and variety; the pork-sausage meat was good and garlicky. Both were juicy, especially when roasted to an internal temperature of 165 degrees, perfectly safe, though way less than the USDA recommends. The three meats and two stuffings making up each Turducken are enough for an entire Christmas dinner in which the banal flesh of the turkey is relegated to its proper role as a wrapper, and the rarely edible cranberry is entirely eliminated. Both Turduckens were roasted in standard roasting pans, and an enormous amount of liquid fat and juice collected around the meat. The fat can be skimmed and the juice made into a gravy, although the sheer volume of liquid shed by the chicken, duck, and turkey was disquieting.

Had I realized that Gourmet Butcher Block's co-owner Leah Mistich had been born Leah Hebert, and that she and her husband, Glenn, had worked in her brothers' business in Maurice, I could have predicted the similarity between these two Turduckens. For variety's sake, I might have substituted another brand. There is a good list of candidates on the Internet at www.gumbopages.com/food/poultry/turducken.html, though I cannot vouch for any Turduckens I have not tried; the author of the Web page has, unfortunately, eaten none of them.

I needed to return to Cajun country to investigate. Immediately, I booked plane tickets to New Orleans and a hotel room near the French Quarter, where my friend Julia Reed—*Vogue*'s celebrated political writer and an expert on Southern food—lives much of the time. Julia had volunteered to be my guide.

With the seductive taste of Turduckens still fresh on my tongue and their juices still dripping down my chin, I disembarked from my jetliner and into the steamy, primeval heat of New Orleans. Soon I was on the phone with Paul Prudhomme, the pioneering Louisiana chef who introduced the world to Cajun cooking 20 years ago—and, by blending it with the urban Creole food of New Orleans and the American family cooking of the Deep South, created a new cuisine, which he called Louisiana cooking. Prudhomme is often credited with inventing the Turducken, and his recipe, or at least an updated version of it, is the one that appears both in *The Prudhomme Family Cookbook* and on his Web site, www.chefpaul.com/turducken.html. Prudhomme's story is that, in the 1960s, as he was traveling the country, working in restaurants and learning to cook all types of American food, he found himself slicing beef and turkey on the buffet line at a resort in Sheridan, Wyoming. Unhappy with the way the turkey looked after the first few servings had disfigured it, he decided to experiment by boning the turkey, stuffing, and roasting it, and then cutting it crosswise into slices. He found the ratio of stuffing to meat much too high; the turkey's shape soon became amoebalike. So he came up with the Turducken. Together he and his partner on a New Orleans radio show in the early 1980s invented the name, and Prudhomme registered the trademark, which he has never enforced. That's his story. Many butchers in Cajun country also claim the Turducken.

People die and memories fade, even memories of Turducken. Verifying Prudhomme's Wyoming story is impossible. But, in my tireless research, I found a story by Charles Michener about the (then) new American cooking in a 1982 issue of *Newsweek* that precisely describes Prudhomme's Turducken! At last, the path before me was illuminated by the pilot light of logic. I simply need to ask every Cajun butcher in south Louisiana who ever claimed to have invented the Turducken how long ago he had invented it. If the answer is consistently less than 17 years, Prudhomme wins and I have my authentic recipe. If not, I am in trouble.

The next morning I strapped myself into Julia Reed's modest automobile, and we sped northwest into Cajun country. This was not an afternoon's adventure—we had already booked rooms at a motel in New Iberia. With us was Peter Patout, a New Orleans antiques dealer and a native of Jeanerette, where his family produces sugar. There is hardly a square inch of territory within a hundred miles of New Orleans that either Julia or Peter has not covered. After an hour, we screeched into a gas station, because Julia has spied in the window a handwritten sign announcing BOUDIN. Nearly every gas station in this part of the world runs a sizable convenience store next to the pumps; Northern gas stations limit their appetites to displays of fan belts and vending machines. Here, nearly every convenience store sells *boudin,* and nearly every *boudin* is made by the owner of the gas station or by a member of his family.

We went inside, and there they were, at the counter, sausage-like objects available in two flavors: pork or crawfish. Around here, *boudin* is pronounced "BOO-dan" and signifies a dressing of rice, broth, pork meat, pork fat, pork liver, and seasonings, all stuffed into sausage casings. Before our story deviates in the fascinating and delectable direction of *boudin,* we should take care of our main business. And here's the end of the story: No specialty butcher we visited claimed to have started making Turduckens more than 14 years ago. This was proof to me that Paul Prudhomme (or some person or persons unknown who preceded him) invented the Turducken. His was the first, and therefore the authentic, recipe.

This is the version I would cook back in my New York kitchen.

My theories about the Cajuns' sharing a French race memory of stuffing things into other things was pretty much a flop. Prudhomme told me that even just boning and stuffing chickens or ducks was not something his or other Cajun families ever did. (A search through my ample Southern-cookbook collection turned up only one recipe for boned and stuffed chicken—in *The Picayune Creole Cook Book*—and there were none that inserted one fowl into another.) It is true that every specialty butcher we visited—Hebert's, Charlie's, Poche's, and others—featured boned, stuffed fowl, but these had become Cajun specialties only 10 or 15 years ago, when supermarkets invaded the area and drew off their straight meat business. Most of the world's Turduckens are made in Cajun country by Cajuns, but Turduckens are not part of the Cajun tradition.

Once we realized that the Turducken mystery had been solved, we were able to turn our full attention to *boudin,* a topic that quickly became an obsession with me. At the end of my telephone conversation with Paul Prudhomme, when I told him that we were about to spend two days in his ancestral territory, he began recommending places where we would find the best cracklins, *boudin,* and *andouille* (pronounced an-DOO-we). In Opelousas there is Ray's, which makes the most delicious *boudin* of all. Billy's in Klotz Springs is worth the detour—you drive through town until you reach the last, perhaps only, Shell station, on the left, under a towering red-and-yellow sign. Billy makes a fine *boudin* but is better known for his wonderfully spicy cracklins. (These are bite-sized chunks of pig—the skin and about an inch of its fat—fried until everything is rendered and crisp, with a little moisture and tenderness at the center.) For the best *andouille* (spicy, smoked Cajun pork sausage), drive to Poche's in Breaux Bridge, which also makes a good *boudin* and other Cajun discoveries. For overall quality, head for the Best Stop in Scott, near Lafayette.

Unlike the French *boudin noir* and *boudin blanc,* these fillings are neither dense nor finely ground; they contain more rice than meat and are moist and somewhat loose. In my experience, their spicing varies from very mild to medium-hot, but I have read about fiery versions. Nearly all Cajun *boudins* are extremely good to eat. For Julia and Peter, eating *boudin* is something they do while cruising around in their cars, holding the *boudin* like a banana and either biting through the casing or squeezing out the filling with their teeth. Few restaurants serve *boudin*. Cajuns have told me that they eat *boudins* at yearly *boudin* festivals, on Saturdays, and also at home, where they cut them in half and pan-fry them in their own fat. My pulse quickens at the happy thought.

So we followed all of Paul Prudhomme's recommendations, those of people we met along the way, and nearly every handmade sign in the windows of gas stations and supermarkets. We did neglect two candidates in Abbeville that we had been told about in some bar, and a red-and-white bumper sticker that read, "Watch My Driving. I Am Eating Diane's 'Hot' Boudin. Try Some. 942-9077."

Our objective was not to discover the best *boudin* in southern Louisiana. Our objective was to eat as much *boudin* as possible. But we agreed with Paul Prudhomme that Ray's is probably the best, partly for the savory, rich taste of pork liver. I later reported to Prudhomme that Billy had recently bought Ray's, about 25 miles away, and makes his spicy *boudin* there, along with Ray's traditional version.

Before I left Louisiana, we had a party. At each butcher in Cajun country, we had bought several frozen chickens stuffed with rice plus crawfish, sausage, shrimp, or pork, and stored them in the large turquoise-and-white plastic coolers that Peter and Julia had brought. Back in New Orleans at Julia's vast and costly home in the French Quarter, we cooked all the stuffed chickens, plus all the meat pies, blood sausages, and *boudins* we had collected. Nothing was short of sincerely delicious.

The time had come to face Turducken. On the plane back to New York City, my luggage was heavier by the weight of a large sack of *andouille* and four bottles of Chef Paul's excellent proprietary seasonings. (These are required in the recipe on Prudhomme's Web site; *The Prudhomme Family Cookbook* has you start entirely from scratch. Otherwise the recipes are identical.) As both recipes are long and arduous, I scheduled the work over four consecutive days: the first to comb the city for everything we needed, the second to make three stuffings and a sauce, the third to bone three fowl and assemble the Turducken, and the fourth to roast it for 12 to 13 hours.

On the first day, I had imagined squandering ten hours in a hired car with my assistant, Kathryn, nudging our way through one Manhattan traffic jam after another, gathering 70 or 80 ingredients, mainly for the stuffing and the sauce. Faced with this unpleasant prospect, Kathryn gathered her wits, typed the ingredients on separate lists, and faxed them to the appropriate shops and markets. By the close of the day, everything we needed had been delivered to us, by their messengers or ours as Kathryn focused on her emery board.

The next day was for stuffings: *andouille*–smoked sausage dressing between the turkey and the duck; corn-bread dressing between the duck and the chicken; oyster dressing inside the chicken; and sweet potato–eggplant gravy to be spooned over every portion. Don't the names alone make your stomach rumble? These stuffings set Prudhomme's Turducken apart from all the others. They show his cooking at its most complex and mouthwatering. Each begins with the Cajun trinity: chopped onions, celery, and green peppers. These are long-cooked at the beginning; then, more of each is added before the end. The idea is to obtain both the tender, caramelized taste and texture of these vegetables, and their fresh and crunchy incarnations. All meat is deeply browned. Each dressing is first cooked over high heat on the stove top, packed into a dish and baked, then roasted in the Turducken, where it is spiced with three colors of ground pepper and moistened by the savory juices of three birds. My kitchen has not smelled this way in years.

Then came the dreaded day for boning the birds and assembling the Turducken, which, in strict terms, does not consist of stuffing a chicken into a duck, and a duck into a turkey. All three birds are relieved of their bones (though, for appearance's sake, the ends of the turkey's leg bones and the two joints of its wings remain), leaving three irregular sheets of skin and meat. The largest, a vast expanse of boned turkey, is laid flat upon the counter, seasoned, and covered with its stuffing. The boned duck is unfurled on top of this, seasoned, and spread with its stuffing. Then comes the chicken, its seasoning, and its stuffing. Now six layers are piled on your counter. At last they are rolled up together and the two open edges of the turkey sewn together. That's the fun part, the culmination of all your days of hard work.

Prudhomme's recipe gives the best turkey-boning instructions I've read, though several hundred diagrams would improve matters further. First we dusted off our turkey (after its spill onto the floor) and balanced it on its nearly spherical breast, the entire backbone exposed. All was at the ready. With one quick masterstroke, I ran the knife straight down the backbone, dividing the skin and meat into left and right. (Then, I executed several smaller masterstrokes to repair the places where the knife had slipped from the center line, into the skin and meat.) Next, we began boning one side of the turkey. The idea is to keep the knife very close to the bones of the body cage as you peel off the skin and meat in one unbroken piece, up to the leg and wing joints. Now comes the trickiest part, as it is far from obvious where and how the sinews attach the flesh to those bones. This is where we could have used Prudhomme's detailed guidance.

On my trip through Cajun country, one of the Heberts told me about a former employee, a 600-pound butcher, who could bone a turkey in just over a minute. He has gone back to Texas. At

Gourmet Butcher Block in Gretna, I met a young man named Chad whose record is one minute and five seconds. Or so he says. It takes Paul Prudhomme fully two minutes; he prizes craftsmanship above mere speed. So do I, but even more so. Thus, the first (and only) time we tried it, Kathryn and I needed just over two hours to debone our 23-pound turkey, but, oh, what a lovely job we did!

I left the duck and chicken to Kathryn, both to help her develop the skill sets she will likely need in her next job and to permit me a nap before the exhausting, though completely fulfilling, hours of stuffing, rolling, and sewing, which I have sort of described already. We waited until the next day to roast Prudhomme's Turducken because you need to be conscious and close by for 12 or 13 hours, as maintaining your oven at a nearly impossible 190 degrees is of crucial importance. Refrigerating the raw Turducken overnight proved as difficult as any task, because the refrigerator door refused to close no matter how I shifted around the gallon jugs of, by now, five-year-old maple syrup, the 30 open jars of jam, the rock-hard chunks of neglected Parmesan, and so forth. In the end, wedging a tilted chair loaded with books under the door handle came closer to creating a hermetic seal than anything else I tried.

"To dream the impossible dream," I murmured musically the next day after our handcrafted Turducken had roasted for six of its appointed twelve hours. A watched pot doesn't boil, they say, but it sure does roast well, and soon the outer turkey wrapper was burnished and golden. "To dream the impossible dream," I repeated, because I couldn't recall the next line. A few repetitions more, and I grew bored and switched to humming.

And then it was done, a total of thirteen and a half hours, to an internal temperature of 165°F. We waited another hour, cut the Turducken in two, lengthwise (which makes it easier to cut crosswise), sliced it, set out two generous servings, and spooned over them Prudhomme's sweet potato–eggplant gravy, which we knew from frequent samplings over the previous 24 hours would be unusually delicious. We should have made a triple order.

I blame myself for the slight dryness of the Turducken's outer layers. If I had let our creation come to room temperature before sliding it into the oven, it would have reached 165 degrees at least an hour earlier. Otherwise, it was the finest and most interesting Turducken I had eaten, and, on balance, clearly preferable to plain old turkey for its wonderfully complex flavors and serving convenience.

After a day or so of snacking, we still had 45 pounds of chicken, duck, turkey, and stuffings left over. I have found it nearly impossible to give away the most excellent and beautiful food to organizations serving the hungry or homeless of New York City—they want you to have an inspected kitchen. So we contributed our mountain of protein to the restaurant Balthazar on Spring Street for their midday staff meal.

Speaking of mountains, I guess I have at last clawed my way to the third of the turkey summits, with time to spare before December 31. Paul Prudhomme has assured me that next time I will be able to debone the turkey in under an hour. But by then I may have other rainbows to conquer.

DECEMBER 1999

IT TAKES A VILLAGE TO KILL A PIG

I went down to Chinatown looking for blood. They say you can buy anything or anyone in Gotham City if you're willing to pay the price, but not this time, not when you're looking for fresh pig's blood and getting desperate. I had shot the morning on the telephone. One of the two French butchers in Manhattan had vanished, and the other pretended not to understand. Ditto the old Italian pork stores on Ninth Avenue, on Bleecker Street, and on Arthur Avenue in the Bronx. "Forget about it," one Italian butcher advised. "Pig's blood is against the law. In Jersey, they make blood sausages with beef blood. If anybody says otherwise, either they got it illegally or they're lying."

And so it was down to Chinatown, where they live by other rules—south on Mulberry, left on Bayard, north on Mott, right on Canal, south on Elizabeth, and right on Bayard. I could have gone directly to Bayard, but I was sure that USDA commandos were following me. At last I darted into the Bayard Meat Market, and there it was, way in the back, frozen and maroon in quart-size plastic tubs. The label said pig's blood, in ballpoint pen. How could I tell for sure it wasn't beef or sheep blood? Is frozen blood as nice as fresh? And after answering these questions I would have to search for *les poumons, le coeur, le rate,* and *les joues* of a pig. I needed a French-Chinese dictionary, and fast. Had I gotten in over my head? I staggered out onto Bayard Street and disappeared into the teeming crowd. Once again, I was faceless in Gotham, and I sighed with relief. I felt like the Icarus of gastronomy. A guy should never hunger for what he cannot have.

It had all started so innocently, as these things often do, with a simple appetite, a modest craving. It was three years ago, and I was at a dinner party just outside Paris. Before we sat down to eat, we drank wine and nibbled on rich charcuterie from Béarn, in southwest France, served with slices of warm rustic bread. There were rillettes of goose, a pork pâté, and *boudin noir,* blood sausage. All three were memorable, but the *boudin noir* was the finest I had ever tasted. It was so phenomenally good that I quickly added it to my list of the hundred greatest foods of the world, tearfully removing the frozen Milky Way bar from my pantheon.

Upon subjecting the remaining scraps of *boudin* to minute inspection, I guessed that it was composed of long-cooked onions, tiny cubes of white pig's fat and skin, and ground pork—all held together by pig's blood, which, when poached, gels into a kind of custard. It was wonderfully spiced with cinnamon, nutmeg, clove, and black pepper (a quartet the French call *quatre-épices*) and, as I later learned, with the hot red Espelette pepper for which the Basque country is famous. Our *boudin noir* had come in an unlabeled gold-tone metal can the size of a medium can of tuna. Its texture was loose, unlike that of most *boudins,* which are densely packed into casings. In southwest France, *boudin noir* has long been preserved in jars and, in this century, metal cans.

Our hosts were Frédérick Grasser-Hermé and her husband, Pierre. Frédérick is a wonderful cook and food writer who has worked from time to time with superchef Alain Ducasse, to whom she addressed her most recent cookbook, *La Cuisinière du Cuisinier.* Pierre is the greatest pastry chef in France, with shops in Tokyo, clients in New York, and an award-winning book in English (written with Dorie Greenspan) called *Desserts.* We three have organized little food adventures all around Europe and in New York City. Fred, as I have come to call her, and Pierre always bring their own salt to dinner—the white *fleur de sel* from Guérande or the pink stuff from the Île de Ré—even to the fanciest restaurants. Pierre also brings his own knife. Yet neither of them is in any way pretentious.

After dinner, in the guise of using the men's room, I rifled through their pantry and discovered that they had a good supply of metal cans filled with blood sausage, which I stopped just short of sharing. A few ounces of this inconceivable sausage meat had aroused in me an irrepressible craving, an appetite that could not long be denied. Frédérick and Pierre agreed. *"Il est top,"* they said, using the French slang popular then. But they were unusually guarded about the source of their *boudin*. They did reveal that it could not be bought in any shop and that the recipe was a complete and total secret. I taught myself to be content with the shards and crumbs of *boudin* to which I was treated at their dinners, and lay in wait.

A year later, Fred and Pierre made an astonishing announcement. Their *boudin* is the famous *boudin* of Christian Parra, they began. Christian is proprietor of the Michelin two-star restaurant Auberge de la Galupe, in the microscopic village of Urt, near the city of Bayonne, in the southwest corner of France. Out of love for Frédérick and Pierre, Christian and his older foster brother, Joseph Bordus (the guardian of the secret family recipe), had decided to pass on their great and incomparable *boudin noir*. When we were ready Christian would arrange the ancient ceremony known as *la tue-cochon,* "the killing of the pig." I pinched myself, as I am sure Frédérick and Pierre had done after they spoke to Christian.

Pork is the most popular meat in France. Grimod de la Reynière, the very first restaurant critic, wrote in the early 1800s, "The pig is an encyclopedic animal. It is a veritable meal on hooves. One throws away nothing." Half the French say, *"Dans le cochon, tout est bon"*: "Every part of the pig is good to eat." The other half say, *"Tout est bon dans le cochon."* By law, most French pigs are now killed in government-inspected slaughterhouses. But, in rural France, traditional pig slaughters are still permitted on farms, where they apparently have changed very little in the last 2,000 years. (After the Romans conquered Gaul in A.D. 51, they so admired the Gallic way with pigs that they brought home both the famous hams of Bayonne and the methods for curing them. These are said to have been the inspiration for Italian prosciutto.)

When a farmer's pig is ready for slaughter, always in the cold months between fall and spring and only when the moon is waning, he confers with his neighbors, and a day is chosen. That morning, the men take charge of bleeding, killing, cleaning, eviscerating, and dismembering the animal. Then there is a *casse-croûte,* a snack in midmorning, which in this part of France is traditionally the pig's liver, sliced and grilled. Meanwhile, the women make the charcuterie (*chair* means "meat" and *cuit* means "cooked")—sufficient sausages, salamis, pâtés, bacon, white and black *boudins,* salt pork, and hams to last the winter. If the village is small, a professional charcutier from a neighboring town may help the family prepare its recipes. Everybody's reward comes that evening at *la fête du cochon,* "the feast of the pig."

In March 1998, Frédérick, Pierre, and I flew from Paris to Biarritz, rented a car, and checked into an exceedingly grand seaside hotel offering low winter rates. With us was Patrice Hardy, a chef who had worked for Pierre, and Patrice's wife. We drove 40 minutes in the gathering darkness to Auberge de la Galupe to meet Christian and his wife, Anne-Marie, and share a preslaughter supper of ham from Spain (an hour's drive away), puff-pastry treats flavored with cracklins, *rillettes* of duck and of goose, small potatoes with black truffles, bluefin-tuna belly bought from Basque fishermen and cooked with hot green peppers, a salad dressed up with pieces of foie gras and more black truffles, ravioli filled with deeply flavored braised duck, a tender shank of veal, and thin slices of crumbly sheep cheese from the nearby Pyrenées. As you might guess, Christian's four grandparents were Landaise, Béarnaise, Basque, and Spanish. Christian's cooking is lighter than its predecessors, and everything was extremely fine.

But where was the *boudin noir*? I spotted it on Christian's menu but nowhere on our dinner table. With each succeeding course, I searched for *boudin.* Even after dessert, I kept the hope alive that someone would soon carry in a huge platter weighed down with all the blood sausage you could ever eat. I knew for a fact that somewhere in this cute little sixteenth-century house of theirs were can upon can of Christian's famous *boudin noir*. Only when we had driven halfway back to our hotel did I dejectedly give up the ghost. I need not have worried. The following day, after *la tue-cochon*, the treasure was to be ours forever.

In France, *boudin noir*, though the cheapest of all sausages, can become an object of veneration and worship. I have an entire little book called *Le Boudin, Récits et Recettes de la Cuisine du Sang*—"narratives and recipes of the cuisine of blood." The author compares *boudin* eaters to Masai warriors, to Aztec noblemen drinking the blood of human sacrifices. The essential formula for blood sausage is equal proportions of onions, pork fat, and pork blood, plus flavorings, and often cream. Every region of France has its own version—*Larousse Gastronomique* lists 16, and my collection of French pig books gives recipes for others. In southwest France and in the Parra family, *boudin* is made from the pig's entire head, neck, and thoracic organs, and thus contains as much pig's flesh as any other ingredient. Unlike some *boudins* in this region, the meat is not stretched with cream or bread (or, as in English black pudding, with rice and oatmeal). I have read that blood pudding was invented by Aphtonite, a cook of ancient Greece.

Christian is a large, jolly-looking man with a well-trimmed salt-and-pepper beard. He received his first Michelin star in 1989. When the great chef Michel Guérard tasted the Parra family *boudin noir*, he insisted that Christian add it to the menu. Christian agreed, and it was surely no coincidence that shortly thereafter La Galupe was promoted to two stars. His is the only recipe for *boudin noir* included in the latest *Larousse Gastronomique*. And, in Christian's own volume, *Mon Cochon*, published last year, it is the very first recipe. The problem is, the two are wildly different, and by intention, I think, neither is correct. Christian made us promise not to publish any recipe that gives precise quantities.

The next morning we rose at dawn and drove back to Urt. Three extremely large, rubicund farmers, in their late 40s, I guessed, wearing berets and rubber boots and rubber trousers or aprons, were standing in a courtyard among several farm buildings, and together we waited for the pig and watched our breaths in the bright, cold air. In one corner, a large copper cauldron had been set on a portable gas burner and filled with water, which had nearly reached the boil. In the center of the courtyard was a rectangular, flat-bottomed, galvanized zinc trough, which would serve as a pig-size bathtub for cleaning the animal. Inverted, as it was now, it was a platform on which to kill and bleed it. Soon Christian, his sous-chef, and Joseph showed up. Someday I may understand why everything involving farms or farmers must begin in the unpleasant hours just after dawn.

I had heard that the killing and bleeding of a pig is pretty rough stuff, and I wondered whether I could take it. I have long felt, at least in theory, that carefree meat eaters like me need to face the reality of slaughter. We shouldn't think of meat as something that originates in shrink-wrapped packages at the supermarket and imagine that we can escape the karma of killing by paying someone else to do it. The more we understand where meat and fish come from, the less we will eat in a casual, mindless way and the less we will waste. Am I wrong?

At last, a large truck arrived. It backed into the driveway, the doors were opened, and a wooden ramp was pulled down into the courtyard. Now, the three farmers dragged a huge pig off the truck against strong resistance. The pig had locked his knees and planted his four feet firmly on the ground. He seemed to know that he was about to die. Maybe he had heard the adage of animal husbandry Christian taught me: When a pig cannot get any fatter, it is necessary to kill it. Put another way, a farmer cannot afford to feed a pig that has stopped growing.

Our pig was over five feet long and weighed 400 pounds, a male castrated at the age of one month or so. He had been trucked that morning from the Pyrenées, where the pigs are twice as large as the local variety, which have been crossed with the smaller *cochon anglais*. Free-range Pyrenées pigs fattened on corn and barley are especially prized for making the finest dry-cured hams and other charcuterie. Our pig's skin was off-white with an uneven growth of dirty bristles, and his eyes were tiny. His ugliness made it easier not to sympathize with him.

The three farmers had tied ropes around the pig's ankles, and with the help of an iron grappling hook, were able to pull him across the courtyard to the inverted zinc trough, and, by tying his feet together, to haul all 400 pounds of him onto the platform, lying on his side. Then, the largest of the farmers pulled back the pig's head with his iron hook, baring its neck from chest to chin. Joseph had brought a broad, deep sauté pan to collect the blood. For the moment, our pig had stopped struggling.

The farmer tugging on the hook held a knife in his right hand. He plunged it in, just above the pig's chest, and drew it up, toward the head. Immediately the blood began to flow, and Joseph caught most of it in his pan. With one hand, he continuously stirred the blood so that it would not coagulate in the cold air. Later he would pour it into a bright blue plastic pail, mix in some salt, and put it in the refrigerator.

The pig began struggling again, and it took four men to hold him down. I became nauseated and dizzy. I had not bargained for his grunts and his hoarse cries. The sounds came close to unhinging me. Pierre and Fred were not doing much better. Once or twice the pig slid off the zinc trough and had to be dragged back onto it. Bleeding the pig took at least 20 minutes, and then he was dead. His tongue poked out of the side of his mouth, just as in a cartoon.

At first, I felt a deep sadness and a sense of shame. But doesn't a pig, a chicken, or a lobster die every day of the week for my dinner? Is there a difference between the deaths I witness and those I don't? It is true that commercially slaughtered pigs are stunned before they are bled. The USDA considers this a humane method of slaughter, required of everyone except kosher and halal butchers, who will have nothing at all to do with pigs but who would bleed their pigs alive if they did. Is the USDA rule more humane? I recently spoke to a friend who years ago nearly bled to death. Her pain had lessened as consciousness drained out of her. With each minute, she became less aware that she was watching her own death.

Cleaning the pig was an elaborate affair. First, he was rolled onto a wooden frame with a sort of stretcher on it. Then, the platform was inverted, and six people grappled with the stretcher to roll the pig into what had now become a trough again, a bathtub. The boiling water in the copper cauldron was poured over the pig as the farmers scraped his skin with the sharpened sections of a retired scythe to remove the bristles; these are saved to make brushes. To speed the process, the pig was dusted with a powdered pine resin, a precursor to turpentine. Then, the rest of the boiling water was poured over him, and the scraping resumed, followed by a singeing with a blowtorch for those problem areas, and then another bath.

The outcome was amazing. What had started as a filthy beast deserving his fate had become . . . a gigantic baby! Its skin was creamy white and spotless, every square inch perfectly smooth and supple, wrinkled only at the joints and neck, and absolutely clean. If he could just have looked this way in life! Only now would the farmers dare to disembowel him.

They rolled the pig onto his back, made one incision from the belly downward, and another up to the chest. Then, they carefully removed the intestines. If these had broken, the waste inside could have contaminated everything else. The breastbone was sawed through and the edible organs removed—the lungs, heart, thymus, spleen, and liver. All these but the liver would become part of our *boudin noir*. Now, the pig's head, throat, and the flaps on both sides of the chest incision were severed, and the pig was opened wide, almost flat. His legs were tied to the four corners of the wooden rack. All three farmers were needed to bring the rack and its pig upright; then, the largest farmer held the rack against his own back, walked it to a barn ten feet away, and rested it against the wall. They covered the pig with a blue-and-white Basque cloth, hosed down the courtyard, and disappeared briefly to remove their blood-spotted boots and rubber trousers and aprons.

Meanwhile, a table was brought out and set with three places for the farmers' *casse-croûte*. Soon, they were feasting on a giant *cèpes* omelet that Christian had prepared—it must have taken a dozen eggs—plus two crisp baguettes and two bottles of red wine. For the rest of us, there was nothing. I had not eaten for 12 hours, and my hunger was becoming bothersome. I question a value system that rewards physical labor with *cèpes* omelets while starving those whose vital work consists of taking notes and contemplating the meaning of blood sausage.

The pig was lowered on his rack and untied, and for the next hour was dismembered into the primal cuts of pork: the shoulder, ribs, loin, filet mignon, belly, legs, shanks, and so forth. In the old days, the filet was given to the village doctor or priest, but today it was destined for our lunch. Joseph immediately salted the hind legs. In 18 months, they would become two top-quality Bayonne hams that would have made the ancient Romans envious. The farmers disappeared again, this time to shower and change into jackets, slacks, and ties.

Work on the *boudin* had begun in the kitchen two hours earlier. The *goula*—the neck or throat—of another pig had been chopped and sautéed in a very large pan for a half hour, until all the fat had rendered out and the solids began to crisp. Great quantities of chopped onion were mixed into the fat and slowly cooked for an hour or so, giving off irresistible aromas. More than a pound of chopped garlic was added, plus fresh thyme and parsley near the end of the cooking.

As soon as the pig's head had been severed, Joseph went to work on it, partially splitting it with a hatchet, removing the tongue and the brain, and cutting off the ears. The copper cauldron had been refilled with 30 quarts of water, along with several onions stuck with cloves and five long, dried, red Espelette peppers, and brought to a boil. Joseph gently released the head into the boiling water, then the lungs, heart, *goula*, spleen, thymus, tongue, and ears. The brain and liver would be saved for other uses. On top of everything went four thick bundles of beautiful leeks from Joseph's garden, trimmed and tied with string.

After an hour, the leeks were done; Joseph squeezed out the excess water and, in the kitchen, fed them through a large electric meat grinder under which the pan holding the onions, garlic, and rendered fat had been placed. After an hour and a half, the ears, tongue, and assorted organs were removed from the cauldron; the ears were skinned and the cartilage discarded; the tongue was skinned and the skin discarded; the organs were chopped into large pieces and their largest arteries and nerves removed; then, everything was fed through the meat grinder into the pan. After two hours, the *goula* and meat from the chest were done and soon afterward, the head. Joseph tested them by seeing how hard he had to press before his finger could pass through the meat.

Standing at his table in the courtyard, he first removed the skin from the head, *goula,* and chest flaps. The skin was lined with a quarter-inch layer of fat, in some places more, and Joseph carefully cut the skin and its fat into hundreds of cubes about three-eighths of an inch on each side, and he slid them directly into the pan under the meat grinder, so that they would remain whole in the *boudin.* Finally, he cut off every scrap of meat and fat remaining on the pig's jaw and skull; the most substantial pieces were *les joues,* the jowls or cheeks. *"Les yeux?"* I asked Joseph—what about the eyes? He looked at me as though I were a barbarian.

We were nearly done. We all crowded into the kitchen as Joseph removed the bright blue pail of blood from the refrigerator. The pan, now full of everything good, had been pulled out from under the meat grinder. Joseph poured in the blood, mixing it with his hand, a process that must have taken at least five minutes and left him bloody up to the elbow. Now, it was time to season the mixture. Joseph added salt, black pepper, *quatre-épices,* and ground Espelette peppers, measuring with his eyes, and mixed them in thoroughly. For the first time all morning, Fortune smiled. To test the seasoning, Joseph needed to fry up a handful or two of the *boudin* mixture—eating raw pork and fresh blood is not considered safe. At long last, I had a taste of the epiphanic *boudin noir.* Then Fortune smiled again when Joseph added a little more of some spice and needed to cook another test batch. The *boudin* was spicier than I had remembered it. Everybody agreed that it would mellow after it was canned.

Now, at two in the afternoon, we returned to La Galupe for lunch, our *fête du cochon,* with the three farmers and several friends. Drinking lots of good local red wine, we ate two pâtés

Joseph had made from the family's recipes, a plate of Bayonne ham, wild freshwater shrimp from the Guadalquivir River delta in southern Spain, and then, the *boudin noir*—a dark-red disk about three inches in diameter and three-fourths of an inch high, sautéed crisp on top and bottom, and served with very fine, rich mashed potatoes and an apple compote, the traditional accompaniments, and a grilled pig's rib. For a minute or so, silence accompanied our eating. The main course was the pig's filet mignon, sliced, sautéed, and served with a vinegar sauce and diced potatoes, crisply browned with garlic and parsley. We finished with sheep cheese, two desserts, and a glass or two of Armagnac. The three farmers sat together and a bit apart from the rest of us, and were, in a sense, the honored guests. They were men of great skill and practical knowledge, but they were also men of few words, you might even say no words. Besides working their own farms, they help friends and neighbors when the time comes to kill a pig. Though they do not expect compensation, Christian sent them off with a gift of money.

All I wanted to do after lunch was stagger into a soft bed and lose consciousness for a day or two. But the *boudin noir* over which we had slaved since dawn had to be immediately preserved. Joseph had cleaned several lengths of the pig's intestines, stuffed them with *boudin,* attached them to willow branches, and poached them in the strongly flavored broth from the copper cauldron. But most of the *boudin* mixture remained. We drove to Maison Montauzer in the nearby town of Guiche, a small factory for the making of traditional, unadulterated charcuterie and prizewinning Bayonne hams. It was M. Montauzer who had arranged for the delivery of our pig that morning.

Christian and Joseph rarely use live pigs when they make *boudin noir;* they buy only the parts they need from M. Montauzer—the head, throat, blood, and organs, the cheapest parts that might otherwise go to waste. On the second floor of Maison Montauzer was a small mechanical canning line. The entire crew from the restaurant had come with us, and Joseph supervised as they spooned the *boudin noir* into 166 shallow metal cans. The cans were then placed on a short moving belt that passed slowly through the sealing machine. Later, M. Montauzer's son would put them into a hot-water bath, maintained at the boiling point, for two hours. This would finish cooking the *boudin*, sterilize it, and solidify the blood.

After dinner on our last evening in and about Urt, Frédérick, Pierre, and I said goodbye to Christian and Anne-Marie, who gave us each 12 cans of the Parra family's peerless *boudin noir*. As to whether we had feasted on the forbidden ortolan or the prohibited *bécasse*, or both, crisply roasted, I have no comment.

Miserly though I was with my cans of *boudin* when I returned to New York City, it was inevitable that before long they would vanish, and this is why I had embarked on my pursuit of fresh, clean, local pig's blood. I now realize that I had become unnecessarily discouraged by the man at the Italian pork store and by my nightmare in Chinatown. Last week I telephoned the USDA in Washington, spoke with Robert Post, director of the labeling and additive policy division, and learned that pig's blood is totally legal! The frozen blood at the Bayard Meat Market was probably genuine after all.

I exchanged frequent e-mails with Frédérick and Pierre, who were suffering the same withdrawal pains as I. There was only one solution: I would fly to Paris, we would buy all the supplies we needed, and we would make *boudin noir* in Pierre and Fred's backyard. Besides the dizzying prospect of getting my hands on 80 cans of *boudin*, this was also the only way to test whether we had learned well the ancient lessons of Urt.

Making the arrangements fell to Frédérick, and even after it became clear that she had bitten off more than any one human could chew, her mood remained cheerful at least half the time. She had to rent and transport a portable gas burner, a huge cauldron, 160 empty metal cans, an industrial-strength meat grinder fitted with screen number ten (just like Joseph's), and a hand-operated machine for sealing the cans. She had to find all the pig parts we needed and make sure they came from a 400-pound pig. She had to shop for leeks, onions, garlic, spices, and herbs. And she had to find seven quarts of clean, fresh pig's blood. It was our good fortune that her local butcher is a distinguished artisan—he supplies several cuts of meat to the restaurant Alain Ducasse. Under Frédérick's constant surveillance, he was able to find all the animal matter we requested.

Three of us had taken detailed notes in Urt—me, Frédérick, and Patrice Hardy. Now, each of us composed a complete recipe and faxed it to the others. Miraculously, our recipes were extremely close, leaving only five or six disputes. The event was set for June 18, 1999, at nine o'clock in the morning. None of us had any idea how to operate a canning machine.

Thankful that we did not have to deal with a live pig, we set the cauldron, really a huge stockpot, over a propane flame and sautéed the chopped onions in chopped *goula,* proceeding as Joseph had done. We were five men and one to three women, depending on their whim, and yet it took us twice as long as Joseph to make the *boudin* mixture, six hours in all. This cannot be explained entirely by the fact that all the men had brought their cell phones—it was Friday, after all, a working day. Whenever there was a ring, all five of us would lunge for our phones.

Frédérick had been in touch with Christian all week. He seemed less than happy about aiding us, probably because he was having second thoughts about letting go of his family's priceless *boudin noir.* After both Fred and I again pledged that we would not publish a recipe giving exact quantities, he relented, remaining slippery on only one or two matters.

Mixing in the blood went without a hitch, but the spicing was initially a problem. We suspected that Christian had not sent us the real Espelette pepper, as he had promised, and we needed to keep reminding ourselves that the spices would soften after we had canned and cooked the *boudin,* but that the salt would not. At long last, those of us who had enjoyed many cans of Christian's *boudin* were able to get the balance of salt, pepper, *quatre-épices,* and hot pepper just right, though in the process we were regretfully forced to fry up and consume many succulent handfuls of *boudin.*

The canning machine was a vivid French blue, and with the aid of a completely confusing French diagram, I finally figured it out—just in the nick of time because the others had already divided all of our *boudin* mixture among 126 cans. Christian and Joseph had produced 166 cans. We were 40 short. Forty times, say, seven ounces per can meant that we had omitted 17.5 pounds of something. Had Christian and Joseph added 17.5 pounds of fat or meat to the cauldron or the meat grinder while our backs were turned? Had our Parisian butcher used a 300-pound pig?

In case you're new to these things, let me tell you that operating a manual canning machine takes much more strength and energy than you can possibly imagine. At 7:00 p.m., 126 cans later, all five men were totally depleted, staring listlessly into space. Frédérick bustled about, collecting the sealed cans and dropping them into fresh, boiling water in the cauldron, where they would remain for three hours of cooking and sterilization. We held our breaths. We had no strong reason to believe that the cans were really, truly sealed. At any minute they could burst open and spill their treasure into the water, or water could seep in and ruin everything. But they held. And one by one, the slightly concave lids became slightly convex as the air and blood inside expanded. Then we all left and went back to the center of Paris. Frédérick stayed up until midnight, taking care of everything.

Before I left Paris with my sanguinary hoard, Fred, Pierre, and I opened a can of our *boudin noir,* sautéed it until it was crusty, and tasted it. We were in heaven, at least at first. Our more mature judgment was that the taste and texture were nearly perfect, but that there was a bit too much blood in proportion to meat. The extra blood had pooled here and there like a crimson custard. Adding those additional 17.5 pounds of pig would surely have done the trick. We were certain we could make an absolutely perfect *boudin noir* in the style of Urt if we tried again, but we were overcome with narcolepsy at the very thought. Perhaps we'll change our tune when we have gone through 60 cans apiece, but for now, the expense and effort seem too awful to contemplate. You might say that it takes a village to kill a pig.

DOWNTOWN AND FAR AWAY

I f my immigrant grandfather had met Butch Cassidy and the
Sundance Kid on the Lower East Side of New York City, it
would have been in 1901, when my grandfather ran a little
grocery there and Butch was staying at a boardinghouse on East
12th Street between Second and Third, planning an escape to
South America, as the Pinkerton detectives closed in.

I feel sure their paths must have crossed. Maybe they sweated
together in the dim inferno of the Tenth Street Turkish and Russian Baths, which had opened for business nine years earlier. I see
them, shoulder to shoulder, waiting patiently for a salami or a
piece of pickled herring at the counter at Katz's Delicatessen,
established in 1888 on East Houston Street at the corner of Ludlow. Except that before his sojourn on the Lower East Side, Butch
had spent most of his life rustling horses and robbing trains
in Wyoming and Utah, where such delicacies were doubtless
unknown, and still may be, and except that my grandfather was
probably a foot shorter than Butch and Sundance, which would
have made rubbing shoulders a feat.

Maybe their paths crossed one bright Sunday at Tenth Street
and Second, as Butch and Sundance headed into St. Mark's-in-
the-Bowery, a stately church already a hundred years old, and my
grandfather, not much of an Episcopalian, walked south, past the
dozen Yiddish-language theaters lining the avenue, giving a
neighborly smile to the Gershwin boys, then only three and five
years old. The remains of Dutch governor Peter Stuyvesant,
whose farm stretched south from East 17th Street and covered
half the Lower East Side, lay in a vault somewhere beneath that

church. He died in 1672, two centuries too soon to meet my grandfather and his new friends from Utah.

Such are my deepest meditations as I stand patiently at the counter at Katz's, waiting for my pastrami on rye, the only still point in a turning world. Outside, everything is undergoing tumultuous and ceaseless rearrangement. Change has always been the essence of the Lower East Side, and each new wave can barely cover up the last before the next wave crashes into it.

Some things stay the same. Only here at Katz's is the succulent pastrami still cut by hand. So what if the place has become a bit of a dump? You should look so good at 110. Peter Stuyvesant still presides over two square miles of nineteenth- and early-twentieth-century houses and tenements built to catch a nearly endless flow of immigrants, first the Irish and the Germans (*Kleindeutschland*, it was called), then the Jews and Italians, and *finally* Hispanics and Chinese, though on the Lower East Side nothing is final for more than a year at a time. Of the numberless Irish saloons, only McSorley's on East Seventh Street is left. Of the Jewish population from Eastern Europe, which reached 400,000 in 1920, only a few of its 500 synagogues and religious schools remain, only one of its dozens of public baths and one of its bakeries—Kossar's on Grand Street, justly famous for its bread of Bialystok—only Katz's and the dairy restaurant Ratner's,* Guss's Pickles, and a creditable newcomer (only 45 years young) the 2nd Avenue Deli. Plus there's Gertel's rugelach baked upstairs at 35 Hester Street and the Streit Matzoh Company at 150 Rivington Street. And best of all, I think, near Katz's on Houston, is Russ & Daughters, which is still called an "appetizing store," now back at the top of its form, lined with spotless cases of smoked and pickled fish and caviar and tangy sweet unadulterated cream cheese that makes the supermarket version seem like library paste.

In the early sixties, the area to the north of Houston was renamed the East Village, probably by some real-estate broker eager to borrow the prestige of the rich establishment bohemia

*As of the year 2000, Ratner's is no longer dairy or kosher.

of Greenwich Village to the west. And ten years before that it had already become, along with parts of San Francisco, the center of the Beat movement. (Jack Kerouac wrote *On the Road* in 1951 in an apartment just north of here.) Then the Beats were succeeded by the hippies, by coffeehouses and music clubs, bookshops and bars, theaters like the Fillmore East, and publications like the *East Village Other* and *Fuck You: A Magazine of the Arts*. Just out of graduate school, I visited the poet Allen Ginsberg in his East Village walk-up to coax him into some project or other. By then his neighborhood was skidding downhill, full of crime, abandoned buildings, and open-air drug supermarkets. Ginsberg, who died in April 1997, never lost sight of the crucial core values. "I have the secret, I carry / subversive salami in / my ragged briefcase / Garlic, Poverty, a will to Heaven," he once wrote.

The lure of cheap housing stabilized the East Village and parts of the Lower East Side in the 1980s, and now they are bubbling with gentrification. A brand-new restaurant or bar or club opens up every day, and I spend my evenings trying to visit them all—an impossible job considering the vertiginous pace of change.

From the corner of Houston and Ludlow, I walk north to meet a young friend on Sixth Street near Avenue A. One block away, between First and Second Avenues, is one of the most amazing streets in the entire area, with 18 inexpensive Indian restaurants along its south side alone, many with tandoori ovens and turbaned musicians in window seats. I recently dined at the two places that seem to have the best reputations, and would not return. Tonight we dine at Raga, an interesting attempt at Indian-American fusion. We eat very well.

Full and happy, my friend and I are ready to move on. She stands and shows off her dress. "Don't you love the lines?" she asks. "I feel it's reminiscent of what Holly Hunter wore at the Academy Awards the year she won for *The Piano*." Her dress is simple and black, and I have no idea what she is talking about. She has worn it so that after dinner we can go on to Lansky Lounge and its Thursday-night swing-dancing party, an event I have dreaded for months.

I decide to pick a fight. Lansky is behind and attached to Rat-ner's Dairy Restaurant on Delancey Street; it is said to be an old speakeasy. A man named Meyer Lansky began his career on the Lower East Side as the most famous Jewish racketeer, along with Bugsy Siegel, before a period of respectability at 211 Central Park West, where he lived happily until Senate hearings exposed him. Was Lansky Lounge named after a murderous gang-ster who probably victimized my grandfather? "Whatever," my friend replies with a giggle, trying to make me feel moralistic, middle-aged, and completely out of it.

In this aim she succeeds, and our plans for Lansky happily evanesce. I stuff her into a taxi, briefly consider returning home to bone up on boating safety by viewing a *Baywatch* rerun, then walk instead down First Avenue to my newest favorite bar, the four-year-old d.b.a., not because it is hip or much to look at, but because, with 150 types of beer, 100 single-malt Scotches, 35 tequi-las, and a very pleasant garden, it is a fine place for a drink or two before, after, or instead of dinner. Some bars serve snacks, some serve up entertainment—comedy or jazz—and some entertain only with amusing themes or decor. A place called Global 33 does all of these quite well and serves many delicious little plates of global fusion. America must be proud as punch that alcohol is back among its youth, washing away all that nasty reefer. There are, however, ominous signs. The popular Drinkland, across from Tompkins Square Park, has a red rope and huge bouncers out front. The red-rope syndrome is slowly and insidiously spreading, and if this continues, the informality and fluidity of nightlife in the East Village and the Lower East Side will come to an end—and the area, for me, will be totally over.

Little Osaka is somebody's name for what is happening on East Ninth Street between Second and Third Avenues and on St. Mark's to the south, an absolutely authentic and spontaneous efflorescence of informal Japanese food—bar food, you could call it. Many is the evening I have constructed an amusing itinerary beginning at the tiny Angel's Share cocktail lounge upstairs at 8 Stuyvesant Street (a fork off Ninth), moving on to Yakitori-

Taisho at 5 St. Mark's Place, returning to Village Yokocho (really the room next to Angel's Share), then down the street to the spiffy Sobaya, and ending up at the down-and-dirty sake bar called Decibel across the street. The customers at all these places are predominantly young, sophisticated Japanese tourists. At Yakitori-Taisho you sit at a long counter, behind which are bearded, headbanded young Japanese cooks at steaming woks and fiery grills turning out skewers of chicken skin and chicken hearts, savory omelets of pork and kimchi, bacon rolls, and deep-fried delicacies of every kind—perhaps a hundred choices in all. And back at Village Yokocho, the menu is similar, but with more raw-fish tidbits like eel roe and more steamed dumplings. And then there's Rai Rai Ken, a new ramen place; just across the street is an oyaku stand (octopus fritters). While you are at it, you can shop for groceries upstairs next door at the Sunrise Mart, the best place downtown for all ingredients Japanese.

Everything on East Ninth Street is savory and inexpensive, and some of it is nearly as weird as the weird parts of Tokyo. As far as I can tell, this phenomenal block is entirely unplanned and spontaneously emerged from the chaos—just as the entire Lower East Side has always been emerging, ever since Peter Stuyvesant bought the farm.

At the southern end of the Lower East Side lies the largest Chinese community outside of Asia, with a population of over 100,000. I have read that the land under Chinatown was a summer fishing and hunting ground for the Manhattan Indians until 1626, when they sold it to the Dutch and moved north. This is where the Dutch put their farms, their *boujery* (later anglicized as Bowery), outside the walled city of New Amsterdam, which was all the way downtown. Peter Stuyvesant, its last governor, had a nephew named Nicholas Bayard, who raised hogs and cattle right around here, on his *boujery*. The livestock business dominated the area even after the British replaced the Dutch in 1664—Joshua Pell and John Mott were prominent butchers—and by 1805, the tanneries had so badly polluted the freshwater pond nearby that a 24-foot-wide drainage ditch was dug to the Hudson

River. Later, it was covered over and named Canal Street. Doyers Street was a private driveway leading from the Bowery to Hendrik Doyers's distillery, where the Chinatown post office is now, across and down Doyers Street from the Nom Wah Tea Parlor, the oldest extant restaurant in Chinatown, founded in the 1920s, and now, I fear, on its last legs, as are the once numerous Chinese coffee shops with their long Formica counters and steam cabinets filled with buns and dumplings.

In the 1840s, the Lower East Side was dominated by German and Irish immigrants. The first Chinese arrived when the seagoing junk *Kee Ying* visited New York Harbor from Canton in 1847, and several of those aboard jumped ship. In the 1880s, Italians, Greeks, and Jews arrived, including my grandparents. Wo Kee, the first Chinese grocery, opened on Mott Street in 1878, and that same year, the U.S. Supreme Court decided that, unlike other immigrants, the Chinese did not have the right to become American citizens. Bigotry against Chinese immigrants, which inspired riots in San Francisco and the burning of the Chinatown there, was at least as powerful as that against other newcomers. Even the great urban reformer Jacob Riis could write these words about the Chinese in *How the Other Half Lives* (Scribner's, 1890): "[The] poison that proceeds from Mott Street puts mind and body to sleep, to work out its deadly purpose in the corruption of the soul . . . [T]he Chinese are in no sense a desirable element of the population . . . they serve no useful purpose here. . . . For the Chinese there is neither hope nor recovery, nothing but death— moral, mental, and physical death."

Do you remember how we were all taught in high school that Jacob Riis was a champion of immigrants and an American hero? Maybe we should actually have read his book, which is condescending to southern Italians and anti-Semitic to boot. Not all Manhattanites perceived or imagined Chinatown the way Riis did. I have seen contemporaneous photographs of swanky uptowners, beautifully dressed, descending from their carriages onto a spotless Pell street to dine at the renowned restaurant Chinese Delmonico's. And in 1891, the popular musical "A Trip to

Chinatown" opened at the Madison Square Theater. It ran for 650 performances and moved to Milwaukee, where its hit song, "After the Ball," was added, the first to sell more than 5 million copies (in sheet music, of course).

It was not until 1943, and our alliance with China during World War II, that the legislative exclusion of Chinese immigrants was relaxed. In 1965, the doors were opened wider, and more than ever, New York's Chinatown became the first stop in America for poor Cantonese, few of whom spoke any English.

I have gone down to Chinatown twice a month for the past 20 years, and I am surprised every time. Last week I began where Mott Street begins and headed south into what used to be Little Italy. Mott Street is now lined on both sides for blocks and blocks with Chinese markets spilling out onto the sidewalks, piled high with emerald vegetables and every kind of fish, and a little store from which you can telephone Hong Kong, Taiwan, and mainland China for between 59 and 79 cents a minute. I have walked on market streets in Asia that felt roomier.

After 20 years I know nothing about this place. Seventy percent of its population is foreign born, many know only the few words of English they need for their jobs and have never carried on an extended conversation with a Caucasian. About a fifth are here illegally, and many never venture outside Chinatown. The only thing I know about the people of Chinatown is a little about their food and their 300 restaurants. Or is it 600?

I cross Canal Street and down into the original Chinatown, eight blocks of tenements that, since 1965, when the U.S. immigration laws were eased, have exploded northward to occupy an area many times that size—two square miles of warehouses, apartments, and factory buildings. I am meeting friends on the corner of Bayard and Mott streets, and I am late. We often eat together in Chinatown, and today we have a massive agenda. First, I have spotted a brand-new vegetarian dim sum restaurant and cannot live much longer without trying it. And then, we will eat two kinds of *lop cheung* and dine at a Cantonese restaurant named Wah Sing Lau. I have heard it is Ang Lee's favorite restaurant in Chinatown, and I need to try it immediately. The opening scenes of Ang Lee's movie *Eat Drink Man Woman* are probably the greatest piece of film about food ever shot—even including the climactic dinner scene in *Babette's Feast,* which comes in second, tied with the fireworks banquet in *Vatel.* Anybody who understands food as profoundly as Ang Lee evidently does must be followed to the very ends of Canal Street.

My friends and I soon come upon Bayard Meat Market. The window is filled with flattened, salted, dessicated animals and parts of animals: five pigs' heads, for example; a whole little pig, with its four paws splayed in the four directions of the compass, plus ducks and geese. Sometimes, the device used to press them seems to have dragged and twisted, and facial features like the little pigs' snouts and cheeks end up grotesquely off center.

Everybody in the shop laughs with great enjoyment when I ask to buy the nicest pig's head of all. I suppose it is their mascot. Pointing to a snow-white, salted, pressed duck hanging next to it, they say, "Same as duck. You cook like duck. You buy duck." So I buy duck, one quarter of a pressed duck for $2.45, and two boned legs and some *lop cheung* as well—the wonderful Chinese sausage, deep red in color (but not so dark as the commonly displayed duck blood sausage), about six inches long, very skinny, and sold in pairs, linked by a white string.

One of my companions is Henry Hugh. Henry, who is waiting outside the shop to avoid embarrassment, is a fine Chinese cook who long ago was head chef at the Yun Luk Rice Shoppe in Chinatown—and earned rave reviews from the newspapers uptown and standing-room crowds downtown. He explains that these pressed ducks began as whole, fresh Pekin (a.k.a. Long Island) ducks; were split in half down the breast (not the back), generously salted, and pressed under a heavy weight; and then here dried for a day or so in the sun and wind on an open Chinatown roof. *Lop cheung* sausage is also dried this way, which is why Chinese sausages are often called "wind-dried." These days, with roofs in short supply, the drying may be performed indoors using electricity.

Henry advises me to boil the duck in several changes of water and then steam it, with some of the meat cut into bite-size strips and some left in large pieces, some on a rack over water in a wok, and some over rice to catch the juices. (When I get home, I follow Henry's instructions. Even then, the duck is very chewy and a bit too salty; it would have been delicious shredded, with vegetables.)

We pass hundreds of shiny, mahogany-hued, Cantonese roast ducks hanging in the windows of Chinatown's many noodle shops. Some of the best restaurants here—New York Noodletown on the corner of Bowery and Pell is a fine example—have evolved from the old noodle shops. My friends at Noodletown gave me a lesson last year in the marinating and roasting of ducks and pigeons and whole pigs and piglets. You lower them into the small round opening at the top of a battered cylindrical fiery stainless-steel oven six feet high and three feet in diameter, and roast them for about 45 minutes.

We next stopped at a place whose name must remain a secret—at the restaurant's request. One of its employees has smuggled in four *lop cheung* sausages from Hong Kong, where you find the best *lop cheung* in the world, and we arrange for a comparative tasting of the local and contraband versions, all cooked in the same traditional way—first steamed, then stir-fried with chunks of unboned, skinned chicken, or with a mixture of vegetables, including snow peas, which to my amazement Henry says are rare in real Chinese cooking except in *lop cheung* dishes. I had never tasted Hong Kong *lop cheung,* which is made with lots of high-proof spirits. It is intensely aromatic and alcoholic and sweet, an astounding new taste epiphany that I will pursue to the very shores of Asia the next chance I get.

We leave our secret eating place, bubbling with enjoyment, though wondering why the local sausage, which was not at all unpleasant, is only a pale imitation of the Hong Kong version. Henry gives me an oral recipe for what is perhaps the greatest *lop cheung* dish, sausage with lotus root and Chinese celery—thin stalks that have a powerful celery taste—stir–fried with just a little sugar, salt, and broth. You add a bit of cornstarch if the starch from the lotus root does not sufficiently bind everything together. As we walk back to the heart of Chinatown, I purchase the required vegetables at one of a thousand little outdoor markets whose rents per square foot have been reported to be higher than Tiffany's on Fifth Avenue.

We spend the next few hours consuming two complete lunches. The brand-new Vegetarian Dim Sum House at 24 Pell Street serves what you might call facsimile food. In the typical style of Chinese vegetarianism, bean curd and wheat gluten are made to look and taste just like meat, chicken, duck, and fish. Chinatown already possesses several restaurants of this sort—though none specializes in dumplings and other snack food. And Vegetarian Dim Sum House stands at a higher level of both quality and dissimulation. The "tasty turnip cake (steamed or fried)" is even better, fried, than the traditional ham-flecked version because the taste of the turnips comes through. The vegetarian shrimp dumplings are astounding in their ability to simulate shrimp and delicious in themselves, as are the vegetarian roast-pork buns, and the stir-fried vegetables with mock smoked ham (a dead ringer), and the mango pudding, made without eggs.

Wah Sing Lau Chinese Restaurant, at 72 Bayard Street, the site of our second lunch, turns out to be a serious and excellent Cantonese restaurant where nobody has ever heard of Ang Lee. (Later, I telephoned the film director himself in the New York suburb where he and his family now live, and he has never heard of Wah Sing Lau. Ang Lee likes the restaurant First Taste, where I have never dined. [Henry tells me that their chef has moved to Lucky's.] He spends more time shopping and eating in Flushing, Queens, than in Chinatown, because he is Taiwanese and Chinatown is Cantonese. Now he mostly cooks himself, except when he is shooting or editing. Much to my disappointment, Ang Lee reports that by making *Eat Drink Man Woman,* he has gotten his obsession with food out of his system, cinematically at least, though I would not call the glimpses of food in *Sense and Sensibility* small potatoes.)

Just as at so many other good restaurants in Chinatown, the printed menu at Wah Sing Lau could have been found at any other Cantonese restaurant. The waiters do not admit to knowing much English, and true specialties appear in Chinese characters on vertical red signs hanging in rows on the wall. Even with Henry Hugh at our table, the waiters are skeptical that we will appreciate the food. Then, when we insist, they suggest more than the usual number of challenging dishes, a way of testing us, I suppose: salted baked whole frog; duck's intestines and tip of pig's stomach (each stomach yields only three or four pieces of tip, so you can imagine the number of pigs sacrificed for our sake), both with black-bean sauce; bamboo fungus in bean-curd skin; eel, shown to us live before it is cooked; and so forth. The meal starts with *lai tong,* or "standard soup," which every customer automatically receives at home-style Cantonese restaurants, long-simmered chicken broth fortified with whatever is left over that day. Nearly everything that follows is delicious, and by the end of the meal our rapport with the waiters and the chef has grown jolly and a little bit raucous.

In the 1980s, when huge flows of flight capital—transfers of money from Hong Kong, Taiwan, and even the Chinese mainland—invigorated the Chinatowns of Vancouver, Sydney, and Toronto ten years ago, only a comparative trickle was attracted to New York's Chinatown, which was considered impossibly downscale by the Hong Kong rich, who would never consider owning a condominium here.

But a host of excellent chefs were attracted to New York, and the result was an entertaining series of garish and glitzy new restaurants—many of them very good but none on the level of those in Hong Kong or Vancouver—plus the improvement of the older restaurants, and the recognition of the noodle shop as a kind of Chinese bistro. Until three or four years ago, there was a new sense of culinary excitement in Chinatown that now seems to have faded as chefs return to work in the booming economies of Hong Kong, China, and Taiwan. It is not hard to find excellent food in New York's Chinatown, but the infusion of new cooking talent has slowed. If you could assemble the best dishes from several places—the crab dumplings *(xiao lung bao)* at Joe's Shanghai (at least as good as any I've eaten in Shanghai), the turnip cakes at the Vegetarian Dim Sum House, the stuffed bean-curd skin at Wah Sing Lau, and the salt-baked flounder or fish cake with preserved vegetable at New York Noodletown, you would have a nearly perfect Chinese dinner.

I leave my friends and walk alone down Mott Street to Chatham Square, named for William Pitt, Earl of Chatham, who tried to prevent violence between Britain and her American colonies. Near here, 350 years ago, black slaves freed by the Dutch started their first settlement, and the Sephardic Jews of New Amsterdam, prohibited from practicing their religion within the city walls, established their first cemetery. I turn left along East Broadway, pass a newsstand where I resist the Hong Kong edition of *Penthouse* for $25 (U.S.), and pause before a poster for Cobra, a five-woman rock group from Beijing performing tonight on East Houston Street. Soon I am walking past the shops and restaurants of Chinatown's newest immigrants, the Fujianese, commonly associated in the press these days with gang violence and heroin trafficking. Outward evidence of extortion, gambling, and gang activity is hidden from tourists' eyes to protect the restaurant businesses so important to the family associations, the tongs, that run Chinatown. The Fujianese have long been considered pirates and brigands.

I walk six blocks north on Allen Street. Just past the Zhen Jui Shi Temple, home of the largest carved wooden Buddha in North America, I reach the corner of Delancey and Orchard streets. This is where my immigrant grandparents lived and where my father was born 91 years ago.

CROSSING THE LINE

The crash of Pacific waves in Rosarito in the Mexican state of Baja California still boomed in my ears as I stood in my Manhattan kitchen, trying to recapture one particular, perfect taco—a translucent tortilla wrapped around a juicy mound of *carne asada,* savory chunks of grilled beef. This is a common enough treat in Baja California, but there is nothing common about the *carne asada* at a taco stand in Rosarito Beach named Tacos el Yaqui, or about the other delicious things that nestle alongside it: the *salsa ranchera,* a medley of precisely chopped, perfectly fresh onions, tomatoes, and cilantro; the *salsa roja,* a thin, powerful homemade chile sauce; and the bright, barely lumpy avocado puree—a slightly liquid version of guacamole. Pinto beans are optional, and cheese melted into the tortilla costs a little more, as does a side order of carefully charred jalapeño peppers. And when your *taco de carne asada* is complete and handed to you on a real ceramic plate, you peek inside only long enough to squeeze the juice of half a lime over everything, close it up again, open your mouth wide, and enter into a high gastronomic state.

It was the tortilla part that was proving the most elusive, and every morning in New York City brought a new and unexpected variety of failure. Yet there was a woman somewhere in or around Rosarito who every day rolled out 30 or 40 *dozen* of the most savory tortillas I had ever tasted. And she still refused to see me.

A few months earlier, a friend in San Diego named Dinah Grisdale had put me onto Tacos el Yaqui. My wife and I had just set up the Southern California end of our newly bicoastal existence. Friends and neighbors warned us not to drive our own car over the Mexican border to Tijuana and points south, not to drive ourselves at all, to take a trolley to the border and walk in, or to hire a military tank complete with crew. Instead, we drove the 18 minutes from our house near the heart of San Diego to the Mexican border and breezed across. Almost immediately, we took the wrong exit and were dumped into the heart of a dilapidated commercial section of Tijuana crowded with car-wash and auto-detailing shops.

Though we lacked a map of this metropolis of 1.6 million people (good maps of Tijuana appear not to exist), it took us only 40 minutes to find our way to the highway again, but in the wrong direction, back toward San Diego, where we discovered an official U-turn lane (we were apparently not the first of 22 million yearly tourists to get confused). Soon, we were roaring down the Pacific coast toward our four planned meals of the day, one each in Rosarito, Puerto Nuevo, Ensenada (where we would also attempt to score a few kilos of illegal and dangerous diet pills), then back to Tijuana for dinner. Now, after 15 trips, we navigate like natives. But, at the time, as dusk descended upon Tijuana and we found ourselves climbing a hill covered with shanties, and lurched into a cul-de-sac populated by a group of late teenagers, I will concede that both of us were silently but frantically trying to remember how *The Bonfire of the Vanities* turned out.

The thrill of exploration tinged with occasional moments of fear kept us cheerful and alert all day, as did the prospect of the famous Pacific spiny lobsters of Puerto Nuevo, deep-fried in savory lard, a local household specialty first offered to tourists in the mid-1950s, and now available at 36 restaurants in a seaside village composed of six crisscrossing streets. In Ensenada, there would be the freshest seafood, raw and cooked, in stands around the port, including amazing black clams sitting in the darkest liquor—though no time for the famous old French restaurant El Rey Sol, or the universally recommended La Embotelladora Vieja. These would come months later.

Our first stop was the taco stand in Rosarito Beach. Dinah's instructions were vague. Leave the narrow pay highway, drive all the way through town, stop at the Rosarito Beach Hotel, and ask for directions to Tacos el Yaqui. Today we know five ways of getting there. But the fact that Tacos el Yaqui is located on the evocatively named intersection of Mar del Norte and Las Palmas is not one of them, because the streets are not marked. Next time you are in Rosarito Beach, drive on the main street to the far south end of town, turn left at the light just before the Rosarito Beach Hotel, and take the first left. On the very next corner, on your right, are the pristine parking lot and white-painted, open-air shed of Tacos el Yaqui, all crowned with the ubiquitous Pepsi sign.

Tacos el Yaqui was crowded when we arrived. We watched as a comical young man named Hugo flipped large sheets of meat over a wood fire and chopped them with a cleaver on a thick slice of oak tree, reheated the tortillas on a griddle, and assembled two tacos for us, starting with a generous helping of meat and a little of its juice. We sprinkled on a little salt and lime juice, bought two Pepsis, and sat down to eat our tacos. Even at this distance in space and time, my mouth waters uncontrollably as I think of that taco.

The chunks of beef had been lightly marinated, and though crisply charred on the outside, were still juicy within and flavored with the aroma of wood smoke. The *salsa ranchera* was crunchy and fresh, the *salsa roja* musky and deeply flavored. The tortilla was chewy, savory, lightly browned, and puffed in spots but nearly translucent elsewhere, and layered within so that it never felt dense or heavy. It was so different from the wheat flour tortilla we knew, the kind you get wrapped around burritos— huge, floppy, nearly tasteless, thick, doughy, and bone white— that we thought it might have been made from corn. Those outsized flour tortillas and the wrap craze they have recently spawned are, apparently, border distortions of the true wheat tortilla of the Sonoran desert south of Arizona, small and quite similar to the tortillas we tasted at Tacos el Yaqui. Gigantic burritos, 12 or 15 inches long and stuffed five inches thick with everything you can imagine, reflect the American preference for triple cheeseburgers and pizzas with everything on them instead of the austerity of the Mexican desert.

Along many streets in Tijuana and the main thoroughfare in Rosarito Beach are strings of taco stands serving corn or wheat tortillas filled with chicken, pork, or beef tongue, tripe and other offal, flank steak or skirt steak, smoked marlin, roast kid. The most famous Baja California taco of all, now ubiquitous over the line in San Diego and spreading through the Southwest (probably because it is tasty and inexpensive) is a corn tortilla wrapped around crisply deep-fried white fish, a tangy white sauce (which can be approximated by mixing mayonnaise with yogurt), shredded cabbage, and a choice of salsas. It was discovered either in San Felipe or Ensenada by a young American entrepreneur, who brought it back to San Diego, opened a restaurant named Rubio's, and developed it into a chain.

I had always considered border food as a massive culinary misfortune, at least until the second or third bite of my *taco de carne asada* at Tacos el Yaqui had altered my entire belief system. Perhaps it was not until my second or third taco. No matter. How could anything so absolutely delicious, so carefully and intelligently made, so truly connected to the rest of Mexico, be condemned as inauthentic or expedient, I asked myself. Not all border food, I now understood, is Velveeta melted over beans and corn chips, or swollen burritos. Aren't the great cuisines of Alsace, the Veneto, the Basque country between France and Spain, and, I have heard, the subtropical region between Thailand and China, all border food? For that matter, isn't all food border food, continually renewed by novel ingredients from the outside, precariously perched on the frontier between yesterday and tomorrow?

It was then that I decided to return to Tacos el Yaqui until I had mastered their magnificent specimen of border food, their *taco de carne asada*.

Baja California is a very long, narrow, arid peninsula that stretches 760 miles south from the southern border of our state of California (Alta California to the Mexicans) and varies between 25 and 150 miles in width. It is separated from the mainland of Mexico by the Sea of Cortés (we call it the Gulf of California) and is linked to it only by a narrow strip below the Arizona border. The peninsula makes up two states of Mexico—Baja California and Baja California Sur. Its largest city is the border town of Tijuana, just off the Pacific coast, and its capital is Mexicali, also a border town, 120 miles across the peninsula to the east. Educated Mexicans do not refer to the state of Baja California as Baja, the way we do (*baja* simply means low, short, or humble), or to Tijuana as TJ (pronounced *tee-jay*), as they do in San Diego. The inhabitants are called *Bajacalifornianos* (or just *Californianos*), and, in English, they refer to their state as Lower California and our state as Upper California.

One day I had lunch in Tijuana with Graciela Sandez de Gutiérrez and her husband, Roberto. Graciela, who was born near the remote southern tip of the peninsula, has spent 25 years researching food history and will soon, one hopes, publish her magnum opus, *Evolución Gastronómica de Baja California*. We met at the excellent Casa del Mole, which specializes in the deeply flavored sauces and soft corn tortillas from the city of Puebla in central Mexico. Graciela explained that corn—the New World staple that has since prehistory supported human life from Texas to Tierra del Fuego—was once unknown in Baja California, which was isolated from the Mexican mainland until Cortés landed there in 1535. The natives were among the most primitive he had encountered in the Americas, living in small, Stone Age settlements isolated both from one another and from the great Indian civilizations on the mainland. They had no agriculture, no corn, and subsisted on reptiles, snakes, and insects. Their vegetables were wild roots such as jicama and yuca. Cortés founded the settlement of Las Cruzes and quickly returned to the mainland.

The first missionaries to establish a lasting beachhead nearly 200 years later were Italians, not Spanish. The Pope had parceled out the various regions of Mexico not among the European nations, but among the Catholic religious orders, and the Jesuits got Baja California, apparently as a sort of punishment. The Italian fathers Juan Maria Salvatierra and Francisco Maria Piccolo disembarked near the southern end of the peninsula in 1697, founded a series of towns, and taught the natives the rudiments of building and agriculture. They brought their own staple wheat, for baking bread and making pasta, and while there are no records of their pasta recipes, Graciela feels sure that the typical, modern-day Baja California dish of noodles with chorizo sausage must derive from those times. When the idea of tortillas developed (or was imported from the rest of Mexico), wheat fit with the climate and agriculture of Baja California as corn had done elsewhere. Epidemics later wiped out most of the natives, and the religious orders that succeeded the Jesuits worked their way up from the south while cattle ranchers and *mestizo* Mexicans from Sonora settled the less forbidding northern part of the state, bringing cowboy cooking and a love for grilled beef. Somewhere along the way, the *taco de carne asada* in a wheat tortilla was destined to emerge.

In the early 1900s, the Mexican government granted copper mining concessions on the east coast of Baja California to the French, who could lure neither French workers nor Mexicans into their sweltering and toxic mines. They turned to Chinese agricultural workers from the United States. These men had stayed after the completion of the railroad to clear the Central Valley of California, working from north to south, where they reached the Mexican border and the city of Mexicali. There are now 80 Chinese restaurants in Mexicali, most of them *cantonesa,* according to Graciela, with hot chiles added, and a bowl of limes on every table.

The most fateful foreign influence on the food of Baja California in the last century came from Italian cooks and restaurateurs who flocked to Tijuana in the early 1920s to establish restaurants near the casino and the racetrack after the advent of Prohibition in the United States. It was Tijuana's heyday, and led by Hollywood stars such as Clark Gable and Jean Harlow (the two names proudly given in every popular history of the time), Southern

Californians (including the 12-year-old Julia Child and her parents) came down for exotic weekends of gambling, drinking, and, after 1924 or 1925, eating Caesar salad, probably Tijuana's most famous culinary creation—romaine lettuce, with croutons steeped in garlicky oil, and a dressing of lemon juice, a little Worcestershire, briefly cooked eggs, good olive oil, salt, pepper, and freshly grated Parmesan cheese.

This is not the place, nor am I the person, to arrive at a definitive history of the salad at Caesar Cardini's famous Italian restaurant in Tijuana. Every newspaper or magazine article giving a recipe for the dish includes one version of its invention or another, and they cannot all be correct. Firsthand research has been done by Julia Child (from both memory and an interview with Cardini's daughter, who lived in Los Angeles), by Diana Kennedy (who attributes the dressing to Caesar but the salad to his brother Alex, who immigrated in 1926 and prepared the dish for her in the 1970s), and by Graciela. Both her parents and Roberto's were friends of Caesar Cardini, and she has interviewed many of his employees. On one central issue, endlessly debated both in the press and the serious food literature, there is no doubt in her mind: A true Caesar salad does not admit anchovies, except for those used in the manufacture of the mandatory Worcestershire sauce.

I have no personal opinion concerning the anchovies, though I would surely trust Graciela. No, my mission in Baja California was more essential, the taco at Tacos el Yaqui. My second visit produced nothing—nobody would even admit owning the place. But soon enough, my elegant command of high school Castilian Spanish and my eagerness to sit there on a bench, eating one *taco de carne asada* after another, broke the ice. I learned that Yaqui is the nickname of Felipe Nuñez, now 47, who came to Tijuana from the state of Zacatecas in central Mexico as a teenager with the triple goal of crossing the border, making lots of money in the United States, and returning to Zacatecas to marry. He accomplished none of these and ended up as a cook in Rosarito. Years later, he opened a little taco stand, which gained a huge following, and soon, with the money he had earned, bought a piece of land one block from the main street and constructed Tacos el Yaqui. His customers are predominantly locals; the taco stands on the main road cater to tourists who will never return.

I also learned that the word for Mr. Nuñez's heavy, rough iron grill is *el asador* and that the butcher shop he uses is Pablo y Alicia, a few blocks north on the main street. On my third trip from New York City to Rosarito Beach, I visited Pablo y Alicia and discovered that the cut of beef they sell to Yaqui is called *arrachera,* which only a Spanish dictionary compendious enough to include words for plumbing supplies and cuts of meat finally revealed to be flank steak. Mr. Nuñez agreed to have an identical *asador* made for me, and a month later, I wrestled it back to San Diego to practice grilling *arrachera.* While other taco places use gas griddles or grills, Yaqui burns aromatic woods—*encina,* both white and red, plus some mesquite and manzanita. *Encina,* known officially as coast live oak, has given its Spanish name to the southern California towns of Encino and Encinitas and its English name to Oakland, where an impressive stand of the trees once stood. Yaqui must drive an hour northeast to Tecate on the U.S. border to find *encina.*

On my fourth visit, I discovered that Yaqui's son, Gerardo, a college student who drives daily into Tijuana, speaks very good English, and soon Yaqui agreed to show me everything—except for his secret marinade, which he would never reveal.

Every morning at 6:30, Mr. Nuñez arrives to make the guacamole, the *salsa ranchera,* and the *salsa roja* in a little kitchen behind the stand; on busy weekends, he makes everything again at around noon, a lucky circumstance for me, as I was able to watch him without having to awake at five in the morning. His helper peeled, pitted, and crushed 18 or 20 Haas avocados (the smaller, tastier, creamier ones in the dark, nubbly skin) with a potato masher, while Yaqui used a blender to make a coarse puree from a large peeled white onion, a small handful of cilantro, and two cups of water. This he poured over the avocados, mashing everything until the texture was only slightly lumpy. For the *salsa ranchera*, Yaqui simply chopped, into regular cubes that measured about a quarter inch per side or a little more, ten large white onions, each about four inches across, and halved 20 three-inch tomatoes. To these he added a handful of cilantro, mainly the leaves chopped pretty fine, and about a quarter cup of salt.

The *salsa roja* was adapted from his mother's Zacatecan recipe. It began with *chiles de árbol*—red, three inches long, available only dried, and extremely hot. After a helper removed the long stem (also called the tail), Mr. Nuñez toasted them on the stove in a burnt-out old pot; as apparently happens every day, the chile fumes forced everybody to run, coughing, from the kitchen, including Mr. Nuñez and me. When the noxious gases had subsided, he boiled a dozen halved tomatoes in water just until the orange foam they gave off covered the surface. (His mother would have used green tomatillos.) He put about two loosely packed cups of the toasted chiles, which had shed most of their seeds through their open ends, into the blender, covered them with tomato cooking liquid, added five or six of the tomato halves and about a teaspoon of salt, and pureed everything until the only solids remaining in the liquid were tomato and chile seeds.

These were the easy parts. But how could I duplicate Mr. Nuñez's perfect tacos without the proper tortillas? The woman who made them was named Estela, and she lived about a mile from the stand. I nagged Gerardo to telephone her. It is sometimes difficult for a New Yorker to understand that not everybody in the world cares about his or her 15 minutes of fame. What if I asked to hire her as a teacher and paid her a fee, I wondered aloud. That would only make things worse, Gerardo replied. But if Estela could see how benign I am, and how interested in her work, perhaps she would relent. Gerardo telephoned. We were free to visit her tomorrow!

Three days in a row, I drove down from San Diego, picked up Gerardo at the taco stand, and drove to Estela's house. On the first day, Estela's daughter cracked open the door by an inch or so and informed us that Estela was at a funeral. I ate two tacos and drove back to San Diego. The day after that, the daughter told us that Estela was at her mother's house, paying a sick call. I had 36 hours left in the San Diego–Tijuana region, and I was getting desperate. So, when we were given the same excuse on the third day, I asked the daughter to telephone Estela at her mother's house and urge her to return home. At last, Estela's daughter revealed that her mother had been inside all along and was simply too shy to see me. And now, Estela was so ashamed of having lied that she could not bear to see me because it was against the Catholic religion to lie.

So, I put forth a brilliant plan, and everybody agreed, including Estela, somewhere inside. Gerardo and I stood by the front door. Estela left the house through the back door, crossed several neighbors' yards, reached the road where her mother lived, and then came walking home as if she had been out all along. We greeted her as though we knew nothing and inquired after her mother, and she welcomed us to her house.

At first, Estela would only describe the process of making wheat tortillas because she had no flour or lard on hand, and the water wasn't right today. Seeing that I was desolated, her daughter urged Estela to give a full demonstration, and soon a 50-pound sack of flour materialized and a kilo of lard, and within minutes there were perfect, savory, bubbly, flaky, six-inch tortillas cooking on the griddle. Estela apologized for lying about her mother and about not having any flour as we ate the tortillas spread with fresh butter and folded in half. She had grown up in Chihuahua, where, like Sonora, tortillas are traditionally made from wheat flour and are six inches in diameter.

I am counting the days until my next trip to San Diego. Now I have it all: the tortilla, the proper cut of meat, the limes, the oak, some sample marinades, the *asador*, and Mr. Nuñez's recipes for guacamole, *salsa ranchera*, and *salsa roja*. After a year's work, I am ready to attempt a masterpiece, a fast-food snack from just over the Mexican border.

TACOS CON CARNE ASADA
(From Tacos el Yaqui)

Every morning at 6:30, Mr. Nuñez (known to everybody as Yaqui) arrives to make guacamole, *salsa ranchera,* and *salsa roja* in a little kitchen behind his stand. The *carne asada* is flank steak; each piece is sliced into two thin, flat sheets, marinated, grilled over a hot wood fire, kept warm briefly in a covered pot, and chopped at the last minute with a cleaver on a piece of wood, as the wheat tortillas are reheated on the warm griddle.

Hugo assembles each taco by holding a tortilla in the palm of one hand while spooning the ingredients into it with the other. First goes in a heaping ¼ cup of chopped grilled beef, and over that 1 tablespoon of *salsa ranchera,* 1 teaspoon of *salsa roja,* and 2 teaspoons of guacamole. Hugo wraps up the tortilla and hands it to you on a plate. Most customers open their taco, sprinkle it with salt and generous squeezes of lime, and wrap it again before eating.

Now for the guacamole, *salsa ranchera, salsa roja, carne asada,* and tortillas, enough for 16 tacos:

GUACAMOLE

1¼ lbs. Haas avocados (the smaller, tastier, creamier ones
with the dark, nubbly skin)
½ small (2-inch diameter) white onion, cut into chunks
5 sprigs cilantro
¼ cup plus 2 Tbs. water

— — — — —

SALSA RANCHERA

½ lb. white onions, peeled
½ lb. ripe, red tomatoes, unpeeled but halved
6 sprigs cilantro
1 tsp. salt

SALSA ROJA

¼ cup dried *chiles de árbol*
1 small tomato (2½-inch diameter), trimmed and halved
¼ tsp. salt

CARNE ASADA

2 flank steaks, about 2 lbs. apiece
½ cup orange juice
2 tsp. cayenne pepper
2 tsp. ground black pepper
2 tsp. salt
1 cup olive oil, or vegetable oil
4 garlic cloves

WHEAT TORTILLAS

1 lb. unbleached all-purpose flour (3 cups measured
by the scoop-and-level method), plus additional flour
for coating the pieces of dough
1 Tbs. (scant) salt
½ cup minus 1 Tbs. lard, at cool room temperature
1¼ cups very warm water

- - - - -

The guacamole in these tacos is thinner, less lumpy, and blander than you would prefer with, say, tortilla chips. Peel, pit, and, in a large bowl, mash the avocados with a potato masher. In a blender, puree together the onion, cilantro, and water. Pour the mixture over the avocado and continue mashing until everything is combined and the remaining lumps are no large than a grain of rice, if that.
Yield: about 2 cups.

For the *salsa ranchera,* chop the onion and tomatoes into regular cubes, measuring about a quarter inch per side. (Each will yield about 1 cup.) Chop the cilantro, mainly the leaves, into fine pieces. In a bowl, combine the onions, tomatoes, cilantro, and the salt.
Yield: about 2 cups.

The *salsa roja* was adapted from Yaqui's mother's Zacatecan recipe. (She would have used green tomatillos rather than red tomatoes.) Snap off the stems or tail ends of the chiles and toast them in a cast iron skillet over medium-high heat, stirring frequently, until they are dark but not black. (Many of the seeds will fall out of the chiles and scorch as you toast them; these are discarded. Those that remain in the toasted chiles are included in the sauce.) Cut 1 small (2½-inch) tomato in half, place in a small saucepan, cover with water, bring to a boil, and cook until it gives off an orange foam. Put the toasted chiles in a blender, just cover with tomato cooking water, add the tomato halves and the salt, and puree until the only solids remaining in the sauce are the chile seeds.
Yield: about ½ cup.

The *carne asada* is made with flank steak. For 16 tacos, you will need 2 of them. Place them flat on your cutting board or counter. Place one hand flat to the top surface of the meat to

– – – – –

steady it. With your other hand, hold a long, sharp knife with its blade parallel to the counter, and slice each flank steak into 2 thin sheets of meat. Prepare the marinade by mixing together the orange juice, cayenne pepper, black pepper, salt, and olive oil. Combine by whisking with a fork. Peel and crush the garlic and place it in the mixture. Twenty or 30 minutes before grilling the meat, immerse all 4 pieces in the marinade. Then, brush off the garlic and grill over a very hot fire, preferably wood or lump charcoal sprinkled with a few wood chips, so that the outside of the meat is crisp and even charred in places but still medium rare and juicy within. As each piece is done, put it into a covered pot kept in a warm place. Then, with a thin, sharp cleaver or heavy knife, chop the meat into small chunks with a maximum dimension of ¼ inch. Some juices will collect in the pot. Spoon a little over the meat as you scoop it into the tortillas.

The tortillas are six inches in diameter, thin and savory, nothing like the swollen, floppy, floury burritos of Arizona and New Mexico and the Taco Bells beyond. Estela grew up in Chihuahua, where, as in Sonora and parts of Baja California, tortillas are traditionally made from wheat flour and not corn. When Estela finally demonstrated her method, she was fairly precise about the measurements. Plus, I had taken 8 tortillas, half of them uncooked, and weighed them as soon as I reached my battery of electronic scales in the big city. It was my inability to recapture Estela's hand techniques—kneading, rolling, and stretching—that robbed me of success until the seventh morning.

For 16 tortillas, put the flour into a large bowl; mix in the salt. Roll the lard in the flour mixture to coat it. Break it up between your fingers into several pieces, coating them also with flour. Continue breaking up the lard as though you were making American pie pastry. When you are done, the pieces of

- - - - -

lard will vary in size between that of coarse cornmeal and that of grains of rice. Again with your fingers, mix 1¼ cups of very warm water into the flour, using about ⅓ of the water at a time to moisten about ⅓ of the flour. Gather the dough and knead it in the bowl for a minute or two, pressing down with both fists, lifting the far side of the dough and folding it toward you, pressing down again, and occasionally turning over the entire mass of dough to get to the bits of dry flour on the bottom of the bowl. The dough will look somewhat shaggy and lumpy.

Divide the dough into 16 2-ounce patties and roll them well in flour. Estela can do this with amazing accuracy just by feel. You and I can forget about it. Instead, take all the dough from the bowl and roll it into a long sausage about 3 inches in diameter. Cut the sausage in half crosswise with a knife. Cut each half in half again; you will have 4 equal pieces. Follow the same procedure again with each of the 4 pieces, and you will have 16 disks. Roll them in flour, lay them flat, and let them rest for 10 to 15 minutes. Then, with a wooden rolling pin, preferably a 10-by-1-inch hardwood dowel like Estela's, roll 1 piece of dough at a time forward and back, turn it 90 degrees, roll again, and continue rolling and rotating until you have a rough 6-inch circle. If you have made the dough correctly, it will not stick or break.

Flop the tortillas from one palm to the other; done right, this will make them more circular. Then, resting each tortilla on one palm, press its edges here and there with your other hand where it may be uneven or thick, pulling on the tortilla where it is less than circular. Toss it onto a large preheated cast-iron frying pan or griddle over medium-low heat on your stovetop. How can you judge the temperature? If it is right, your tortilla will puff in several places in under a minute, and will brown lightly in several spots in 2 minutes or a little longer, after which you will turn it over. If the brown spots are

- - - - -

dark and the tortilla becomes white and dry, the flame is too
high. When you remove the tortilla from the heat and let it
cool for a moment or two, it will become nearly translucent in
places. Estela makes 40 dozen in 4 hours, or about 30 seconds
per tortilla including breaks. When they cool, she stacks them
up and wraps them in plastic bags, ready for Yaqui to pick up in
midmorning. He reheats them on his griddle as he needs
them.

Yield: 16 tortillas

WILDERNESS ENOW!

I had never seen the desert in bloom. Neither had my wife nor our resplendent golden retriever, Sky King. Three times I had traveled to the American Southwest for that very purpose. In all, I saw one or two tiny, crushed, dusty yellow specks on the ground and a small red flower improbably attached to a scarred and weary saguaro cactus. Plus, it was not even a proper desert, the kind with boundless, golden, undulating sand dunes and long, stark shadows. Instead it resembled a vast and vacant lot as far as the eye could see, pocked with anthills and snake holes, and lacking even one reddish mesa or purple canyon. This was all before Sky King was born. I am grateful he was spared the disappointment. Sky King does not yet handle disappointment gracefully.

Everybody promised me that this time would be different, and, as our story will reveal, they were right. The enormous Anza-Borrego Desert Region, two hours' drive northeast from San Diego, is famous for its wildflowers in the first weeks of spring. It has a Web site and a telephone number you can call for sometimes accurate wildflower bulletins and alerts. Two friends had just returned from the Anza-Borrego Desert Region, and it was certifiably in bloom.

The only vexing question was what to cook and eat in the desert wilderness. Nothing is more splendid than a picnic under a huge, spreading tree, even if the ants insist upon sharing your sandwich and the bees would like to put you into anaphylactic shock. The problem is, there are no spreading trees in the desert. One thing was certain—fully grown and several months past his third birthday, Sky King was finally old enough to learn that there is no such thing as a free lunch. His years as a purposeless and parasitic puppy were over. He was bred to be a work dog, a gun dog, a bird dog, a retriever, and he had already shown major talent in that direction. He had learned in only two tries to bring my *New York Times* from the end of the driveway just after sunrise, through the front door, up the stairs, and into the bedroom; drop it next to my sleeping head; and expect to be fed. I had resolved that, at the very least, he would carry his own food and water into the desert, and maybe some of ours.

My resolve was stiffened by the big albino bouncer blocking the entrance of the largest camping superstore in the country, as we approached with Sky King at our side. No dogs allowed, he announced, unless you're getting your dog fitted for a pack. We immediately decided to explore the wide world of dog packs. They are designed like horses' saddlebags and made of lightweight fabric and webbing. We loaded each pack with heavy objects from around the shop, attached them in succession to Sky King—some strapped around his chest or his belly, some padded to cushion the weight—and let him wander around the busy store, grinning self-consciously. As he showed no strong preference among them, we bought the least expensive, in blue, for $28. If the camping industry had offered the same model in a silvery fabric with titanium on the list of ingredients, we would have paid eight times as much. That's what titanium does these days to the price of museums, cafeterias, and camping equipment.

Turning our 85-pound puppy into a beast of burden was diverting enough, but that's all it was, a diversion. The crucial question remained. *Whatever would we eat in the California desert?* This, in turn, depended on where and how long we would stay. Twenty-five years had passed since my wife and I had mastered what today might be regarded as extreme backpacking. The idea of returning to the sport was tempting, perhaps more to my wife, who does Pilates twice a week, than to me. So we slid into one of the 20 tents set up all around the camping superstore, and

Sky King crawled in after us, and we lay there staring through the skylight at remembered stars and reminisced about dining on the trail.

Back then, we had started out cautiously with a few days of car-camping in Canada, and the next month took a three-day walk in the Adirondacks, carrying all our food, shelter, rain gear, sleeping bags, and kitchen. (Apart from the spiritual and aerobic virtues of sleeping in the wilderness, camping gives one an entirely free hand to research, shop for, and operate a parade of really cool toys.) Next it was Big Sur and the Rockies, and, finally, after three years' practice, an 11-day hike in the Grand Tetons in Wyoming, which was as long as anybody besides a trained athlete could walk without replenishing food and fuel. It had started as a ten-day hike, but on day nine we began reading a novel just published in paperback and were unwilling to move camp for the next 36 hours—until we had both finished *One Hundred Years of Solitude.*

Eliminating every unnecessary ounce of weight is essential to the extreme backpacker. That had been our primary principle. (My second favorite rule was "Never lose altitude unnecessarily," which enabled me to hold the moral high ground while subverting many of the exhausting side trips my wife regularly proposed.) Real food was out of the question, apart from the odd treat, because *real food contains much more water than nourishment.* A potato is 80 percent water. Our brains are 80 percent water. Some vegetables are 90 percent; most meat is 60 percent. Plus, a good fraction of real food goes into the trash—stalks, peel, fat, gristle, and bones. We bought Euell Gibbons's books (such as *Stalking the Wild Asparagus*) to see if we could live off the land. My wife identified a leaf or two and popped them into her mouth. I often did the same with pieces of dark chocolate, which I had identified early on as the most virtuous backpacking treat, for it contains less than 1 percent water and no waste. Otherwise, we carried freeze-dried and dehydrated dishes manufactured specially for backpacking, plus instant coffee, tea bags, packets of hot chocolate, and Quaker instant oatmeal, to all of which you just add boiling water. We always camped close to flowing water (and stopped for lunch near water) to avoid lugging it around and because it makes a lovely sound. Our stove was the all-brass Svea, an ancient classic using a liquid fuel called white gas, which you vaporize by pressurizing the fuel tank with a tedious hand pump.

All our weeks of extreme summer backpacking were training, we felt, for a trek in the Himalayas. In those days, athletes and campers tended not to dramatize or glorify themselves with words like "assault" or "extreme." And besides, we weren't going mountain- or rock-climbing, just taking a three-week walk through Nepal, with vistas of Everest and Kangchenjunga, to the Annapurna Sanctuary and back. (This is a spectacular valley about 14,500 feet above sea level surrounded by Annapurna I, Annapurna II, and several other of the tallest mountains in the world.) We could not afford a highly organized trek and would not have enjoyed one anyway, and so, after we landed in Kathmandu, we paid a nominal sum to the most illustrious organizer of expeditions, Mountain Travel, to plan our route and hire a head Sherpa, who would hire other Sherpas, and together they would guide us and carry most of our stuff.

We rendezvoused in a city called Pokhara, at the market, where Pasang Tsering Sherpa, our head guide, helped us buy food—lots of flour, rice, and lentils, six cabbages, spices, three dozen eggs, and canned goods, including canned cheese. And so we set off. Pasang knew some English; given his high status, he carried only a light day pack. Behind us were the head bearer—a huge and gentle Buddhist who carried all the food and cooking equipment and our tent and sleeping bags; a sweet, clownish male cook with a high voice and red nail polish; and two women, who carried the other Sherpas' baggage. We were way over-staffed. Pasang explained that an Air India strike had kept tourists away that spring and there was great unemployment among the Sherpas, which we were doing our part to cure.

Our staples were curried rice and chapatis stuffed with cheese—the dough was mixed, kneaded, rolled, filled, and griddled twice a day—supplemented with eggs and canned goods, which we had stridently resisted because it seemed wrong to bring canned shrimp and roast-beef hash onto the snowy peaks of the Himalayas. We had not yet discovered that there would be little food to buy in the villages along the way, although whenever we stopped, the Sherpas did try to collect a few wild greens. After a week, everything was gone except the chapatis and cheese, the rice, and our oatmeal breakfasts, which we cooked ourselves on the little Svea stove, just outside the doorway of our bright blue high-tech tent from home.

After two weeks, even the cheese was gone, and we were getting hungry. I had read that in the days before inmates are released from prison, many of them can think and talk about nothing but food—the best meals they have ever eaten and what they will eat as soon as they get out. With civilization only five days away, the same symptoms overtook my wife and me. One afternoon, as the shadows began to lengthen, I could control myself no longer and persuaded Pasang to find us a chicken when we reached the next village. As Pasang and the villagers were Buddhist and kept chickens only for their eggs, upon which they depended for their sustenance and very existence, the negotiations proved protracted and difficult. Then Pasang disappeared for a half hour (during which I silently contemplated various procedures for slaughtering, bleeding, and plucking chickens, about which I knew nothing) and returned with a bony and anemic fowl. My wife petted it, clutched it to her heart, and began sobbing. Villagers gathered round. Cannily sensing that I was no match for this ugly crowd, I surrendered the bird, left the farmer with his money, and made Pasang lead us in the gathering darkness to the next village, hoping that we would arrive ahead of the news of my humiliation.

In the four hungry days it took us to trudge back to Kathmandu, my wife and I were overcome by a sort of madness. We spent nearly every minute making precise and elaborate plans to take a detour on the way back to New York City and spend a week feasting in the south of France. As soon as we reached Kathmandu, she and I headed off in opposite directions.

Although her garments were tattered and torn and her skin crusty with weeks of Himalayan grit, my wife went straight to the French embassy, borrowed a copy of the most recent *Guide Michelin,* and phoned my parents for a large loan. I went on to Air India to change our tickets. As our fare had been very cheap and its terms highly restrictive, I stuffed a wad of Nepalese money into the ticket envelope, my first attempt at a bribe.

We met back at the hotel. My wife had succeeded in both of her assignments, and I had completely failed in mine, either by miscalculating the exchange rate or by stumbling over an unimpeachable employee. And then something miraculous happened. During dinner that night at a mediocre Chinese restaurant, the more we ate, the less fixated we became on food, so that by the end of breakfast the next morning we were even able to make small talk about the three weeks of unutterable beauty we had just shared. By lunchtime, all thoughts of La Côte d'Azur had vanished.

I have never forgotten this profound lesson—that hunger can scramble your brain as powerfully as any controlled substance or pretty woman. This is why the last time I allowed myself to become extremely hungry was on that very path from the Annapurna base camp to Kathmandu in the spring of 1975.

Back in the titanium tent on the floor of the camping superstore, Sky King had lost interest in our reminiscences and was softly snoring. It was decision time. My wife proposed that we should immediately and completely return to the art of backpacking, and she craftily dangled the idea that we would certainly need the lightest, totally state-of-the-art, two-human-one-dog tent either currently on the market or in laboratory development, and that I would be in charge of that complex purchase. I saw through her bribe with the speed of a Nepalese airline clerk. Our old tent—bright blue nylon and state-of-the-art in 1975— which had been stored away with our sleeping bags, packs, and cooking equipment for many years, shared all the vital statistics of today's top backpacking tents: seven and a half pounds in total weight, 58 inches high in the center, a floor area of 48 square feet, no center pole, and so forth. It had been made by a Colorado company named Gerry, now apparently and unjustly defunct. What kind of industry is this, anyway, that has made so few technical advances in 25 years? I exclaimed as I sprang from the tent, followed by Sky King.

We three made our choice. We would go backpacking into the desert and sleep there two nights—but only if we found our old tent and sleeping bags in good condition. If not, I would propose a secret alternative plan, which I had already formulated. Meanwhile, I was authorized to make one or two little purchases, while my wife and Sky King, whom the big albino bouncer was eyeing hungrily, retreated to the car. I bought a pair of lightweight Lowa hiking boots and, still wearing them, spent an hour in the food and cooking department, where I filled two of those oversize shopping carts with dehydrated and freeze-dried (marginally lighter) meals from every manufacturer, one brand having a built-in source of heat in every package; cooking pots—one set of featherlight titanium and one of black, nonstick aluminum; a kit that was advertised to allow you to do baking on the trail; a dozen cans of cooking gas, a mixture of butane and propane; and the most magnificent and satisfying purchase of them all—the coolest backpacking stove in the world, the tiny, titanium, three-ounce, costly Primus Alpine, with built-in piezoelectric lighter!

Later that day, while my wife searched for our decades-old equipment, Sky King and I played with our new Primus Alpine stove, no larger than a pack of cigarettes. First you screw it into the top of a gas canister, which serves as its base. Next you unfold and rearrange three vanes attached around the burner, so that they can support a pan as wide as 10 or 12 inches. Then, you simultaneously turn on the gas and click the starter, and a fierce circular blue flame spurts into life while emitting a continuous miniature roar. We boiled a quart of water in a titanium pot, and timed it at four minutes. We selected a packet of food at random, Potatoes Au Gratin from Backpacker's Pantry, emptied the contents, which were bright orange, into one and a half cups of boiling water, weren't told whether or not to cover, and cooked them slowly for 10 to 15 minutes, stirring as needed. The gratin was awful—thin little tesserae of barely cooked potato in a watery sauce, truly repulsive in taste and texture, and feloniously mislabeled: the surface of a gratin must be crisply and deliciously browned. That is its mission in life.* In a nearly unprecedented turn of events, Sky King refused even one taste, even one lick.

Other candidates for lunch and dinner in the Anza-Borrego Desert Region were more encouraging, including the Classic Three Cheese Lasagna from Natural High, which you prepare by adding boiling water to the plastic package, resealing with the plastic zipper, waiting awhile, and stirring. You eat it right out of the pouch, avoiding a messy cleanup. In common with other backpacking lasagnas we tried, here was another violation of the labeling laws; the dish was simply noodles in sauce. At a minimum, lasagna means a long, very wide noodle; typically, several of them are stacked and separated by sauce, and they are browned on top, like a gratin.

The Mountain House freeze-dried green beans reconstituted amazingly well, and would be sufficient to keep you going on the trail for about 30 seconds. With AlpineAire's Self Heating Meals, you pull a string, lay the package on its side, watch steam emerge from the end, wait 20 minutes, tear open the package, and remove a sealed pan filled with a warm and tasty stew. (The package is heavy and bulky, but you save the weight of a store and its fuel.) MSR's Mountain Gourmet Garlic Fry Bread with Basil made 16 round and soggy biscuits with the unhappy taste of dried basil; their Organic Alfredo Pasta & Cheese took 10 minutes of steady boiling and could have used 20, plus at least twice the amount of sauce supplied.

At last, our backpacking equipment was unfurled in the sunlight outside the garage. Everything was clean and intact. We examined our supertent of a generation ago and in five minutes remembered the complex process of setting it up. Now only a single thing stood between us and the Anza-Borrego Desert

*For proof of this statement, please turn to "Scraping By," page 187.

Region. One has great difficulty phrasing this delicately. It relates to the odor of our tent, sleeping bags, ground sheet, ponchos, and packs. Everything made of fabric or plastic smelled like . . . how shall I put it? I'm afraid there is no word more decorous than . . . vomit. Everything smelled like vomit. Not just a little dab of vomit, but lots and lots of vomit.

I revealed my secret fallback plan: We would rent an RV, a recreational vehicle, and live in the wilderness for four or five days. San Diego County seems to be one of the world's capitals of recreational vehicle sales and rentals, at least compared to my native Manhattan. Where better to explore the fascinating mobile world of RVs? Plus, there was an RV show in progress at Qualcomm Stadium, a major RV appliance and gadget store called Camping World 20 minutes to the north on Route 15, and Norm's RV Rental halfway in between. The rest of that day and part of the next brought us very close to renting a 31-footer, complete with a four-burner stove and refrigerator, a queen-size bed, a portable charcoal grill, air conditioning and television, a hot-and-cold shower with a skylight, and the capacity to remain parked in the desert for three or four days without hooking up to water or waste pipes, or electricity or gas.

I had it completely figured out. We would spend the first night in our driveway testing out everything and retreating to the house for supplies, tools, and e-mail. On the second night, we would park in a far corner of one of San Diego's countless shopping mall parking lots. And, if everything went right, we would set out the next morning for the desert. The only impediment to slipping into this exciting new lifestyle was my wife's terror of driving a 31-foot RV. She refused to budge. I might have overcome her reluctance by offering to do the driving myself, but I had absolutely no intention myself of getting behind the wheel of a vehicle the size of a school bus. Sky King would have loved it.

My wife was sure that a vigorous scrubbing and a day or two in the sun and fresh air would cure the problem. We used the downtime to perfect our wilderness cooking skills. We drove to 99 Ranch, one of a chain of huge Asian supermarkets, where there are entire aisles devoted to dried noodles and noodle soups, some in their own paper cups, others in pouches or sold in bulk. And then we combed two regular supermarkets for nearly weightless food. A Chinese noodle soup made in Taiwan and labeled "black peppered beef flavor" won our award for tasty and satisfying; I'd reveal the brand if I could decipher Chinese characters. In the Caucasian-pasta category, Lipton Noodles & Sauce: Parmesan was surprisingly good. The standard for gastronomic comparison should be, I believe, airline food in economy class.

For the shakedown cruise of our new Backpacker's Pantry Outback Oven, we had bought several Betty Crocker and Duncan Hines cake and brownie mixes, realizing too late that most require you to add fresh eggs. Without a head Sherpa, bringing fresh eggs into the wilderness is impractical. One mix expects you to supply your own icing, but the Betty Crocker Stir'n Bake Carrot Cake with Artificially Flavored Cream Cheese Frosting seemed perfect, requiring only the addition of two-thirds of a cup of water. We poured the batter into the Outback Oven, which consists of a nonstick frying pan and its cover. These are placed on top of a metal heat diffuser that goes over your camping stove to protect the pan from the bare flame; around everything is an insulated, padded, foil shroud or tent to keep in the heat.

Everything was going famously until I noticed that the plastic parts of my costly new Primus Alpine stove—the gas knob and the clicker of the piezoelectric igniter—appeared to be changing shape. I poked them with a long fork. Yes, as the heat had built up under the foil shroud, the plastic had actually begun to melt. When I tried to turn off the stove, the now molten knob revolved without shutting the valve, then attached itself to my sizzling skin. As I violently recoiled from this source of excruciating pain and from the reek of burning flesh and hair, both my own, the Outback Oven flipped into the air and onto the floor, where the barely cooked carrot-cake batter spread into a pink semicircle four feet in diameter. Sky King has five or six fleece beds around the house, one of them under the kitchen table. He can always be counted on to detect and clean up every food or beverage spill, but the scent of the Betty Crocker batter did not rouse him.

My state-of-the-art titanium Primus Alpine stove was ruined, and I was plunged into the deepest of depressions. The proud product of two incredibly successful Freudian psychoanalyses, I quickly understood why: My Primus Alpine had been the single most perfect thing in my life—the only perfect thing.

The camping store maintained that it must have warned us against using the Outback Oven with the Primus Alpine. Besides, they pointed out, our disaster was nothing compared to that of another customer who, deep in the woods somewhere, had suffered a fuel-tank explosion when the foil tent concentrated the heat and reflected it downward. Fortunately, the customer and the surrounding trees around him were sufficiently distant that their sole injury was the humiliation of getting covered with liquid brownies. Only when I mentioned that my hand might have to be surgically reattached did the store agree to replace the Primus Alpine stove.

There are larger questions. Do we really want to bake carrot cakes in the wilderness? Isn't the only excuse for eating dehydrated food the need to save weight? What do we truly yearn to eat in the desert and the woods, and amidst the peaks of the Himalayas? My picture has always been of a campfire encircled by rocks on which you can balance a grill and two cast-iron skillets for cooking eighteen-egg omelets stuffed with roasted potatoes and wild mushrooms and pounds of bacon, and the kind of biscuits you drop into sizzling butter. And fish, grilled or fried, and sausages. All of these are heavy and require a big cooler packed with ice, the type you can carry in an RV or the trunk of your car but not on your back. (Plus, campfires are not popular among wilderness regulators.) Backpackers out for more than a day or two care about the number of calories in each ounce they carry, including all packaging and the fuel they'll burn making dinner. Some dehydrated products require eight to ten minutes of continuous boiling while others have you just add boiling water, stir, and reseal for a while. Nobody provides you these calculations.

Two days later, our camping equipment smelled as sweet as my wife had predicted, and the next morning we departed, a maximum-size package of Oreos in the trunk for emergencies. Once we had cut free from the freeways, the two-hour drive was lovely, through rolling ranchland, Indian reservations, and several towns with genuinely rustic-looking suppliers of hay and farm machinery in place of the ubiquitous SUV dealerships and tract housing of Southern California. Then came the long and windy descent into the rocky Anza-Borrego Valley, not a certified desert of rolling sand dunes but a desert of rocks and wildflowers.

On the park radio station, we learned that this is one of the few "camp anywhere" state parks in the country. "At last!" we three sighed in unison, "a wilderness free of all those silly governmental restrictions, a chance to regain the primal man, woman, and dog in each of us!" But once we had parked at the Visitors' Center, we saw that we had been stupendously fooled.

The first danger sign was their attitude toward what they refer to as "pets." "The desert can be a dangerous place for your pet," they tell you, feigning concern. "Leave it at home if possible." They don't really mean pets. They aren't thinking of the parakeet or the gerbil. They are thinking only of dogs. They are against dogs. Warning signs at the trailheads show an animal halfway between a large normal dog and a monstrous mastiff with a slanted line through it; the warning signs do not show a kitten or an ant farm. During the day, "pets" must be on a leash measuring no longer than six feet; at night they must be confined in a vehicle or tent. And here's the worst thing of all: Dogs are not allowed off the main roads, nor, officially at least, in the Visitors' Center. Yet there we were, the three of us, standing together in front of the long list of rules in the Visitors' Center, growing more heartsick with each one.

We reeled and stumbled out into the sunlight. I tried to reason with the park masters. What damage could Sky King cause on the trails? Get this: His urine might confuse the territorial markings of the native coyotes. Please! They apparently allow—even encourage—motorcycles and four-wheel-drive SUVs on their 500 miles of backcountry roads, but not a little 85-pound, late adolescent golden retriever. I have a suspicion that Anza-Borrego, and God knows how many other state parks, have been captured by an off-road automotive ethic. I can picture the scene in late spring with hundreds of gasoline cowboys sitting behind the wheel in their souped-up SUVs and reconstructed pickups, behind the handlebars of their chrome monstrosities kicking up clouds of impenetrable dust in daredevil stunts and drag races. Where do you think those television commercials are filmed, showing SUVs climbing nearly vertical hills, then sailing through the air to the next one? That's why the desert can be a dangerous place for your pet! I remember some official in the Reagan administration saying that our national parks would not be held hostage by a small, elitist band of backpackers. He proposed "balanced development." Now I know what he had in mind. And another park rule: Open fires are allowed only in metal containers. I am not sure what this means, but it probably envisions that you will carry an entire barbecue grill in your SUV. Our replacement Primus Alpine would not even qualify.

A "Park Interpreter" (that's what twenty-first–century park rangers or guides are called) mollified us with directions to a nice, easy, and unregulated wildflower walk. We left the park and drove through the town of Borrego Springs to a road on the edge of the desert. It was a vacant-lot style of desert, to be sure, but lovely nonetheless, carpeted with low purple flowers, sand verbena, I think; and many little yellow ones and white ones, and beautiful light green things. We tromped around without constraint, yet did no damage to our desert garden. Sky King was in heaven, off the leash, off the road, with a boundless panorama before him and lots of large holes to poke his snout into. At last he could reclaim his inner dog. We were pretty happy, too.

We drove back into the park and up to the trailhead of the Borrego Palm Canyon walk, and reviewed our options. We could not leave Sky King in the car for 36 hours while we backpacked up Palm Canyon and camped overnight near the palm oasis at the end of the trail. We *could* drive a hundred feet further and pitch our tent in one of the dusty campgrounds just off the main road—really unpaved parking lots—which were already filled with dozens of recreational vehicles, and spend the night, sharing our freeze-dried backpacking food with the ants and the scorpions. Or we could do the five-hour Palm Canyon round-trip walk without Sky King, grab a bite to eat, drive home, and be in bed by midnight. This would represent a total capitulation to both the rigid wildlife bureaucracy and the internal-combustion engine. After pondering these ethical issues for a few seconds, we opted for total capitulation.

The hike was spectacular. We followed a rocky trail that wound among high, rough hills, really piles of ancient boulders, some painted with centuries of bacterial colors—slow going but without superfluous or painful gains or losses in altitude. Yes, the desert here was in full bloom—trees, shrubs, bushes, and low-spreading plants, some delicate and striking like the indigo bushes with their gray-green leaves and intense blue-purple flowers, others truly silly like the ocotillo with its thick, green, six-foot stems waving in all directions, each one tipped with a large red flower, plus flowering cacti and prickly pears, white sage and desert lily and bright red bushes of little chuparosas. We arrived back at the car as the sun was setting. Sky King snoozed expectantly in the backseat. All three of us were ravenous, but not ravenous enough to crouch down in the parking lot over a pot of dried spaghetti and dehydrated meatballs. We headed out of the park and drove through a cool and magical twilight toward civilization, which, after an hour's travel, was manifest in an increasing concentration of fast-food and pizza joints.

We were about to choose among these—we had eaten next to nothing all day and were feeling the first dangerous and deranging symptoms of actual hunger—when we spotted signs for the Barona Indian Reservation. Surely, in their food shops and canteens, perhaps in a tribal restaurant, we would find basic, essential food that had naturally evolved over centuries in harmony with the surrounding countryside. For many miles, perhaps a half-hour's drive, we passed through dark woods and ranchlands, until in the far distance we perceived a white glow emanating from behind a cluster of hills. As we drove on, a regular, rectilinear pattern of white lights emerged from the mists, almost like a landing zone constructed to welcome the starships of an alien civilization, or, even less likely, a vast parking lot dropped down into the wilderness. Indeed, it *was* a vast parking lot, with cars and people streaming to and fro. Beyond it a low, wide, spotlighted building came into view. We parked and followed the others toward the light, hoping that our now painful hunger would soon be slaked.

It was the Barona Indian Reservation Casino, and immediately upon entering, we found ourselves in a vast, bright room filled with slot machines, hundreds and hundreds of them, and just as many happy people sitting at them. The sound was transporting—each machine emitted a brief electronic song whenever there was a payoff, and the air was filled with sweet, unearthly, ever-changing music. We hastily surveyed the food on offer, a little too hastily, as it turned out. To the left was a Las Vegas–style buffet, which I believe is supposed to be a good thing. To the right was a coffee shop. Straight ahead was a bare-bones food court where Subway and DaBoyz Pizza were way outclassed by the presence of Krispy Kreme. And there were little kiosks here and there, one for Asian food, mainly a dark gray shade of fried rice, one for shrimp and crab cocktails, another selling giant half-pound hot dogs. There was no alcohol.

We temporized with a handful of Krispy Kremes, watched the action in a small area devoted to table games, and then, to accommodate my wife's wishes, searched among the 2,000 slot machines for the one made just for her. Would it be the one labeled Fireworks or the machine known as Boom? Or Break the Spell, Cast for Cash, Double Diamond Deluxe, Elephant King, Filthy Rich, Joker Poker, Monopoly, Quartermania, Stars & Stripes, Ten Play Poker, Wheel of Fortune, Wild Cherry, or Volcano Island? Only the poker slots seemed comprehensible. We pulled ahead by several dollars, after which we fell several dollars behind, whereupon we quit. None of the food tempted us. Had we only investigated the situation more professionally, we would have discovered the Jackpot Dining Menu (Buffalo wings, chicken tenders, spring rolls, and taquitos) and the High Stakes Dining Menu (beluga caviar, dim sum, roasted duckling, seafood Louie), which allows you to dine on the casino floor while you gamble.

Ignorant of these treats, we three unanimously declared an emergency, opened the Oreos, and headed home, arriving just minutes before the scourge of hunger would have scrambled our brains, perhaps forever. Fortune and foresight were smiling, for the refrigerator was bursting with several pounds of relatively fresh leftover take-out Sichuan food from our favorite Chinese restaurant in San Diego County, and we devoured them in pro-portion to our body weights, though with Sky King getting slightly more than his portion, as he had not shared equally in the Oreos. Yes, we had failed miserably in our quest for the ideal wilderness diet, though for just a moment, reheated hot-spicy twice-fried pork belly seemed to come awfully close.

JUNE 2001

FLAT OUT

Tuesday, 8:27 a.m. Flight 148 lands at Fiumicino Airport south of Rome. We are 18 minutes early. Good. My schedule for the next six days has been planned with military precision. By me.

8:56 a.m. The air is clear and warm, the sky a brilliant blue. In the taxi, I check out my bag of technical equipment. One oven thermometer, mercury. One instant-read thermometer, digital. One tape measure, metric. Ten heavy-gauge plastic bags, suitable for carrying bread flour across international boundaries. Four plastic half-liter bottles. Measuring cups and spoons. Six rolls of fast color film. A dozen electrical and telephone adapters. Twelve hundred dollars in unmarked bills, small denominations. Four half-pound bars of dark French chocolate in case of nutritional emergencies. Never did think much of Italian chocolate.

9:44 a.m. Arrive at the hotel, six minutes early. A room has been readied for me. Its window opens onto a dark courtyard resounding with the clangs and crashes of the kitchen. This is not good.

Back in the lobby, I lubricate the concierge with 10,000 lire and suggest a view of the Borghese gardens, the pines of Rome. He ostentatiously rolls his eyes toward the exchange-rate chart overhead. Ten thousand lire equals $6. I count out 50,000 more. For this I get a view of a sunny neo-Renaissance wall across a narrow street. My schedule is slipping.

10:12 a.m. Martina Simeti telephones from the lobby. A graduate student in nineteenth-century Italian history, the niece of a friend in Sicily, Martina will be my lieutenant in Rome. On the basis of several transatlantic interviews, I hired her for her bilingual abilities, love of food, and husky voice. She is three minutes early, an auspicious omen. I wonder what she looks like.

I must keep both Martina and Rome at bay for 40 minutes while I plug in my computer, shower and shave, flip on the TV. Gianni Versace has been murdered in Miami. *Assassinato! Omosessuale!*

In the shower, the shampoo refuses to lather. This means that Roman water is high in minerals, which can be good for the color and texture of bread, but slows fermentation and tightens the dough. I reach for my scuba diver's underwater writing slate, as seen on *Baywatch,* indispensable for recording those flashes of insight that so often strike one in the bath. We must test the water of Rome.

I have come here to learn how to bake two of the greatest breads in all of Italy, in all the world. For three years my thoughts have returned almost daily to *pizza bianca,* also known as *pizza alla Romana,* and to *pane Genzanese,* also known as *pane di Genzano* or just *pane Genzano.* Each is a high gastronomic achievement, enough to make any bread lover dizzy.

No two breads could look less alike. *Pizza bianca* is thin, flat, bubbly and golden; six feet long, nine inches wide, and less than an inch thick, crisp and tender, brushed with oil and sprinkled with salt, cut across into rectangles, held in waxed paper and eaten warm at any time of the day as a crunchy, savory snack, or folded into a happy little sandwich. *Pane Genzano* is huge and round and dark, an ancient loaf of substance and gravity, more than a foot in diameter, its thick, hard crust covered with bran and baked until it nearly burns, its insides chewy and open in texture—shot through with air bubbles of varying sizes—nearly five earthly pounds of primordial goodness.

Will they soon be mine? Despite backbreaking labor in past years, I have been only guardedly successful at duplicating bread discoveries from Europe, North Africa, and the Middle East. This time I want nothing left to chance. This time there will be no errors, no ambiguities, no slipups.

10:52 a.m. Martina and I meet downstairs and walk to a café on the via Veneto for an espresso while I brief her on the theory and practice of bread. Martina is tall, beautifully tanned, and 25. I discover that, even with her appreciation of food, she is sadly deficient in her technical knowledge of bread. And so, despite the extremely economical manner in which I typically express myself, my instructional briefing stretches on, and our schedule slips a little more.

I explain the origins of my mission. Italy can boast of an illustrious tradition of bread-making. But, in most Italian towns and cities these days, as in large swaths of France, you cannot find a decent loaf or flatbread or bread stick without knowing exactly where to look, and sometimes not at all. Yet, three years ago, on a brilliantly sunny day like today, these two magnificent breads literally fell into my lap. In truth, only the *pane Genzano* did. Friends and I had gathered at one of Rome's fine fish restaurants, the table was crowded with food, wine, and olive oil, and a basket of bread overturned onto my lap. What could I do but eat a slice? I knew immediately that my quest to find a truly great Roman bread had been fulfilled. It was *pane Genzano,* the owner said, baked at the Antico Forno, a shop nestled in one corner of the nearby market square, Campo de' Fiori.

The next morning, our last in Rome, several of us began our search for the Antico Forno in the wrong corner of the square, wasted a half hour before realizing our mistake, finally found it, and were soon watching six-foot-long strips of *pizza bianca* being pulled from the deep hearth ovens. For the next hour we were completely distracted by slice after delicious slice of *pizza bianca*. Only then did we inquire after the *pane Genzano* on the shelves and learned that the Antico Forno buys theirs at Venanzio Conti's bakery on the via di Pettinari, several blocks away. Just two of us had the vision and sense of mission to find Venanzio's, and when we arrived, there was only enough time to ask a few questions, view the brick oven, and purchase as many two-and-a-half-kilo loaves as we could carry. We were due in the ghetto for a lunch of crisply fried artichokes.

It was then that I pledged that before the Earth had made another circuit around the sun, I would return to the Campo de'

Fiori and the via di Pettinari and bring home the secrets of these two great breads. So I lied. It took three years.

This time there will be no distracting artichoke lunches. Or very, very few.

11:45 a.m. Our taxi pokes its way through the traffic jam that is noontime Rome. We were expected at the Campo de' Fiori a half hour ago, Martina's briefing is only half finished, and I am growing increasingly anxious. I barely glance at the Pantheon, the Column of Marcus Aurelius, or even a covey of teenage Danish schoolgirls, late teenage. I force myself to relax.

The best breads are the simplest, I explain to Martina. Like both *pizza bianca* and *pane Genzano,* they all contain flour, water, salt, and sometimes yeast. That's about it. These four ingredients can become a thousand—ten thousand—distinct breads. The differences come from the kind of wheat the baker uses, the water, the mixing and resting of the dough, how he forms the loaves, and how he bakes them. These differences are what Martina and I must capture.

And so, we will spend our waking hours at the two bakeries. We will watch every motion of the bakers, take photographs, clock the revolutions of the mixers, measure the temperatures inside the ovens. We will collect samples of flour and have them analyzed back home; we will telephone flour mills in Italy and ask for their own analyses. And we will fill plastic bottles with the water of Rome and the water of Genzano—or at the very least, obtain chemical analyses from local laboratories. I will then return to New York, produce an absolutely authentic *pane Genzano* and a perfectly Roman *pizza bianca*—and write foolproof recipes for my readers. By the time my oration is finished, Martina's nutty skin has turned a ghostly white. At last she has grasped the heavy responsibility that now weighs upon her young shoulders.

Church bells peal all over Rome to signal either our arrival at the Campo de' Fiori or the stroke of noon, I do not know which. Over the doorway of a little pink building at one corner of the piazza, the letters say, simply, *forno* (oven). We are greeted by Signore Roscioli, the owner, and Osvaldo Palamidesse, one of two bakers who have worked here for the past 15 years. Somebody hands us warm strips of *pizza bianca* wrapped in thin waxed paper, and we munch and watch as Osvaldo carries in a long wooden plank from an adjoining room. The pizza is delicious, barely crisp on both top and bottom, and tender inside with a sweetness that great bread somehow achieves without the help of sugar. Osvaldo's plank is covered with a thick bed of white flour, and on it sit four puddles of dough—mixed several hours ago, divided into two-and-a-half-kilogram chunks (over five pounds each), rolled up loosely, sprinkled with salt, and left awhile to ferment and spread. Now Osvaldo lifts one of the puddles with both arms and plops it down on another plank, this one covered in thick canvas impregnated with years of flour, and begins dimpling the dough with his fingertips, then stretching it out as though he were shaking a blanket, then dimpling again—until it nearly covers the entire plank, six feet long and ten inches wide. He brushes it with golden olive oil.

How Osvaldo gets six feet of soft dough into the oven is one of the most amazing feats in all of bread-baking. He places a peel— a thin two-and-a-half-foot rectangle of wood attached to a ten-foot-long pole as its handle—on the bakery floor in front of the oven. Then, he lifts the plank on which he just spread the *pizza bianca* dough and tilts it down onto the peel, skillfully shaking and sliding the plank until all six feet of pizza dough have folded up on the peel like an accordion! Finally, he lifts the peel and thrusts it through one of the dark glass doors of the multileveled hearth oven and deep into its interior. As he withdraws the peel, alternatively shaking and pulling it toward him and watching very carefully, the dough unfolds to its original length and beyond, stretching out on the floor of the oven to a length of nearly seven feet!

Osvaldo turns to the other puddles of dough, now and then checking the first oven. Eight minutes later, the first *pizza bianca* is ready, and he slides a long, thin slat between it and the hearth and pulls out the *pizza,* beautifully browned and aromatic. When the *pizza* has cooled slightly on one of seven wooden racks mounted like shelves on the wall, Sig. Roscioli briefly abandons his post at the sales counter in the little room next door, again brushes the *pizza* with olive oil, and cuts it into strips for the hungry noontime crowd that fills the shop. There are businessmen in suits, housewives in cotton dresses, tourists in T-shirts, and two models in skintight leggings, all clamoring for their pieces of *pizza bianca,* for which Sig. Roscioli charges by the weight. The five-year-old girl who lives in the next piazza ignores them all, walks right into the baking room, as she does every day, and waits patiently for Sig. Roscioli to appear with her *pizza bianca* lunch, neatly folded in half so that she will not get oil on her dress.

If you had come upon me standing near the oven at the Antico Forno in the Campo de' Fiori and were ignorant of my dogged investigative purpose and the precision with which I was pursuing it, you might have guessed that I had entered a *pizza bianca*–eating contest and had a fair chance of winning. But you would have been gravely wrong. For during the two hours we spend at the bakery that noontime, Martina and I minutely observe the dimpling, stretching, folding, and restretching of 20 *pizza biancas,* measuring their length and breadth, at one point counting the dimples. In the back room, we watch the mixing of the next batch of dough, counting the revolutions of the giant mixer. We check the temperature of the water, and of the air in the mixing and rising room, record the information printed on the bags of flour and the half-kilo brick of fresh yeast (and the bag of *farina di malto di frumento,* which feeds the yeast and enhances the color of the pizza). We feel the dough at various stages and try to memorize the sensation. I snap many photographs.

We make an appointment for nine o'clock the next morning to watch the mixing of another batch and to scrutinize the rising, dividing, and weighing of the dough. And to settle, once and for all, the ancient question of whether *pizza bianca* eaten at the beginning of the day tastes better than *pizza bianca* eaten at noon and every ten minutes in between.

But now Martina and I are due at the bread bakery of Venanzio Conti, where the best *pane Genzano* I have tasted in Rome can be found. We walk down a pleasant, narrow street and into the brilliant sunlight of the vast and elegant piazza Farnese, take a right on the via di Pettinari, find the bakery, and duck under the metal gate that Mr. Conti is about to lock. He remembers my visit years ago—from which I had emerged empty-handed and disconsolate—and introduces us to Aldo (who, like other Italian bakers, wears shorts and a T-shirt, or just shorts).

It is here that Martina and I will spend at least half of our time—because the mixing, forming, and baking of the huge *pane Genzano* seems a complicated process. (The dough is mixed, rested, and augmented several times; it is leavened with dough from the baking of the previous day, plus a little yeast; and the surface of the loaves is studded with tiny, charred flakes of wheat bran—the hard, shiny coating of the wheat kernel that is sifted out in the milling of white flour.) Saying this does not quite capture the hour upon endless and agonizing hour we will stand next to the merciless wood-burning brick oven (this one is currently fueled with hazelnut shells, which burn hotter than wood), watching Aldo at his work, helping him form his loaves, offering to pay him back for the loaves I helped him form, asking question after fascinating question, watching him slide my thermometer ten feet to the back of the oven and back out again. Nature has favored me with the rare gift of being able to produce a gallon of perspiration every 15 minutes under the proper conditions, which are easily met today at Venanzio's—principally an ambient temperature reaching, according to both of my thermometers, a steady 105°F with high humidity. Ordinarily, I would have become comatose within minutes. But the exhilaration of bagging the biggest game among Roman breads lends me a sort of godlike and heroic strength, humanized with a surplus of cheerful goodwill. Martina—young and strong, her whole life before her—must be led to a rickety wooden chair, her breathing shallow, her pupils unresponsive to the beam of my professional titanium flashlight.

Between our happy hours amid flour, water, salt, and fire, Martina and I visit several other bakeries around town, often returning to the hotel to continue our investigation on the telephone. Soon, she has located the municipal office responsible for the Roman water supply. Sure, I already know that the water at the hotel is highly mineralized, but what about the rest of Rome? And what are the specific minerals? When I return to New York City, where the water averages only 60 parts per million of dissolved solids, will I have to find a bottled water to replicate the water in Campo de' Fiori? And what is the cheapest, fastest way to send four samples of flour totaling 12 pounds in weight to Knoxville, Tennessee, home of The White Lily Foods Company— known among biscuit lovers as the only source for the soft and creamy flour so indispensable to all baking in the American South—which has very generously offered to analyze the bread flours of Rome? And 50 other questions.

Pane Genzano is named for a town in the lovely hill region southeast of Rome called the Castelli, the fortresses, among which the most famous is Castel Gandolfo, the pope's summer residence. There are 60 wood-burning ovens throughout the Castelli, and ten of them are in Genzano, where, I have been told by one of the principal bakery owners, they bake the only bread in Italy recognized by the Ministry of Industry, Commerce, and Artiginato with the prestigious badge of *Denominazione Origine Protetta,* usually reserved for extraordinary regional foods. It was not until the 1950s that *pane Genzano* came to be widely produced in Rome itself. Now the brick ovens are disappearing, one after another, and the bread along with it. But not in Genzano itself. Under the laws of the Italian Republic, the Genzano bread on the via dei Pettinari (and even my own) probably can not be called Genzano bread; Venanzio's price list does not use the word *"Genzano."*

By emptying my pockets into those of the concierge, I try to persuade him to arrange reasonably priced transportation to the Castelli. Despite our round-the-clock negotiations, he offers us only the most costly car service in Rome. So, we hire an ordinary cab for a circuitous, four-hour trip to the airport, which includes a wide swing in the opposite direction, to the southeast: We have only a half-day left. As we pull up to the airline terminal, our taxi is bursting with massive, dark, round loaves alternating with smaller, longer *filoni* formed from the same dough. Without even

the slimmest pretext, the young and hulking cabdriver, repudiat-
ing our advance agreement, refuses to take Martina back to
Rome unless I throw in an extra 60,000 lire. In the end, I give him
the money, but dizzy and blinded with anger, I forget our yeasty
treasures in the trunk of the taxi, and storm off to London without them. But, as I have already tasted every loaf en route and
have become quite an expert in the wood-burning ovens of the
Castelli, I am ready to bake the moment I land home in New York
City, preheating the oven before unpacking. Then I turn off the
oven. It will not be needed until the dough has risen and rested
for at least a day.

My very first attempt is an astounding, glorious, unaccount-
able success, a rusty, rough-textured, puffy, misshapen pillow of
greatness. I have even figured out how to simulate the bitter ashes
of carbonized hazelnut shells that are strewn across the broad
Roman brick hearths by infernal convective currents. But everything else is taking longer than I expect—White Lily's analysis
is only half complete; papers documenting the beatification of
Genzano bread in 1993 have yet to arrive from the Consortium for
the Protection of Pane Casareccio Genzano; and the city of
Rome has yet to replace the meaningless, pro-forma water report
they gave us with the real thing. On the other hand, the excellent Ecosystems company of Rome faxes me not one but six
complete water reports from Genzano, each from a different
pozzo (a well or spring). Their water is even more mineralized
than I would have guessed. Martina would still be hard at work
on these matters, I am sure, had she not slunk off with her dollar-
denominated salary for a languid August idyll on the Isola d'Elba.

We *have* cleared up one long-standing mystery. European
bread flours have a reputation for softness—for possessing far less
of the proteins that produce gluten, which makes dough springy
rather than extensible. Yes, the special creamy flour used to make
true French baguettes is very soft, but not the flour in crusty
French country breads, which is typically supplemented with
hard Canadian or U.S. wheat. The situation in Italy is similar.
Flour there is identified as "1," "o," or "oo" on the side of every

bag of flour. These grades refer only to how refined a flour is—how finely it has been milled and how much of the dark bran and germ have been sifted out, and not how much protein it contains. "oo" or *doppio zero* (double zero), the most refined, is used for making egg pasta, which requires flour that is *both soft and refined,* and which American cooks sometimes simulate, with some success, by adding very-low-protein cake flour to all-purpose flour for some or all of the *doppio zero* in pasta recipes. Thus a confusion was created, especially in this country, under which all *doppio zero* flour, even when used for baking bread, was thought to be *both soft and low in protein.* But there are many versions of *doppio zero* flour, which, while always highly refined, can vary dramatically in protein and the gluten this produces—low gluten for pasta and higher gluten for bread. The 50-pound bags of flour in Italian bread bakeries give not only the grade but may also say *"panifiable,"* suitable for making bread—higher in protein. In the bakeries we visited in and around Rome, the "oo" flour proved, in chemical analyses, to be higher in gluten than the less refined grades.

With all of this additional information, my version of *pane Genzano* will no doubt improve. Sure, it is a bit too white on the inside and a little feeble in taste. But it is nonetheless one of the finest breads ever to emerge from my oven—a huge, dark crackling five-pound loaf.

Pizza bianca is another thing entirely. What seemed childishly simple in Rome becomes a daily humiliation when I try it at home. Nothing works.

I begin by scaling down the large amounts of flour, water, salt, fresh yeast, and malted wheat flour from the Campo de' Fiori, so that I will have enough dough for exactly one *pizza bianca* rather than 40. Then, I find some handy substitutes for the fresh French yeast and the malt from Brescia. Obtaining a fitting substitute for the type "o" flour milled by Alimonti in Abruzzo, however, becomes an arbitrary matter; the initial analysis from White Lily says that it contains 9.26 percent protein; Alimonti itself estimates it at 12 percent; and a worker at the bakery was pretty sure it came to 11.3. I compromise on a strong, unbleached all-purpose flour, and ignore the high mineral content of the water of Rome. The dough comes together sloppily and does not handle well.

I clear off the longest countertop in my kitchen, six feet long, and press out one full *pizza bianca,* which does gratifyingly resemble the one at Campo de' Fiori. My plan is to cut it crosswise into five sections, and bake each separately. But as soon as I cut it, the segments shrink and the others glue themselves so firmly to the counter that getting them into the oven is out of the question. Even after I have learned to handle the dough, the pizzas are tough and misshapen and require double the baking time of the original—even though I have regulated my oven with the same mercury thermometer I brought to Rome.

Morose and dissociated, the bitter taste of defeat stinging my tongue, I telephone Jim Lahey for help. Jim is co-owner and head guy at Sullivan Street Bakery in New York City, an excellent and very successful three-year-old venture and one of the few bakeries in America that bake genuine Italian hearth breads. And among these is the *pizza bianca* that Jim learned several years ago at the Antico Forno in the Campo de' Fiori in Rome, Italy, from Signore Roscioli and his bakers! All of them had acted like proud parents or older brothers when we talked about Jim and his fine Italian bakery in New York.

The next day, Jim comes over, his arms filled with warm *pizza bianca* (one a sweet version dotted with champagne grapes and anise seed) and a dark, crusty *pane Pugliese,* and we set to work, making four doughs in all. Immediately we deviate from the Roman formula—Jim has me use stronger bread flour, lots more water, and only a little yeast. We form individual pizzas, each about six by twelve inches, then stretch them out on the hot baking stone on my oven shelf.

Twenty minutes later we are munching on a totally terrific *pizza bianca* and congratulating each other. Our work over the next five hours only serves to improve matters, except every once in a while.

Jim is slightly too amused by my project in Rome—what he calls the mimicry approach. Bakers for whom bread is a way of life adapt their methods to changing conditions and schedules several times a day. I had recorded the motions of only four bakers, in three bakeries, on only two days during one season, he says. No wonder my *pizza biancas* failed.

Then why is my *pane Genzano* so perfect? Jim's reply is only, quite frankly, an appropriate expression of awe.

TWO ROMAN BREADS

These recipes make wet and sticky doughs that are nearly impossible to knead by hand. That's why a mixer is called for, and why your counter and hands must be heavily dusted with flour. The resulting doughs are wonderfully soft and elastic and bouncy and full of air bubbles—a joy to handle—and when they have been baked at a high temperature, they become very crisp on the outside, and both light and chewy on the inside.

I have chosen King Arthur Unbleached all-purpose flour, not because it is absolutely the best flour you can buy, but because it works consistently and well, has a good taste, and is roughly comparable to the combination of flours at Venanzio's. I have also specified SAF-Instant yeast from France (not active dry yeast) because SAF does not need to be dissolved in warm water, and it performs extremely well. Both are readily available by mail order if you call The King Arthur Baker's Catalogue at (800) 827-6836. You can also find SAF-Instant yeast in Williams-Sonoma's stores and catalog. Recently I have been trying King Arthur's European-style bread flour, which has the same level of protein as all-purpose but a bit more taste.

If you use King Arthur all-purpose flour and SAF-Instant yeast, you will get about the same results as I do. If you vary the ingredients, especially the flour, you must make adjustments. Both flours are about 11.7 percent protein—which is more than most other all-purpose flour and less than most bread flours. A flour with more protein will absorb more water. If you prefer, you can substitute American-style bread flour (with about 1 percent more protein) for half the all-purpose; then you'll need about ¼ cup more water. In every case, the dough should be very wet, but not so slack that the loaf refuses to rise impressively.

Weighing flour and even water is the most accurate way of measuring them. But for the sake of convenience, I have also given flour and water measurements in cups and tablespoons. The assumption is that you will dip your measuring cup deep into the flour and level it off with a straight edge or with your hand. I traced the problem of inconsistent results to the older flour at the bottom of my plastic storage barrel; this had had a year or two to dry out dramatically. So I recommend using only fresh flour, at least at first.

PIZZA BIANCA

1 cup extra-virgin olive oil
3 cups King Arthur Special Bread Flour (480 g), measured
by dipping a cup measure deeply into the flour and
leveling it off with a straight edge
1 tsp. salt plus 3 scant teaspoons
1¼ tsp. white sugar
2 cups minus 1 tsp. water (470 g)
1 tsp. SAF-Instant yeast
½ cup cornmeal or semolina, for dusting the peel
Special equipment: An electric mixer designed for kneading bread,
such as the KitchenAid 5-quart mixer. A rising bowl or bucket with
a 3-quart capacity or more; it should have straight or nearly
straight sides and be translucent or transparent. A pastry brush or
soft paint brush, about 3 inches wide. A wooden baking peel or
piece of stiff, smooth cardboard, about 12 inches long. One or
2 large, heavy baking stones (the ideal is rectangular, with an
18-inch diagonal to allow the pizza to be stretched to this length).

─ ─ ─ ─ ─

Place the baking stone(s) on your oven shelves and preheat your oven to 500°F for at least an hour.

This recipe yields about 3¾ cups of dough, which will rise 2½ to 3 times. Fill your rising bowl or bucket with 9 cups of water and mark this level for the minimum rise. Add 2 cups of water and mark the maximum. Empty and dry the bowl, then brush the inside with 2 tablespoons of the olive oil.

In the mixer bowl, stir together the flour, the yeast, and 1 teaspoon of salt. Pour the water over this mixture. Fasten the bowl and the dough hook to the mixer, and mix at a slow speed for 5 minutes to combine the ingredients. Over the next 3 minutes or so, gradually advance the speed to high (speed 6 or 8 on the KitchenAid), and knead for about 10 minutes, until the gluten has developed sufficiently that all of the loose, wet dough gathers around the dough hook. At this point and every 2 minutes hereafter, turn off the motor (the dough will sag and liquify), scrape down the bowl and dough hook, and check the dough.

The dough is ready when: 1) it is shiny and very smooth; 2) a piece can be stretched between the fingers of both hands into a thin, translucent sheet at least 4 inches on a side without lumps or holes; and 3) a little handful of dough pulled from the bowl will stretch at least 1 foot before breaking. Total kneading time at high speed will be between 12 and 18 minutes.

Scrape the dough into the oiled rising bowl. Cover with plastic wrap and let rise at a warm room temperature for about 1½ hours, until it reaches 2½ to 3 times its original volume.

Heavily flour your countertop and turn out the dough onto it, top side down. It will spread into a rough circle or oval. Fold this in half to enclose the sticky upper surface, forming a long, wonderfully soft and wobbly and bouncy roll of dough. With a knife or metal dough scraper, cut the dough crosswise into 3 equal pieces.

Flour your hands and stretch one of the pieces of dough into a long rectangle about 1 foot by 4 inches. Place it on the

— — — — —

counter with its length extending away from you. Fold the farthest edge an inch toward you and press to seal. Then, roll up
the dough, starting with that edge, tightening as you go. The
easiest way is by placing the backs of both thumbs behind and
against the far edge of the dough, rolling them and the dough
one turn toward you, then pushing them away from you to
tighten the roll. Repeat, again placing your thumbs behind the
far side of the growing cylinder of dough and rolling them forward. Soon, the entire rectangle will have been transformed
into a rough, puffy, elastic cylinder about 8 inches across. The
harder your thumbs press against the dough as it rolls, and
the harder you push them away from you, the tighter the roll
will be.

On another region of your countertop, sprinkle out 3 thick,
oval cushions of flour. Place the first roll of dough, seam side
down, onto one of them. Continue with the 2 other pieces of
dough.

Liberally brush the 3 rolls of dough with olive oil, about 2
tablespoons each. Sprinkle each with a scant teaspoon of salt.
Allow them to rise for about 30 to 40 minutes until about double their original volume—when you poke a finger deeply into
the dough, it will not spring back much. Each piece of dough
will be 4 to 5 inches wide and about 10 inches long.

Now form your first *pizza bianca:* Very liberally dust your
peel or cardboard with the bran, semolina, or cornmeal. (They
use flour at Campo de' Fiori and Sullivan Street, but in the
home oven this results in a soft, unpleasant layer of uncooked
white flour on the underside of your pizzas.) Lift 1 roll of
dough onto the center of the peel with its length at right
angles to the leading edge of the peel—the edge away from the
handle, the edge that will go into the oven first. Now, dimple
the dough, pressing down firmly with the fingers of both
hands 6 to 8 times, using the forward curve of your fingertips,
not the very tips. With your brush, dribble about a tablespoon
of olive oil in and around the dimples you have just made,

avoiding the edges of the dough, which may otherwise stick to the peel.

Now dimple and stretch the dough 20 to 30 times more—including all four edges—so that it ends up rectangular, about 8 by 12 inches, with one of the shorter sides on the leading edge of the peel. The dimples should be deep—but not penetrating the dough—and the dough between them should remain nearly as puffy as when you began. While you may occasionally stretch the dough by flapping and pulling it, for the most part the expansion of the pizza is accomplished as you press and dimple it. If the dough keeps pulling back to its original shape, let it relax for 10 minutes and then try again. Avoid dimpling the dough in the same places twice.

Now transfer the pizza to the hot baking stone in the oven: Rest the leading edge of the peel on the far corner or edge of the stone and jerk the peel toward you until the dough begins to slide onto it. Alternatively pulling and jerking the peel, continue until the pizza lies entirely on the stone—and has stretched out to a full 16 to 18 inches. The lower the angle of the peel to the stone, the more the dough will stretch; the higher the angle, the faster the dough will slide onto the peel. With a rectangular stone, stretch out the pizza on the diagonal for the greatest length.

Bake until the pizza is puffy, crisp, tender, and varies between golden brown and darker shades of brown. This can take between 12 and 20 minutes, depending on your oven. Rotate the pizza once on the baking stone if the browning is uneven. The pizza should feel light when you lift it: in the oven it will have lost over a fourth of its weight. Its thickness will vary between ¼ inch (where it has been deeply dimpled) and 1½ inches (where the bubbles are puffiest).

Let the pizza cool briefly on a rack. After a minute or two, again brush the top with olive oil, about a tablespoon. Cut the pizza crosswise into strips. It will be very, very good to eat.

Note: To save time and prevent the dough from overrising, use two baking stones on separate oven shelves. After the first pizza has begun to bake, form a second one and slide it onto the other baking stone. Then form the third pizza, so that it is ready for baking when the first one is done.

Yield: 3 rectangular pizzas, each 6 inches wide and 17 to 18 inches long.

PANE GENZANESE

This is the best bread I've ever baked, and when it turns out just right, one of the best I've eaten: huge (14 inches in diameter and 3 inches high), with a crunchy, dark reddish-brown crust and a moist, creamy interior shot through with irregular holes and air bubbles; and full of delicious flavors, from the sweet, barely tangy interior to the nearly bitter crust. I have made this Pane Genzanese many, many times since returning from Rome. At first, the outcome was unreliable and frustrating. I grew depressed. Slowly, however, I arrived at a method that seems to work well nearly every time.

Making the starter dough:
½ cup fresh King Arthur all-purpose flour
1 pinch SAF-Instant yeast
¼ tsp. (scant) salt
¼ cup water

The purpose of this step is to obtain the rough equivalent of five ounces of fully risen, day-old bread dough, with which the bakers of Genzano start the ten-hour process of mixing, building, fermenting, shaping, and baking their current day's bread.

— — — — —

If you happen to have a half cup of leavened bread dough on hand, you can move on to the next stage.

Otherwise, the day before you plan to bake the bread, stir together the flour, yeast, and salt in the bowl of a mixer designed to knead bread, add the water, and stir vigorously with a wooden spoon to form the dough. Knead for a minute or two on a floured surface (or with the paddle of a mixer) until smooth, cover the bowl with plastic wrap, and leave it at room temperature, overnight, for 12 to 18 hours.

Making the biga:
One batch of starter dough, above; or about ½ cup (5 ounces) of
day-old bread dough
1 cup cold water
2 cups King Arthur all-purpose flour
Special equipment: A heavy-duty mixer designed for kneading bread
(for example, one of the Kitchen Aid 5-quart or 6-quart models)

The next morning, pull the starter dough from the mixer bowl and set it aside on a plate. Put about half the flour and all of the water into the bowl, attach the bowl and paddle to the mixer, and beat well to combine, starting at the slowest speed and gradually increasing to medium. Now add a piece of the starter dough, about the size of a walnut, and in about 10 seconds, when it has pretty much disappeared into the mixture, add another. Continue until all the starter has been incorporated and the dough is smooth. Turn off the mixer, remove the beater, add the rest of the flour, and stir for a minute with a wooden spoon; this will prevent the flour from splattering. Attach the beater again and, gradually increasing the speed to medium, beat the dough for about 3 minutes until it is smooth and stretchy.

This is the biga. Remove the bowl and beater, gather the biga into a rough ball in the mixer bowl, sprinkle with a tablespoon of flour, and cover the bowl with plastic wrap. Let the

– – – – –

biga rise at a warm room temperature for 5 to 6 hours. It will at least double.

The bread:

1 batch of biga, above

3 ⅓ cups cold water (770 g)

7 cups King Arthur All-Purpose Flour (1036 g)

1 ¼ tsp. SAF-Instant yeast (about 3.5 g)

1 ½ Tbs. (22 g) salt

About two cups additional flour for sprinkling the dough, covering the counter, and rubbing the cloth

1 cup of wheat bran flakes, milled fine so that few flakes are longer than ¹/₁₆ inch (available at health-food stores)

Special equipment: A heavy baking stone (round, square, or rectangular) with its smallest dimension no less than 14 inches

A square container (a baking dish, casserole, cardboard box, or plastic food storage box) 10 to 11 inches on a side and 3 to 6 inches deep

A large, clean cotton or linen kitchen towel

A wooden baking peel or a square of stiff, smooth cardboard no smaller than 15 inches on a side

A plant sprayer filled with water

In one bowl, mix together the yeast and about half the all-purpose flour. In a second bowl, mix together the remaining flour and the salt.

Remove the biga from the mixer bowl and set it aside on a plate. Pour the yeast-flour mixture and all the water into the mixer bowl and stir briefly with a wooden spoon. Attach the bowl and paddle to the mixer, and following the method we used to make the biga, combine the flour and water well, beginning at the slowest speed and gradually increasing to medium. Next, pull apart the biga and beat it into the dough one piece at a time. Then turn off the mixer and stir in the salt-flour mixture with a wooden spoon (detaching the bowl from the mixer if this seems more convenient), and resume beating, gradually increasing the speed of the mixer to high. All or most of the dough will gather around the paddle.

Continue at high speed for 5 minutes. Halfway through, stop the machine and scrape down the bowl and paddle; then continue beating. The dough will probably climb over the top of the paddle.

Now scrape down the paddle and check the dough. Bread dough is fully kneaded if it is shiny and smooth, stretches for at least a foot when you pull a handful of it from the bowl, *and* forms a smooth, unbroken, translucent sheet four or more inches across when you take a piece the size of a lemon, roll it in flour, and gently spread it like a rubber sheet between the well-floured fingers of both hands. Continue beating at high speed until these conditions are met, scraping down and checking every minute or so. The initial 5 minutes may be enough. If not, 2 to 4 additional minutes will probably be all you will need. The dough should stretch properly, but need not look perfectly smooth; the next step will miraculously take care of the texture.

When the dough is ready, simply leave it in place for 10 minutes. Then give it ten turns of the paddle at high speed. Scrape down and remove the paddle, scrape down the bowl, and sprinkle the dough with one to two tablespoons of flour.

Let it rise, covered with plastic wrap, in the mixer bowl at a warm room temperature (about 80°F) for between 45 and 60 minutes. Its volume should increase by between one-quarter and one-third (just over an inch in the Kitchen Aid 5-quart bowl).

Heavily flour your countertop in a rough 18-inch circle, using at least a cup of flour (which can be sieved and used again). Tilt the mixer bowl into the middle of the circle as you pull out the dough, keeping the floured top side down. The dough should spread into a rough circle about a foot in diameter. If necessary, stretch it slightly to form a neater circle. Let it rest for ten minutes.

Meanwhile, place the baking stone on a shelf in the lower third of your oven and preheat to 500°F. Rub ½ cup flour into the kitchen towel and line the square container, casserole, or cardboard box with the towel, draping its edges over the sides of the box. Then sprinkle about 2 tablespoons of ground flakes onto the part of the towel lining the bottom of the container.

When the dough has rested, form it into a round loaf as follows, taking care not to deflate the dough any more than you need to: With floured fingers, gently grasp the edge of the circle anywhere along its circumference, fold it two-thirds of the way to the other side, and press to seal. Repeat, continuing all around the circle of dough. Then go around again to fold in any badly protruding corners.

Sliding the palms of both hands under opposite edges of the wonderfully puffy loaf you have created, flip it over. Again, with both hands lift the loaf and place it into the box, still smooth side up. This will require some manual dexterity. Sprinkle the loaf with two tablespoons of bran and press firmly. Cover with a baking sheet. Let the loaf rise for 40 to 45 minutes in a very warm place (about 85°F)—it will both spread and rise nearly an inch.

When the dough is ready, briefly open the oven door to sprinkle 2 tablespoons of bran flakes onto the hot baking stone; it will soon blacken and smoke a little, simulating the burned hazelnut shells of Rome.

Now place the wooden peel or stiff cardboard flat on the countertop and sprinkle another 3 tablespoons of ground bran over it. The task now is somehow to transfer the loaf from the rising box onto the peel, keeping it smooth side up. The only way I've mangaged to do this is by inverting the loaf and then inverting it again, as follows: Uncover the rising box. Place one hand on the countertop, next to the peel, palm up. With the

— — — — —

other hand, tilt the rising box and invert the loaf onto your palm. Pull off the towel. Then, with both hands, invert the loaf again onto the peel so that it comes to within an inch of the peel's leading edge (opposite the handle), smooth side up.

Stretch the loaf about an inch all around so that its diameter goes from about 11 inches to about 14 inches. (Don't just pull on the edges; slide your hands, palms up, under the bread and stretch out from the middle.) Sprinkle another tablespoon of bran over it and press lightly. The loaf will now resemble a fat pancake.

Open the oven door and pull out the shelf holding the baking stone. Slide the loaf onto the baking stone by placing the leading edge of the peel or cardboard near the far edge of the stone and alternately jerking and pulling the peel toward you. Liberally spray the surface of the loaf with water. Slide it into the oven. Spray the inside of the oven twenty times and close the door. Reduce the heat to 450°F.

Bake for about an hour and 10 minutes (70 minutes). This loaf wants so much to rise and expand that within 15 minutes it will nearly have doubled in height so vigorously that it will curve up and off the baking stone all around the bottom. After about 7 minutes, open the oven door briefly and quickly spray the loaf another 20 times. After about 40 minutes, rotate the loaf front to back, and if areas of the crust are beginning to burn badly, lower the oven temperature to 425°F. When the bread is done, it will be a beautiful, very dark russet shade, and its internal temperature, when tested with an instant-read thermometer thrust into its center, should measure 210°F. Let it cool on a rack for 2 hours.

EXPLAINING ESPRESSO

Have you ever counted the number of coffeemakers you've collected over the years? I just did, and there are 18, including two electric drip machines, a Melitta plastic filter holder, an old Chemex, two French-style plunger pots, three electric espresso machines (two gathering dust), a Napoletano (heat the water in the bottom, then flip it over), two and a half elegant glass-and-Bakelite Cona coffeemakers based on the vacuum-pot principle (which I've never satisfactorily learned to operate), a tall, chipped, red enameled pot with a spout and a little rusted hinged cover, and an old percolator, which I threw out five minutes ago. Percolators may be the worst way ever invented to make coffee, except for chipped red enameled pots.

This will amaze you: The market for coffee is the second largest in the world, after the trade in oil! Sometimes steel and grain jump ahead of coffee; sometimes they fall behind. We were told this when I visited the Lavazza Training Centre in Turin, Italy, two years ago. The people of the world love coffee more than almost anything else. Did you have even an inkling or intimation?

Less amazing but nonetheless interesting: Nearly half the adults in the United States drink coffee every day. Another quarter drink coffee occasionally. Each of us averages three cups a day, more than they drink in Italy! The world's heaviest coffee drinkers live in four of the five Scandinavian countries, which may explain the Seattle phenomenon. Then come the three Germanic nations, plus the Netherlands, then France and us. Here's a theory: The colder the weather, the more coffee we drink. Sure, coffee is a drug-delivery system for caffeine, but we really drink it for the warmth. Here's a contrary theory: In the land of the midnight sun, everybody needs caffeine to stay awake through the dark and gloomy winters. People who drink coffee have been shown to commit suicide less frequently than people who don't.

It's no wonder that humankind's most persistent activity over the past few hundred years has been inventing new ways of making coffee. How many coffeemakers you have at home depends on 1) your age, 2) your love of coffee, 3) your love of toys, and 4) your total inability to throw anything out. I get high scores in all four. But most important is factor number five—call it the spiritual factor, if you must. Have you ever felt that coffee—in the roaster or the grinder, in the can or in the bag, in the coffeemaker or the cup—*nearly always smells better than it tastes?* This is the cause of our eternal torment and discontent, us coffee lovers. We never stop searching for the impossible, *for a way to drink the heady, complex, incomparable aroma of coffee.* That is why we buy 18 coffeepots and are always ready to buy another. And why so many of us turn to espresso.

Right now there are 14 brand-new, state-of-the-art, home espresso-makers in my house, all borrowed from their manufacturers and arranged along the circumference of my large, round, dining-room table, all facing outward, all plugged into one of two power strips in the center. I have two La Pavonis, two Saecos, two Gaggias, and one each from Krups, Starbucks (the Barista), Faema, DeLonghi, Rancilio, Briel, and Lavazza. A new Pony from Unic has just arrived. After an evening and early morning stumbling around in the dark every time the fuses blew, I decided to plug in only four espresso-makers at a time. With my table taken over, I have been eating standing up for the past few weeks. It is like dining on the subway.

Why espresso? Because it has the potential to deliver more of the incredible taste and aroma of roasted coffee than any other method. Espresso is not a kind of bean, a method of roasting, or a particular grind. It is a way of making a cup of coffee. A prototype device was introduced in Paris in the mid-1800s. *It works by forcing hot water under high pressure through well-packed, finely ground coffee.* The result is a dark, smooth, almost syrupy liquid covered with a thick, fine-grained, reddish-brown foam called *crema*. The taste of espresso is bittersweet, with an initial impression of acidity. From your first sip, the aroma is intense and explosive. Afterward, you are left with a very pleasurable coffee taste that can last for half an hour. The predominant flavors are caramel, flowers (including jasmine), fruit, chocolate, honey, and toast—but only if you do everything exactly right. One false step and you are totally doomed. One false step and you will never taste the jasmine.

How does espresso get its aroma, its body, and its *crema*? The force and turbulence of the hot brewing water as it forces its way through the packed, ground coffee reduces the coffee's oils to the tiniest droplets, which can then both become suspended throughout the hot water in your cup and form the foam on top. The evanescent and volatile aromas that might otherwise escape into the air are dissolved in (or fixed onto) these oils. They await your first sip. The water pressure must be high enough to turn the oils into droplets so small that they will not separate from the water and end up floating on top of the coffee. This is what people mean by "emulsification." (Oil and water do not mix, but they can coexist—as when you whip up a vinaigrette.) The *crema* also forms a lid on the espresso underneath (keeping in much of the aroma), and is a sign in itself that everything else has gone just right. Roasted coffee also contains lots of carbon dioxide, which under the pressure of the espresso machine disperses into the espresso as innumerable tiny gas bubbles, lending it further body.

The *crema* should be fluffy, about one-eighth of an inch thick, and long lasting. Here's a terrific test: slide a small spoonful of granulated sugar onto the *crema*. The sugar should sit there for two seconds or so before disappearing under the surface.

If you order an espresso in a restaurant, and it comes without a very good *crema*, send it back. You will thus benefit not only yourself but also that portion of humankind that patronizes the restaurant after you.

I have read that there are 114 variables to worry about when you make espresso. Many of these concern plant genetics, agronomy, roasting, and packaging—things that happen to coffee beans before you buy them at the store. Of the 114 variables, there are maybe seven we can try to control at home: water temperature, water pressure, the amount of coffee we use, the grind of the coffee, how firmly we compress (tamp) it, the number of seconds we allow hot water to flow through it, and the amount of espresso we draw into our cup.

The general idea is this: If the water pressure or temperature is too low, if the coffee is ground too coarsely, if we tamp it too tightly, if we let the water flow through it for too short a time, if we draw no more than a tablespoon or so of espresso into our cup, then we have extracted very little from the coffee beans. We will have produced what is called an underextracted espresso. The *crema* will be pale and thin, with large bubbles, and it will disappear quickly. The espresso underneath will lack body, taste, and aroma.

If we reverse these conditions, if the water pressure or temperature is too high, if the grind is too fine, if the water runs though the coffee for too long a time, then we will have drawn too much out of the coffee beans, including the most bitter and woody tastes and aromas. This is an overextracted espresso. The *crema* will be dark, with a white spot or a black hole in the center. The coffee will taste astringent—that puckery feeling in the mouth—and may even have a peanut flavor. Beware that peanut flavor.

Here's what the experts, nearly all the experts, say. To brew a perfect espresso, you should heat the water to 192°F, give or take a few degrees. (Water boils at 212°F.) The water pressure must be nine bars—nine times the atmospheric pressure at the Earth's surface—or about 132 pounds per square inch, which is equal to the same massive compression your eardrums would feel at 297 feet under the sea. Not many home machines are capable of this combination of temperature and pressure. The steam-driven espresso-maker is guaranteed to fail, producing excessively hot water under too little pressure. It makes espresso that lacks body and aroma, has little or no *crema,* and tastes excessively bitter. The only espresso machines to buy are pump driven. They are more expensive, but then at least you have a fighting chance.

You must use seven grams of coffee. This is one-fourth of an ounce, if that helps, or the weight of the yeast in one of those little yeast packets, if you're a baker, or one tablespoon if you are not fanatical about accuracy, though I will concede that the margin for error here may be small and that weighing seven grams is a real bother. The coffee must be ground very finely and packed very firmly. I could tell you what the experts say about average particle size, but this would probably be as meaningless to you as it is to me, and anyway, they disagree. An inexpensive grinder with a whirling blade will not do, though you can use it when you brew coffee in other ways. Some of the particles will end up much too large and others too small, clogging the filter. You need an expensive burr grinder, which crushes the beans in one pass between two knurled disks, or use coffee that has already been ground and immediately sealed, preferably with an inert gas.

A shot of espresso must take 25 seconds to draw, measured from the moment the first drops plop into the cup. An ideal shot of espresso is two to two and one-half tablespoons. If you want a double espresso, draw two regular-size shots into the same cup; if you let the machine run for twice the time, and try to compensate by using twice the coffee, you will end up extracting the bitter, woody, and peanut-tasting components. For the same reason, if you want a diluted espresso, make one correctly and add hot water.

It's as simple as that: Two tablespoons of 192°F water forced through seven grams of finely ground coffee under nine atmospheres of pressure for 25 seconds, and you'll have a perfect espresso. You will drink the fantastic aroma of roasted coffee beans. You will taste the jasmine.

When I bought my first home espresso machine 15 years ago, I spent hours pondering details as small and insignificant as, say, the tamping down of the ground coffee into the metal filter basket (also known as the brewing basket or portafilter or filter holder) before attaching it to my machine. How hard should I press? Should I tap the basket sideways to dislodge stray particles of coffee and then press them down again? Should I just press, or press and twist? What if the top of the compressed coffee is perfectly flat and smooth but slanted? As time passed, I began to feel that obsessions like these were unhealthy and twisted.

Then, a few months ago, I began reading in earnest about espresso and found page upon page dealing with tamping techniques. Some even have names! Espresso experts are more obsessive about everything than I have ever been about anything. I vowed not to get drawn into this madness. I would not allow espresso to ruin my life. Yes, I have let 14 espresso machines take over my dining room and make my life otherwise unlivable. But this is only temporary. For when I am through, I will have answered the one question that can free me forever from obsessing about espresso: What is the easiest and most mindless way of making nearly perfect espresso at home?

I will admit that, having made this pledge, I allowed myself to be distracted by one little experiment, unfinished business. I put my bathroom scale on the kitchen counter, placed the filter basket from my active espresso-maker (the chic FrancisFrancis!) on it, and measured the pressure I exerted on the ground coffee with my black plastic tamper. My measurements were all over the place, depending on how much I leaned into it.

I telephoned Dr. Ernesto Illy in Trieste, Italy, one of the world's most knowledgeable and eminent espresso experts. Illy is 75 years old, a chemist, and chairman of Illycaffè, which produces what for me is the finest of all the widely available espresso coffees—one blend, one flavor, in beans or ground coffee, decaf or regular, medium roast or dark. As I discovered at dinner with Illy a few years ago, he knows more about espresso than I know about everything else put together. Tamp the coffee as hard as you can, he advised; 40 pounds of pressure is a minimum. The key thing is, the tamped coffee must contain no more than 64 percent air; it must occupy at least 36 percent of the space. Any fluffier and the hot, pressurized water will race through it too quickly. Of course, there's no way for you or me to measure this 36 percent. We must tamp through trial and error. Or switch to pods.

A pod is a premeasured, pretamped packet of ground coffee—simply insert into your espresso machine and let 'er rip. The grinding, tamping, and measuring have been handled by unseen experts. That leaves only water temperature and pressure to worry about. But, as home machines have no adjustments for water temperature or pressure, all I need care about is that my machine produce a little more than two tablespoons of perfect espresso in about 25 seconds.

There are three pod systems: Nespresso, Lavazza, and E.S.E. (Easy Serving Espresso); this last is supported by a consortium of many machine manufacturers and coffee roasters. Nespresso pods work only on the Nespresso espresso machine. They are truncated metal cones and come in a variety of flavors, the strongest of which is called *Ristretto,* the Italian word for a short, strong espresso. The French love Nespresso (including at least one world-famed, Michelin three-star restaurant) because they dislike the bitterness of Italian espresso and find, as I often do, that it interferes with their perception of the subtler flavors in coffee. I should mention that I taste Italian-style espresso both before and after adding two demitasse spoons of sugar, about a half teaspoon. (Ninety percent of Italians put twice this amount of sugar in every cup.) To my taste, this prevents the other aromas and flavors from being overwhelmed by bitterness. With most American blends, sugar is unnecessary.

The Lavazza pod machine takes only Lavazza pods, which are made of translucent plastic. It's a heavy, good-looking, all-metal machine without any resemblance to other espresso-makers because it lacks a filter holder with its long black handle. You pull back a metal lever, pop in the pod, close the lever, and press a button.

I have been using the E.S.E. pods with my FrancisFrancis! for more than a year with good results, until recently. They are flat, well-tamped, two-inch disks of ground coffee sealed between two sheets of white filter paper, and packaged in either individual foil pouches or cans. The Illy company seems to have been the technological and organizational force behind these pods, which are now produced by coffee roasters ranging from the local (the much-admired Moka d'Oro in Brooklyn) to the national (Starbucks) and international (including Illy and Lavazza). I found ten brands for sale in the United States. Two other coffee roasters may also be manufacturing E.S.E. pods, but they refuse to return telephone calls.

The 14 machines on my dining-room table were chosen in this manner: My assistant, Gail, and I made a list of all brands available in the United States, based on reading, searching the Internet, asking the people at Illy and the SCAA (Specialty Coffee Association of America) in Long Beach, California, and trips to Zabar's, which carries a wide array of models. I also dusted off the Nespresso machine in my closet, which takes only Nespresso pods. I requested a machine from Lavazza. Then we telephoned all the other companies and asked if any of their machines accept E.S.E. pods. (Often this requires nothing more than a shallow metal insert for the standard filter basket.) If they did accept them, I asked for the least expensive model that made good espresso. I was looking for a model without the costly cosmetics and conveniences of the upscale versions.

On two occasions, I deviated from this rigorous scheme. While on the telephone with La Pavoni, I requested one of their famous lever machines (even though it does not accept pods) because I had never played with one before. And the man from Saeco persuaded me to go beyond their E.S.E.-pod model and try their superautomatic as well, which has a built-in grinder. For this and several other experiments, I bought roasted beans from Peet's, Torrefazione, J. Martinez, and others.

So. Fourteen machines. Sixteen types of coffee. That makes 224 combinations. We could not test more than four machines at a time because of the fuse problem. Plugging and unplugging them in order around the table was not difficult, but an espresso machine needs to heat up for a good period of time, maybe an hour. (Unless the metal parts in contact with the coffee and the water are hot enough to burn your hand, they will allow the water to cool, ruin the *crema,* and produce an underextracted cup.) Comparing 224 combinations is humanly impossible if you don't want espresso to ruin your life, and maybe even if you do. Plus, you probably also want to know how well each machine steams milk. Forget about it.

I narrowed down the trials. I sent back the lever-operated La Pavoni. To test the E.S.E. machines, I used pods only from Illy and Starbucks because these well represent the Italian and American ideas about blending and roasting.

And here are some conclusions:

1. The Saeco superautomatic has an edge over the pod machines when it is working properly—about 30 percent of the time—because it grinds the beans right before brewing them. It makes a fine *crema* that can support a spoon of sugar for a record four seconds. The results, however, were quite inconsistent. I do not know how the Saeco stacks up against other superautomatic models; all are much more expensive than simple pod machines and have plenty of mechanisms and electronics that can go haywire. The Saeco allows you to use any beans you wish and to fiddle with the fineness of the grind and the volume of the espresso. It is thus well suited to the espresso lover like me who likes to obsess, but only a little, and without getting his or her hands dirty. Last-minute grinding seemed to preserve some of the heady aromas that disappear with all other methods.

2. The best single cup of espresso came from the Unic Pony, a heavy, all-metal semiprofessional machine that uses E.S.E. pods and was sent to me instead of the simpler, less expensive version I had wanted to test but which had not yet arrived from Europe. Using an Illy

dark-roast pod, it produced the strong and incredible scent of jasmine, sip after sip. It was an epiphanous moment. When I drew another cupful, it was gone. The next day, it was still gone.

3. The Nespresso makes a nice cup of espresso nearly every time, with a good, thick *crema*. But you have to use Nespresso's own coffee, and have no control over anything but how long you let the water flow through the pod. The most crucial flaw is that Nespresso uses only five grams of ground coffee. (Believe me—on two occasions, I took apart ten pods and weighed their aggregate contents.) This is not enough coffee—you can taste the dilution.

4. Two E.S.E. pod machines produced, out of the box, as good espresso as anything I can make at home with roasted beans, a burr grinder, and a bathroom scale. These were the La Pavoni (PL-16) and the Saeco (Via Veneto). Close behind were the Starbucks Barista, the Rancilio Silvia, and the Briel (ES200A). I can give only a provisional recommendation to my own espresso machine, the FrancisFrancis! Recently, it has not been producing the proper amount and type of *crema*. One reason could be that its pump is putting out insufficient pressure. I had a brainstorm. What if I attached a small water-pressure meter to the spout at the center of the filter holder? After several hours wasted at my local hardware store, I telephoned Roy Forster, quality-assurance manager for Illy USA, for help. It turns out that he and his technicians use a water-pressure meter that mounts on the filter holders of professional machines, which contain powerful, adjustable, centrifugal pumps costing more than an entire home machine. With home machines, even fancy ones, either the pump works right, he feels, or it doesn't work at all. But he sent me a pressure meter anyway, and I discovered that my FrancisFrancis! is not

perfectly sealed, allows the pressure to escape, and
thus presumably cannot properly emulsify enough of
the oils! I believe that my wife, the least of whose
countless virtues is mechanical aptitude, may have
injured the machine a few months back when she
chose brute force over dexterity to ram the filter basket into its holder while my back was turned. The
screech of tearing metal still rings in my ears.

Have I forgotten to mention that the water you use is said to
have a dramatic effect on the quality of the espresso, especially on
its body? Hard water, water with more minerals, makes a thicker
espresso, which contributes to the velvety texture and the long
aftertaste. But even Illy and his laboratories have not figured
out which minerals are important and just how hard the water
should be. Forster loves the nearly brackish water in Scottsdale,
Arizona, for making espresso. Illy prefers Los Angeles, where
nearly everybody drinks bottled water because much of the tap
water tastes awful.

On my next trip to San Diego, I will have a list of experiments
in hand. Out there the water can be so high in minerals as to vio-
late federal standards and taste nearly brackish. I use bottled
water even for Sky King, our incomparable golden retriever. The
espresso should be magnificent. On the other hand, maybe I'll
leave my experiments back in New York City. In San Diego, the
jasmine grows on trees.

NOVEMBER 2000

THAILAND

The plunder from our three weeks in Thailand was spread out on the kitchen table. There was a clear plastic bag of bamboo worms—crunchy, deep-fried, pale yellow—and my brand-new Kom-Kom Miracle Zig Zag, a four-function kitchen tool with an orange plastic handle with which you can peel and shred green mangoes and papayas in no time flat. Plus six books on the fruits and vegetables of Thailand and the rest of Southeast Asia. A fine round bamboo sieve and a ladle made from a polished coconut shell. A bag of fresh mangosteens, thought by some to be the most delicious fruit in the world. A solid-brass wok, for making Thai sweets. Disks of golden palm sugar, which tastes a little like maple syrup, wrapped in palm leaves. A sack of green rice, a delicacy; the grains are picked early and pounded flat. And a bag of wild black peppercorns, said to be pepper's most ancient form, not small and round but nearly two inches long and skinny, about the shape of bamboo worms, if you know what I mean.

There were also 500 photographs of lunches and dinners and how they were prepared, in homes, at restaurants, and in the street, and photos of markets—fresh-food markets, night markets, all-sweets markets, a jungle market with nearly a dozen species of fried and roasted insects (it was late January, the height of the season for red-ant eggs, which are snowy white), and prepared-food markets so vast that you think you can follow the curvature of the Earth as you peer down the long rows of soups and curries; noodles and salads; delicately fried pork rinds worthy of the finest gas stations in the American South; snacks of thin, sweetened water-buffalo jerky; bloodred water-buffalo tartare; banana-leaf packages stuffed with sweet or savory concoctions and steamed or roasted over charcoal.

Sadly, I have no photographs of the Chinese man who on most evenings for the past 44 years has cooked *phad Thai*, the national noodle of central Thailand, in the parking lot of a temple in Bangkok known as Wat Raat Burana. That's because, several hours earlier, I had left my camera, notebook, and exposed film in a taxi. His is the best *phad Thai* I've tasted, chewy instead of sloppy, savory instead of entirely sweet. The *phad Thai* man begins at around six and goes home when he has run out of eggs; he prepares each portion with the attention and interest he must have lavished on his first attempt. When I heard of an allegedly superior version two hours from Bangkok, at a shack in the shadow of another temple, I arranged for transportation and companions. We ventured forth and arrived in time for lunch. Fortune frowned that day—the shack was empty and a careful search of the temple grounds produced not a trace of *phad Thai*, though there *were* signs of recent cooking. Yes, we should have called ahead, but as a matter of definition, I believe, shacks don't have telephones. We did find 11 other good things to eat in the neighborhood.

Here are some amazing statistics: Thirty-five meals in Thailand and only one flop among them. (That was at a swanky French restaurant.) One hundred fifty Thai dishes, almost no repeats, and all but ten delicious, interesting, memorable. How could I have let my Thai friends maneuver me into a French restaurant in Bangkok?

My travel trophies were not confined to food. Far from it. There were several rolls of obligatory photographs showing golden temples, scenic vistas, famous mountains, whatever. And beautiful pieces of handwoven silk. (The Thai silk industry was rebuilt after World War II by American expatriate Jim Thompson—today still a hero in Thailand—who enlisted the advice and influence of his friend Edna Woolman Chase, editor of *Vogue* magazine in New York City. This, according to my new friend William Warren, a 40-year American expatriate in Thailand, who has written 38 books about the country, including one about the mysterious disappearance of Jim Thompson.) And there was a bootleg MP3 disk containing 432 Beatles songs from 26 albums, every song but "Revolution 9," all on a single disk costing $4. As I earn my livelihood from what, even in my case, is referred to as intellectual property, I am bitterly opposed to this kind of thing and was truly forbearant when a friend in Bangkok took me to an mini-mall completely devoted to pirated CDs, DVDs, and the latest software. Only the adult titles were homegrown.

My most prized and cherished treasure is a gray granite mortar and two pestles, one of palm wood, the other of stone. The mortar weighs 20 pounds and measures ten inches across, and in my mind it stands at the heart and core of true Thai cooking, the first step in preparing curries, sauces, dips, and soups. It signifies the irreducible and irreplaceable manual labor demanded by this remarkable cuisine, the magical release of flavors and aromas, the meditative rhythm of the pestle in a communal Thai kitchen, and the enduring closeness of Thai cooking to the forest and the jungle, to the Neolithic era, when food was gathered as much as grown.

But hold on a minute. Maybe I'm wrong. Did late Stone Age people know how to make stone mortars and pestles? (Now I learn that the Thais changed over from terra-cotta to stone mortars in 1769, way after the Stone Age, at the start of the current royal dynasty.) Wasn't the greatest Thai food created by cooks in the royal palaces and not in the jungle? And doesn't Thailand export more rice than any other country in the world, surely a sign of agricultural prowess? There should be a law against people who formulate grand culinary theories based on just 35 meals.

I did at least learn a little about how to pound and blend, with my mortar and pestle, the fragrant ingredients that define Thai cooking. One old woman told me I would make a fine daughter-in-law because of my skill in pounding. This may have been a profound insult. Real men don't pound, she seemed to be saying. But Thai men are famous cooks. King Chulalongkorn, who reigned from 1868 to 1910, was considered one of the greats. And the very sophisticated Thai man who took care of us in Phuket, M. L. Tridhosyuth Devakul (Tri for short), a busy Bangkok architect with a noble title and a degree from the Harvard Graduate School of Design, cooks all his family's meals.

Since returning from Thailand, I have not been in the mood for Western food, or for most of the Thai-restaurant food here in Manhattan. As cooking Thai food seemed beyond my capacities, I initially lived in fear of starvation or, at the very least, malnutrition, so I shifted to a subsistence diet of rice and noodles. Sometimes, I feel that I could live the rest of my life eating this way, and so could the rest of the world. But, most of the time, to be perfectly frank, I pray this is only a phase and that I will get over it soon. Last night I nursed myself halfway back to health with a little soft food, a tiny foie gras flan at a hot new restaurant, and I was actually able to keep it down.

In a related development, I have also not been much in the mood for Western people. While in Thailand, I became powerfully aware of the contrast between the predominantly compact and graceful Thai people, notably the young women, the most beautiful I have ever seen, and most Caucasian tourists, who increasingly struck me as large, pale, fleshy, sweating, clumsy, clueless, loud, bulging, ill-dressed, thick-boned, red-faced, lumbering, hirsute, and dull. I concluded that there is no reason for any human to take up more space than the average Thai or to be less delicate. I am contemplating a race-change operation, and will soon inquire whether our health plan at *Vogue* covers the cost.

I spent three weeks traveling around Thailand, eating and learning about Thai food. I could not have had better teachers. One generous friend led to another. If only they had had a cleverer student.

My paramount leader was Su-Mei Yu, a Thai native born in Bangkok to Chinese parents, who, since the age of 15, has lived in the United States, now in La Jolla, California, where I first met her. In 1999, I had spent a few days in Thailand and quickly recognized that here was some of the most satisfying and complex food I had ever eaten. Su-Mei was there, too, finishing the research for her book; we overlapped for a day and pledged to return together. Su-Mei recently published *Cracking the Coconut* (Morrow), an extremely valuable guide to Thai home cooking that has been so well received, I think, because while it is authentic and highly knowledgeable, it also understands the situation of the American home cook.

Su-Mei introduced me to Bob Halliday, an American who has lived in Bangkok for the past 30 years. Bob is an amazing man, fluent in spoken and written Thai, a polymath who is both music critic and food critic at the *Bangkok Post,* and who knows more excellent Bangkok restaurants—familiar and obscure, high and low—plus food shops and street vendors, than you could visit in several years, including one to which he has justifiably awarded the title "The Tour d'Argent of the Noodle." Even when Bob's choice for the evening appeared to be a total dump, the food would be superb, and there were often several Mercedeses lined up outside. At one place specializing in fish-ball soup, we were told that we had just missed the governor of Bangkok. Before you leave for Thailand, you can collect Bob's reviews from the *Bangkok Post* Web site, www.bangkokpost.net. He writes under the name of Ung-aang Talay, which is Thai for *sea toad,* an imaginary animal.

It was also in 1999 that I first met Kobkaew Najpinij, a woman in her middle age, who heads the authoritative government cooking school at the Rajabhat Institute Suan Dusit. I can still picture the lush and surprising tableau of Thai herbs and vegetables Khun Kobkaew had set out for us in a classroom filled with graceful Thai girls practicing the intricate art of carving fruits and vegetables. (Need I mention it was heaven?) On our recent trip, Khun Kobkaew and her lovely daughter Ning arranged lunches and dinners for us in restaurants and people's houses and were able, of course, to answer any food question of which I was capable. (*Khun* is a polite form of address.)

Su-Mei had also introduced me to her childhood friend, Vithi Phanichphant (whose last name I have never tried to pronounce), now professor of Thai fine arts and folk arts at Chiang Mai University, a proud chauvinist of northern Thailand and of the jungle (some Thais prefer the word "forest"), and a friend of the elephant. Vithi invited us for lunch at his family's house in Lampang, two hours to the south of Chiang Mai. On the way, we stopped in the town of Hang Chat at the large Tung Kreung market—created to bring a little income to Thais who still gather edible insects and wild plants in the surrounding forest—which is where we bought red-ant eggs for a soup, plus other delicacies, and searched for a fitting granite mortar and pestle for me.

The next evening, we had dinner with Vithi at an outdoor vegetarian restaurant he likes, and, during dessert, a mahout and his elephant, unemployed during the winter, sadly wandered into the courtyard to beg for food and money. Have you ever played with an elephant's trunk and felt the little lips at its tip as it takes a banana from your hand? And then you remember you're in the middle of Bangkok or Chiang Mai and standing only half a block from a cybercafé.

Do you see what I mean by the closeness of the Thai jungle? It unfortunately grows more notional and symbolic by the day, like the British countryside and the American wilderness, all supposed sources of these countries' deepest values. Still, so many Thai greens and vegetables are gathered and collected instead of grown. And most Thai sweets are based on the coconut in its various forms, palm sugar, and bananas and their leaves, usually in combination with jasmine rice or sticky rice. I wonder if the jungle theory will offend my sophisticated, urban Thai friends.

Also in Chiang Mai, we were introduced to the national noodle of the north by Bob Halliday's friend Kit Young, a concert pianist whose husband is in our foreign service and whose father was ambassador to Thailand under Kennedy. It's called *kao soy*— thin delicious egg noodles resembling Italian *tagliatelle,* served in a soupy, dark, and savory sauce flavored with chiles, chicken, and many dry spices. Although a vast variety of delicious noodle dishes can be had cheaply on nearly every city street, and Thais eat noodle snacks and complete noodle meals at the drop of a hat at any time of day, noodles were brought to Thailand by the Chinese, and are still considered Chinese food. That's why noodles are the only food in Thailand regularly eaten with chopsticks. (Otherwise you eat with a fork and spoon; the fork is used only to deposit food on the spoon and is never put into the mouth.) Vithi believes that *kao soy* is a northern Thai transformation of a Central Asian dish; the predominance of dry spices is evidence of a Muslim influence.

Circumstances and friends often conspired in the foolish hope that I might someday be able to understand Thai food. (Even on a side trip to Cambodia to clamber over the ruins at Angkor, we met up with Sottha Khunn, recently retired as head chef at Le Cirque 2000 in New York City, who was visiting his family in nearby Siem Reap, where his mother cooked us a wonderful Cambodian lunch that included a delicious turtle salad and little deep-fried birds the size of your thumb.) One night, M. L. Sirichalerm Svasti, one of Thailand's leading food personalities and a graduate of the Culinary Institute of America, held a delicious and instructional banquet for our growing group, complete with demonstrations and recipes (in Thai, later translated by Su-Mei), all outdoors on the Chao Phraya river, a half hour upstream from Bangkok. We learned to make a luxurious green curry with chunks of roasted duck, savory skin and all.

My friend David Thompson, owner of the best Thai restaurant in Australia, Darley Street Thai in Sydney, was in town; we dined together several times, and he e-mailed me 200 pages—the general and historical sections—of his forthcoming *Thai Food* (Viking). David believes that the golden age of Thai cuisine was in the late 1800s, and much of his research is aimed at recapturing it. We were introduced to Dr. Kanit Muntarbhorn, a physician and food historian who arranged an excellent dinner in Bangkok at My Choice restaurant, where every dish was new to us. At my request, Kanit organized a little comparative tasting of fermented fish sauces. And we discussed, into the next morning's early hours, the likely origins of Thai peanut sauce (could it be Bolivia?) and the appearance of the coconut in Thai cooking. Kanit believes that the golden age of Thai cuisine was 250 years ago, when the capital of Siam was the city of Ayutthaya, by British report the most splendid court in Asia, and he pledged that, after only a few more years of his research, we would be able to dine in the Ayutthayan manner. I can't wait.

For Bob Halliday's friend Nutchanand Osathanond (friends call her Pao), the golden age of Thai cooking was in her childhood. Her grandfather was the son of a court physician, was educated in England, became a high Thai official and governor of several provinces, won the Irish sweepstakes, employed many cooks, and took notes on their cooking. Pao spent the better part of her childhood in the kitchen, talking with her grandfather's renowned cooks, and, with her mother's help, filled her notebooks with their advice and instructions. These notes have become recipes for her remarkable dinner parties, and we were invited to one of them in Pao's large stone house, built in the style of eighteenth-century France. Pao cooked many new dishes for us, including a novel form of green curry and a wonderfully tangy beef soup, hot with chiles. Days later, in the market, Pao showed me how to select the best mangosteens, that indescribably delicious fruit. Khun Pao is also fluent in French, and visits Paris every month or two.

Back in New York City, my addiction to real Thai food and the troublesome withdrawal symptoms had me totally mystified. Thai cooking is in many ways completely foreign to us. I'm not just thinking of the truly exotic food I learned to eat, such as various insects in northern Thailand, those light and crispy bamboo worms, the platter of roasted wasp larvae at a Yunnanese restaurant in Chiang Mai, or the red-ant eggs, which Vithi calls "jungle caviar." Not to mention Yunnanese pig's brains, which are truly delicious, not when they are sliced and deep-fried as we had them in one restaurant, but mashed up with mild flavorings and steamed in a banana leaf. (Yunnan is the most southerly province of China and the probable origin of the Thai people, who migrated south and overwhelmed the ancient Mon.) I drew a line in the sand just this side of winged four-inch water bugs, battered and fried.

No, even some of the simplest Thai flavorings and ingredients and the principles of combining them are alien to the Western palate. I am thinking of my big stone mortar, just like the one in nearly every Thai kitchen, and the things you pound together in it, the strong tastes in nearly every Thai sauce and curry. ("Curry" is from the Tamil word *kari,* meaning a sauce or relish for rice; the Thais may have made curries long before Indian cooking and its multitude of spices arrived; today, only a few Thai curries taste like Indian ones. Premixed curry powder was invented by the British.)

You start preparing a curry paste by pounding together garlic and salt, and some sliced purple shallots. Here the similarity to Western food grows thin. Nearly every curry paste also includes coriander root (in U.S. supermarkets, coriander, also known as cilantro, usually comes with the white roots lopped off), dried and fresh chiles, galangal (a milder, smoother member of the ginger family), sliced lemongrass stems, turmeric root, the rind of the kaffir lime, and shrimp paste, often strongly fermented. You will also add dry spices—coriander and cumin seed, maybe cinnamon, and possibly cardamom—which you have earlier roasted and ground. Pounding all this together will take 20 minutes. Thai pounding is performed up and down, up and down, not grinding in a circle.

The resulting paste is a typical mixture of the tastes and aromas that underlie a Thai dish. (In most European cooking, the flavor base is often made up of finely chopped onions, garlic, parsley, and sometimes celery and carrots, slowly sauteed in butter or olive oil.) In many recipes, the curry paste will first be sauteed in vegetable oil, especially for making the jungle curries of the north, or sautéed in the rich cream skimmed from a bowl of fresh coconut milk, especially in central Thailand. Coconut milk is not the liquid you find inside a fully mature coconut. Nor is it the wonderfully sweet and fragrant nectar you sip through a straw from a green coconut. Coconut *milk* is made by shredding fresh coconut, massaging it 89 times in hot water (the number is traditional), and straining. This is then repeated with additional water. When the resulting coconut milk is boiled or left standing, the fatty coconut *cream* rises to the top; the thin liquid on the bottom is sometimes called "coconut cream tail" by the Thais. When the cream is used for sautéeing, the oil it contains gets very hot, like any other cooking fat.

The main ingredient of any curry will be pieces of fish, meat, fowl, or vegetable. These will be added directly to the curry paste or cooked first in a pot of boiling coconut cream tail. Later, you will add fermented fish sauce and probably palm sugar. A fresh and vivid top note will come from the aromatic leaves of the kaffir lime and of basil (and coriander leaves in dishes without coconut), added at the last minute—though coriander is used much less in Thailand than here, and these days, basil appears everywhere far more often than it should, according to my Thai experts.

And that's just for a start. Everywhere you go in Thailand, cooks use types of leaves, stems, roots, and flower buds that you have never tasted, heard of, or imagined. Morning-glory stems appeared somewhere in half of our meals; they are hollow and delicious and stay crunchy even after they are cooked. A friend of Su-Mei's named Lady Sirin (please don't ask me to explain the Thai system of entitlements) took us to a fine lunch in Ayutthaya; we made packages with the leaves of what was called the cumin plant to wrap and eat a fiery pork mixture, made from the chopped ribs, soft bones and all, of a baby pig, and garlic grown as individual cloves and pickled. And somewhere, we ate a cassia-leaf curry. (Lady Sirin generously lent us her van and driver whenever we needed to travel a good distance for the purpose of eating, and gave us bags of young, green rice, a crop on which she is basing a business.)

Now Bob Halliday swears that cumin leaves are bitter, fibrous, and awful to eat. Do you see what it's like trying to find out the simplest things about Thai food?

For a while, my favorite exotic leaf was *phakchee farang,* which uncannily combines and amplifies the flavors of lemongrass and coriander leaves. Bob Halliday's colleague on the *Bangkok Post* is Suthon Sukphisit, a great expert in traditional Thai ways, and one day, Suthon guided us for an hour or two outside of Bangkok to a beautiful little village that runs for about a mile on both sides of a meandering river. There, at a vegetable seller's stand, I discovered the delicious *phakchee farang* (which is apparently used in Thai cooking to neutralize the odor of certain cuts of beef). Now I am told that, in season, whenever that is, you can find *phakchee farang* in Chinatown, right here in New York City. My copy of *Plants from the Markets of Thailand,* by Christiane Jacquat, shows about 200 other green things you'll never find here.

Everybody in Thailand tells you the importance of balance in every dish among sweet, sour, salty, and bitter. Cooks in other cuisines often seem to promote principles like this, but the Thais are truly serious about it, even dipping slices of fresh fruit in a mixture of ground chiles, salt, and sugar, and flavoring their sweet fruit juices with salt.

Sweetness comes mainly from palm sugar and granulated sugar; Thai rice, known as jasmine rice either for its fragrance or its snowy color, seems naturally sweet. Sour tastes derive much less from vinegar, except in dishes derived from the Chinese, than from tamarind, wild plums, lime juice (they do not grow lemons in Thailand), and green (unripe and acidic) mangoes. The salty ingredients are principally white table salt itself, shrimp paste, and fermented fish sauce, which, we realized at Dr. Kanit Muntarbhorn's comparative fermented-fish-sauce tasting, not only contains 25 percent straight salt, but also adds an indispensable rounded, savory flavor to the dish. Bitterness is introduced by a variety of leaves and greens, lime or bitter orange rind, and little eggplants.

You know those tiny, round Thai eggplants the size of large peas? I had always thought that if I cooked them properly, they would lose their unpleasant bitterness; Westerners, and especially Americans, generally avoid foods that taste bitter. I had totally missed the point. These miniature eggplants are added to Thai dishes expressly for their bitter taste—plus a nice crunch.

Most dishes contain hot chiles—ground, dry, or fresh—sometimes as a piquant undertone, at other times as an enveloping experience that for a time takes over your mouth. Yet, among 150 dishes, only one was too hot for me to eat, and I am not one of those macho hot-chile guys either. Here's a handy tip: If you discover that the food in your mouth is painfully hot and spicy, keep chewing but do not swallow it right away. The heat will dissipate. If you swallow immediately, your throat will also be seared, you will gasp and cough, and your food will spray all over the table.

Real Thai food is the most intensely flavored I know, even without the chiles. A Thai meal is an immersion in a large and complex system of tastes and fragrances, one layer upon another. Some of the ingredients might even be unpleasant eaten on their own—bitter eggplants, for example, or fermented-fish sauce, or shrimp paste; in combination, they create a powerful sense of pleasure. Trying to make a dish taste Thai by adding coriander leaves and lemongrass to Western food pretty much misses the point. There is only one thing left for you and me to do. Get hold of a book that does not cut corners, such as Su-Mei Yu's *Cracking the Coconut*. Buy a giant granite mortar with a smooth bowl measuring at least six inches across, plus a pestle and some wonderfully aromatic Thai ingredients. And just start pounding.

APRIL 2001

An Intense Hunt for the Facts

I was able to acknowledge how little I truly understood the life cycle of the lobster, especially the sex part. An intense hunt for the facts ensued.

On a Roll

Supergoose

Perfection Pizza

Red Wine and Old Roosters

Where's the Boeuf?

ON A ROLL

As I am fairly sure God intended for all animal species, including humans, the male lobster practices serial monogamy, remaining faithful to his mate for between one and two weeks. The female lobster spends most of her adult life being in one way or another pregnant and thus gets interested in sex only once every two years, if that. While love lasts, the male is supremely tender and protective. And then it is time for him to move on. In actual fact, it is time for her to move on because he owns the apartment (or "shelter" in lobster terminology), and she doesn't.

How, you are silently wondering, does a lobster couple practice sexual intercourse? That is a question I had often asked myself but, until a few weeks ago, lacked the mettle and initiative to investigate. For it was then that, lost in the trancelike state into which eating a lobster roll with french fries and the tiniest green salad at the Pearl Oyster Bar on Cornelia Street in Greenwich Village had plunged me, I was first able to acknowledge how little I truly understood the life cycle of the lobster, especially the sex part. An intense hunt for the facts immediately ensued.

The simple answer is this: The female molts. She sheds her shell to have sex, while the male keeps his armor on. A more complete and vivid account follows somewhere below.

Those of you who spend little time in the northeastern United States may have some difficulty appreciating the spiritual qualities of the lobster roll. You may never even have heard of it, though it is one of the central culinary discoveries of the New England region. At its most schematic, a lobster roll is a toasted hot-dog bun filled with lobster salad. (There is an alternate, so-called *hot* lobster roll, relatively rare but favored here and there throughout New England, and by Jane and Michael Stern in *Real American Food* [Knopf], in which both bun and boiled lobster meat are sautéed in lots of butter and then somehow assembled.) As you can imagine, the variations are infinite—there are numberless formulas for lobster salad, innumerable types of hot-dog rolls, and countless ways to prepare them for stuffing. But there is one best way, and the recipe, the somewhat austere Pearl Oyster Bar version, appears at the end of this piece. You'll need four special hot-dog buns, their *sides* browned in butter, a pound of lobster meat, finely chopped celery, Hellman's mayonnaise, and a little lemon juice. You will not regret the effort spent on shopping. And on cooking some lobsters.

Lobsters are the only animals we slaughter ourselves at home before cooking them—unless you include oysters or belong to some weird ethnic group. Before this project, I had never killed a lobster by driving a heavy knife between its eyes as so many books tell you to do. I had never microwaved a lobster alive or dismembered a lobster alive the way the French do, first tearing off the claws and then the tail. I still haven't. Whenever I boiled or steamed lobsters—and hundreds of them have died for my dinner—I shook them out of their brown paper bag into the fuming stockpot as they tried to catch their claws on the rim. Then, I left the kitchen to escape the clatter they made as they tried to push the cover off the pot. I had never held a live lobster and looked at it face-to-face with equanimity and fascination. Now I can tell you: The more you kill, the easier it gets.

Is there a humane way to kill a lobster? A method of killing is considered humane if it results in instant death, or relatively quick death with a minimum of discomfort to the animal.

The ASPCA doesn't do lobsters, they said when I telephoned, only pets, which they call companion animals. Their animal-science-and-behavior expert, however, guessed that a knife to the head is probably most humane because it is said to kill the lobster instantly.

The British Universities Federation for Animal Welfare advocates plunging lobsters into already boiling water. They cite experimental evidence that the creature dies in 15 seconds; its continuing movements are just nervous reactions. (As I later learned, it is the muscles and not the nerves that keep on thrashing; most animals die this way.) Everybody there was too squeamish to plunge a heavy knife through a living lobster. Fifteen seconds of what must be intense suffering is the best they can do.

The Australian Royal Society for the Prevention of Cruelty to Animals finds boiling unacceptable. "An animal is humanely killed," they say, "by first making it insensible to pain and killing it before it regains consciousness." They advocate anesthetizing lobsters in an icy slush for at least 20 minutes. Crustaceans are cold-blooded and their physical activity slows to nearly nothing when they are chilled. But, as they are heated in the boiling water, don't they pass through at least 15 seconds of misery?

I again telephoned the British Universities Federation for Animal Welfare to ask about this disagreement. James Kirkwood, their scientific director, feels that the conflicting positions taken by various humane societies, including his own, are based on outmoded research from the seventies and eighties and on anecdotes. Miriam Parker, his counterpart at the Humane Slaughter Association, put me on to a scientist at the University of Bristol who has been doing studies on the humane killing of lobsters. He asked me not to use his name, because members of his department have been physically threatened by animal-rights advocates, even though his work aims at relieving animal suffering; a few months ago, a bomb went off under one of their cars, doing no damage to the scientist but hospitalizing a little girl walking by.

How can we tell that a lobster has died and no longer feels pain? "Sensibility" is the test, said the Bristol researcher—whether the animal can still react and respond. In higher animals, brain death is the criterion. But lobsters and crabs lack centralized brains. Their nervous system is distributed all around their bodies in nerve bundles called "ganglia." Crabs are easy to kill humanely because they have only two ganglia. Lobsters have eight. A lobster is still sensible if it pulls away when you touch its antennae, if it grasps your finger with the little pincers at the end of its walking legs, if it responds when you touch the sensitive little hairs that cover its underside. The Bristol scientist has determined that lobsters take a relatively long 45 seconds to die in boiling water, much longer if you begin with cold water and bring it to a boil. This will first drown them in fresh water, and they will struggle only briefly, but he feels that this must nonetheless be a long and painful death. As I once was, he has been too squeamish to kill lobsters with a heavy knife first to the head and then down the body. Accurately done, though, he imagines that this could take out all eight ganglia nearly instantaneously. I have more or less perfected my technique for killing lobsters this way. They do not remain sensible, but you cannot steam or boil the resulting lobster halves. For this, I slide the whole lobsters in the freezer for a half hour or more before popping them in the pot.

The Bristol researcher has been experimenting with electrocution, stunning lobsters electrically, as the slaughter industry does with pigs and sheep, and then killing them with a knife or by cooking. Electrocuting them from start to finish causes carcass damage. With existing technology, the lobsters are stunned individually, out of water, in a machine resembling a microwave oven.

Whew! Now you know why some people avoid cooking lobsters.

It must be among the hundred sharpest ironies of culinary history that the lobster roll was made possible by a man who could never enjoy one, a Moses denied his promised land. The lobster has been standing in the wings to play its starring role since the mid-Jurassic period, 195 million years ago, but the evolution of the hot-dog bun was much more recent. Anton Feuchtwanger was a Bavarian sausage vendor at the St. Louis Exposition of 1903 who lent his customers white gloves to keep their fingers clean as they ate his sausages. The gloves kept disappearing. He asked his brother, a baker, for help, and the long, soft, spongy roll we love today was born. As Anton and his brother were Jews, eating lobster was out of the question. They could not even have imagined such a treat as the lobster roll!

There are other versions of this story and many other stories as well. The *Oxford English Dictionary* says that the use of "hot dog" to mean "good or superior" (giving rise to all sorts of surfing and skiing slang) dates back to 1896, which *preceded* by several years its appearance as "a hot sausage enclosed as a sandwich in a bread roll." I find this nothing short of astounding.

H. L. Mencken attributes the hot dog to Harry Mozely Stevens, caterer at the New York Polo Grounds around 1905, but gives him credit only for warming the buns and adding assorted condiments, saying that "the sale of sausages in rolls was introduced in this country many years" earlier. I'll stick with Anton, as food historian Joan Nathan calls him, or Antoine, according to Waverly Root. I'll also stick with Joan Nathan.

Here I sit surrounded by hot-dog buns, 20 or 30, all of my own making. We did it for you, my assistant Kathryn and I, because, unless you live in the Northeast, you will be unable to find the top-sliced Pepperidge Farm Frankfurter Rolls favored at Pearl Oyster Bar. Frankfurter rolls are indispensable because they are soft and quite sweet, which brings out the sweetness and crunch of lobster. But the important thing is *top sliced*. Top-sliced buns are baked side by side, and when you pull them apart, all but the ones on the ends emerge with two rough, torn surfaces that brown especially beautifully when you panfry them in butter. The bottoms are flat and square and only the top is sliced, so that even when you load the bun with five ounces of lobster salad, it sits erect and proud on the plate. It is an oddity of our language that "hot-dog bun fried in butter" cannot convey the fine, rich, sweet taste to which it gestures.

A few days' investigation revealed that Pepperidge Farm produces top-sliced frankfurter rolls only in the New England and mid-Atlantic states. Even in New York City, you have to hunt and peck from neighborhood to neighborhood until you find the one D'Agostino or the four Food Emporiums granted the honor of carrying them. While I doubt it was mere chance that put a top-sliced location within easy walking distance of my house and a thousand miles from yours, I was still willing to squander several hours trying to find a solution for you. Having failed to locate a supermarket eager to mail you—at any price—a package of Pepperidge Farm Top-Sliced (or even of an inferior top-sliced brand we discovered), it was into the kitchen. Of the three recipes we tried for hot-dog buns, Marion Cunningham's (in *The Fannie Farmer Baking Book* [Knopf], a variation of her hamburger bun) won hands-down in a blind taste test. They are different from store-bought—better-tasting, but denser and more substantial. They need more lobster salad for the proper taste balance.

Marion Cunningham uses lard. Lard is far less bad for you than butter or a hydrogenated solid shortening like Crisco or margarine and makes for a lighter, tastier bun than life-extending canola oil ever could. Yet so many of you would never consider buying even a teaspoon of the stuff that I telephoned Marion, who had been my very good friend until the phone call, to ask whether I could monkey with her recipe and substitute Crisco or oil. Both work, but are inferior to lard in taste and texture.

I am avoiding something. That's what you are thinking. All this fussing about hot-dog buns must signify a phobic turning away from a psychically painful subject. Yes, I have been putting off the sex part. We'll ease into it very soon. But first let's talk about cooking.

So many fine cooks have worked with lobsters all their lives and have still come up with conflicting cooking advice. Are female lobsters more tender and sweeter than males? Is steaming better than boiling? Is it 10 minutes for a two-pounder or 20 minutes or what? Are hard-shell lobsters sweeter than soft shell? Regardless of one's preference for humane killing, are lobsters more tender if you freeze them first or drown them in fresh water?

How many lobsters would I have to cook before coming to conclusions more reliable than the experts'? Maybe 200, I figured, maybe more. Anything less would be anecdotal. I briefly toyed with the idea. There is a terrific shop near my house at which to buy lively lobsters, the Lobster Place at the Chelsea Market. They must keep a thousand of them at all times in their saltwater tanks. But no, I would follow Jasper White, who has written the best book about cooking lobster at home. It's called *Lobster at Home* and was published last year by Scribner. Jasper once had the best restaurant in New England, and has worked around fish and seafood ever since. I'd swear by Jasper. Everybody should buy his book. And yet . . . I do like my lobster a little less cooked than he does. Maybe I'll do an experiment or two. But no more than 30 lobsters' worth.

Jasper boils his lobsters in seawater. If none is available he steams them, rather than boil them in salted water. He loves the ocean taste, though he feels that steaming yields sweeter and more tender lobster. He's right. Steaming is easier, cleaner, and safer, and the results are better than boiling. My recipe follows, with Jasper's timing and my own. Here's a useful guide: Lobsters yield between 20 percent and 25 percent of their live weight in meat—tail, claws, and a little from the arms, known in the trade as the "knuckles." Soft-shell (recently molted) lobsters are fine but hard-shell are even better and less watery. Jasper's absolute favorites come to market from southwest Nova Scotia, in Canada, beginning November 15. Jasper finds no consistent difference in the flesh of the male and female. Neither have I.

If you like the coral, which runs along the shell on both sides of the female's body (and is black or dark green when raw and vividly coral-colored when cooked), you'll still need to tell them apart. So, we're back to male and female. I haven't really been avoiding the sex part, just putting it at the end, to hold your interest.

The American lobster, also known as Maine lobster, Canadian lobster, and *Homarus americanus*, can be found from Newfoundland to North Carolina. Unlike the various species of spiny lobster and rock lobster, the American lobster (and a smaller cousin in Europe, but no others in the world) has large, edible claws. Lobsters grow by molting, by shedding their shells, then taking in seawater and temporarily swelling up so that their new shell will harden at a considerably larger size. They grow about 20 percent with each molt. By the time a lobster is capable of mating, it will have molted 20 to 30 times and probably be between five and seven years old. (We can't be sure, because you cannot easily tag a lobster that sheds its shell.) Then it slows down to about once a year. It will weigh one pound, the minimum legal weight for capture.

Immature lobsters live in burrows in the sea floor, older ones in close-fitting shelters in the rocky coastline. Their shelters always have two or more entrances, at least one barricaded and one ready for an escape. Adult lobsters spend most of their time at home, venturing out after sunset to look for food. Some lobsters migrate. The record is nearly 500 miles. Others have been clocked at nearly six miles an hour. For the most part, lobsters are *not* scavengers but are predators that feast on mussels, sea urchins, crabs, and worms, plus a minuscule amount of vegetation. They need powerful crushing claws for the first, and armor against the second and against each other. They are extremely aggressive with other lobsters and are even capable of cannibalism, though not while mating.

In the summer, before she molts, the female enters the dominant male's shelter, where they engage in a boxing ritual for several seconds or minutes. The female may become violent. One hour before molting, the female faces the male and rests her claws on his body. There is much touching of antennae. Then her carapace, her main body shell, splits from her tail and she pulls herself out. Her claws have already shrunk, and now she pulls them through her narrow arm shells. She is completely naked and vulnerable, barely protected by a thin, soft covering that will harden very slowly over the next two months. She can hardly stand on her own legs.

Mating follows molting by a half hour. The male stands over the female, holding himself up by his claws and tail, and turns her over very gently with his ten legs. Copulation lasts between eight seconds and a minute, during which he places a sealed packet of his seed into a pouch in her abdomen, employing the world-famous thrusting motion. Then he stands guard over her for a week or so while eating her discarded shell. She leaves, burying herself in the sand until her shell is hard enough for protection. She will not use the stored sperm until the next summer or whenever she feels like it. After about a year, she will produce between 5,000 and 100,000 eggs, somehow fertilizing them herself, and attaching them to the underside of her tail, where they will remain for a year before hatching.

That's the sex part. It carries important lessons we can use in our own daily lives.

As lobsters generally molt in the summer, nearly all those caught between July and September have soft shells. Since these lobsters are extremely numerous, more likely to die when transported, and earn a lower price at market, many are placed into "pounds," fenced-off areas of the ocean where they must be fed scraps of fish for several months. Lobsters trapped between October and December are among the best, with hardened shells, well fed and fat. From February through mid-April, though, when the weather is awful and the icy water puts lobsters into a kind of hibernation, drastically reducing the number that will wander into traps, most lobsters that arrive at your fish market come from pounds. They are fine to eat but lean and bland because they have not been dining particularly well.

And then comes spring. The sun is bright, the water sparkles, and the lobsters are active again, swimming about, eating like kings, and vying for a place in your butter-browned top-sliced frankfurter bun.

LOBSTER ROLLS
(adapted from Pearl Oyster Bar)

1 lb. freshly cooked lobster meat, cut into ½- to ¾-inch chunks
(see recipe below)
¼ cup very finely diced celery, or more to taste
⅓ cup Hellman's mayonnaise, or a little more
2–3 tsps. fresh lemon juice, to taste
1 very large pinch of salt or more to taste
8 grindings black pepper
4–6 Tbs. unsalted butter
4 Pepperidge Farm *Top-Sliced* Frankfurter Rolls
1–1½ tsp. very finely sliced chives

Mix the lobster meat, celery, mayonnaise, and lemon juice. Taste for salt and pepper. Delicious! Melt the butter in a frying pan over medium-low heat. Lightly brown both sides of the four frankfurter rolls. Fill each with a quarter of the lobster salad. Sprinkle with chives. Garnish with potato chips, preferably homemade, or thin French fries, and a small green salad. Serves four.

STEAMED LOBSTER

Most lobsters that I prepare this way come out sweet and tender. Follow it and cooking lobsters will cease to be a mystery or a bother.

Try to shop at a fish market with high turnover of lobsters. If you live at a far distance from the Northeast, you might order lobsters by mail. Handle lobsters very gently. Their claws should be banded, not pegged. Grasp them around the body, just behind the claws. They should wave their claws and

- - - - -

flap their tails when you pick them up. Their antennae should be pretty much intact. Do not cook a lobster you did not see alive. Keep live lobsters in your refrigerator for a maximum of 36 hours, wrapped in wet newspaper. Despite what you may have heard, lobster meat has fewer calories, less saturated fat, and less cholesterol than skinless chicken breasts.

This recipe yields 1 *pound* of lobster meat.

4½–5 lbs. live lobsters (see note)
a 20–32-quart stockpot or lobster steamer
Special equipment: a steaming rack (the type with a ring of
metal petals works well) or enough rockweed to keep
the lobsters out of the water

Place the lobsters in the freezer in a paper bag for 30 minutes or more, or head down in a pot of fresh water for 20 minutes or more. These treatments produce sweeter and more tender meat.

Put an inch or two of cold, fresh water in the stockpot. Set the rack or the rockweed onto the bottom of the pot. Cover and bring to a very lively boil over high heat. Uncover the pot, and with a long pair of tongs or an oven mitt set the lobsters on the rack or rockweed. Cover and begin timing. Five 1-pound lobsters will require eight to nine minutes of steaming. Four 1¼-pound lobsters need 9 to 10 minutes, and three 1½-pound lobsters need 10 to 11. (An instant-read thermometer thrust into the thickest part of the tail should read about 140°F. Jasper White feels that lobsters are more succulent if steamed about a minute or 2 longer.) Larger lobsters should be saved for eating whole.

If you plan to make lobster rolls, cool the lobsters under ice to stop their cooking. Twist off the tails and claws. Use kitchen shears or light garden shears to cut along the center of the

– – – – –

translucent shell on the underside of the tail and remove the meat. Crack the claws and the knuckles, which have the sweetest flesh, with the back of a heavy knife. The fluffy substance that resembles cooked egg whites is congealed blood and is perfectly fine to eat. The greenish tomalley (liver and pancreas) and reddish coral (roe) in the body cavity are delicious but are not used in lobster salad.

Note: For lobster salad, the least expensive 1-pound lobsters are perfect. For your cooking convenience, the lobsters should all be about the same weight.

AUGUST 1999

SUPERGOOSE

This year all the signs and portents pointed to goose—a burnished, glistening, savory, crispy, crunchy, crackling, aromatic, roasted goose. I had traveled down the turkey trail as far as I could go, at least for now. I planned for pig, but backed out of the deal when the farmer at the Greenmarket was only hours away from killing the poor little pink thing—I assume it was pink—just when I should have been preheating my oven and polishing my carving knife. The farmer fed the animal for another few months and slaughtered it anyway for bacon and sausages and pork chops.

My aspirations shifted to game birds, grouse and woodcock in particular, and maybe even teal. I love woodcock—in France they are *bécasse* and, though illegal, are esteemed above all other birds except maybe ortolan—and I feasted on grouse in London last fall, and now I have discovered with childlike delight that American woods and ponds are bursting with them. But in our country, as in France, hunters are generally prohibited from selling their quarry. Thus, my only option was to take up shooting from square one, to devolve from shopper-gatherer to hunter. It took just three visits to Holland & Holland on East 57th Street to conclude that just choosing an outfit would require weeks of study.

Which left me with goose. I had ignorantly believed that roasting a goose in winter was some musty and otiose British custom lacking all gastronomic value, an eccentric quirk given unjustified immortality by Charles Dickens or somebody.

Then I began reading amongst the myths of all the world's cultures. How deluded I had been to question the inevitability of goose. Has any other edible bird been more prominent in the legends of mankind? In one creation myth of the ancient Egyptians, a celestial goose laid a cosmic egg, which, as luck would have it, contained Ra, the bird of light, who then hatched and created the world. The migratory goose's affinity for the sun put it at the center of ritual meals near the winter solstice that ensured the return of the sun on the darkest day of the year. Christians later adopted this day for Christmas. The promise of enduring light is one of the meanings of Hanukkah, which is when my grandmother always roasted a goose. Maguelonne Toussaint-Samat, in *A History of Food*, writes that "almost all civilizations of the world which encountered geese regarded them as intermediaries between heaven and earth." Sacrificing (and feasting on) geese at the change of seasons was traditional in Europe, Central Asia, and among the Berbers of North Africa and the North American Indians.

Despite their later connection with the bird, the British were laggards in the cooking of goose. Julius Caesar wrote that they avoided geese and hares, presumably on religious grounds, though they apparently enjoyed arranging cockfights among the ganders. Meanwhile, the nearby Gauls, Scandinavians, other Germanic peoples, and Slavs relished nothing more than a nicely cooked goose. Or so I have read.

Reeling from my newfound appreciation of the goose's cosmic and earthly prestige, I understood why a midwinter feast must include roast goose. The problem is that I had never roasted a goose I cared to eat. And I was not in the mood to spend the autumn months in training, all so that on some dark December evening I could bring a glistening, golden-brown fowl to the dining-room table, flaunt it for 30 seconds, collect a round of obligatory compliments, and then carry it back to the kitchen for carving. But I simply had no choice.

The potential flaws of a roasted goose are many: soggy skin; tough, stringy, and flavorless (or bitter-tasting) meat; overdone and desiccated breast meat; barely cooked, unrendered fat in pouches and pockets and thick layers everywhere beneath the skin. I had tried numerous recipes over the years, but none had solved more than one or two of these problems at a time.

Here was my project: First I would roast a series of geese, striving each time to conquer just one of the potential defects. I would then assemble all my solutions into one grand cooking method. It was possible, though still not entirely likely, that I might create a Supergoose.

Problem #1: How to establish a reliable supply chain of geese from the farm to the *Vogue* Test Kitchen and Food Laboratory, which has for the past decade has temporarily occupied half my loft in New York City. I telephoned Ariane Daguin, co-owner of D'Artagnan, Inc., and a native of Auch in southwest France, which, by most measures, is the world's goose capital but where, I have read, the goose was never much romanticized, mystified, venerated, or worshipped. Ariane explained the problem of supply. Nearly all baby geese are born in and around the month of June. (Shifting the timing through artificial insemination has not been a huge success.) Geese are ready to be eaten five or six months later, the first at the beginning of November, with the most plentiful supply coming around the winter solstice. In late August, when my experiments began, Ariane could not guarantee a steady daily shipment. I could find only two butchers in Manhattan, an island which I feel certain has the highest per capita concentration of true butcher shops in the country, that offered to deliver a parade of plump, full-grown, fresh, never frozen geese weighing 11 pounds each, starting immediately. These were the famed Citarella and the celebrated Lobel's.

Solution #1: The Amish. The first specimen from Citarella came, I'm afraid, only partially defrosted and the second was scrawny. The geese from Lobel's were handsome and plump, and they cost only twice as much as any others in the city. The Amish farm in Pennsylvania that supplies Lobel's thus saved the day. How the Amish can come up with plump geese at the end of summer is a mystery. Incidentally, I just checked with the U.S. Bureau of Labor Statistics. Manhattan has four times the national average of butchers and butcher shops.

Problem #2: Roasted goose never tastes as good as, say, a pastrami sandwich on rye.

Solution #2: Brine your bird. Everybody these days is brining whatever they can get their hands on. This means putting your goose or turkey or pork shoulder into salty water and leaving it in your refrigerator or cellar or on a wintry windowsill for a day or two. The water can be further flavored with sugar, herbs, and spices. Brining can be fun and gives you something new to do for the holidays. All those recipes for braising goose in a well-flavored stock, so popular in France and China, are attempts to get some soft, rounded tastes into this dark, gamy bird, and make it juicier and more tender. Yet I had never heard of anybody brining a goose.

So. I eased a 12-pound bird into a plastic bucket half filled with water, plus a cup of salt for each gallon, and spiced it up with cloves, cardamom, bay leaves, cinnamon sticks, and black peppercorns. The bucket was now very heavy and would not fit into my refrigerator, which was already home to three other raw geese and their prospective garnishes. I simulated an open window in winter by putting the bucket next to an air conditioner set on turbo-freeze. Repeatedly carrying 50 pounds of goose and sloshing brine for 60 feet and lifting them onto a high windowsill proved unexpectedly taxing. After taking a painkiller and a restorative nap, I walked to the nearby industrial hardware store and shopped for a handcart, one of those four-foot-high, L-shaped metal things with big rubber wheels, commonly used to move refrigerators. I was a nanosecond away from buying the lightest, best designed, and most expensive handcart in Manhattan—I have always wanted to own a handcart—when, inwardly illuminated by a flash of insight, I realized that the vegetable drawers in my refrigerator are precisely goose-shaped. I raced home to test my brainstorm. Eureka! Now I can semiprofessionally brine two geese at once, at the proper temperature, using only half the water, salt, and spices, and without having to run the air conditioner in October.

The effect was magical, especially on the taste. Having found no logical explanation in the popular press of how brining works, I e-mailed my friend Harold McGee, whose two books, *On Food and Cooking* and *The Curious Cook,* are indispensable to people who enjoy scientific explanations for what goes on in their kitchens. It's all about osmosis, Harold explained. I have never understood osmosis. I must have missed that day in elementary school. Now, after learning how complicated osmosis is, I feel it should be taught only at the very end of college, if then.

Here's what happens. First, salt in the brine draws water out of the goose and itself seeps into the goose flesh, which it flavors and where it dissolves some of the muscle-fiber protein, tenderizing the flesh. At the same time, the increased concentration of dissolved solids in the goose's juices somehow pulls water back from the brine, increasing the juiciness of the meat. In the process, the flavorings and aromas in the brine hitch a ride into the goose. Brining has become a fascinating hobby and is essential to the creation of a Supergoose.

TO BRINE A GOOSE

Find a container that will hold your goose with enough space around it to allow the brine to move freely. Slip in the goose and cover it with water, *which you should measure as you add*. Then, for each gallon, put into a saucepan 1 cup of salt and ½ cup of sugar. Add a few cups of water and bring to a boil to dissolve. Off the heat, add whatever flavorings you'd like. A blend I've enjoyed is 5 crushed black peppercorns (lightly crushed), ½ cinnamon stick, 1 clove, ¼ tsp. ground cardamom, and ½ bay leaf, for each gallon of water. Let cool and pour into the water surrounding the goose. Refrigerate for about 24 hours, longer for a giant bird. Then remove the goose, pat it dry, and either use immediately or store in the refrigerator for up to 2 days. Before proceeding with any roasting method, be sure to pierce the goose's skin all over with 100 quick thrusts of a small, sharply pointed knife. The knife must be held nearly flat to the surface so that it pierces the skin and fat without puncturing the meat. Then concentrate on areas where you see large pools of fat under the skin. Let the goose come to room temperature for 3 or 4 hours before roasting.

Problem #3: Roasting a goose whole, or a turkey for that matter, is the method least likely to produce perfectly cooked flesh or accomplish much of anything else except for crisping the skin, which is nothing to sneeze at, but not the only thing. Plus, one always burns oneself in several places when roasting anything larger than a chicken.

Solution #3: There is no solution. I roast something or other two or three times a week, even just for lunch. But roasting is still a mystery to me. You need a high temperature to crisp the outside, but a lower setting to keep the flesh juicy. Most recipes have you start high and finish low; some do the reverse. The breast gets done before the legs, because of both its prominence and thinness and the kind of flesh it is. This is why many French recipes for goose and turkey, and even for chicken and squab, have you dismember the bird and cook the legs separately from the breast. Later, some people try to reassemble the bird for purposes of display, hiding the seams with parsley or something.

But gathering as a tribe or clan, and killing, roasting, and sharing an entire animal is a primal, atavistic ritual, a secular communion that cannot be duplicated by divvying up a low-calorie turkey breast, a goose-meat stew, or a giant roasted squash. And that is why the 30-second display at the table of the whole roasted goose is indispensable. Thanksgiving dinner is the most intense and extreme example of this primeval need. Not only do we share a single roast turkey at our own table, but everyone else in the United States—in truth, it's 91 percent—is eating the same thing at the same time whether we like it or not. Turkeys are served at public kitchens for the homeless, even if the homeless would prefer a Quarter Pounder. I can't think of a meal that even comes close, anywhere. To accomplish it, 45 million turkeys are killed for one dinner, the most bloodcurdling example of ritual animal slaughter in the history of the world. That's how important it is to us.

But here's the problem: All domesticated poultry, besides the chicken and the guinea hen, descend from migratory fowl, which need thick breast muscles designed for endurance. Active muscles designed for endurance are dark with the pigment myoglobin, which is used for the storage of oxygen. So, ducks and geese are entirely dark meat. Their breasts, which operate their wings in flight, will always be chewier than, say, a nicely roasted chicken's. What makes goose and duck legs extra tough (and turkeys', too) is the large amount of connective tissue between their muscle fibers. That's why we can enjoy a medium-rare, thinly sliced duck breast but never a medium-rare leg. The connective tissue in the legs is dissolved by braising them, moist and slow, and, in southwest France, by poaching them in goose fat for confit.

What internal temperatures would make for the most deliciously roasted Supergoose? I dismembered a goose or two and roasted one breast and one leg at a time in a 325°F oven, taking the temperature of the flesh and tasting it at regular intervals. To my astonishment, the goose breast was most delicious in only 20 minutes, at about 130°F on the instant-read meat thermometer, like a steak. This is medium-rare, and the meat ran with delicious, deep-pink juices, softly flavored by the spicy brine. I am not the first to discover rare goose. Ariane Daguin tells me that in southwest France, while the huge, tough legs of the foie gras geese are preserved in fat, the breasts are often grilled or griddled like magret duck breasts, the skin and fat scored and placed face-down over the heat.

Is there any way to achieve, in the same oven at the same time, a roasted goose whose breast is medium-rare and whose leg and thigh are well done? Not that I can find or, after several attempts, even imagine. Harold McGee has a solution for turkeys. He believes that the ideal temperature for turkey breast is about 155°F, and for turkey leg, at least 180°F. Harold achieves this with an extreme measure: He straps ice packs to the bird's breast as the rest of it comes to room temperature; because the breast starts out much cooler than the legs, it ends up that way, too, but his method does not produce sufficiently differing temperatures in a goose. The closest I came was by standing up a goose in a stockpot, hooking its wings over the rim, pouring broth up to the bird's waist, and trying to poach its bottom half—before briefly roasting the whole bird at a high temperature to cook the breast and crisp the skin. The first time, all the flesh and skin from the bottom half of the goose fell off into the broth. The second time, the entire goose succeeded in reaching the oven, where the bottom half turned blue.

At higher temperatures, the goose's breast becomes a mound of gray rubber until it is way overcooked, when it softens again. In Alsace, roasted goose is the traditional meal on St. Martin's Day and on Christmas. Cooks often use a combination of roasting and braising. The goose is first browned all over in its own fat, roasted at a high temperature for a short while, and finally surrounded by stock and vegetables for four hours of slow cooking. When I prepare goose this way, I stuff it loosely with apples and crisp the skin at a high temperature at the end. Not one part of the goose emerges in absolutely perfect gastronomic condition, but for a traditional goose, it is very good to eat.

Incidentally, a 12-pound goose yields three pounds of boneless meat, enough to serve eight if you include lots of side dishes, and four to five cups of liquid fat. Goose fat is one of the world's greatest fats.

Problem #4: How can one achieve superskin? If the flesh of a goose cannot be perfectly roasted from beak to tail, the condition of its skin becomes all the more vital—it should be taut over its entire body, translucently golden brown, free of most fat, incredibly delicious to eat, and a model of crispiness and crunch. Turkeys are bred to be nearly spherical—with huge, round breasts and skinny legs—which, as we all remember from high school, produces the lowest possible ratio of surface to volume, of skin to meat. The reason is that Americans strongly favor white meat. As the turkey's main asset is its skin, it should instead have been bred to resemble a two-foot pizza with vast surfaces of skin covering both top and bottom, tiny wings and legs at its circumference, and very little meat in between. The goose comes close to this because its central cavity is so large that (except for its excessively bulging drumsticks) it resembles a hollow cylinder covered with skin over a layer of fat and a layer of meat.

Solution #4: Paradoxically, three very different cooking methods produce the most perfect skin: extremely quick (one hour of roasting at the highest temperature), very slow (nine hours of roasting at the lowest possible temperature), and using my Roto-Broil '400,' a shiny, chromed, electric countertop rotisserie produced in the mid-1950s. I have become a minor collector of Roto-Broil '400's, having acquired two by gift, two by purchase, and four by auction—on eBay. (I now have two in active use and two in reserve for spare parts.)* In my investigations, nothing manufactured since 1957 even comes close. It cooks a 12-pound goose with absolutely perfect skin in less than two hours, truly a midwinter miracle. The downside was that a few inches had to be amputated from both the drumsticks and the bird's shoulders before it would fit into even the rare King Size Roto-Broil '400,' the largest model.

The first step in all these methods is to pierce the bird's skin and fat in many places. This will allow large volumes of fat to melt and flow out of the openings, basting the surface—almost frying it—and leaving behind a thin layer of crispy solids lining the skin, a kind of crackling. The perfect skin is not paper thin. Incidentally, stuffing your goose can compromise the skin, as steam from the stuffing softens it near the end of roasting.

Problem #5: Does all this add up to Supergoose?

Solution #5: Super breast meat is medium-rare and juicy. Super leg is well done and yet somehow still juicy. Super taste comes from brining. Super skin is taut and crisp.

Mankind has not discovered a way to achieve all four in the same bird at the same time, at least around my house. If you give up the idea of medium-rare breast meat and are willing to settle

*For more on the Roto-Broil '400,' please read "As the Spit Turns," page 36.

for something moist and tasty but quite well done, try gently steaming the entire brined, pierced, unstuffed goose until it reaches about 170°F in the deepest part of the thigh, which will take about an hour; then dry it off and immediately roast it on a rack at 425°F to crisp the skin, about 30 minutes. Steam a whole goose? It's a breeze in that huge, black-enameled lobster pot you've used only once. Just put the goose in a large shallow bowl to collect its juices, and set the bowl into the steamer.

Yes, Supergoose is a work in progress. Confidentially, I have very high hopes for my latest discovery. It is now being deep-fried in a gallon of bubbling, golden goose fat.

Just a word about ceremony. After roasting it, always show your guests the beautiful, beautiful goose, intact and on a platter. Pause as you all share a universal, primordial tremor. Then return the goose to the kitchen, where you will carve it. Unless you are very talented, avoid carving a large bird in public.

ALSATIAN ROAST GOOSE

1 fresh goose, 11–12 lbs.
2½ lbs. sweet apples, peeled, cored, and
cut into ¾-inch pieces, about 6 cups
1 cup each peeled and roughly chopped carrots,
celery, and celery root
8 small pears, peeled but with the stems left intact
zest of 2 well-washed or organic oranges
½ tsp. ground cardamom
3 cups low-salt chicken stock, homemade or canned
3 cups white Alsatian wine, Gewürztraminer, for example

At least one day in advance, wash the goose inside and out. With a cleaver, chop off the first joint of both wings and reserve them along with the neck, the heart, and the gizzards.

Save the liver for another use. Pull all the excess white fat from the goose's cavity and reserve. Cut off the neck skin flap, leaving only a few inches of it.

Brine and pierce the goose by following the preceding recipe.

Preheat the oven to 425°F.

Choose a heavy roasting pan just large enough to hold the goose comfortably on the diagonal. (Mine measures 12 inches by 15 inches, is nonstick, and works perfectly.) Cut half the reserved fat into ½-inch pieces and melt it in the roasting pan over medium high heat on the stove top.

Rub a little fresh black pepper into the cavity of the goose. Add the cubed apples but do not crowd them. Pull together the 2 skin flaps at the opening, push short skewers or even toothpicks through them, and secure the skin by lacing with string. (Or loosely sew the opening shut.) Wrap and tie 2 separate lengths of string around the goose's body, 1 around the breast to keep the wing joints close to the body, the other around the fattest part of the drumsticks.

Remove the solids from the melted fat and brown the goose on all sides, regulating the heat to avoid burning the fat. This will take between 20 minutes and ½ hour. Balance the goose on the sides of the roasting pan or hold it by the drumsticks to get at irregular surfaces. Meanwhile, chop the reserved neck, wingtips, and innards into 1-inch pieces.

When the goose is nicely browned, remove from the heat, set the goose on its back, and scatter the pieces of neck and wing around it. Slide the roasting pan into the preheated oven and roast for ½ hour, basting after 10 and 20 minutes. Pour and spoon off the fat into a bowl; I like to use 1- and 2-quart Pyrex measuring cups for all tasks like this. Scatter the vegetables and pears around the goose. Moisten them with a little of the goose fat you have just removed and roast for 15 minutes. Using a bulb baster or a spoon, remove as much of the fat from the pan as you can.

— — — — —

Sprinkle the orange zest and ground cardamom over the pears, pour half the stock and half the wine over them, and return to the oven for 15 minutes. Lower the heat to 300°F, pour the rest of the wine and stock over the goose, and roast for about an hour longer (removing the pears to a baking dish after a half hour), until the thighs reach 170°F on an instant-read thermometer thrust into the thickest part of the meat.

Remove the roasting pan from the oven. Turn the heat up to 400°F again. Lift the goose to a plate and immediately remove the apple stuffing to the baking dish holding the pears. Strain the roasting liquid into a saucepan, skim off most of the fat, and reduce to about 1 cup on the stovetop. Wipe out the roasting pan and put the goose back into the oven for 15 minutes to crisp its skin. Spoon a little goose fat and some of the half-reduced roasting liquid over the pears and the apple stuffing and put them in the oven with the goose to rewarm and brown slightly.

Let the goose rest for 20 minutes and serve on a large platter, surrounded by the little roast pears and the apple stuffing.

Note: This general method appears in published recipes by Alsatian chefs such as Christine Ferber and Antoine Westerman. The brining is mine (a mixture of soft, warm spices popular both in Alsace and, at Christmastime, throughout northern Europe). The fruit garnish and confidential hints are Christine's; the apple stuffing is a lighter, traditional Alsatian alternative to the more common, heavyweight ground pork and veal mixture that would have enabled this goose to satisfy 12 celebrants.

PERFECTION PIZZA

The dull gray, snub-nosed gun wavered in my trembling hand. The laser sight projected a blazing red dot onto my prey. I held my breath and squeezed the trigger. Ugh! It was even worse than I had feared!

My gun is exceedingly cool. It is a Raynger ST-8 noncontact thermometer made by Raytek of Santa Cruz, California. From several feet away, you point it at anything you wish and pull the trigger, and it instantly tells you the temperature of that thing within a tenth of a degree. My gun goes up to 1,000 degrees Fahrenheit! Sure, it cost way too much. Yes, I should have used the money to upgrade my footwear instead, or have a makeover. But everyone turns green with envy when I demonstrate my ST-8, especially men and boys, girls maybe a little less.

I have recently been going around New York City, taking the temperature of the best commercial pizza ovens, plus my own ovens at home, gas and electric, and my array of barbecue grills. Do you go through phases when you simply can't get pizza off your mind? I certainly do—and more often than I would care to admit to anybody but you. As you may have guessed, I am going through such a phase right now, a pretty serious one, though I have hopes that I will soon pull out of it. For I feel I am at long last ready to hoist my pizza-making to an entirely new level. I believe I am close to a pizza breakthrough for the American home.

Here's the idea. Pizza is a perfect food. From Elizabeth David to Marcella Hazan, all gastronomes agree. It is high on my list of the hundred greatest foods of the world. Though it is the most primitive of yeasted breads—a flatbread baked on stones heated by a wood fire—pizza is today made in pretty much its primordial form on 61,269 street corners in America.* In New York City at least, it is still typically handmade, from scratch. Flour, water, yeast, and salt are kneaded into dough, given plenty of time to rise, patted and stretched into a circle, and baked to order in a special oven. A Neolithic bakery on every block—do you find this as astonishing as I do?

I have made thousands of pizzas at home. I have boldly faced the challenges that fate has thrown at me and overcome most of them. The most important thing about pizza is the crust. Toppings are secondary. (Both at home and in restaurants, cooks who don't know how to bake a good pizza crust become wearily creative with their toppings; they aim to distract us from their fundamental failings, the way poor bread bakers add cilantro and dried cherries to their mediocre loaves.) Over the years, I have spent hours in renowned pizzerias trying to learn their methods. I have experimented with a hundred types of dough and by now have pretty much got it right. I'll give you the recipe later.

And yet my pizzas are not perfect, not even close. There are two perfect pizzas. One is Neapolitan. Pizza was not invented in Naples, nor probably in Italy. But around 1760, when tomatoes replaced lard and garlic as the principal pizza condiment, Naples—both the nobility and the poor—went mad for this ancient flatbread, and devised the greatest pizza in the world. It is about 10 inches in diameter and one-fourth of an inch thick, with a narrow, charred, puffy, sauceless rim, crisp but tender and light; it is made with about seven ounces of dough prepared with soft flour; and it is most often topped, very lightly, with tomatoes, garlic, oregano, and olive oil (this is the *pizza marinara*) or with tomatoes, olive oil, mozzarella, and a leaf or two of basil (this is the *pizza Margherita*, named in 1889 for the visiting queen of Italy, and notable for the red, white, and green of the Italian flag). The mozzarella is usually made from cow's milk, sometimes from water buffalo's milk. In Naples, pizza toppings are not cooked in advance—only by the heat of the pizza oven.

*61,269 is the number of pizzerias in America, not the number of street corners.

The other perfect pizza is Neapolitan-American. Pizza came to the New World just before the turn of the twentieth century with the arrival of immigrants from Naples. Though Gennaro Lombardi, at 53½ Spring Street, was granted the first license to bake pizza, issued by the city of New York in 1905, his justifiably proud yet fair-minded descendants reveal that Neapolitan bread bakers in New York had been making pizza with their surplus dough for at least the previous ten years. In my experience, the perfect Neapolitan-American pizzas are made in New York City, and in New Haven, Connecticut, at the towering Frank Pepe's Pizzeria and Sally's Apizza. (For all I know, the three other cities where Italian immigrants predominantly settled—Providence, Philadelphia,* and Boston—are unheralded treasure troves of pizza, but I have never heard anyone brag about them.) Lombardi's reopened several years ago, at 32 Spring Street, because the oven there could be repaired by the one company in Brooklyn that still knows how. The oven at 53½ was gone. Through both anecdotal evidence and photographic proof on the walls of today's Lombardi's, we know that Gennaro Lombardi taught both Anthony "Totonno" Pero and John Sasso the art of pizza; these men would gain metropolitan and, yes, nationwide renown with their own pizza places, John's Pizzeria on Bleecker Street and Totonno's in Coney Island.

The mystic hand† of evolution somehow transmuted the true Neapolitan pizza of 1889 into the perfect Neapolitan-American pizza of today, which is 14 to 18 inches in diameter, rimmed with a wide, puffy, charred circumferential border; heavier, thinner, crisper, and chewier than the Neapolitan original; made with

*Though the population of Providence, Rhode Island, remained quiet, the voices of several Philadelphians were raised, recommending Tacconelli's.
†As there used to be two seriously authentic Neapolitan pizzerias within taxi distance of my house—Gemelli and Pizza Fresca—one could set side by side a direct descendant of the original pizza next to its American cousin and, alternately chewing and thinking, ruminate on the process of evolution and wonder how one became the other. This I did several times. Nothing to report.

Gemelli was destroyed on September 11, 2001.

high-protein bread flour; and topped with lavish quantities of cooked tomato sauce, thick slabs of fresh cow's milk mozzarella, olive oil, and most often—36 percent of the time—pepperoni, an innovation of the 1950s and still America's favorite topping, for which there is little excuse. The perfect Neapolitan-American crust is about $\frac{3}{16}$-inch thick. Viewed in cross section, the bottom $\frac{1}{32}$-inch is very crisp and nearly charred. The next $\frac{3}{32}$-inch is made up of dense, delicious, chewy bread. And the top $\frac{1}{16}$-inch is slightly gooey from its contact with the oil and sauce. The outer rim is shot through with huge and crunchy bubbles. *This is the crust I have been after for as long as I can remember.*

Serious pizza places here and in Naples have brick ovens fueled either by wood or, in New York City and New Haven, by coal. Yes, coal—large hunks of shiny, blue, bituminous coal. Authentic Neapolitan pizzas take from 80 to 120 seconds to bake, authentic Neapolitan-American pizzas maybe five minutes. Mine take 14 minutes. It seems obvious that what stands between me and perfect pizza crust is temperature—real pizza ovens are much hotter than anything I can attain in my own kitchen. Lower temperatures dry out the dough before the outside is crisp and the topping has cooked.

I have confirmed all this with my new Raynger ST-8. At the reasonably authentic Neapolitan La Pizza Fresca Ristorante on East 20th Street, for example, the floor of its wood-burning brick oven measures 675°F; the back wall (and presumably the ambient air washing over the pizza) pushes 770°F, and the domed ceiling 950°F. The floor of Lombardi's Neapolitan-American coal oven soars to an amazing 850°F measured a foot from the inferno, less under the pizza itself. My ST-8 and I have become inseparable.

I have tried a wide variety of measures to reach such breath-taking temperatures. Laypersons may possibly feel that some of these measures are desperate. I own a creaky old restaurant stove with a gas oven that goes up to 500°F, no higher. The hot air is exhausted through two vents in back. What if I blocked the vents with crumpled aluminum foil and kept the hot air from escaping? Would the oven get hotter and hotter and hotter? No, this experiment was a failure. As I could have predicted if I had had my wits about me, the oven's thermostat quickly turned down the flame as soon as the hot air I had trapped threatened to exceed 500°F.

How to defeat the thermostat? More than once, I have skill-fully taken apart my stove and then needed to pay the extortion-ate fees of a restaurant-stove-reassembly company. This time, I had a better idea. Way in the back of the oven you can see the thermostat's heat sensor, a slender rod spanning the opening to the exhaust vents. How, I wondered, could I keep this bar artifi-cially cold while the stove tried harder and harder to bring up the temperature and in the process exceeded its intended 500°F limit? I folded together many layers of wet paper towels, put them in the freezer until they had frozen solid, draped them over the tem-perature sensor with the oven set to high, shoveled in an unbaked pizza, and stood back.

The results were brilliant, especially in concept. My oven, believing incorrectly that its temperature was near the freezing point, went full blast until thick waves of smoke billowed from every crack, vent, and pore, filling the house with the palpable signs of scientific success. Yes, the experiment had to be cut short, but it had lasted longer than the Wright brothers' first flight. Inside the oven was a blackened disk of dough pocked with pud-dles of flaming cheese. I had succeeded beyond all expectations.

And not long afterward, I slid a raw pizza into a friend's elec-tric oven, switched on the self-cleaning cycle, locked the door, and watched with satisfaction as the temperature soared to 800°F. Then, at the crucial moment, to defeat the safety latch and retrieve my perfectly baked pizza, I pulled out the massive electri-cal plug and, protecting my arm with a wet bath towel, tugged on the door. Somehow, this stratagem failed, and by the time we had got the door open again half an hour later, the pizza had com-pletely disappeared, and the oven was unaccountably lined with a thick layer of ash. I feel that I am onto something here, though as with the controlled use of hydrogen fusion, the solution may remain elusive for many years.

Then came the breakthrough. The scene was the deck of my Southern California house. The occasion was the maiden voyage of my hulking, rectangular, black-steel barbecue, which has an extravagant grilling area measuring 18 by 30 inches. I had built my inaugural fire, using hardwood charcoal and wood chunks; hours later, a thick steak would go on the grill, but for now I was just playing. At some point, I closed the massive hood and watched the built-in thermometer, as the temperature climbed to 550 degrees. And then it struck me. Why not double the fuel, the wood and the charcoal? Why not 650 degrees? Why not 750? Why not pizza?

I dashed into the kitchen and prepared my excellent recipe for pizza dough. It must be understood that this was not to be the popular grilled pizza introduced by Johanne Kileen and George Jermon at their Al Forno restaurant in Providence, Rhode Island, in which the dough is placed directly over the fire. My barbecue grill was to be used only for its ability to generate great amounts of heat.

As the pizza dough was completing its mandatory three-hour rise and one hour's refrigeration, just as the sun was setting over Charles A. Lindbergh Airport, I built a massive fire using 18 pounds of hardwood charcoal, two bulging bags that filled the firebox to overflowing. In 45 minutes, when gray ash had covered the charcoal, I lowered the hood and watched the thermometer climb to 600°F—and go no further! Where had I gone wrong? I opened all the air vents and the large front door that lets you add fuel and remove ashes. Huge volumes of oxygen flowed in, and bingo! The needle climbed past the 700°F red line and into uncharted territory. Using oven mitts, I fitted a thick round baking stone onto the grill, waited for advice from my ST-8, slid a raw pizza onto the stone, and lowered the hood.

This is when I learned that a pizza stone can get much hotter than the air around it if you put it directly over fire, causing the bottom of the pizza to burn to a crisp before the top is done. I also learned that when your ST-8 noncontact thermometer tells you that the barbecue grill has reached 900°F, the electrical cord of the rotisserie motor you left attached to its bracket will melt like a milk-chocolate bar in your jeans pocket or, more aptly, like the huge plastic all-weather barbecue cover you just as slothfully left draped over the shelf below the grill.

These were mere details, for victory was mine. And it can be yours as well. If you scrape the fiery coals to either side of the baking stone, taking care not to singe your eyebrows again, you can reduce the stone's temperature to the ideal 650°F while keeping the air temperature directly over the pizza near the perfect 750°F or even higher. Use all the hardwood charcoal you can carry, and between pizzas, add more to maintain the heat. Just before you slide the pizza onto the stone, throw some wood chips or chunks onto the coals to produce the aromatic smoke of a wood-burning oven near the Bay of Naples. And in the light of day, feel no regrets that you have burned the paint off the sides of your barbecue and voided the manufacturer's limited warranty.

This remains my favorite and best way of making pizza. Although the procedure is tricky, three out of four of the pizzas that emerge from my barbecue are pretty wonderful—crisp on the bottom and around the very puffy rim, chewy in the center, artfully charred here and there, tasting of wood smoke.

Very little time had passed, however, before I became uneasy and discontented once again. How could I complacently feast while others went without? Very few American families possess my monstrous barbecue. How could I bring my pizza breakthrough to the average American home?

It was time to exhume my Weber Kettle, which without a moment's hesitation or research, I knew to be the most popular charcoal grill in the country. As I had long ago discovered that the Weber Kettle (which lacks a mechanism for raising and lowering the fuel or the grill, admits only a trickle of oxygen when the cover is closed, et cetera, et cetera) is of extremely limited use for cooking, I had exiled it to the garage, where it held two 50-pound bags of French bread flour, the gems of my collection, off the moist concrete floor.*

I filled the Weber to the brim with hardwood charcoal, let the fire go for a half hour, plopped on the baking stone, and put on the cover. The internal temperature barely reached 450°F, and

---

*The nearly identical sentiments expressed in "Cast Party," page 44, reflect depth of feeling concerning the Weber Kettle, not lack of imagination.

the baking stone even less. I dumped ten pounds of additional charcoal into the center, fired it, produced a conflagration measuring 625°F, with the stone at an even higher temperature, and in no time at all had achieved a pizza completely incinerated on the bottom and barely done on top. Despite the vast amounts of ingenuity I had brought to bear in half a day of exhaustive tests, I simply could not get the Weber Kettle to heat the air above the baking stone to anywhere near the desired heat. The Weber is simply not wide enough for enough of the heat to flow up around the baking stone and over the top of the pizza. Once again, the Weber proved itself incapable of producing gastronomic treasures. Back into the garage it went.

By all means, experiment with your own charcoal grill. Like me, you will not regret the hours and days spent on backyard exploration. And to forestall the obloquy to which you may be subjected if the results are not good enough to eat, remember to make a double dose of dough and preheat the oven in your kitchen as a backup. Indoor pizzas can still be awfully good. Meticulous instructions follow.

Author's note: Norwegian food writer and personal friend Andreas Viestad, aware of the dangers of igniting wood and charcoal on a fire escape in New York City, hand-carried from Europe a bright red Pizza Express countertop pizza oven manufactured by G3 Ferrari in Modena, Italy. Looking vaguely like a huge waffle iron, it has a ceramic baking stone with a heating coil underneath and another coil in the cover, which you lower over the uncooked pizza. With the assistance of a huge 30-lb. electrical converter, and with thanks to Andreas's unprecedented generosity, the results, at 850°F, are delectable.

NEOPOLITAN-AMERICAN PIZZA

2 lbs. (about 6½ cups) flour, half all-purpose unbleached and half
bread flour, both preferably King Arthur brand (see note)
1⅛ tsp. SAF-Instant yeast or 1½ tsp. active dry yeast
1 Tbs. plus 1 tsp. salt
3¼ cups cold water
6 Tbs. extra-virgin olive oil, plus a few teaspoons more to oil the
measuring cup and plates used to hold the rising dough
½ cup cornmeal or semolina
1½ cups tomato sauce (a good recipe follows), or crushed, drained,
canned plum tomatoes (empty a large can into a strainer set
over a bowl and squeeze the tomatoes with your hand, using
only the solids left in the strainer)
½ lb. fresh cow's milk mozzarella, cut into 12 slices
1½ tsp. salt (or 3 Tbs. grated Parmesan)
Special equipment: an electric mixer suitable for kneading dough;
a thick ceramic baking stone, round or square, at least 14 inches
across; a wooden peel (a flat paddle for transferring unbaked
breads and pizzas) or a rimless baking sheet

In the mixer bowl, stir together the flours, yeast, and salt.
Pour in the water and stir vigorously with a wooden spoon
until the ingredients come together into a shaggy dough.
Mount the bowl on the mixer and attach the beater (not the
dough hook—this dough is too wet for conventional kneading). Mix on slow speed for about 1 minute, then increase the
speed to high and beat for 3½ minutes, scraping down the
beater and bowl halfway through.

Here is a good way to tell when the dough is properly developed. With well-floured fingers, pull off a piece of dough
about the size of a walnut and roll it in flour. You should now
be able to stretch it with the fingers of both hands into an
unbroken sheet at least 3 inches across.

- - - - -

Scrape and pour the dough onto a heavily floured work surface. (The only way to handle dough as moist and soft as this is to keep your fingers, countertop, and the dough itself very well floured; whenever it sticks to the counter, use a metal pastry scraper or a long, wide knife or even a paint scraper to detach the dough without pulling and tearing it more than you have to.) It will spread into an irregular blob. Fold the far end over to the near end so that half the floured underside covers the rest of the dough. Let it rest for about 10 minutes.

With a dough scraper, divide the dough into 4 equal pieces. (Each will weigh about 14½ ounces, should you use an accurate electronic scale, as I always do.) Shape each piece into a smooth ball. Place 3 of the balls on well-oiled, 8-inch plates, generously dust their tops with flour, and cover loosely with plastic wrap. Put the fourth ball into an oiled, 1-quart glass measuring cup and cover tightly with plastic wrap. Let everything rise at warm room temperature until the balls have doubled in volume, which should take between 3 and 4 hours.

With this proprietary and surely patentable method, the markings on the side of the 1-quart measuring cup will tell you when the ball inside, and by inference the 3 others, have doubled in volume, from 1½ cups to 3. Now refrigerate all 4 balls of dough—for a minimum of 1 hour, an ideal of 3 hours, and a maximum of 24 hours.

At your own risk and following the procedure described in this article, prepare your outdoor grill to achieve a temperature of 750°F, regardless of the warranty. Clear an area in the center of the coals and place a heavy baking stone over it.

Alternately, preheat your oven for at least 1 hour to its maximum temperature, 500 or 550°F, with your baking stone inside. In a gas oven, the baking stone goes right on the metal floor of the oven; in an electric oven, on the lowest shelf.

Set the peel on a level surface and dust with about 2 tablespoons of cornmeal. Take 1 or more of the balls of dough

– – – – –

(now disks) from the refrigerator. On a well-floured surface, pat 1 into a neat, 8-inch circle. Now stretch its rim all around (the center will take care of itself) by draping the dough over your fists, knuckles up, and, passing it from hand to hand, keeping most of the dough resting on the counter—until the circle of dough reaches a diameter of about 12 inches. With your fists still under the dough and held apart, quickly bring the circle of dough over to the peel, plop it down, and pull it into a neat circle between 12½ and 13 inches across.

Put a heaping ¼ cup of tomato sauce or crushed, drained canned tomatoes in the center of the pizza and spread with the back of a wooden spoon, but only to within 1½ or 2 inches of the rim. Sprinkle with freshly ground pepper. Arrange three slices of mozzarella over the tomatoes. Sprinkle with a generous ¼ teaspoon salt (or 2 teaspoons of grated Parmesan) and 1½ tablespoons of olive oil. Shake the peel back and forth to see that the pizza is not sticking to the peel. Bake immediately: Open the oven door, place the leading edge of the peel just short of the far edge of the baking stone and at about a 45° angle to it, and by a combination of jerking and pulling the peel toward you, evenly slide the pizza onto the stone. This will be difficult at first, child's play with practice.

Bake for 5 to 8 minutes at 750°F or for 10 to 15 minutes in the oven (rotating the pizza midway so that it will bake evenly), until the rim of the pizza is very well browned, the topping is bubbling and the cheese is golden brown, and the underside is crisp and charred here and there. Cut into sections with long scissors or a pizza wheel.

Note: I have called for King Arthur flour because it is of good quality, and widely available in supermarkets and at (800) 827-6836. Flours differ widely in their ability to hold water, which depends largely on their protein content. (Protein also determines the ideal mixing time.) If you use the flour I use, your

- - - - -

results should be similar to mine. The combined protein level of these two flours is 12.27 percent; if you especially like a particular bread flour having about 12.27 percent protein, by all means substitute it for both King Arthur flours. If your preferred flour has more or less protein, increase or decrease, respectively, by a few tablespoons the amount of cold water you add.

King Arthur also sells inexpensive plastic rising buckets marked on the side in quarts and liters.

TOMATO SAUCE

¼ cup extra virgin olive oil
1 3-inch onion, finely chopped
4 cans (28 oz. each) whole Italian plum tomatoes
1 head garlic, cut in half crosswise
any loose outer papery skin removed
2 Tbs. coarsely chopped fresh herbs (basil, oregano, marjoram)
or 2 Tbs. dried herbs
2 tsp. salt
Freshly ground black pepper

Heat the olive oil in a 4- to 5-quart saucepan and gently cook the chopped onion in it until just translucent. Empty the tomatoes into a large strainer set over a 2- to 3-quart bowl. Squish the tomatoes with your hands until no large pieces remain. This should be quite enjoyable. Empty the tomato solids in the strainer into the saucepan. Add 1½ cups of the tomato water and stir in all the other ingredients except the pepper. Bring to a snappy simmer, cook for about 20 minutes, and remove from the heat. Add about 16 grindings of pepper. When it cools, the sauce should be very thick. Makes one quart.

RED WINE AND OLD ROOSTERS

H ow could I have been such a blockhead, I asked myself, rhetorically. It had been right in front of me all these years, or right inside of me, to be more precise.

You know how sometimes you bite into a forkful of breakfast, lunch, or dinner—or even sometimes just a snack—and suddenly an eternal truth or universal law reveals itself to you? That's just how it happened this time. There I was, in Oxford, England, in a restaurant called Le Petit Blanc, eating a plate of *coq au vin*. This is, of course, one of the most famous of all traditional French country dishes—at its most essential, pieces of chicken stewed in red wine. I had eaten *coq au vin* maybe 200 times before. It was the first complicated dish I had ever cooked, taking many times longer to get on the table than a hamburger and requiring the purchase of what then seemed unusual ingredients—a slab of unsliced bacon, dozens of tiny white onions, several bottles of red wine. I had borne the expense and effort in hopes of impressing a pretty blond female classmate in graduate school. As I remember, it worked but not quite well enough.

Where did I go wrong? While the sauce—really concentrated cooking broth—was lovely, dark, and deep, the chicken itself came out tough, dry, and stringy. Maybe that was the problem. Or was it those slippery little white onions that worm their way into nearly every *coq au vin*? They are the size of marbles, take forever to peel, and are nearly impossible to bring to the lips, because when you try to spear them with your fork, they fly off your plate and onto your pretty, blond, female classmate's fluffy white angora sweater. Perhaps it was the excess of bouncy, nearly tasteless, cultivated white mushrooms known as champignons de Paris, or just champignons, that litter most latter-day *coq au vins*?

The Oxford version might just have done the trick. There the chicken was juicy and meaty and full of flavor, and I finished every morsel. For the first time, I understood why people have been eating *coq au vin* for hundreds or thousands of years. (The French believe that Julius Caesar was served *coq au vin* in the Auvergne in south-central France during his campaign to subdue Gaul around 54 B.C., and became a total fan.) How was the Oxford *coq au vin* different from mine?

And then it came to me. *Coq au vin* means "rooster with wine." They must have used an old rooster, a bird possessing a rich and profound flavor and flesh that stands up to endless stewing. A writer on the history of French food who happened to be at the table confirmed my hunch: Yes, of course, authentic *coq au vin must* be made with a rooster. *Coq* means "rooster." How could it be otherwise? He peered into my plate and examined the scattered molecules remaining there, but he could establish nothing. I asked the waiter to ask the chef, but the chef had left for the evening.

Stewing an old rooster in wine makes perfect sense. When making chicken soup, whether my grandmother's incomparable recipe or the broth the Chinese call "superior stock," we buy a mature stewing hen weighing between six and eight pounds, whose flesh is full of savor but far too tough to roast or fry or broil. Mature hens and roosters lose their chief function when their reproductive powers fade. Something must be done with all that flavorful flesh. And the alcohol in wine is a famous tenderizer. Somehow, even then, I knew that when I returned home, my chief mission would be to bring true *coq au vin* to America, where nearly everybody has eaten something called *coq au vin*, but where nobody, I felt sure, had ever eaten an old rooster cooked in wine.

All I needed were a recipe and a rooster.

But first I had to check one fundamental fact. I telephoned my indefatigable friend Mira, who is seeking a Ph.D. in classics at Princeton. Was Julius Caesar really fond of *coq au vin*? Mira turned to Caesar's *Commentarii de Bello Gallico* (you know, the famous one that starts, *"Gallia est omnis divisa in partes tres"*), which I read as a boy in Latin class and which Caesar had written as a kind of campaign biography to gain popularity among stay-at-homes both in Rome and in high schools in the suburbs of New York City. There is not one bite of *coq au vin* in *Commentarii de Bello Gallico*. Caesar mentions chicken only once, and that's later, when he gets to Britain, where the people refuse to eat fowl but enjoy cockfights. As for French wine, Caesar tells us that the Gauls had a great weakness for it (though their neighbors in Brittany and Germany banned the beverage in the belief that "it makes men weak and womanish") but does not mention tasting it himself. Where do the French get these ideas?

The restaurant in Oxford had promised to fax me their recipe. Nothing arrived. If there is a cookbook written in English that tells you what to do with old roosters, I do not own it. A few of my French-language books do tell you; what shocks me is that the others use young, female birds and still call it *coq au vin*. When you make a chicken stew with a young (even female) bird, you can skip the marination, or use white wine, leave out the bacon, forget about the bouillon, and cook everything in just over an hour. This can be a tasty dish. But how anybody who speaks French can continue to describe it as *"coq"* escapes me. My disillusionment with France and its people continued to mount until I could bear it no longer.

So, I hopped on a plane and awoke in Paris. My first stop was dinner with Mary and Philip Hyman, an American food-historian couple who have lived in Paris for 30 years and recently began work on *The Oxford Companion to French Food*, an incredibly prestigious assignment. They brought me a chapter from a book entitled *Droit* [Law] *et Gastronomie* (1999), by one Jean-Paul Branlard, who grapples with the legal identity and denomination of *coq au vin*. As you might imagine, considerable litigation has been brought on the subject. The two main issues are whether the word *"coq"* can include a *poule, poulet, coquelet,* or *chapon,* and whether dealcoholized wine counts as *"vin."* Beginning with a government decree of March 17, 1967, and continuing through a decision in Bourges in 1982, culinary justice remained unblemished: The word *"coq"* was officially limited to "a male domestic fowl of the genus *Gallus,* having attained its sexual maturity." But then, in 1986, the Court of Appeals in Rennes scandalously admitted both *poule* and *poulet,* claiming to prefer a definition based on actual practice over one grounded in what the judges called "semantics." A few years later, the government opened the floodgates, decreeing that it is not fraudulent "to offer under the title *coq au vin,* elaborated dishes made from any of the fowls of the genus *Gallus: poule, poulet, chapon, coquelet,* or *coq."* (All statutory translations are by the present author.)

Some writers believe that the similarity between the words *Gallus* and Gallia, the Latin word for "Gaul," explains why the *"coq"* became the symbol of France. You can be sure that this symbolic *"coq"* still includes only the proud and swaggering rooster, not the effeminate *poulet* or castrated *chapon.* Why have an academy to protect the French language and then carry on like this, I asked the Hymans. They shrugged like French people in the movies and handed me their own formula for *coq au vin,* using an eight-pound rooster. The Hymans can usually dig up a 300-year-old recipe for nearly anything, but the oldest they've found for *coq au vin* comes from 1912. They explain that before this century, cookbooks were about fine food, not about country dishes. But how do they know that *coq au vin* was not actually invented in 1912?

And what about those ubiquitous, cultivated white mushrooms? Surely country cooking like this would call for a wild and rustic fungus, if indeed the dish is centuries old. Yes, but the Hymans tell me that the French were growing white mushrooms in large volumes by the late seventeenth century! Paris was the center of production (which explains why they are still called *champignons de Paris*) until just over 100 years ago, when it migrated to caverns in the Loire Valley.

My second stop was Le Coq Saint-Honoré, one of the two or

three superpremium butchers in Paris specializing in pedigreed chickens, turkeys, and geese, most of them raised in open pasture and fed according to written guarantees. (The shop supplies, among other places, the Plaza Athénée, Taillevent, L'Espadon, the Crillon, Gérard Besson, Le Pré Catalan, and Pierre Gagnaire.) My friend Frédérick Grasser Hermé met me at the shop, which she had already telephoned with an order for two substantial roosters. Our plan was to watch and interrogate the butcher, then rendezvous at Frédérick's house two days later to cook the *coq au vin* for eight friends who were planning to assemble for her birthday. (Frédérick is consulting chef in charge of the menu at the hot year-old Paris restaurant Korova; her latest book is *Mon chien fait recettes* [Editions Noesis].)

The shop was spotless, all white tiles and refrigerated cases, and flooded with daylight. Our butcher was a cheerful woman named Marie-Louise Desrimais, and she brought out two 12-pound specimens, both around two years old. Anything smaller, she said, would not be right for a true *coq au vin*. Our roosters had grown up on a farm in Sarthe, near Le Mans, an area as prized for fine fowl as is Bresse. Marie-Louise removed the two crests and four kidneys—prized morsels to which such extreme food lovers as Catherine de' Medici have become addicted—and discarded the heads. The long necks were chopped and saved for our bouillon, but their skin and the birds' feet were removed and discarded, not what you would do with young, tender chickens but apparently advisable in the case of old roosters. Marie-Louise then disjointed the birds, cut each meaty section crosswise into several pieces, and chopped up the carcass and wings into small chunks. We asked Marie-Louise about her own recipe for *coq au vin*. "Normale," she replied, and we knew just what she had in mind.

In the end, as often happens, over the course of the next three days Frédérick did most of the cooking for her own birthday. Traditional, full-bore *coq au vins* start with a marinade made up of vegetables, herbs, and a powerful red wine. The meaty pieces of rooster—the legs and breasts resemble those of a small turkey—are steeped in the marinade for a day or more. Meanwhile, a broth is prepared from the wings, neck, carcass, and backbone, all chopped up. Some bacon—fresh or salted or smoked—is melted and the meaty pieces of rooster are browned in the fat, then covered with wine and broth, and stewed very slowly until the rooster is wonderfully tender. This can take six hours. And then those little onions are boiled or browned or both, and added, along with white mushrooms and the crisp pieces of browned bacon. At the end, the cooking liquid, now deeply aromatic with browned vegetables and rooster flesh, is concentrated into the most savory sauce you can imagine, and poured back over the pieces of rooster, bacon, mushrooms, and onions.

Frédérick's was certainly a full-bore *coq au vin*. But 24 pounds of rooster for ten eaters? She explained that over the years she has become increasingly unhappy with the breasts of the rooster, which no matter what she tries, come out inedibly tough and dry. Now she uses only the dark meat, the legs and thighs. To make up for the blandness of white Paris mushrooms, she adds dried wild mushrooms to the sauce, early in the cooking.

If I felt any reluctance to disembark at JFK, it was only because the task of finding the necessary ingredients in New York City was bound to be grueling and enervating. I needed a rooster, and I needed a big one, and not just one but many, if a delicious recipe was to divulge itself. I tried my typically patient, expert, and reliable sources for animal flesh, Lou at Balducci's and Stanley at Lobel's; both took longer than usual to conclude that a rooster was an impossibility.

My assistant Gail and I angrily telephoned the USDA to find out where all the roosters had gone. Thomas Kruchten gave us the full story. Last year, 8.4 billion chickens were slaughtered in the United States (yes, a huge number but, after all, only 31 chickens a person). Most chickens, male and female, were killed and eaten young, seven weeks old on average, and sold without reference to gender. Only 165 million of them, about 2 percent, were allowed to grow to sexual maturity. The vast majority are hens, assigned to laying eggs, some of which produce chicks. Only 5 percent of mature chickens appear to be roosters—eight million a year, one-tenth of 1 percent of all chickens. What becomes of the other male chickens? I grew anxious and queasy at the thought that a billion of them are killed as chicks. A billion boys a year.

Gail despaired of ever finding enough roosters for our important work among this one-tenth of 1 percent. Me, I saw that we were practically home free. There were eight million mature roosters in America, and we needed to find only a fraction of these. I called Victoria Granof, our food stylist and a food writer in her own right, who suggested that I start with an establishment on Linden Street in Brooklyn called Knickerbocker Live Poultry Market. As so often happens, whenever you open a new door in this city, an entire world awaits you on the other side.

Michael Lane, 44, a graduate of NYU film school, bought Knickerbocker with his father 13 years ago, carrying on a family trade that his great-great-grandparents had brought from Russia more than a century before. On a good day, Michael has a thousand live fowl on hand, in cages. Roosters are child's play for him—he sells between 40 and 50 each week—but never for *coq au vin*. Most of his rooster customers are from India (or of Indian descent, from places like Guyana), who make a special rooster curry, or are Hispanics, who prepare a rooster soup. For years the New York City government had limited the number of live-poultry markets to 30. Then, with so many immigrants coming here from places where people simply do not buy dead chickens, the city lifted the numerical limit while stiffening the hygiene requirements. Sounds Solomonic to me. Now we have 76 live-poultry markets here. The USDA hates it.

Soon, Knickerbocker and I had established a steady traffic in big old roosters from Brooklyn to my house, near Union Square in Manhattan. Each rooster cost $10 and arrived as I had requested it—properly dismembered with only the head, feet, and internal organs missing. Many experiments lay ahead.

First we tried Frédérick's recipe, but using both dark and light meat. She was right. The breasts were stringy and dense and dry, even when cooked ten hours. We moved on to the Hymans' method, though with dark meat only and with smoked bacon, which lent depth and complexity to the sauce, but maybe too much smoke. Then we ordered several large stewing hens on the theory that they would be more available to you, my readers, and might yield equivalent results. The theory was piteously wrong.

Next we tried a combination—dark meat, more wine, smoked bacon (but blanched to soften the smokiness), Frédérick's dried mushrooms—plus we browned the bony rooster pieces and vegetables to flavor the bouillon more richly. This was the best version so far.

Coq au vin is served on the same plate as a fitting starch to sop up the incredible sauce—steamed potatoes, noodles, spaetzle, or rice. Having enjoyed many meals of *coq au vin* over the past month or two, I would recommend nearly any form of boiled or steamed potatoes. Noodles don't absorb.

It is universally agreed that black pepper boiled in a soup or stock or stew for longer than ten minutes turns bitter and loses its aromatic and pungent properties. Yet few people correct and enhance the old recipes by leaving out pepper until the end. I rigorously held back most of it, grinding it in a peppermill over the sauce a few minutes before serving; in delightful and unexpected ways, very fresh black pepper transforms a sauce into something both perfumed and piquant.

There followed several days of mission creep. Two goals were added. As the recipe had become just a tiny bit arduous, I rearranged it so that most of the work can be finished the day before dinner. Besides, like most stews, *coq au vin* seems better the next day. The second goal was more pressing. The longer we cooked the rooster, the more the meat fell off the bones, leaving a pot of savory and lip-smacking rooster wreckage.

To tenderize the rooster in advance and thus shorten the stewing time, we increased the period of marination in red wine from one day to one week, and even longer. Results? Ambiguous. Our next solution was to cook the rooster pieces all in one layer and to hold down the stewing activity to a bare simmer—too gentle to agitate the meat. Our *coq au vins* improved.

The French, especially in restaurant cooking, use a low-temperature method called *sous vide,* in which the food, cooked or uncooked, is sealed without air, and then very gently heated in

388 AN INTENSE HUNT FOR THE FACTS

a water bath. At an incredibly low 144°F and with lots of time, even the toughest protein is said to emerge smooth and tender. I've had enough experience trying to maintain these stylish French slow-cooking temperatures to know how tedious and uncomfortable it is to stand at the stove for hours at a time, staring at a thermometer. But what about a Crock-Pot? I had never used a Crock-Pot and have always made fun of both Crock-Pots and of people who use them. I throw out every Crock-Pot cookbook that comes my way.

We telephoned several manufacturers, discovered that they all claim minimum temperatures no lower than 190 degrees. Although not as mild as 144 degrees, this *is* nonetheless below the bubbling point, will not jostle the pieces of rooster, and may result in a smoother, creamier protein, as when you poach a chicken instead of boiling it. We bought the largest Crock-Pot we could find, a six-quart Rival. Interrupting an ongoing *coq au vin* experiment at the postmarination stage, we poured everything into our new Rival, and tried to choose among the three temperature settings, "serve," "low," and "high."

Rival's flimsy user manual warned "DO NOT cook on SERVE setting." So, I flipped the dial to SERVE, waited two hours, got out my digital thermometer, took the temperature of my *coq au vin* twice, and learned that the Rival's absolutely minimum temperature is an admirable 180°F. Eleven hours passed, most of it spent watching the immobile Crock-Pot plus additional time for reducing and defatting the sauce, and we were eating one of the two best *coq au vins* we had produced, deeply flavored and tender. I'll never again make fun of Crock-Pots. I apologize.

In France, *coq au vin* is traditionally thickened with rooster blood or, when that is unavailable, pig's blood—widely available there and sometimes found in New York City's Chinatown. These days, softened butter mixed with flour—called *beurre manié*—is usually substituted for blood. One day, when I cut myself while chopping an onion for the marinade, I briefly considered adding human blood. You need barely more than a quarter cup. But that was after a long day's cooking had diminished my powers of reasoning. I had forgotten to ask Knickerbocker about rooster blood and when I finally thought of it, they said, Sure, we have rooster blood. The Chinese often require a little container of blood with their ducks. Sadly, it was too late to embark upon a new series of experiments.

Several days ago, when our experimental work reached a feverish peak of activity, we received a fax asking for donations of food, raw or cooked, for the rescue workers and volunteers at the World Trade Center site. The nearest collection point was two blocks away at a restaurant named The Tonic, and just before dinnertime we walked over with 18 servings of extremely fine *coq au vin* made from four old Brooklyn roosters and five bottles of Australian Shiraz, plus a plastic tub of extra sauce. It was rumored that the chefs at the restaurant Balthazar get a police escort whenever they deliver their creations to the volunteer center at Chelsea Piers, but we didn't mind. For we had succeeded in capturing the true and ancient *coq au vin*. How it compares to the Oxford rooster is lost in the fogs of memory. Ours emerges intact but tender, and its sauce is deep and layered and makes your mouth water just thinking about it.

COQ AU VIN

2 mature roosters, about 18 months old, 11–13 pounds each,
gross weight, which is 9–11 pounds each, net weight, including
the crest and the kidneys but discarding the other internal organs,
the feet, and the head. Explain to your butcher that you will be
eating only the dark meat and using the rest for bouillon.
So, the drumsticks should be separated from the thighs and the
thighs cut crosswise into 2 pieces each, for a total of 12 pieces.
Everything else should be chopped into 2-inch pieces.

For the bouillon:

4 Tbs. vegetable (canola) oil
3 medium carrots, scraped and thinly sliced, about 1½ cups
1 medium-large onion (about 3½-inch diameter), peeled
and roughly chopped, about 1½ cups
2 large leeks, only white and light green parts; leaves separated,
carefully washed, and sliced crosswise, about 1 cup
1½ large ribs celery, leaves discarded,
washed and sliced crosswise, about ¾ cup
1 large bouquet garni (2 European bay leaves, 6 sprigs of fresh
thyme, and 12 sprigs of parsley, bundled and wrapped around with
one of the discarded dark green leek leaves, and tied with string)
½ tsp. salt
3 whole cloves

For the marinade:

2½ bottles hearty, young red Burgundy or domestic Pinot Noir.
Remember—don't cook with a wine you wouldn't drink.
There is no need to go overboard: $10 a bottle should suffice
½ tsp. salt
15 black peppercorns

10 turns of a peppermill containing black peppercorns
1 head garlic, unpeeled, cut in half crosswise
2 medium-large onions (about 3½-inch diameter), peeled and
roughly chopped, about 2 cups
2 large carrots, peeled and sliced crosswise every ⅛ inch,
about 1 cup

For cooking the coq au vin:

¼ cup vegetable (canola) oil, as needed
1 lb. smoked slab bacon, cut into cubes ¾-inch on each side
Salt and freshly ground pepper
3 Tbs. all-purpose flour
½ cup cognac
2 oz. dried *cèpes* (porcini in Italian), soaked in hot water
for ten minutes and squeezed to expel the water

For finishing and serving the coq au vin:

½ tsp. granulated sugar, if needed
1 lb. white "Paris" mushrooms. (Choose them all yourself;
try to buy only the tiniest ones, ideally ½ inch across the cap.)
Juice of one lemon
salt
2 Tbs. vegetable (canola) oil
Freshly ground black pepper
1 lb. steamed, small, peeled potatoes; or spaetzle;
or lightly buttered egg noodles
Special equipment: 2 large roasting pans; a stockpot having at least
8 quarts' capacity; a large frying pan; a bowl having at least
6 quarts' capacity; a large strainer; and a large, heavy roasting pan
or stew pot at least 4 inches deep, large enough to accommodate all
(or nearly all) the pieces of rooster in one layer without much space
between them—enameled cast iron is ideal.

— — — — —

Between 2 and 4 days before dinner: making the bouillon from the bony pieces and breasts of the roosters. Begin by arranging the chopped-up pieces of rooster in one layer in two large roasting pans, dribbling a tablespoon of oil over each one, and browning well in a 425°F oven for about 1 hour. Halfway through, turn the meat, add the carrots, leek, onion, and celery, and dribble with another 2 tablespoons of oil.

Lift the roasted rooster parts and vegetables into a stockpot with a capacity of at least 8 quarts. Add the bouquet garni and cloves. Tilt the roasting pans, spoon out any oil, and discard. Pour a total of 1 quart of water into the roasting pans, bring to a boil on the stovetop over medium-high heat, scrape up the coagulated meat juices and vegetables from the bottom of the pans, and pour into the stockpot. Add barely enough water to cover the pieces of rooster and vegetables, about 2½ quarts more. Add the salt, the peppercorns, and the cloves. Bring to a boil over medium-high heat, reduce to a bare simmer, and cook, covered, for 3 hours. (If the liquid evaporates too quickly and exposes the other ingredients, pour in a little boiling water.) Let cool for several hours or overnight. Strain and measure. Reduce over high heat to 2 quarts.

Between 2 and 5 days before dinner, marinate the meaty pieces of rooster: Put the 4 drumsticks, the 8 pieces of thigh, and the 2 pieces of lower back into a bowl with at least 6 quarts' capacity. Add the vegetables and the salt. Pour in enough red wine barely to cover, about 2½ bottles' worth. Cover tightly with plastic wrap, refrigerate, and let marinate until 1 day before the dinner.

The day before dinner, cook the coq au vin *and prepare the garnishes:* Bring about 1 quart of water to the boil in a 2- to 3-quart saucepan, add the bacon, and simmer for 5 minutes. Drain and dry with paper towels.

Remove the pieces of rooster from the marinade and dry with paper towels. Pour the marinade through a large strainer

— — — — —

set over a 4- to 6-quart bowl. Press the vegetables against the strainer to expel more of the wine and dry the vegetables between paper towels.

Over medium-high heat, in a frying pan large enough to hold half the rooster in 1 layer, brown the bacon in the oil until it is crisp on the surface and barely cooked within. With a slotted spoon or wire skimmer, remove the bacon to a bowl. Spoon out all but 2 tablespoons of the bacon fat and reserve it in another little bowl for subsequent batches of frying. Salt and pepper half the pieces of rooster, put them into the frying pan, skin side down, and brown well on both sides over medium-high heat. Put 2 teaspoons of the flour in a strainer and shake it over the rooster pieces. Turn and brown the floured side. Dust the upper side with flour, turn, and brown that side. Add more of the bacon fat as needed. Remove to a plate and blot with paper towels.

Repeat with the other pieces of rooster. Then brown the vegetables strained from the marinade, dust with flour, brown again, remove to a plate, and blot with paper towels.

Choose a large, heavy pan at least 4 inches deep, large enough to accommodate all (or nearly all) the pieces of rooster in one layer, closely packed. Spoon in the bacon and the browned vegetables and set the pieces of rooster on top of them. Pour the cognac over all, put the pan over high heat, and when you hear it sizzle, carefully light the vapors above the pan with a long match or igniter, and shake the pan until the alcohol has burned away. Then pour the wine from the marinade over everything. Pour in enough of the bouillon just to cover the solid ingredients. Over high heat, bring to a boil and immediately reduce to a simmer.

Skim the surface of the liquid for about 10 minutes. Add the dried, revived *cèpes* or porcini. Reduce the heat further to the barest simmer, cover tightly, and cook for 5 hours.

Check frequently and adjust the heat when necessary. The

– – – – –

pieces of rooster should be tender when pierced with the point of a knife but still offer a little springy resistance. Then let the pan and its contents cool overnight to room temperature.

On the day of the dinner, preferably in the morning: With a slotted spoon or wire skimmer, very carefully remove the pieces of rooster from their sauce to a platter or rimmed cookie sheet. Strain the sauce into large glass bowls (2-quart Pyrex measuring cups are extremely handy and let you measure as you go along; I own several), let settle for 10 minutes, and skim off as much fat as you can. You will have about 3 quarts of sauce; reduce over medium-high heat to just over 2 quarts.

Meanwhile, wash the white mushrooms. Cut off their stems to within ¼ inch of the caps, and discard. In a large saucepan, cover them with 2 quarts of water, 2 teaspoons of salt, and the lemon juice. Bring to a boil and cook until the mushrooms are crisp-tender. Drain and blot dry; then season them with salt and pepper and brown them over high heat in a frying pan or saute pan, using any remaining bacon fat and adding vegetable oil.

Choose a casserole capable of holding the pieces of rooster in 1 layer. (The rooster will have shrunk and will fit into a much smaller pan than before.) Spoon in the reserved bacon and the sautéed mushrooms and nestle the pieces of rooster atop them. Pour in the broth, bring to a boil over medium-high heat, uncovered, and immediately reduce to a simmer. Cook very slowly for 10 minutes, skimming frequently.

After 5 minutes, taste the sauce and if it is markedly acidic (from the wine you have chosen), add ¼ teaspoon of sugar. Repeat a few minutes later. Then turn off the heat and cover until dinnertime.

One hour and a half before dinner, bring the *coq au vin* very slowly to a simmer and cook for ½ hour. Meanwhile, prepare the potatoes, spaetzle, or noodles, and begin cooking them.

Once again, gently remove the pieces of *coq* to a serving dish. Strain the sauce and scatter the bacon and mushrooms over the rooster. Cover with foil and hold in a warm place. In a 3-quart saucepan over medium-high heat, reduce the sauce to about 3 cups. (It should have thickened and be able to coat the back of a wooden spoon [see note], but not have become syrupy or sticky.) There will be more than enough to coat the pieces of rooster and flavor the potatoes, noodles, or spaetzle. Add ample black pepper to the sauce—which will transform it in a surprising way—about 20 grindings of the mill, taste for salt, and pour over the rooster. Serves 8 to 10.

Note: Have you ever wondered what recipes mean when they say that a sauce should be thick enough to coat the back of a spoon? Here's what they mean: Dip a wooden spoon into a sauce, remove, and run your finger horizontally across its back, making a wide gap or trail in the sauce. If the sauce is thick enough to coat the back of a spoon, it will not immediately run down and fill in the gap. There must be an easier way to explain this.

WHERE'S THE *BOEUF*?

S teamed broccoli is the root of all evil. I am pretty sure of this. I feel it is a major cause of mad-cow disease, hamburgers poisoned with *E. coli,* high cholesterol, and what is called "variant Creutzfeldt-Jakob disease," the human version of mad cow—about which the industrialized world is in an uncontrolled panic, as I write.

Here's why. We would all be glad to eat more vegetables and less beef, birds, and fish if vegetarian meals were sumptuous, seductive, artful, delicious, et cetera. And if vegetarian chefs understood that cooking vegetables requires at least as much artistry as roasting a chicken. Then there would be less need for factory farming, growth hormones, and all the other desperate measures that agribusiness uses to boost the production of animal flesh and lower its price. The worst of these (so far, at least) appears to have been the use of cheap, high-protein animal feed (including British cat food) made by grinding up the inedible parts of dead cows—bones, scraps, and innards. This is how mad-cow disease (also known as BSE, bovine spongiform encephalopathy, or spongy brain disease) was turned from an old and isolated bovine illness into an epidemic, though a small one, to be sure.

You can imagine my frenzied excitement upon hearing, at the turn of the year, that one of France's greatest chefs had banned meat from his menu, or so he had told the French newspaper *Libération*. He is Alain Passard, and his restaurant is the three-star L'Arpège, one of only 21 restaurants in France to which the *Michelin Red Guide* has given its highest rating. Could this be the dawning of a new epoch of human civilization, I wondered, the Age of Aquarius at last? Only minutes passed before I had made plans for the journey to Paris. One of the Western world's great chefs had gone vegetarian!

I have been a full-time vegetarian twice in my life and have no desire to become one again. But it seems obvious that vegetable cooking in the Western world needs to get much better. There are, after all, splendid vegetarian cuisines in Japan and China, and several in India alone. Why can't we do as well? It seems inevitable that our meat supply will be threatened from time to time, as it is now in Europe; yet, if we are forced to subsist, even intermittently, on steamed broccoli, this will surely drive us crazy. Even flesh fanciers, such as me, would be happy to eat lower down on the food chain more of the time and take some pressure off the factory farms that raise third-rate cows, chickens, and fish.

I had hardly recovered from my flight to Paris when I headed over to the weeklong Salon International de l'Agriculture, a vast exposition near the Porte de Versailles on the southwestern edge of the city. How were the French people, aside from Alain Passard, feeling about cows? Until last October, the French considered *la vache folle* an Anglo-Saxon problem, caused by the British and restricted to England. Then a French animal trader and his son were arrested for trying to pass off an infected cow at a slaughterhouse in Normandy. The veterinarians who caught them learned that the rest of the herd—first estimated as a ton of meat, then eight tons—had already been sold to the Carrefour chain of 39 supermarkets, plus at least three other stores. Sales of beef throughout France dropped by 50 percent, at least for a little while. More disturbing to some French diners was the government's ban on the use of beef intestines for making sausage and its ban on T-bone steaks (crosswise slices through a steer's backbone, which houses both marrow and spinal cord, two of the most likely carriers of mad-cow disease).

At the Salon, I was looking for the reported explosion of interest in organic farming and for palpable signs of hysteria (are we allowed to use that word again?) over animal diseases. I headed into the first exhibition hall I came to, the largest of eight. Instead of being surrounded by bewitching 16-year-old girls dressed as organic carrots and Japanese cucumbers in really short skirts, as you would see at American trade and agriculture fairs, I immediately found myself in the midst of cows, scores and hundreds of cows, beautiful, lovingly groomed, happy, sleepy, gentle cows, each with his or her own portable stall and private pile of hay, cows from France, Germany, Switzerland, Italy, and beyond, all seeming as harmless and innocent as immense and sluggish puppies. Plus there were sheep and goats. At first I gasped in fear and horror at being in the same enclosure with so many live cows and steers. But then, imitating the trusting behavior of the French children around me, I petted several of the loveliest bovine animals I have ever seen. These were called Brown Swiss, and their appearance owes something to the Brahman breed, in their softly rounded humps and their huge, profound, and liquid eyes.

This was all in stark contrast to the small area and even smaller crowds devoted to organic farming in one of the other buildings. One could easily find piles of pamphlets explaining the countless ways in which beef contributes to good health, but pamphlets about mad-cow disease were scarce—until I demanded one at the hospitality center of the Ministry of Agriculture and Fisheries. There were several displays showing the constituents of French cattle feed, indirect assurance that French farmers are entirely unlike the British, which seems less true than the French want to believe.

(Did you know that the English word for an epidemic among animals is "epizooty," from the French *épizootie*? Among the first authors to use the word in English was Thomas Malthus, the great and gloomy economist who argued that the world's population will inevitably outpace its food supply. Among his many reasons was the epizooty: "Great and wasting epizooties are frequent among the cattle," he prophetically observed in 1798.)

Nobody knows how mad-cow disease is transmitted. Some say it is a virus. Others favor prions (pronounced "PREE-ons")—runaway proteins that, though not alive, are somehow capable of replicating and are very difficult to destroy. (This is the scariest theory.) We do not even know for sure whether eating mad cows causes the human form of spongy-brain disease—variant

Creutzfeldt-Jakob, or vCJD. (The phrase *spongy brain* refers to the pits and holes that appear in the patient's brain, which first disable him or her and then bring on dementia and finally death.) Just three people in France have died of vCJD, compared with 90 in England. (Even 90 represents an average of only 15 cases a year in a population of nearly 60 million.) The animal-feed problem in England and the rest of Europe is nearly cleared up, and the epidemic of BSE is waning.

But everyone in France has watched a young English girl named Zoe Jeffries on television as she died of vCJD. Nobody knows how long a cow or a human can harbor the disease without showing symptoms. The federal Centers for Disease Control and Prevention in Atlanta has said that, depending on the incubation period in both species—somewhere between 5 and 15 years—the mathematical models predict anywhere from fewer than a hundred to several hundred thousand additional deaths in Europe from vCJD. Then we read that the British, worried about the *economic* health of their slaughterhouses, are still producing the banned feed and its constituents but shipping it all to Eastern Europe, the Middle East, Southeast Asia, and Africa.

Fortunately, I had already gotten deep into the vegetable cuisine of Alain Passard. On my second day in Paris, I walked from my hotel to L'Arpège, Passard's tiny restaurant on rue de Varenne, in the 7th arrondissement, right across from the Rodin Museum, to meet my friend Patrick for lunch. L'Arpège is a beautiful place, with curving pearwood walls and stylish modern lighting set into a soft-rose ceiling. It is probably the most intimate and personal of the three-star establishments in France. At 44, Passard cuts a glamorous figure—handsome, medium tall, medium thin, and rugged-looking. He lives on a *péniche,* a barge, on the Seine.

I had enjoyed some very fine meals at L'Arpège over the years, and suffered several agonizing ones. I fondly remember a fine though whimsical dinner in the early nineties, before Passard won his third star; he had decided to revive the elaborate tableside service of 50 years ago, and the room was bustling with twice as many waiters as usual, all wheeling around trolleys heavy with roast ducks and saddles of lamb on metal platters over alcohol flames—each one meant to serve two or three diners. Our food was wonderful—an entire roasted foie gras sliced and sauced next to the table, and a buttery apple tart in the form of a vast flat disk covered with a fine grid of caramelized puff pastry, prepared from scratch and baked just minutes earlier. Passard was famed both as a *rôtisseur,* an expert in the roasting of meats, and also as an experimentalist with a distinctly modern temperament.

Patrick and I spent a half-hour with the brand-new vegetarian menu, which Passard had introduced on January 16. (Overnight, 12 of his famous fleshy dishes were gone.) Then we gave up and asked for every vegetable dish on the list. In truth, the menu is neither strictly vegetarian nor entirely new. There are always two or three fish or seafood dishes, and Passard has kept his famous pigeon, roasted rare under a spicy coating of crushed *dragées,* sugared almonds.

So: A martini glass holding a bright wedge of avocado Bavarian cream is sprinkled with a rare oil pressed from grilled pistachios and set over a spoon of smoked black herring caviar from Aquitaine—nearly vegetarian but not quite. A small, delicious side dish combines leeks and black truffles. Deep-red baby beets are flavored with fine balsamic vinegar, spooned over melting red onions; around all this are wiggly concentric swirls of white-onion mousse, brilliantly green parsley-coriander sauce, and purple beet juices. (How did Passard discover such amazing flavors in white onions and in the cooking juices of a beet?) Then another side dish arrives: sautéed spinach with a carrot-and-orange puree. And happy yellow slices of rutabaga (one of the "lost vegetables," as Passard calls them) next to the pale wintry green of apples. Following this are two of his major plates: A wide, tender circle of celery root, paved with chestnut slices, crisply gratinéed, and set in a puddle of black truffle sauce. And delicate ravioli stuffed with a horseradish cream and a sage-leaf stripe, on and under a sauce made with vegetable cooking juices, salted butter, and aromatic argan oil, pressed from the seeds of a Moroccan evergreen.

Dessert is two thin slices of roasted pineapple with a layer of black truffles in the middle. My least favorite dish.

The food was stunning, original, precise, provocative, and very delicious. These are the five things we ask of modern cooking, aren't they? There are novel tastes and new ideas in Passard's cooking but nothing tricky. As a near-vegetarian, Alain Passard is still, or again, one of the finest cooks of France. Fear of mad-cow disease could not inspire such food; nor could an aversion to meat, to fowl, to carnality, to blood. This is the motive behind so many vegetarian restaurants—and their cooks. Their inspiration should instead be their love of cooking and eating vegetables, every kind in every way.

After lunch Passard sat down to talk. He explained that L'Arpège is not a vegetarian restaurant—he loves lobster and pigeon too much for that. At most, fear of animal flesh may have sped along his dramatic change. "I have not eaten meat for several years," he said, "and I have no more desire to cook it." Passard has gradually been adding vegetable dishes to the menu for the past 12 months—filling notebooks with the results of his experiments, and sometimes serving vegetarian, or nearly vegetarian, meals to habitués, regular customers who are willing to give him a free hand. "So it is not so much that everybody in France became afraid of beef at the same time. But, yes, I am very unhappy about the way our agriculture is going, especially the way we have turned herbivores into cannibals."

He knows and trusts several fine organic producers of beef and lamb, and butchers who are personally acquainted with every animal they sell. But Passard has made it his mission "to help invent a new cuisine for France," and he talked happily about the colors and aromas, the luminosity of vegetables. "I want to rethink vegetables," he said. Other chefs make fine vegetable dishes, but they are all prisoners of what he considers the Provençal cliché of vegetables in olive oil. "I am from Brittany, and so I love the taste of salted butter." Has he invented a new vegetarian cuisine? "No," he said, "but I have made a beginning." I pointed out to him that eventually this would require more grains or beans or lentils, sources of plant protein. He knows this. "Maybe next year or the year after," he predicted.

The news that Passard had gone vegetarian shook the French food world. What would become of the haute cuisine without fish, fowl, and meat? Was Passard an opportunist, they asked, playing on the new French dread of beef? Surely Passard was risking not only his third star but perhaps also his second, which he had won at 26, the youngest ever. Gastronomes would never pay $200 or $300 apiece for food that doesn't go with wine, they warned. The day after Passard's new menu was introduced, the newspaper *Le Monde* ran a psychological analysis of his motivation. He had been depressed, gossiped *Le Monde,* the way some people get when they win the top honors early in life. "Vegetables are his instruments against boredom."

Passard shrugged. He was not worried. He had met with the Michelin people, and they seemed content with what he had done. Besides, wine lovers have a wide range of distinguished whites to pair with their vegetables. On my second day at L'Arpège, *Le Figaro* scooped everybody with news of Michelin's ratings for 2001. Passard had kept all three stars.

For the next few days, I dined at *L'Arpège* for lunch or dinner. (The 690-franc tasting menu at lunch is one of the greatest three-star bargains around. That's about $90 at today's exchange rate, plus wine, for six courses, including two fish dishes, which I am sure you can replace with vegetables.) And I spent hours in the kitchen with Passard and his second-in-command, Gunther Hubrechsen. Every morning, their suppliers appeared at the kitchen door with the day's treasures. First there was a woman carrying a small cardboard box filled with aromatic black truffles. Then M. Didier Pil arrived from the town of Allonnes with the most perfect vegetables imaginable; he has supplied L'Arpège for the past four years. "It is not possible to disguise an imperfect vegetable, the way you can with a piece of beef," Gunther explained. All the fish is wild, caught by Passard's friends in Brittany. Only one type of salted butter will do, the one made by Jean-Yves Bordier. Passard rarely uses the central wholesale market at Rungis.

Gunther bravely tried to teach me some of Passard's dishes, especially the baby beets, the celery root, and the ravioli. Back in New York City, I had very good results with the beets and the celery root, and I will give you the recipes below. My countless tries with the horseradish-cream ravioli were unavailing. No, Alain Passard does not steam broccoli, or any other vegetable for that matter. "Steaming is too violent," he tells me. His beautiful mixed vegetables, sometimes served in a *vol-au-vent* of the lightest puff pastry I have ever eaten, illustrates his basic method. First, each of eight or ten species of vegetables is peeled and trimmed (always with a little of their stems left attached), and cooked separately in barely simmering water or vegetable stock or *jus de légumes,* frequently with a little salted butter. Now their colors are naturally vivid, and their texture falls between crisp and tender. At mealtime, they are combined in one pan and glazed for a few minutes in salted butter and a little of their mingled juices. And then they are arranged in an artful pile along with cabbage, beets, and black truffle (which are not cooked with the others) alongside little pools of intense green, pale gold (a raisin sauce), and deep beet red.

All of this takes an enormous amount of work. My time in Passard's kitchen was a reminder that one reason we avoid cooking vegetables is that they require back-breaking care and attention in shopping, washing, peeling, and precise cooking, all before we even get to the imagination part. Maybe vegetables are simply too much for home cooks. Perhaps we should leave them to restaurants like Passard's and their huge kitchen brigades, and do the really easy stuff at home—the foie gras, the pressed duck, and the venison. You can be the judge.

CELERY ROOT WITH CHESTNUTS
AND WILD MUSHROOMS

1 really large celery root weighing at least 2½ lbs.
(and at least 5 inches in diameter)

½ lb. salted butter, kept cold

8 oz. wild mushrooms, especially *cèpes* (porcini in Italian),
chanterelles, and black trumpets; to save money,
include lots of portobellos

¼ clove garlic

1 cup *jus de légumes* (see note)

¼ tsp. *quatre-épices* (see note)

Salt, preferably *fleur de sel*

40 chestnuts, shelled and cooked in water until tender, or,
to be more realistic, peeled and steamed and sold in otherwise
empty jars under the Eric Bur label, available at Balducci's in New
York City. Avoid the mushy canned variety packed in water.

2 Tbs. coarse bread crumbs, made by letting bread (preferably
dense white bread, not sourdough, with crusts removed) dry out for
a few days, and then grinding it, not too finely, in a food processor

Peel the celery root and cut it in half. Cut 2 slices from each
half, about ¼-inch thick and 5 to 6 inches across. (To cut celery
root evenly, carefully run a small knife around the circumference, making a ½-inch-deep cut exactly where you want it.
Then, with a larger knife, deepen the cut all around, and finally
slice through.) Put them in a baking pan or roasting pan large
enough to hold them in one layer. Pour in enough water to
come nearly to the top surface of the celery-root slices. Add a
tablespoon of the butter. Press a sheet of parchment paper
down into the pan so that it covers the celery root and presses
against the sides of the pan, preventing excessive evaporation.
Simmer on the stovetop for 5 minutes, turn over the celery

- - - - -

root, simmer for another 5 minutes, and continue until the slices are tender.

Meanwhile, prepare the wild mushroom sauce. Clean the mushrooms with a stiff brush and without using water. Chop them into ¼-inch pieces or smaller. Melt 2 tablespoons of the butter in a sauté pan, add the mushrooms and garlic, increase the heat to medium-high, toss everything together, and cover tightly. In 2 minutes, remove from the heat. The mushrooms should be wilted and surrounded by a little of their juices. Discard the garlic. Scrape into a blender or food processor along with ½ cup of the *jus de légumes,* a pinch of *quatre épices,* and a pinch of salt, and puree finely. Add the rest of the *jus* and up to ½ cup of warm water or even more, if needed to thin the sauce so that its texture resembles very heavy cream. Taste for salt.

Now slice the chestnuts into oblong, ⅛-inch-thick pieces. Pave the surface of the celery root circles with chestnut slices, all of which should be aligned in the same vertical direction. Begin by laying them all around the circumference and then fill the center with horizontal rows.

Preheat the broiler. Cut the cold butter lengthwise into very thin slices, less than 1⁄16-inch thick, and cover the celery-root-and-chestnut disks with them. Sprinkle ½ tablespoon of bread crumbs on each one. Brown under the broiler. Season each with a pinch of salt and a pinch of *quatre épices.*

Spoon generous pools of wild mushroom sauce onto four very warm plates. Place a celery-root-and-chestnut disk in the center of each. Serves 4.

BABY BEETS WITH RED ONIONS

3½ lbs. baby beets (weighed complete with their greens),
or just under 2 lbs. trimmed

2 Tbs. granulated sugar

2 Tbs. white distilled vinegar

½ lb. white onions, peeled and very thinly sliced

6 Tbs. salted butter

1 cup *jus de légumes* (see note)

2 medium-size (2½-inch diameter) red onions, peeled
and very thinly sliced

Juice of ½ lemon

1 Tbs. very fine (and expensive) balsamic vinegar

2 tsp. finely sliced chives

Trim the beets, removing the greens and roots, but leaving a
scant ½-inch of stem attached to each one. Wash the beets
meticulously, especially between the stems. Peel the beets.
Scrape and cut off the dark, rough ring between the beets and
their stems. Rinse under cold water. You should have about
1 pound of arduously trimmed baby beets. Halve or quarter
the beets, depending on their size. (You should end up with
about 64 pieces.) Try to include a little part of the stem on each
piece.

In a 4-quart pan, cover the beets with water by ¼ inch, and
add the sugar and vinegar. To reduce evaporation, press a
sheet of parchment paper down into the pan, touching the
water and the sides of the pan. Bring to a boil and reduce to a
low simmer. Cook for 2 hours, until very tender, adding hot
water if necessary, so that no more than the tops of the beets
are exposed. Remove from the heat but leave the beets in their
juices, covered with parchment paper until you need them, as
long as several hours.

- - - - -

Meanwhile, make the white-onion mousse, really a foamy sauce. Slowly cook the sliced white onions in 1 tablespoon of the salted butter until they are soft and limp, about 20 minutes. Puree in a blender, adding enough of the *jus de légumes* to thin the sauce and make it foamy. Strain into a small pan. Taste for salt.

Now there are 4 steps left before you can eat: cooking the red onions, glazing the beets, foaming up the white-onion sauce, and arranging everything on four very warm plates.

Melt 2 tablespoons of the salted butter in a sauté pan and add the sliced red onions. Press a sheet of parchment paper down into the pan, touching the onions and the sides of the pan, and cook slowly until the onions are still slightly crisp, about 7 to 10 minutes. Remove from the heat, discard the paper, and stir in the lemon juice. To your amazement, the onions will turn a lovely pink.

Meanwhile, with a slotted spoon, move the beets to a sauté pan, leaving the juices behind. Over high heat, reduce the juices to about ¾ cup (or add water if they have cooked down too far). Reserve ¼ cup of the juices to decorate the plates, and pour the rest over the beets. Add 3 tablespoons of the salted butter, and over medium-high heat shake the pan and toss the beets until the juices have reduced to a tablespoon or two and the beets are glazed and shiny, 3 to 5 minutes. At the last minute, stir in the balsamic vinegar.

Warm the white-onion sauce and blend with a hand mixer. Divide the red onions among the plates, setting them in a rough circle in the center. Cover the onions with the glazed beets.

Spoon a wide circle of white-onion puree (about ½ table-spoon each) around the red onions and beets, and a thin wig-gly circle of beet juices around that. Sprinkle some chives onto the circle of white-onion puree. Serves 4.

Note: At L'Arpège, the celery root paved with chestnuts is set onto a pool of black-truffle sauce; at Passard's suggestion, I have substituted wild mushrooms and prepared them as he and Gunther recommended. And I have left out the parsley-coriander sauce—it is simply too much work—and used Gunther's idea of adding a nice green sprinkling of chives.

Jus de légumes can mean a variety of things; at L'Arpège, it is light and sweet, and relies mainly on the wealth of vegetable juices left over from preparing various dishes. Here, we must start from scratch. To make 2½ cups of *jus,* enough for both recipes: In a 4-quart saucepan put 10 cups of roughly chopped vegetables (carrots, celery, onions, black radishes, turnips, leeks, rutabaga, and in the winter, celery root). Cover with cold water, about 6 cups. Add 2 tablespoons of salted butter. Bring to a simmer, partially cover, and cook for 40 minutes. Strain the liquid and reduce it by about half to 2½ cups. Taste it and smile. Add any pan juices left over from cooking the red onions and the celery root.

Quatre-épices: This common French combination of four spices, used especially in charcuterie, typically includes black or white pepper, nutmeg, cloves or cinnamon, and ginger, and is sold already prepared in bottles. Passard makes his own, using white pepper and going heavy on the ginger. To follow him, use a (clean) electric coffee grinder, the kind with a whirling horizontal blade, to pulverize 2 tablespoons white peppercorns. Add ¼ teaspoon ground clove, ¾ teaspoon ground nutmeg, and 2 teaspoons powdered ginger, and grind them all together until the mixture is extremely fine.

The Most Perfect So Far

But here's the point: Alain Ducasse's transcendent tuiles—*the most perfect* tuiles *so far—are now a minimum standard, a floor below which a baker may sink only at his or her peril.*

POT SHOTS

There is no spleen in Paris and very little shin. From butcher to butcher we buzz about in my friend Frédérick's little car, covering most of the city's center. Her mission is simply to prepare tomorrow's dinner, while mine is to conquer, once and for all, to subdue and subjugate, the *pot-au-feu*. For this is not just the national dish of France—the foundation of Empires, as one French statesman has put it. More important, it is the foundation of my winter entertaining plans.

We find a parking space on the Faubourg Saint-Honoré, right in front of Les Boucheries Nivernaises, and walk inside. "Got any *pot-au-feu*?" Frédérick asks the bright-eyed, immaculate butcher. She is not requesting a takeout or frozen version of the national dish but, in abbreviation, the beefy ingredients for making one. We try to appear casual, though in truth we are suffering from great inner panic because this is the last butcher on our list, and all we have found in the French capital are some knucklebones, the *crosse* and *nourrice* (knee and ankle or ankle and knee, I can't remember which), and *macreuse*. I have pored over French and American maps of dismembered cows for many a year and still cannot figure out where the *macreuse* fits into the picture. But we have plenty of it, or them, in the car.

"No *pot-au-feu*." The butcher shrugs, turning back to his block, where he hacks away at a mountain of red flesh.

"You have oxtail?" Frédérick persists.

"Um," the butcher answers, turning to enter the walk-in refrigerator. He brings out several long, red animal tails.

"You have *paleron*?" I ask.

"Whoosh," the butcher answers, disappears for a minute, and comes back with the entire front leg of a cow. He does not really say "whoosh." This is my way of spelling the special Parisian way of pronouncing *oui*—a noisy inhale with the lips pursed.

And so it continues. In truth, the butcher has everything you could want for a *pot-au-feu* except the *rate,* the spleen, which nobody ever seems to carry unless you order it way ahead, but which a French writer upon whom Frédérick and I are relying swears is indispensable to the flavor of the broth and to its golden color. I suppose you must show your seriousness to a butcher before he will sell you these humble cuts of meat, which have become increasingly rare in an age of steak and roast beef—even in Paris. Or maybe, at the end of summer, the cold-weather ingredients for a *pot-au-feu* are in short supply, hoarded for regular customers.

Before long, the butcher and I are pals, drawing diagrams of the foreleg and hind shank, leaving bloody fingerprints on my French and American cow maps. He labels his diagrams with the Latin names of the various bones—the *cubitus,* the *humerus,* and the *scapula*—the universal language of educated French butchers. I think I almost have it figured out.

Paris has never been lovelier than on this bright September day, but my thoughts are stuck in the depths and darkness of winter, as I imagine the perfect holiday dinner party. *Conviviality* is the point, warmth and bright conversation, eight or ten of us around a table, candles all about and a smoldering fire somewhere near. The scent of cloves and oranges, of cinnamon and apples, is in the air. Through the window, we can see the snow swirling under a street lamp.

But wait. There is nothing truly convivial in this picture, not yet at least, no food, no drink. Until the modern era, conviviality meant "feasting and drinking together," nothing more nor less, and a "convive" was a fellow feaster. Maybe joviality and candles played a minor part. ("Convive" is an English word taken directly from the Latin. Somehow, in the nineteenth century, the British decided the word was French and began italicizing it.

They had obviously lost a good part of their *joie de vivre*.) Now, oddly, conviviality has come to include nearly any festive group activity with or without carousing or feasting. I prefer the older definition. True conviviality is where *pot-au-feu* comes into the picture.

Pot-au-feu (literally, "pot on the fire") is theoretically a simple dish of vegetables, marrow bones, and meats simmered in a clear, golden broth, eaten with sour little pickles and onions, several mustards, coarse gray sea salt, and perhaps a sauce or two. The meal starts with a bowl of hot bouillon more delicious than you have ever tasted, poured over a toasted crouton. Next there is a marrow bone or two, the insides scooped out and spread like butter on pieces of grilled rustic bread and sprinkled with coarse sea salt. And then comes the *pot-au-feu* proper, sections of oxtail, perhaps a piece of chicken, slices of tender boiled beef taken from the humblest cuts, leeks and carrots and turnips. I have read that the French eat more carrots than any people on earth, and that leeks are the heraldic device of the Gauls.

The *pot-au-feu* is what the French call a *plat unique*, a one-dish meal, and also a *plat convivial*, a dish for sharing, for feasting, for celebration. In these ways, it is like bouillabaisse and cassoulet, like an Alsatian *choucroute* or a southwestern *garbure* (a soup so thick and so full of nourishment that a fork stands up straight in it). In the United States, we have the grandest *plat convivial* of them all, the holiday turkey, which we share with 245 million other Americans, including the members of the armed forces, for whom the government spares no expense in jetting turkeys about the globe. There is an uncanny and intoxicating sense of oneness in enjoying a dish with a quarter billion of your fellows. No fussy eating allowed, no irrational preferences or aversions, no cultish diet fads or hypochondria. Just feasting and drinking together, essential and fundamental nourishment, plus lots of trimmings.

Somehow, *pot-au-feu* always ends up only theoretically simple. First you must choose a recipe. Both Frédérick and I have tried countless of them. There is Michel Guérard's famous version, served at his first little restaurant (itself called Le Pot-au-Feu) in a grimy Paris suburb in the seventies, long before Guérard's genius won him three Michelin stars at Eugénie-les-Bains. And Marcel Rouff's favorite, made with poached foie gras, described in his famed 1924 "novel of the table," *La Vie et la Passion de Dodin-Bouffant, Gourmet*. And Mme. St. Ange's long chapter on the subject in her 1927 bible of French home cooking. And a thousand other recipes for *pot-au-feu*. Whole cults have formed around one or the other, bound together by the belief that one cut of beef is superior and indispensable, all others being vulgar and out of the question.

Second, you must organize the meal. The result is nearly always a logistical disaster. You seem to need five pairs of hands in the kitchen, especially at the last minute. And even then you end up covering every surface, every piece of your clothing, your arms, your head, and every pot and pan you own with meat and broth and rendered fat.

Finally, a multitude of technical questions have never been authoritatively answered: Should you clarify the bouillon or leave it cloudy (and perhaps full of richly flavored particles)? Should you start with cold or boiling water? When do you add the salt? The French come to blows over issues like these, too.

Having learned a bit of butchers' Latin and collected everything we needed except dessert, Frédérick and I return to her house on the outskirts of Paris. (As her husband, Pierre Hermé, is the greatest pastry chef in France, we are not worried about the end of the meal.) We immediately put the knucklebones and shin meat into a huge stockpot, pour in six quarts of water, set it over a moderate flame, and go about trimming the other meats and the vegetables during the hour it takes for everything to come to the boil.

Here is the problem: Kitchen lore in France, Italy, and the United States is nearly unanimous that starting with cold water and adding salt at the beginning results in both a rich and savory broth and tasteless meat that has been leached of all its flavor. Yet, if you do the opposite—boil the water first to "seal" the meat and withhold salt until the end—the broth will be thin and anemic. This is a vital issue because it is the bouillon that matters most—French writers have called it the soul of home cooking. Many recipes—Guérard's, for example, and one of Mme. St. Ange's—have you make a broth a day or two ahead and then introduce a new round of meats and vegetables for the final feast. Frédérick and I follow a brilliant compromise proposed by Brillat-Savarin in the nineteenth century: Put the bones and meats for the bouillon into cold water. A few hours later, add the meats and vegetables that you plan actually to eat. And several hours after that, or the next day, remove and discard the first round, now gray and tasteless.

You need a giant pot, and you will spend lots of time skimming the surface of all its fat and foam because the broth and most of the meats should by the end be entirely lean. No matter how you do it, a *pot-au-feu* is a great labor of love. I leave Frédérick at six for a dinner back in Paris. She continues cooking until midnight. Or so she later tells me.

Several *pot-au-feu* issues are nearly settled the next day after our friend Hervé This arrives for dinner. Hervé is the leading French writer (and TV personality) on the science of cooking. He announces that he has demonstrated experimentally that the amount of flavor that is leached from the meat to enrich the broth is the same whether you start out with cold water or hot—as long as you cook the meat for many hours. (Hot and cold water have different effects only after brief cooking.) But there is another aspect to the problem. If you start with cold water, Hervé has found, the bouillon ends up golden and beautifully transparent; otherwise it may be gray and cloudy. The reason, he thinks, is more mechanical than chemical—strenuously boiling water loosens tiny particles from the surface of the meat.

Hervé has brought a laboratory flask, a vacuum pump, and a set of filters made of paper or glass. Tonight, we will evaluate three methods for clarifying broth. First is Herve's scientific technique. Second is the ancient method of the French *bonne femme*, the traditional home cook, who knows that after a very long, very gentle simmer, the larger meat particles fall to the bottom of the pot while the less visible contributors to flavor remain suspended, presumably making for a rich-tasting but still golden broth. And third is the lofty technique of French haute cuisine; at the very end, the broth is simmered with egg whites and, sometimes, additional meats and vegetables (to add back flavor), for an hour or so.

Hervé, Frédérick, and I sip the three resulting liquids. The *bonne femme* wins, at least tonight. The haute cuisine method leaves the bouillon beautifully clear and golden but vapid in taste when egg whites alone are used to collect the particles that would make it cloudy; when ground beef and leeks are added for flavor, the broth has a raw taste—hamburger meat boiled for an hour cannot compete with knuckles and shins simmered for two days. Hervé's laboratory filters lose badly, but they have requested a rematch: One is clogged with the leftovers of a massive tomato consommé experiment Hervé recently conducted in Alsace, his ancestral seat.

Frédérick's dinner is magnificent. To the primordial and profoundly nourishing tastes of beef broth and root vegetables, Frédérick adds hors d'oeuvres in the form of tiny white ceramic cups filled with cucumber granité and foamy, cold tomato soup, and a dreamy pork pâté made by her friend near Bordeaux. Pierre serves a sweet *vin de paille* to start with and a powerful Morgon with the beef, and he has concocted an unimaginably delicious raspberry dacquoise with pistachio cream.

But Frédérick is exhausted. The overall procedure we have followed left her with too much labor after the guests have arrived. Back in New York, I figure out another way—by spreading the effort over three days and combining a few steps here and there, nearly everything can be done ahead, at least on paper. Then I trudge down to my favorite butcher in Greenwich Village with sheaves of cow maps and my own verbal body-part descriptions.

How many times have I made this hapless journey, only to conclude that we Americans slice up our cows in shapes and directions so different from the French that there is no hope of replicating what one has eaten in France? For *pot-au-feu,* the French usually require at least one lean piece, one gelatinous cut, and one in the semifatty category. Our domestic meat industry finds alternate uses for choice but either gelatinous or fatty morsels such as beef cheeks—they end up in dog food, in commercial hamburger, or in frozen shipments to Latin America.

First, I try a *pot-au-feu* with the nearest I can come to the traditional French cuts. The result is mediocre. You will understand that these two brief sentences sum up several days of messy effort and the considerable bitterness that ensued. Somehow, the French cuts of American cows are not as succulent as I remember them from Paris. Not for the first time in my life as an amateur cook, it is time to start at square one. With the aid of my indefatigable assistant, Kathryn, I make a quadruple dose of bouillon and spend the next week slowly simmering every American cow part that can possibly benefit from such treatment, each alone in its own pot. We test short ribs, boned and unboned, front shin and rear shank, upper leg and lower, arm pot roast and neck pot roast, rump pot roast and mock tender, hanger steak and trusty oxtail.

And the winners are three. The most juicy, savory, and rich of all of these are full-cut short ribs, nearly the equivalent of the essential French *plat de côtes couvertes.* Favored for their unique flavor and famous shape are sections of oxtail. And, just in the nick of time, I discover that the American "tip steak" from the cow's upper rear thigh is the *plat de tranche,* a very close neighbor to Mme. St. Ange's absolute favorite, mouthwatering cut for *pot-au-feu,* the *point de culotte*!

The results are magnificent, and the simple, lengthy, and very detailed recipe that came out of all this follows. Sadly, there is no spleen in New York City this winter. But conviviality reigns—carousing and feasting, abundance and generosity, friendship and reunion, sighs and laughter, all around a pot upon the fire.

POT-AU-FEU

Pot-au-feu is usually prepared, served, and eaten in one excruciatingly long day, or in two pretty rough ones. The recipe below is spread over three, so that your labor on the day of the dinner—always a problem with *pot-au-feu*—is minimized. When the recipe calls for refrigeration, you may take the term loosely because you are unlikely to own a refrigerator large enough to hold everything. It is winter now, and you can use a porch or cellar, a fire escape or open window.

2 oxtails, cut into 2½-inch sections by your butcher

8 lbs. veal and beef soup bones, from the knuckle or ankle (not marrow bones), cracked or sawed by your butcher into 2-inch or 3-inch pieces

9 quarts cold water, plus additional water kept hot over low heat in a covered pan or teakettle to replenish some of what is lost to evaporation

5 lbs. shin or shank meat, off the bone, cut into 2-inch cubes

10 medium leeks

1 bunch parsley

4 bay leaves

3 sprigs fresh thyme

3 cloves garlic, peeled and lightly crushed

½-inch piece of peeled fresh ginger

1 stalk celery, with leaves if available, washed

4 medium onions (each about 3 inches in diameter), peeled

9 whole cloves

Coarse sea salt

Black pepper in a peppermill

2 pinches ground cloves

2 pinches grated nutmeg

2 pinches ground cinnamon

4 lbs. of short ribs, preferably full-cut short ribs

all in one piece, 10–12 inches long

3 lbs. of neck pot roast, in one piece, or, if unavailable,
rump pot roast
1 3–4 lb. chicken, preferably free-range
16 sections marrow bone (each about 1¼-inch thick)
8 medium carrots
8 small turnips (each about 2½ inches in diameter)
8 round, ¼-inch-thick slices of baguette, grilled, toasted,
or lightly browned in butter, for the broth
16 large slices of French country bread, toasted or
grilled—8 cut into quarters for the marrow,
and 8 cut in half to accompany the *pot-au-feu*
A few branches of fresh tarragon and fresh chervil
Condiments: a tiny bowl or 2 of coarse sea salt;
peppermills or tiny bowls of coarsely ground black pepper;
2 or more mustards in small bowls, one a strong Dijon style,
another with the seeds left intact; cornichons—
the very sour, small French pickles; horseradish sauce
and green sauce; and, optionally, sour cherries
pickled in vinegar, or currant jelly or chutney
Special equipment:
2 baking sheets with raised edges (or 2 large, shallow
roasting pans) for browning the bones
A 20-quart stockpot or soup kettle
Kitchen string
A large tea kettle or covered 2-quart saucepan
2 packages cheesecloth, a total of about 50 feet in length
A skimmer, made with closely woven wire mesh
A large strainer with fine or medium mesh
An 8-quart pot or bowl (or 2 smaller ones)
A large ladle
8 soup plates
8 dinner plates, preferably wide and deep
1 huge or 2 large platters
8 small spoons or seafood forks

— — — — —

Day One (Elapsed time: 10 hours. Working time: 3 hours). Preheat your oven to 450°F. Rinse the oxtail pieces, select the eight largest, and refrigerate them in a covered bowl of cold water. Roast the smaller oxtail pieces and the soup bones for about ½ hour or until they take on a good golden color, turning them once. Turn off the oven and transfer the bones and oxtails to the stockpot, along with any reddish-brown juices in the roasting pan. Add the shank or shin meat and pour in 9 quarts of cold water. Mark the water level on a wooden skewer or chopstick plunged to the bottom of the stockpot. Set the stockpot over medium heat and bring slowly to a boil. This can take up to 1 hour.

Meanwhile, get the vegetables ready. Cut each leek crosswise to separate the white part (including an inch or 2 of light green) from the tough, dark green leaves. Wrap the white sections in plastic and refrigerate. Discard half the dark leaves; wash and trim the rest, and tie them together with a piece of kitchen string. Cut off the stems from the bunch of parsley, wash them, and lay them on the leek leaves, along with 3 of the bay leaves, the thyme, garlic, ginger, and celery stalk. (Save the parsley leaves for another use.) Wrap up everything in a large piece of washed cheesecloth, folded into a double thickness, and tie securely with kitchen string. Here and throughout this recipe, leave a 2-foot tail of string that will drape nearly a foot over the rim of the stockpot, making the bundle easy to remove.

Stick 3 of the peeled onions with 3 cloves each.

As soon as the water in the stockpot comes to a boil, lower the heat so that the water maintains a *moderately low boil*—considerably more active than a simmer but much less than a rolling boil. Cook for 45 minutes more. As scum and foam rise to the surface, remove them with the metal skimmer. (I find it convenient to keep a bowl of warm water nearby for rinsing off the skimmer.)

— — — — —

After 45 minutes, add 3 cups of cold water to the stockpot; this should bring more fat and foam to the surface. When the water returns to a boil again, skim until there is nothing left to skim, about ½ hour. Add the cheesecloth package of herbs and vegetables, the onions, 1 tablespoon of the salt, 6–8 grindings of black pepper, and 1 healthy pinch each of ground clove, grated nutmeg, and ground cinnamon. Lower the heat to maintain a very gentle simmer—hardly more than a shiver (or as the French call it, a smile) of movement on its surface. Cook, uncovered, for 3 hours.

Meanwhile, rinse the marrow bones, submerge them in a bowl of cold, lightly salted water, cover with plastic wrap, and refrigerate for at least 1 day, changing the water 3 times.

After 2 hours, fill a kettle or saucepan with 2 to 3 quarts of cold water and place over low heat. This will be used to replenish the water evaporating from the stockpot. Remove the oxtail pieces, short ribs, and neck pot roast from the refrigerator. Drain and rinse the oxtail pieces; wrap and tie them in a cheesecloth package. Tie the 2 other pieces of beef with kitchen string in several places to help them keep their shape. Remember to add on 2-foot tails of string.

When the 3 hours are up, add enough boiling water to bring the level of the broth to its original level, using the mark on your chopstick as a guide. Add the wrapped and tied meats to the stockpot. Turn up the heat to medium and bring the water to a moderate boil. Now, following the procedure we used before, cook for 45 minutes more, skimming often; then add 3 cups of cold water; when the broth returns to a boil, skim until there is nothing left to skim, about ½ hour. Then lower the heat to maintain a very gentle simmer for the next 3 hours.

After one hour, preheat the oven to 450°F. Remove the chicken from the refrigerator. Discard the innards, if any. Wash the bird inside and out with warm water, pat dry, stuff with the fourth peeled onion and the fourth bay leaf. Truss the chicken with kitchen string, leaving a long tail. Set into a small roasting pan and into the oven for 25 minutes until the skin colors lightly and some fat and juices are released. Remove the chicken, turn off the oven, and wipe the chicken with a paper towel to remove any fat that has been released.

After the meats have simmered for 2 hours, add the chicken.

An hour later, turn off the heat, and if you are as strong as I, remove the stockpot to a cool place. Add the 15 black peppercorns, and cover. Let cool to room temperature overnight.

Day Two (Elapsed and working times: 2 hours). Pull the meat and the chicken from the stockpot by their strings and set aside. Lift out and discard the cheesecloth package of vegetables and herbs and, with tongs, enough of the bones to make the stockpot manageable. Put the strainer over the 8-quart bowl or pot. Line it with a double layer of moistened cheesecloth. Pour the remaining contents of the stockpot into the strainer. Discard the bones and solids. Wash the stockpot and pour back in the strained stock. You should have about 6 quarts.

Untie the meats and chicken. Remove the skin and all visible fat and gristle from the chicken, and cut it into 8 serving pieces. With your fingers, remove all gristle and fat from the oxtails and short ribs. Remove the bones from the short ribs and slice the meat into 8 or 10 portions. Tie the chicken pieces in a large piece of doubled cheesecloth and the meats in another. Submerge them in the broth, cover, and refrigerate.

Prepare the sauces and condiments, cover, and refrigerate.

Day Three (or the second half of Day Two, elapsed and working times: 2 hours). An hour and a quarter before dinner, remove the stockpot from the refrigerator, fire escape, or other cold location. Lift off the thick layer of fat that will have solidified on the surface of the broth and discard it (or save for making French fries, mixing this beef fat with an equal amount of canola oil). Set the pot over medium-high heat. As soon as the gelatinized broth liquifies, stir in another good pinch each of ground cinnamon, ground cloves, and freshly grated nutmeg, and several grindings of black pepper. Bring to a simmer; this can take 45 minutes. Skim as necessary.

Meanwhile, prepare the vegetables. Remove the tough, discolored outer layers of the reserved leeks (white and light green portion), and slice off the roots, removing as little as you can. Slit the green ends by 2 inches and wash out any sand and dirt. Tie the leeks into a bundle with kitchen string. Peel the carrots, trim their ends, cut in half both lengthwise and crosswise, and tie the resulting pieces into a bundle. Peel the turnips and cut them in half. Cut a large piece of cheesecloth, fold it in half, and tie it into a package around the leeks, carrots, and turnips. This might be a good time to grill or toast the slices of baguette and French country bread.

Remove the marrow bones from their cold-water bath, rinse them, trim the gristle and fat from their outer surfaces, rub their ends with coarse sea salt, and place them in a saucepan or sauté pan just wide enough to hold them in 2 layers.

As soon as the broth comes to a simmer, submerge the vegetable package in it, reduce the heat, and cook at a low simmer for ½ hour. After 10 minutes, ladle enough simmering broth over the marrow bones to cover them, bring to the barest shiver, cover, cook for 20 minutes, then turn off the heat. After another ten minutes, add eight grindings of black pepper to the broth. Warm the soup plates and dinner plates in a low oven. When the vegetables have simmered for ½ hour, turn off the heat under both the stockpot and the marrow. You are ready to eat!

For the first course, place a round of baguette in each of the warm soup plates and spoon about a cup of broth into each

– – – – –

one. Float a few fresh tarragon and chervil leaves on each portion, and serve. This will probably be the most delicious thing you have tasted in weeks.

For the second course, lift the marrow with tongs to 8 small plates, sprinkle the upper end of each bone with a little coarse sea salt, place 1 or 2 quarter slices of toasted country bread on each plate, and serve with very small spoons or forks. Your guests will scoop out the marrow, spread it on their bread like butter, sprinkle with more salt, and eat with glee.

The third course is the *pot-au-feu* itself. Set the condiments and sauces on the table along with a basket or two of grilled bread, along with a bowl of hot broth. Remove the cheesecloth packages of meats, oxtails, chicken, and vegetables from the stockpot, cut them open, and arrange everything on 2 or 3 platters. Moisten everything with several soup spoons of broth for each platter, and either place the platters on the table, carry them around to each guest, or put them on a sideboard or buffet table. Or, if you have a helper, arrange each plate yourself, putting a little of everything on it, and moistening with broth. Then arrange the remaining meat and vegetables on one platter, cover with a kitchen towel well moistened with hot water, and place in a very low oven for 10 minutes or so, whereupon you will bring it to the table for second helpings.

Serve with a robust red wine.

MY WAY OF PREPARING MARROW BONES

When I combined the principles that gave rise to Sky King's Roasted Marrow Bones, page 85, with a delectable marrow-bone dish at Michael Jordan's Steakhouse in New York City, the result was an alternative, untraditional, and perhaps more desirable way of preparing the marrow-bone course for *pot-au-feu*. Frédérick has adopted it as her own. Buy one entire marrow bone, 6 to 8 inches long, for each guest. Have the butcher saw each bone lengthwise into 2 halves, each flat on the marrow side and curved on the other, uncut side. Either steam or microwave the bones, flat side up, until the marrow is just tender. Then, immediately before eating, brown under a hot broiler, and sprinkle with coarse salt. Serve 2 sections to each guest, along with country bread.

DECEMBER 1997

DECODING PARMESAN

S tanding on the corner of Grand Street and Mott in New
York City, in what remains of Little Italy, in front of Di
Palo's Fine Food, on a sunny, subzero afternoon, I stamped
my feet, watched my breath, and reconsidered the puzzle of
Parmesan. Parmigiano-Reggiano, Parmigiano for short, is one
of the two or three greatest cheeses in the world—ancient,
incomparably delicious, delicate, savory, and complex. Boccaccio
relates a dream of Parmigiano in his *Decameron* in 1348, in which
there is a "mountain of grated Parmesan cheese on top of which
there were people who did nothing but make maccheroni and
ravioli." Samuel Pepys hastily buried his supply to protect it from
the great fire of London in 1666. In the last years of his life,
Molière would eat nothing else. It is the only cheese whose flavor
underpins an entire cuisine.

Parmigiano-Reggiano falls into a category of Italian cheeses
called *grana,* because the texture of a fine, aged specimen is
grainy, with crunchy little white crystals and long, thin flakes
that radiate out from the center of the cheese. Grana is made
throughout the provinces of northern Italy, which for centuries
waged a chauvinistic war over whose grana should be considered
the most valued and prestigious. For reasons good and bad, the
cheeses of Parma and of Reggio Emilia won out, and those
of the other regions were lumped under the name of Grana
Padano, after the word for the Po River Valley. The best of these
can be excellent cheeses, though they are typically inferior to
(and less expensive than) the 700-year-old cheese now known as
Parmigiano-Reggiano. *Parmesan* is the French word for *Parmi-*

giano. The British adopted it in the early 1500s, spelling it any way they pleased—*parmasian, parmazene, parmasent, parmizant, permoysaunt*—and applied it both to the cheese and to the citizens of Parma. The powdered Parmesan in those green canisters in the supermarket is a salty, dry, repellent condiment that should not be called Parmesan.

Parmigiano-Reggiano is produced by nearly 700 dairies (using milk from 12,000 farms) in the contiguous Italian provinces of Parma, Reggio Emilia, and Modena (plus slivers of Mantua and Bologna), and its texture and taste and aroma vary from dairy to dairy and from month to month. Each giant golden wheel weighs between 70 and 90 pounds, has a street value exceeding $1,000, and is branded with the month and year of its manufacture and the code number of the dairy that produced it. For years, I have been trying to unlock the mystery that lurks behind these markings so that whenever I shop I will be able to find, in the most mathematically precise way, the ideal wedge of Parmigiano-Reggiano. And I think I have finally cracked the puzzle. Or maybe I haven't.

I started with the idea that the oldest dairies, which presumably produce the most authentic cheeses, are those with the lowest code numbers. Then I learned that when a dairy goes out of business its number can be reassigned to the newest entrant—and anyway, that each region has been given its own range of numbers, so that, for example, all the dairies around Parma have numbers from 2001 to 2500, and 3001 to 3500, with Modena in the middle. Back to square one. I worked tirelessly to wangle a copy of the rare and treasured booklet "Caseifici Produttori," which translates the numerical producer codes into the names of individual dairies. I succeeded. But it was a Pyrrhic victory. Even if I now had the ability to name the cheesemaker of any wheel of Parmesan I came across, I still did not know which producers to look for.

Could I choose a wheel of Parmesan by the month when it was made? Cheese is concentrated milk—17 pounds of it go into each pound of Parmesan. Whatever a cow eats flavors her milk and any cheese made from it. In winter, cows are given dry hay and alfalfa; in spring, they feast on tender, young, aromatic herbs and grasses, at least if they graze in mountain pastures; by midsummer, the meadows are parched and burned by the hot Italian sun, and not very appetizing. So, I thought, the most delicious and complex milk for cheesemaking must be the milk of early spring.

But we must also keep our eyes on the butterfat. Parmesan is a relatively low-fat cheese, varying from 28 percent to 32 percent. Within this narrow range, more butterfat means that the cheese can be aged longer, which produces a more complex flavor, a wonderfully long "finish" or aftertaste, and the prized flaky texture—all without the cheese becoming sandy, dried out, and bitter. Most cows give birth to their calves in late winter or early spring. Butterfat is lowest at calving time and then rises gradually. (That's why, in bygone years, only cheese made from mid-April through mid-November could be called Parmigiano-Reggiano. Cheeses made in the winter, called *invernengo*, and in early spring, called *testa*, commanded lower prices. Now, partly from crass commercial motives and partly from modern methods of bovine manipulation, milk throughout the year is considered good enough.) This all pointed to cheeses produced in late spring and early summer, wheels with Giugno or Luglio stamped on the side—high butterfat plus fresh herbs and flowers.

But when I telephoned the knowledgeable Leo Bertozzi at the Consorzio del Formaggio Parmigiano-Reggiano in Reggio Emilia, he explained that the protein level of the milk is the thing to watch. Parmigiano is a partially skimmed-milk cheese. Each day's cheese is made from two milkings, evening and morning. As the evening milk rests overnight, its cream rises to the surface. In the morning, some of it is skimmed off. Then the milk is poured into a copper cauldron with the full-fat morning milk. As cheesemaking begins, some whey from the day before is mixed in to start the fermentation, the milk is heated, rennet is added, and after a while the casein (the main protein in milk) coagulates into clumps known as curds, which are broken up, cooked briefly, drained, packed into molds, dried, salted, and aged—cheesemaking in a nutshell. It is the clumps of casein—the curds—that form the underlying structure or network of the cheese, holding the butterfat, minerals, and water.

But if more butterfat allows longer aging and more complex flavors, why skim off any of the cream? The reason is that the casein structure in Parmesan cannot hold more than its own weight in butterfat. As milk always has more butterfat than casein throughout the year, some of the fat must always be skimmed. Butterfat may reach its maximum in June, but then the casein is so low that nearly all of the fat from the evening milk has to be skimmed off. I should have been watching the casein graph!

So I did. Casein starts at about 2 percent at calving time, and then climbs in a straight line to reach 2.6 percent 10 months later. By September, October, and November, the casein graph has climbed quite smartly, allowing the cheesemaker to skim much less. These are the months when a wheel of Parmigiano-Reggiano will have the highest and most luxuriant level of butterfat and the greatest potential for aging. But how appetizing is the cow's diet in the fall?

Just fine, as it turns out. Bertozzi explained that as the cruel sun of Emilia Romagna retreats in late September, a new crop of mountain grass appears, a second growth! Cows living in the valley may not benefit from this grass—and having lived through a sweltering, suffocating lowland summer, they are more subject to bacterial infections, their milk will not be at its purest, and undesirable types of fermentation can occur. But cows that spend the summer frolicking in cool, sub-Alpine mountain pastures and dine in the early fall on the fresh second growth of grass are both the healthiest and the most aromatically fed.

In truth, the frolicking ended years ago. All milk cows in Emilia Romagna live in barns, and forage is brought to them. But mountain dairy farmers cut their fresh grass, herbs, blossoms, and clover twice a day and feed them directly to the cows. In the valley, the cows eat dry forage—often one or two uninteresting species like alfalfa and hay brought from distant fields.

But does mountain milk always go to mountain cheese producers? Fortunately, the answer is mostly yes. By and large, Parmigiano-Reggiano cheese is handmade by small producers who average eight cheeses a day and use milk from cows living nearby. As with farmhouse cheeses elsewhere in Italy and in France, but unlike most handmade cheeses in this country, the cheesemaker is proud of his territory and wants the flavor of his cheese to reflect the character of his land, its vegetation, and its climate—to reflect what the French call *terroir*.

There you have it. I had to get my hands on some October or November Parmesan from a mountain producer. How to discover which cheeses are made from mountain milk—which numerical codes go with the mountain cheesemakers? I had read that all cheeses from the province of Reggio Emilia (with numbers from 101 to 999) come from the mountains. But Leo Bertozzi set me straight. Four of the five provinces produce both mountain and valley cheeses; only Mantua has no mountains. And I could find no map, chart, graph, or table separating valley producers from those in the mountains. I knew that certain Parmesan wholesalers or brokers—Rocca, Magnani, Gennari, and Greci—specialize in mountain cheeses. But how could I identify these cheeses in America? I had already tried asking the cheese sellers at some of the fancy shops uptown where their Parmesan came from, but the clerks did not have the slightest idea what I was talking about. One of them even made me the object of fun.

Bertozzi faxed me a list of the winners of this year's Parmesan judging, the nine dairies making the best cheeses. They were numbers 361, 602, 934, 1415, 2115, 2188, 2322, 2873, and 2924. I roamed the city for several hours, Bertozzi's fax clutched tight in my hands, hoping to spot one of these numbers in the window or on the counter of some cheese shop. I came up dry.

Which is why I was standing on the frozen corner of Mott and Grand, in front of Di Palo's Fine Foods, gripping an illustrated map of the Po Valley, shivering violently, and talking to myself. I was ready to head into the tiny shop and take my place at the end of a long line.

Di Palo's is one of the few latticini left in Manhattan. (In Italy, a dairy shop is called a *latteria;* its window would advertise *latticini,* dairy products. Somehow, in Little Italy, a dairy shop ungrammatically came to be called a latticini from the word painted on the window.) These are establishments that make their own fresh mozzarella and ricotta and cheesy Italian delights such as scamorza and burrata, and sell ripened cheeses imported from Italy such as Parmigiano-Reggiano and Gorgonzola, Fontina and Taleggio, and occasionally, less expensive domestic imitations. Di Palo's is now run by the third generation of brothers and sisters, Louis (born Luigi), Marie, and Sal, and they are great specialists in Parmesan.

Louis had assembled an impressive collection of uncut wheels (or "forms") of cheese. He opened each in the same way, first scoring a deep groove into the tough golden rind across the flat top of the wheel, and continuing this groove down the sides, and then across the bottom of the cheese. Now he plunged another knife, thin and sharp and triangular, deeply into the groove. And finally he wedged and twisted a third knife, this one the familiar almond-shaped blade (also described as resembling an olive leaf or a laurel leaf), down into the deep incisions he had just made— until the entire cheese slowly split in two like a massive boulder, revealing a striking horizontal grain dotted with tiny white crystals. Perfect Parmesan has a uniform, straw-yellow color, without brownish signs of oxidation or the pink or red tinges of unwanted fermentation. The color can vary from deep gold in spring to a paler hue in late fall and winter, when the fodder is dry and lacking in pigmentation.

When you bite into a piece of Parmesan, it should break like a cracker and not bend like rubber or Swiss cheese. After a little chewing it should practically melt in your mouth and the crunchy crystals dissolve like salt or sugar. The first taste should be lactic, the flavor of cultured butter or milk, and slightly acidic. There can be vegetable or fruity overtones, especially that of pineapple, but not of coffee or nuts, or of the barnyard. And there should be very little bitterness, no hint of sulfur or ammonia—

signs of excess age. Perfect Parmesan is intense, delicate, complex, and persistent, as Mr. Bertozzi puts it.

First, Louis split open his two favorite wheels, produced within days of each other in early October 1994, both excellent and beautiful cheeses. The first, made by Caseificio La Maestà (number 3075) in the hills around Parma, had a deep golden color with only a moderate grain and few white crystals—it seemed almost too smooth and yielding for Parmesan, more like an aged cheddar in texture—and its flavor was fine and sweet but mild. The second, made in the plains near Modena by the renowned Caseificio Albareto (number 2720), was grainier, lighter in color, stronger and more complex tasting, more acidic, and more lactic. Mountain cheeses need more time for their flavor to develop.

Several customers had entered the shop and joined us for the tasting. Louis broke off thick chips of Parmesan and passed them around. He preferred the mildness and elegance of the cheese from Parma, though I favored the more complicated taste of the Modena cheese and its flakier, crunchy texture. But both of us agreed that neither, each excellent in its own way, could stand up against the complexity of the long-aged Parmesans of years ago. He then opened wheels from April and June 1993, each well over three years old. June was grainy, crunchy, and powerfully strong, with hints of pineapple. April was pink and harsh. Both had grown far too bitter for use as eating cheeses—Louis would sell them to restaurants for grating.

Bent under the weight of five generous wedges of cheese, I made my way home. (If you find a good wheel of Parmesan, and you don't live near Di Palo's or another trusted Parmesan specialist—if there are any others left—buy a good-size wedge, two or three pounds, and store it in the bottom of your refrigerator the way Louis does: Wrap it tightly in parchment paper and then in aluminum foil, which allows the cheese to breathe a little. Some people use just aluminum foil. But Louis would never allow the taste of metal to touch his best Parmesan.)

Twenty years ago, hardly anybody would have bought Parmesan younger than three or four years. With each year of aging, the flavor intensified and deepened, the texture became flakier without getting dry and acrid, and a multitude of tiny, savory, crunchy crystals appeared, as the casein broke down into its constituent amino acids, particularly tyrosine. But today's highly economical dairy cows, especially the Friesians that live in the valley and are known as milk machines, give huge amounts of milk with inferior casein that ages poorly beyond two years. The brown Swiss cows of the mountains have a lower yield with better aging properties.

But nothing is said to compare to the traditional red cows of the Reggian breed, known as the Razza Reggiana or Vacche Rosse, famous since the Middle Ages for their role in making Parmesan, but rare today. Their casein molecules gather into larger particles in a way that makes for a dense aggregation of fat, minerals, and protein—perfect for cheesemaking. But their milk production is low and therefore more expensive. The Consorzio Parmigiano-Reggiano seems to be guiding its ancient cheese, its sacred trust, in directions to please a worldwide market that prefers its foods bland and banal and universally appealing.

Our tasting had reinforced Louis's belief and my calculations that October cheese is the best—everything else being equal— and that anything else aged much more than two years becomes harsh and unpleasant. The advantage of October mountain cheese is its supposed aging potential—its high casein and butterfat levels. It should be able to ripen for three years, unlike the harsh cheeses from April and June 1993, and a little more like the Parmesan of our youths. After I had subtly nagged Louis for about 10 minutes, he agreed to search for a form from October 1993. How Louis would find one wheel of Parmesan in the haystack that is the New York metropolitan area, I could not imagine. But I was far from idle while I waited.

I had read that some farmers are again raising the magical, nearly mythical red cows, which now number about 1,500 out of the 200,000 whose lives are dedicated to the production of Parmesan. I telephoned Leo Bertozzi again, and he told me that one producer, Caseificio Notari, number 101, in the plains near

Reggio Emilia, uses only red-cow milk to make its unique Parmesan. After the most subtle hints on my part, Bertozzi offered to send me some of Notari's cheese.

And a three-pound wedge arrived just a week later. The man from DHL pretended not to know how momentous was the event in which he had played a vital though tiny part. I kept the wedge in its thick plastic shrink-wrap until Louis called to say that no October 1993 cheese could be found anywhere, but that he had secured an entire wheel of the next best thing, November 1993. Back on the corner of Mott Street and Grand, each of us unwrapped his treasure.

We were right about the buttery, long-aged fall Parmesan—it was more like the cheese of 20 years ago, crunchy and grainy and moist at the same time, and it was powerfully flavored, though without any sweet hints of fruit. It was just a few months, we thought, from being over the hill, from becoming harsh and sandy. But these are the cheeses to look for—three-year-old October and November Parmesan from a good cheesemaker.

The wedge from Notari was a revelation. It was nearly two years old but tasted like an adolescent—soft, deeply golden, lacking nearly all grain, deliciously fat, and just starting to develop its *punti bianchi,* the tiny amino-acid crystals. It had a wonderfully sweet, complex flavor that only hinted at what it could become. It had the strength to age at least two years more.

Now, the search is on for what should be the ultimate modern-day Parmesan—a four-year-old cheese made entirely with the milk of the antique red race as they vacation at a mountain resort in the early fall. Whether such a cheese will be created before the millennium, I cannot predict.

MARCH 1997

PRICKLY PLEASURES

It had all started so gaily, so innocently, a year or two ago. We were in Southern California, at a party catered by a sushi chef named Kawasaki. A friend possessing a nearly infallible palate handed me an oval clump of rice topped with a strip of bright yellow sea-urchin roe. It was a piece of *uni* sushi. "This is the best thing you've ever tasted," she said. I was skeptical. Nearly every sea urchin I had previously encountered was slimy and gooey and tasted of rotting seaweed—rank, bitter, and full of iodine—even when, minutes out of the ocean, it was scooped from its spherical shell right into my mouth.

But my friend was, as is nearly always the case, completely right. The roe were firm, and their taste was sweet and fresh— almost floral, with the aroma of rose petals. No, I'm not getting precious and overheated. It *was* one of the best things I've tasted. I tried to eat my fill, but all that sushi rice got in the way.

It was then that I pledged to track down these magical sea creatures to their watery lair. I telephoned Kawasaki. He was happy to tell me that his *uni* are gathered off the coast of Southern California, in the waters near San Diego, and that he buys them from a place called Catalina Offshore Products. I checked the Web site of the famed Tsukiji fish market in Tokyo. Yes, red sea urchins from Southern California bring the highest prices in the world—except for something called Japanese White, which I think are from Hokkaido. I spoke, on deep background, with several Japanese fish buyers on the East Coast. Catalina Offshore Products' sea urchin is *the best in the world,* they confirmed. I ordered several trays from Santa Barbara and Northern Califor-

435

nia. Yes, they were sweet, but Santa Barbara's had a more bitter iodine taste than Catalina's, and the sea urchin from Northern California was sweet but bland and watery. Not a scientific tasting, of course. Sea urchins all along our Pacific coast are of the same species, so their diets, particularly the varying types of kelp they eat, and the way they are handled make all the difference.

Sea urchins are found in every ocean of the world. On the Pacific Coast of North America and Mexico, from Sitka, Alaska, down through Baja California, two types of sea urchin predominate—the exquisite red (which are often so dark you might mistake their color for black) and the smaller purple (which are nearer to lavender). Red sea urchins are the principal commercial species. They attach themselves to rocks; eat huge volumes of kelp, a giant seaweed; bristle with long and venomous spines; and fear (if, primitive as they are, they are capable of fear) two main predators—sea otters and humans. Unlike the green sea urchins of the north Atlantic coast in both America and Europe—which have short spines, inhabit the gravelly coastal sea floor, and are commonly collected by dredges that drag along and damage the bottom—red Pacific sea urchins are harvested one by one, by divers who pry them from their rocky perches, put them into large net bags, and haul them to the surface. Except for the mechanized air supply—sea-urchin boats have a compressor and a long yellow tube, several hundred feet long, to carry air down to the diver—the hunt for sea urchins hasn't changed much since that day thousands of years ago when the first early human convinced herself that she needed to risk her life to eat the inside of a sea urchin. Maybe she was imitating a sea otter.

I telephoned Catalina Offshore Products and arranged a visit, and the next day pulled up to a large, white, one-story building in a light-industrial pocket of central San Diego. Dave Rudie— a former diver who, with his wife, founded the company—took me on a tour of what looked to be a model operation. Then again, I've never seen a model operation when it comes to sea urchins.

There are 22 divers in San Diego, and they sell all their urchins to Catalina Offshore Products. Most divers return to harbor with their catch in the late afternoon or early evening. Catalina floats its own boat (the kind with trailer wheels underneath) alongside theirs, and with a winch, lifts and weighs the heavy baskets of urchins. Back at headquarters, these are emptied into huge refrigerated tubs labeled so that each diver's catch is segregated until the next day, when the yellow and orange strips of roe have been removed, cleaned, firmed up, and tasted. The divers are paid between $.50 and $1.50 a pound for the live, whole sea urchins they bring in, depending on the amount and quality of the roe. On a rare and perfect and frenetic day, a diver can make as much as $1,500.

I watched a worker pry open the shells with a triangular blade plunged into the sea urchin's mouth. I tried it myself until I had the hang of it and was able to eat the sweet roe with my fingers, just seconds after the animal had died—that is, just seconds after, frankly, I had killed it. The animal itself is a nearly empty sphere, between two and five inches across, and covered with spikes that, in the Pacific, increase its span to ten inches or a foot. Inside the shell you see five bright strips or skeins of "roe," yellow or orange and arranged in a star-shaped pattern—the sea urchin is related to the starfish. Each strip is covered with tiny bumps and is ridged down the center so that it resembles a little tongue, which is what the French call them, *les langues.*

Male urchins are more likely to have orange roe and females yellow, but not always. (Dave showed me the real way to tell the difference. I'd rather not go into that right now.) The strips of "roe" are really male or female gonads, the testes and ovaries. We use the word *roe* because it sounds nicer. On the outside of the shells, little tubular feet with suckers poke through rows of tiny holes, and there are pincers, sometimes venomous. You can't eat either of them.

Everything was directed by Alex Castillo, the production manager, who had been trained by a Japanese specialist. Women sat in rows before long, shallow tanks of salt water and cleaned the roe, which were then passed through a mild preservative bath of

potassium alum (also used to firm up pickles), drained, refrigerated, and sorted into six grades. Alex is the definitive taster and
judge. We stood outside the chilled packing room and ate one
strip of ethereal roe after another, discussing their virtues. By
now, Alex can predict the flavor of a tongue just by looking at it.

The wooden trays are shipped by air that same afternoon. Several years ago, when the Japanese were rolling in money, most of
Dave's production went to the Tokyo wholesale market. Now 75
percent goes to New York City, where it will fetch the best price.

The amazing thing is that ordering perfect sea-urchin roe—the
finest specimens of one of the world's famed delicacies—is an
easy and relatively inexpensive proposition. Am I beginning to
sound like a salesman on late-night TV? I don't care. Dave Rudie
charges $68 for 400 grams, nearly a pound, packed on five small
trays. (Some French recipes call for the saline liquid within the
shell, for which you can order living sea urchins.) Catalina
has a Web site, www.catalinaop.com, and a telephone number
(619-297-9797). You can eat the urchins straight, or put them on
cooked rice, or you can cook them. Over the past year, I have
been ordering sea-urchin dishes everywhere I've gone, and the
winners are: Nobu's unique tempura; a traditional pasta dish
from Sicily; and a quivering custard invented by Alain Ducasse at
his grand New York City restaurant. The recipes will come later.

You can imagine how powerful was my need to go diving for
sea urchins. I needed to taste them underwater. As the idea met
with amusement and derision whenever it was bruited, I soon
sublimated my drive into a plan to go out with one of the local
divers.

Dave Rudie put me together with Clifton Hawk. Cliff is about
40, of medium height, handsome, and dark-haired. He was a
championship swimmer in his youth (he swears that between the
ages of 6 and 12 he was raised in a famous nudist colony east of
San Diego) and a sea-urchin diver since the age of 18, and unlike
other divers I've met, still loves nothing more than spending
every working day hunting for the largest number of top-quality
sea urchins he can find. He cracks some of them open underwater to taste them and assure himself of their quality.

My memory of the next few hours is hazy, for reasons that will become apparent. My notes and photos have us leaving Dana's Landing on Mission Bay and bouncing along, slamming against the swells for about half an hour until we were opposite La Jolla, about two miles from shore. So striking a juxtaposition, I remember thinking, to practice the most primitive form of hunter-gathering within view of this fabled playground of the rich. But as Cliff observed, sea urchins live on rocks and eat kelp, and that's where we'll find them.

Cliff anchored the boat, suited up (including knee pads and double gloves), turned on the noisy air supply, and dived down 50 feet through the thick brown kelp forest. And now I was completely alone on the deck of an ancient, weathered boat anchored two miles from shore, my only companions the wind, the odd pelican, the slapping of the bow against the rising swells, and the first subtle signs that I would soon be overcome by a truly major case of seasickness. The queasiness and vertigo part had arrived, along with the seedlings of mental confusion. Next would come a deepening depression and then the conviction that I would do anything to get out of there. I had paid good money for that little round scopolamine patch plastered behind my ear, guaranteed to prevent seasickness. I would bring suit, a class action, with lots of punitive damages. This entire sea-urchin diving business is so primitive, I thought, so atavistic.

Time slowed nearly to a stop. If the first human ever to dive for a sea urchin were alive today, I would throttle her to within an inch of her life. And then my anger turned to fear. I could no longer see Cliff's hose or his float. Where had he gone? How long could I suffer this misery? What if he never came back up? I could hardly stand. My watch refused to move. I toyed with cutting Cliff's silly yellow hose and racing to shore. This is completely true. But he had taken the keys.

At last he surfaced, smiling and cheerful and energetic. I suppressed my hatred until it passed as my seasickness retreated bit by bit. Cliff pulled up an 80-pound basket of beautiful, perfect urchins, and at my urging, off we went without tasting one of them. Ordinarily I would now know everything about his combined sonar and GPS monitor, where he stores hundreds of likely diving spots, and about his diving suit, which had all sorts of gadgets attached, and his air compressor and winch, and pink float, and all the other toys such as real men bond around. But I know nothing, except that I could not think straight until both feet were on dry land.

Two hours later, safely home, my head cleared by a nap and a big glass of whisky, I impressed and entertained my wife with mariners' tales of courage and peril as I opened my La Jolla sea urchins. And then the cooking began.

LINGUINE WITH SEA URCHIN
(from Trattoria Piccolo Napoli)

A few weeks ago, as I was passing through Palermo, a detour taken solely for the purpose of eating, I was taken to this excellent seafood trattoria on the Piazzetta Mulino a Vento 4 (091-320-431) by Mary Taylor Simeti (celebrated author of *On Persephone's Island* and *Pomp and Sustenance*). Their Sicilian seafood pastas were delicious, especially a version of this traditional dish. Every pasta with sea urchin includes the roe, olive oil, garlic, and dried hard-wheat pasta; most add chopped parsley and pepper, black or red; some have tomatoes. Mary helped me pin down the details of owner Pippo Corona's linguine by returning to the restaurant long after I had sadly left Palermo. I am sure I saw and tasted tiny flecks of hot red pepper in the sauce. Pippo disagrees, and the chef remains silent.

2 Tbs. salt

9 oz. (approximately 250 g) dried linguine—thin, flat, narrow noodles—made from semolina, without eggs

3 Tbs. fine-quality extra-virgin olive oil

2 cloves garlic, peeled and sliced very thinly

7 oz. (approximately 200 g, ⅞ of a cup) very fresh, cleaned, rinsed sea-urchin roe

½ tsp. very finely chopped red pepper flakes (optional)

2 Tbs. very finely chopped Italian (flat-leaf) parsley

In a 6- to 8-quart pot over the highest heat, bring four quarts of water and the salt to a vigorous boil. Meanwhile, before the pasta water comes to a boil, put a 4-quart saucepan containing the oil and garlic over low heat and cook very slowly until the garlic becomes translucent but has not begun to color, about

10 minutes. Stir in the sea-urchin roe and the chopped red-pepper flakes and remove from the heat.

Add the linguine, and as the water returns to a boil and the linguine soften, press and bend them with a wooden spoon until they are submerged. Cook the linguine at a full boil for about six minutes. After four minutes, start testing the linguine by tasting them. They should be extremely firm—you will cook them more later; the hard starchy center of each noodle should just have disappeared. Scoop out and reserve 1 cup of the pasta water. Drain the linguine.

Pour the linguine into the saucepan containing the sea urchins. Add ½ cup of reserved pasta cooking water. Put the saucepan over medium-high heat and cook for 4 to 5 minutes, tossing the linguine with 2 forks to separate the strands and coat them with sauce, and scraping the bottom of the pan with a wooden spoon to prevent the sea urchins from sticking. You may add the remaining pasta cooking water. When the sauce is thick enough to coat the linguine, but before it becomes gummy, you are finished. Taste for salt, and mix in the parsley. Divide among 4 warmed pasta plates. Serves 4 as an appetizer.

SEA-URCHIN TEMPURA
(from Nobu)

A little mound of sea-urchin roe is wrapped in a spicy *shiso* leaf, rolled in thin, crisp *nori*, dipped into tempura batter, and deep fried. Like so many of Nobu's dishes, this one is simple, very delicious, and, incomprehensibly, found nowhere in the world besides the far-flung outposts of his empire—Los Angeles, New York City, London, Tokyo, Aspen, Las Vegas, and soon, Miami and Paris. Toshio Tomita and Edwyn Ferrari taught me how to make it in New York.

4 cups cottonseed oil or soybean oil

2 sheets dried *nori*, each about 7 by 8 inches

12–20 *shiso* leaves

½ lb. (scant) fresh, cleaned sea-urchin roe (200 grams, ⅞ cup)

2½ cups tempura-batter mix, available in gourmet shops,
Asian groceries, and the Asian section of some supermarkets

1 egg yolk

2 cups ice water

Salt, pepper, lemon juice

Heat the oil to between 360°F and 380°F in an electric deep fryer or a deep saucepan; the oil should be about 3 inches deep.

Meanwhile, trim the rough edges of both sheets of *nori*. Cut each sheet crosswise into six equal strips, each at least 1¼ inch wide. Place 1 strip on the counter with one narrow edge nearest you. Arrange 1 large *shiso* leaf with its base along the near edge of the *nori* and its point aiming away from you; or 2 smaller leaves, pointing outward in opposite directions and overlapped in the center of the *nori*. Either way, the *shiso* should extend beyond the edges of the *nori* by nearly 1 inch on both sides. Put a heaping tablespoon of sea-urchin roe onto the *shiso* leaf, and roll it all up in the *nori*. Seal the end of the *nori* with a dot of tempura batter. The result will be a cylinder, with *shiso* and *uni* protruding from both ends. Continue with the remaining eleven strips.

In a broad 3- to 5-quart bowl, thoroughly mix the egg yolk into the ice water. Pour 2 cups of the tempura flour into the bowl and just barely combine them. This is done with chopsticks, a few strokes at a time, whisking a little of the flour from the sides of the bowl into the water. Continue until no dry flour remains on the surface of the batter, a ring of dry flour still surrounds the batter, and many small lumps remain in it. Dip your finger into the batter—it will emerge lightly coated with a thin liquid plus several little lumps of flour. Use the batter soon; after ½ hour it will not behave properly.

Dredge the sea-urchin packages in the remaining tempura flour. Then, holding each one with chopsticks, dip it into the tempura batter and gently lower it into the hot oil. Fry in batches of 2 or 3 until they become very crisp but before they take on much color, about 90 seconds. Maintain the temperature of the oil. Drain on a rack. Serve with small dipping dishes of salt, black pepper, and lemon juice. Makes 12 pieces, enough for 4 to 6 people as a little appetizer.

ROYALE OF SEA URCHIN WITH VELOUTÉ OF LOBSTER
(from Alain Ducasse and Didier Eléna)

My nomination for best dish of the new millennium goes to this sea-urchin custard (topped with a cappuccino-style lobster foam) and its accompanying velvety lobster soup or *velouté*. When Ducasse's executive chef, Didier Eléna, showed me how to make them, I was reminded that nothing is simple in the haute cuisine. The custard (also known as *flan* and as *royale*) is child's play itself, but requires both a lobster bouillon and uncooked lobster coral. It is the kind of weekend project I used to love before I became a food writer—several hours for the lobster bouillon, plus an hour for the custard and the soup, both sublimely delicious. I asked Ducasse whether he and Didier had really invented it. "There are no inventions in cuisine any longer," he said. "All the knowledge is now available. It's how you use it." Easy for him to say.

For the lobster bouillon:

4 female lobsters, each 1¼ pounds
6 Tbs. extra-virgin olive oil
½ medium onion (about 3 inches in diameter)
½ carrot
1 rib celery
½ bulb fennel
3 medium tomatoes, cored
6 unpeeled garlic cloves, crushed
1 scant cup cognac
2 cups white wine
1 Tbs. tomato paste
6–8 cups salt-free veal stock or salt-free chicken stock,
homemade or canned, or water
3 slices lemon
1 basil stem

- - - - -

For the sea-urchin flan:

2½ oz. (70 g) sea-urchin roe, a very generous ¼ cup

¼ cup whole milk

1 egg

1 pinch sugar

1½ tsp. uncooked coral from the lobsters

For the lobster velouté:

1 cup heavy cream

1 Tbs. butter

2 Tbs. whipped heavy cream

Salt and black pepper

2 tsp. finely chopped chervil

First prepare the lobster bouillon. This can be done a day in advance. The French dismember their lobsters live. If you're as brave or cruel as they are, go right ahead and pull off the claws and the tails. If you're squeamish, immobilize all four lobsters in one or more paper bags in your freezer for an hour. Remove them one at a time and plunge a heavy knife or cleaver through their bodies from their heads to the joint where the tail begins; this will kill them. Then twist off the tails and claws. (If even this is too much for you, first steam the lobsters in a big pot in the standard manner, but for the shortest time it takes to turn them partially red and stop their movement, probably between 2 and 4 minutes.)

Refrigerate the claws and tails. Cut the bodies in half and with a small spoon scoop out the coral into a small bowl. (The coral is the black or dark green substance that lines the body shell on both sides and turns a coral color only when cooked; the lighter green stuff nearer the center of the cavity is the tomalley, the liver.)

Chop the onion, carrot, celery, fennel, and tomatoes into medium-fine pieces, each about ¼ inch on a side, or a little

– – – – –

smaller. Put a heavy saucepan over medium-high heat, pour in 3 tablespoons of the olive oil, and mix in the garlic and chopped vegetables. Reduce the heat to medium-low and allow to cook very slowly, uncovered, stirring occasionally, until the onion and celery become translucent—but before they take on color, about 10 minutes.

Meanwhile, with a cleaver roughly chop the 4 lobster bodies. This is a messy task. Cook the resulting lobster pieces in 3 tablespoons olive oil in a very heavy pan over medium-high heat, until the shells take on a roasted aroma and color, 10 to 15 minutes. While they are cooking, alternately stir them and, with a large stone or wooden pestle, crush them further.

When the vegetables and shells are cooked, combine them in the heavier pan. Add the cognac and cook over medium-high heat, continuously stirring and scraping until only a little liquid is left on the bottom of the pan. Add the white wine and reduce by half, stirring occasionally. Mix in the tomato paste and cook slowly for 10 minutes. Pour in enough veal or chicken stock or water so that it tops the level of the shells and vegetables by about 2 inches. Cook over medium heat, uncovered, for 25 minutes—no longer.

(Use this free time to cook the reserved lobster tails and claws: Slide a chopstick or dinner knife between the shell and flesh of each tail to keep it straight, and steam in the normal manner for 9 minutes. After 2 minutes, add the claws. [Subtract any time the tails and claws may already have spent in the steamer.] As soon as they are done, cool in ice water and refrigerate.)

When the lobster broth is ready, pour it through a very fine strainer—a conical chinois is ideal—into a bowl. Add the lemon slices and the basil stem and let their flavor infuse into the liquid for 15 minutes, off the heat. Strain again into a saucepan, and over medium-high heat reduce by about half to just under 2 cups. Reserve 2½ tablespoons of the lobster bouillon for the flan; the rest will be used in the velouté.

Now for the sea-urchin flan: Preheat your oven to 250°F. In a 1-quart bowl, combine the sea urchin, milk, egg, sugar, coral, and reserved lobster bouillon, and allow them to come to room temperature. Whip with a hand blender until homogeneous. Divide evenly among 4 espresso cups, nearly ¼ cup in each. (You will probably have enough for five.) Set the cups into a small roasting pan, pour in enough boiling water to come halfway up the sides of the cups. Bake for about 25 minutes, until the the custard is almost set; it will cook further as it stands. A toothpick plunged into the one of the custards halfway between the center and the edge will come out clean.

The velouté: While the flan is baking, warm up 4 small, flat soup bowls. Shell 2 of the reserved, cooked lobster tails and cut each into eight slices. (Save the other 2 tails for a delicious lobster salad, two lobster rolls, or whatever.) In a 1- to 2-quart saucepan, bring the lobster bouillon to a bare simmer over medium heat. At the same time, reduce the heavy cream by half in a small saucepan over medium-high heat, whisking constantly. Stir the reduced cream, the butter, and the whipped cream into the lobster bouillon. Taste for salt and pepper. Try not to faint.

With a hand blender, whip up the soup over low heat until it is covered with a frothy foam, easily accomplished by tilting the blender so that the blade is only half submerged. Using a soup spoon, skim off the foam and distribute it among the 4 baked custard cups so that they look like cups of cappuccino. Arrange 4 lobster slices in each of the 4 warm soup bowls and pour a generous ½ cup of velouté around them. Decorate with the chervil. Serve the soup with the sea-urchin royale on the side. Serves 4.

HIGH STEAKS

There was an eighth of a cow in my refrigerator; I watched it grow older by the day. Okay, maybe it wasn't quite an eighth, but it was huge nonetheless, an entire 30-pound rib section still covered by all the layers of fat and gristle with which Nature had protected it. Beside it were a blue plastic fan and a little dial from the hardware store for measuring humidity. Together they had taken over half my refrigerator, converting it into a miniature room for the dry-aging of beef and crowding out a host of other treasures. Seven weeks had passed since this giant chunk of cow had arrived from Balducci's in Greenwich Village, where Lou (Lucio) Arena runs one of the finest meat departments in New York City. One more week to go.

What had driven me to this audacious act? My hunk of beef was a major thrust in a five-pronged investigation that has increasingly occupied me over the past few years: Whatever has become of the great American steak house, not to mention the great New York steak house? And, even more profoundly, what has become of the great American steak? Until recently, I felt I could answer these questions in my sleep. Now I'm not so sure.

Neither steak nor steak houses are peculiarly American. The word "steak" arrived on British shores in the early 1400s from Old Norse, but steak houses didn't. The London tavern, transplanted to New York City in the 1700s, looks to me like the predecessor of the modern steak house, and is in some ways still the model for it. James Boswell used the word for the first time: "Went into the City to Dolly's Steak-house in Paternoster Row and swallowed my dinner by myself." But it is here in America that the steak house has achieved its most developed and elaborated form.

449

Here is how I once would have defined the great American steak house: a restaurant specializing in dry-aged, long-aged, USDA Prime-grade steaks, often oversize; where the waiters are typically (though not necessarily) men with rough exteriors and hearts of gold, and the decor (whether humble or grand) is old-fashioned; and where an atmosphere of liberality encourages each customer to order three or more helpings of fried starch, nicely salted, such as hash brown potatoes, French fries, cottage (or steak) fries, shoestring potatoes, matchstick potatoes, hand-made potato chips, and deep-fried onion rings. Some people love steak houses for their mandatory bonhomie. Others welcome the excuse to carouse; *Wine Spectator* notes that outside major cities, some of America's finest restaurant cellars (and biggest wine bargains) can be found in steak houses.

For me, it is and has always been the beef that matters most. Most restaurant reviewers treat the beef like a side dish, and exhaust their cleverness on everything but the meat—the plank floors and the waiters who tread upon them, the precise origins and social position of the other customers, how daunting it is for a reviewer to consume so much succulent and costly beef (oh, please!)—so that by the time they get to the steak itself, their vocabularies shrink down to words like *tasty, rich,* and even the dreaded *sinful.* They write sentences like "Dozens of places know how to cook a perfect hunk of meat, but we wanted something more" and go on to praise the imaginative garnishes, the sweet-potato puree with jalapeño cream. They nonchalantly report that a given steak house serves wet-aged USDA Choice when they should be sounding the klaxon. They write about the "total steak-house experience," which, I guess, includes things like the carpet.

I like carpeting as much as the next guy, and after I have sated myself on steak, I do lift up my head from the plate and look around the room. I am not insensible. Far from it. I can tell you that the best steak-house waiter I have ever met is George Justis at Ben Benson's Steak House in New York City; he is knowledge-able, efficient, intelligent, attentive, fun, and fascinated by his work. And that the best waitress is Vanessa Villarroel at Bern's Steak House in Tampa. That the best creamed spinach is served at db, not a steak house at all, but Daniel Boulud's new "bistro modern" in New York City. And that the best hash browns I've eaten in quite some time were at MarkJoseph, a new place in downtown Manhattan. See, I notice these things. But only after my raging hunger for the consummate steak is satisfied.

Dozens of places *used* to know how to buy and cook sublime steaks, but very few do any longer. This became tragically apparent as I revisited many of New York City's famed steak houses over the past three years and tried some new ones as well. Nearly everywhere, the beef was unsatisfying. It was usually tender enough but did not truly taste like beef. New York City steak houses once were paragons, the finest in the land, and it made me proud as punch to have grown up in and around them. Among my prized teenage dining experiences were lunches with my father at Christ Cella, perhaps the greatest of them all, the acme and zenith of steak houses, an expensive businessman's place on East 46th Street, with discreet, no-nonsense waiters, and the most memorable beef of a lifetime. Even today, New York City's meat wholesalers handle a dominant share of the best USDA Prime beef carcasses in the country. But something is very wrong.

At newer steak houses, I've asked the well-educated young chefs about the beef they buy. None had ever tasted beef aged for more than three weeks. I repeatedly telephoned the Culinary Institute of America (CIA) in Hyde Park, New York, to discover just what they teach their students about the grading and aging of beef. I have yet to hear back. Both compendious cookbooks published by the CIA deal only perfunctorily with the subject.

Have you ever felt that you were the last person on Earth in possession of a secret truth? And people looked at you in a funny way whenever you revealed this? And you feared they would drag you away and put you in a little room and keep you there until you admitted that you never had been in possession of any secret truth? That's how I was beginning to feel. And then, six months ago, I started to fight my way back. It was then that I formulated my five-pronged attack:

Prong One: A Guided Tour. Having systematically eaten my way around beef carcasses for nearly a lifetime, and having recently made my way through the technical meat literature, I think I have figured out a thing or two. America's principal sources of steak are the steer (the young unsexed male of the species), and the heifer (the young female, who, while not unsexed, is forever kept away from bulls). Old cows and bulls become hamburger. The steer and the heifer spend about seven months on mother's milk, the next four to six months grazing in pastures, and the final four or five in a feedlot, fattening up on grain. While nobody would think of cows as hyperactive types, all that standing around, grazing, and ruminating does develop the muscles of their legs, shoulders, and hindquarters, which consequently become tough and require extended cooking in stews and braises to make them tender and bring out their deeply beefy flavor. The same goes for other delicious cuts, such as the brisket and the short rib.

Plump and juicy steaks generally come from the animal's back, from the area that runs from the shoulders (the chuck) and the rump (the round). Grazing leaves these middle cuts largely unexercised and tender. A cow has thirteen ribs on each side. The first five are in the shoulder. Then comes the rib section, really ribs 6 through 12, the home of rib roasts and rib steaks. The next section is the loin, which commences with the final rib out of 13, and progresses to two long and valuable cuts running side by side and separated by a thin bone—the filet and the shell. The shell can be boned out and sliced crosswise into the steaks known as shell steaks or strip steaks or New York strip. The filet is also often removed whole and sliced. When the shell and filet are left on the bone and the entire loin is sawed into steaks, the result is several T-bones and several porterhouse steaks, both made up of a shell steak and a filet steak on alternate sides of the center bone. T-bones start just beyond the thirteenth rib, where the filet begins in a narrow little tail; they contain only a small amount of filet meat and much more strip. And beyond the loin comes the sirloin or hip.

Thick, well-marbled, amply dry-aged rib steaks, rib-eyes (as they are called when the bone has been removed), strip steaks, and porterhouses are the most flavorful and succulent steaks a steer or heifer has to offer. The sirloin is less expensive and is usually less marbled and too chewy for absolute perfection. And the cheaper cuts, such as hanger steak and skirt steak, are wonderful to eat, rich and flavorful in themselves (especially when sautéed) and full of beefy essence, but are too thin to yield the luscious and tender interior of a perfectly grilled steak. The filet mignon, the paragon of tenderness, is often disappointing because it lacks a full, beefy flavor, and its texture can approach mushiness. In a true steak house where beef is king, it is the thick porterhouse that most smacks of manly, bovine romance. But the rib steak offers the most succulent and flavorful muscle of them all: the *spinalis dorsi*. "You can't beat the *spinalis dorsi*," is what cattlemen and meat scientists say to each other in hushed tones as they finish up a fine steak dinner. Sometimes they just call it the *spinalis*. It's the curve of heavily marbled meat topping the rib-eye.

Most butchers do not know the words *spinalis dorsi*, though they acknowledge this strip to be the most flavorful and tender and juicy beef you can eat. Some deny that it has a name at all. Can you think of anything so good that has never been given a name? The knowledgeable James O. Reagan, Ph.D., a former beef academic now at the National Cattlemen's Beef Association, gave its common or vernacular name as the "rib-eye cap" or "top of the rib." One very expensive New York City butcher, who with psychic ability was able to sense the extent of my gluttony, proposed selling me a whole seven-rib section for $250 and slicing off the entire *spinalis dorsi* for a special feast. To such extreme lengths neither I nor my employer was willing to go.

Do you remember that a steer (or heifer) has thirteen ribs on each side, of which the rib section occupies seven? The rib-eye muscle next to the loin at rib number 12 has no *spinalis dorsi* to brag about, or very little of it. This area is known as the "first cut," and your butcher may try to force it on you, often at a higher price, because the central rib-eye muscle predominates here and there is less visible fat. Don't listen to a word of it. As you move back toward the shoulders, the *spinalis dorsi* grows thick and plump. But near the chuck, the distinct muscles in a rib steak become more numerous and varied, with large chunks of fat and gristle among them. And worst of all, the *spinalis dorsi* there thins down to a quarter-inch in thickness as it begins to fan out over the animal's entire shoulder area.

So, it is the three steaks cut from the center of the rib section, ribs eight, nine, and ten (counting from the front of the animal) or three, four and five (counting from the back end of the rib section), that have the thickest piece of *spinalis* (though number seven is nothing to be ashamed of) plus a fine rib-eye, and only moderate deposits of separable fat at their center. Ribs eight, nine, and ten: These are the three greatest steaks, the very summit and apogee of beef. Plus, of course, the paradigmatic porterhouse.

Prong Two: Steak Quality: Beef is not really good for us, especially fine, fatty, juicy, expensive beef. The environment is certainly not improved by the sheer number of cattle we raise. World hunger will never be solved by our eating so much so high on the food chain. And, according to some feminists, beef-eating is somehow connected with testosterone and the hideous control of human society by guys. But to deny our occasional need for the chewy, bloody, raw, primeval, primordial, ferrous, feral, slightly rotten taste of beef is to deny our very chromosomes, our human inheritance. We should consume beef infrequently, but when we do, we should buy only the most tender, rich, juicy, and flavorful beef we can afford, and grill it over wood or charcoal.

USDA quality grades are aimed at predicting these desirable qualities by having an inspector look at the carcass of a steer or heifer a day or two after slaughter. Aging is aimed at enhancing these virtues in the days and weeks that follow. The main physical characteristic the USDA looks for is the amount of marbling— the streaks and dots and squiggles of white fat running through a piece of beef. More is better. A carcass is graded by matching the marbling on the surface of the meat between the twelfth and thirteenth ribs with one of six full-color steak photographs (or, more probably, one's memory of them). The fat should run not in thick veins but in delicate traces. More marbling means more flavor, more juice, and more of one type of tenderness. More about that later.

Meat without intramuscular fat can taste meaty—full of the mineraly, metallic hemoglobin taste—but not taste beefy. Many studies have shown that lean lamb, beef, and veal completely devoid of fat all taste the same. Melted marbling fat is juicy in itself and stimulates our saliva, which creates as much of a subjective impression of juiciness as the juice that oozes from a piece of beef when we bite into it. Tenderness depends on many factors, some not yet discovered. We do know that marbling fat lubricates the muscle fibers in beef, so that they can slide past each other as we sink our teeth into them. But there are at least two other kinds of tenderness. One is the general background tenderness of the meat, which seems to come from the amount and type of connective tissue in it—the transparent and white membranes of collagen and the stretchy fibers of yellowish elastin. Cooking melts collagen into gelatin—but only above 140°F. This works wonderfully when you braise or stew flavorful, gristly cuts of beef, but 140° is way hotter than the temperature to which I would ever bring the rosy interior of a perfect steak. The second is the ease with which you can chew through and sever the muscle fibers; this has more to do with the cut of meat, the breed, and the aging process, which we will come to later, than it does with marbling. (Aging has no effect on connective tissue.)

From the moment the USDA's quality-grading program was formally put in place in 1927, there have been 12 degrees of marbling: extremely abundant, very abundant, abundant, moderately abundant, slightly abundant, moderate, modest, small, slight, traces, practically devoid, and devoid. The USDA's set of official color photographs of rib steaks shows nearly life-size rib-eyes and is coated with plastic to make it easier, I presume, to wipe off the blood. (Japanese beef inspectors use three-dimensional plastic models of steaks, similar to the plastic food in their restaurant windows.)

I am the proud owner of an official set of these photographs, which came in a handsome zippered black leatherette pouch. They run only from "slight" through "moderately abundant," leaving out the extremes. When my set arrived, I was dismayed to find only six cards in the handsome leatherette pouch. Where were my "devoid" card, my "practically devoid," and my "traces"? Even more galling, where were "extremely abundant," "very abundant," and "abundant"? The sad truth is that none of these missing cards is needed anymore. Nearly all meat better than moderately abundant ceased to exist years ago, except in Japan, so the top three cards are rarely needed. The photograph of a "slightly" marbled steak is so pitiful that no self-respecting steer would ever admit to the even lower-end "traces," "practically devoid," or "devoid." That leaves the six photographs in my black leatherette pouch.

Over the years—in 1939, 1941, 1949, 1950, 1956, 1965, and 1973— the USDA grade definitions have been changed, most often to make it easier for a mediocre carcass to win a higher grade and fetch more money. The meat industry was perfectly happy to make marbling the chief criterion for quality when the grading system began, because the same farmers who raised or fed cattle also produced an abundance of grain and welcomed a way to sell it more profitably in the form of luscious meat. But by the 1930s, cattlemen could often be seen lobbying congressional committees to legislate this sort of grade inflation. Congress was only too happy to go along, at first in response to apparent grain shortages, then in the name of health.

I have read most of the congressional hearings on proposals to weaken the USDA's standards. The year that will live in infamy is 1950, when USDA Prime and USDA Choice (the grade below Prime) were lumped together and labeled Prime. As a result, when you buy a Prime-grade steak today, it need have only "slightly abundant" marbling. So, you may end up paying top dollar for what 50 years ago was considered third-rate beef—what is sold today as USDA Prime is no better marbled than the upper half of the cheap Good grade back in 1927.

They did it to us again in 1965 and 1976. And in 1987, the term "Good" was changed to "Select," solely for the purpose of tricking hapless Americans into accepting extremely lean beef. Half of all beef is now graded Choice—a label that has therefore become meaningless. In response, there are now many special grading programs, conducted by the USDA but paid for by companies or organizations within the meat industry. So, labels like "Certified Aberdeen Angus" usually mean that the beef has been selected, by USDA inspectors, from the high end of the USDA Choice category, and is not as good as Prime.

You will read in magazines and newspapers, especially when they have fallen under the influence of the beef or nutrition industries, that leaner beef, graded by the USDA as Choice or Select, is just as flavorful as Prime, just as tender, and much less fatty and expensive. Please don't be a chump. Most USDA Choice or Select grade steaks are simply not worth grilling. As one USDA official confided to me, "At the supermarket level, it's hard to find something you want to take home." The USDA itself!

One consequence of all this is that consumption has in recent years been shrinking at home as it rises at steak houses. Even the meat industry has grown worried. As a recent taste test organized by the National Cattlemen's Beef Association demonstrated, only well-marbled USDA Prime steaks are guaranteed to please the consumer. Yet no more than 2 or 3 percent of the beef in America earned the Prime grade. Most of it was sold to restaurants, to Japan and Korea, and—yes, there is a God—to ten or more retail butchers in New York City, the last bastion of Prime beef in the entire country. In most other towns, you cannot purchase Prime steaks even if you are rich as Croesus. But you can now buy them through mail order.

I have heard old-timers say that the fabled marbling of Japan's costly Kobe beef today looks just like a USDA Prime steak did fifty years ago. The downgrading of American meat is a major scandal, a venal conspiracy first to deprive every American of her right to dine on a profoundly savory, plump, and juicy steak, and then to deny her the knowledge that something far superior ever existed. The few excellent butchers and beef buyers remaining in this country (Stanley Lobel on Madison Avenue, for example, and the three presiding women at Peter Luger) not only insist on buying only Prime beef. They also talk of low, medium, and high Prime—the unofficial grades of the cognoscenti. The rich cognoscenti. Perhaps the ratings correspond to "very abundant" and "extremely abundant."

And now to the matter of aging. Even USDA Prime beef right off the hoof tastes bloody, not particularly beefy, and will be extremely tough, or gummy if the animal has not passed through rigor mortis. In the few days or week it takes to reach the supermarket, beef ages enough to develop a minimal degree of tenderness and flavor. The meat industry would prefer selling its products straight from the slaughterhouse—get a faster return on its investment and eliminate the cost of storage. But if you keep meat just above freezing temperatures for several weeks, it becomes more tender and under some conditions more flavorful. Aging goes more quickly at higher temperatures, but microbes develop even faster.

Upscale meat wholesalers, many butcher shops, and some supermarkets with real butchers in their meat departments sell only what is known as "dry-aged" beef, whose flavor is commonly described as buttery, rounded, roasty, brothy, toasted, and nutty. (Food writers use the word "nutty" to describe nearly everything; but occasionally a bite of dry-aged beef does taste to me like a cross between a hazelnut and a peanut.) In dry-aging, entire wholesale cuts of beef (known as "primal cuts") or even complete carcasses are placed, uncovered, in a refrigerated room or locker—on racks or on giant hooks—for weeks or even months. The temperature must be kept between 32° and 36°F. The relative humidity should never stray from between 80 to 85 percent. And the air around the cow must move at about one and a half meters a second, which, I figure, comes out to about three miles an hour.

Dry-aging dramatically improves the flavor and tenderness of beef, especially in the higher USDA grades. These effects are brought about by the beef's own enzymes, not by external bacteria or mold. The temperature, humidity, and air circulation are aimed at letting the beef age in peace. The low temperature keeps down the bacteria. The humidity prevents the beef from shrinking excessively. If the air around it moved faster, it would dry out the beef; if it moved more slowly, humidity might condense on the beef and encourage bacterial spoilage.

As enzymes break down the meat's long muscle fibers, the meat becomes easier to chew; as the protein molecules are broken down into their constituent amino acids, the meat becomes more flavorful. Protein itself has little flavor—as you can tell when you taste a thin slice of raw steak—but the amino acids that make up the protein itself are full of flavor. Scientists are not absolutely certain about either of these mechanisms, especially why dry-aging enhances flavor. But it certainly does.

The only problem with dry-aging is expense. The beef shrinks and forms a dark crust, which must be removed before it's eaten. Sometimes a mold forms that can be thicker than the crust. (The mold is no more toxic than the mold you scrape from a Smithfield ham. I've found a paper claiming that the mold on fine Spanish ham, *jamón ibérico*, the best in the world I think, is necessary to its flavor and may be cultivated, like cheese mold, by its manufacturers.) Between shrinkage and waste, a carcass or a primal cut can lose 25 percent or more of its weight. And then there's the cost of energy, capital, labor, and the real estate occupied by the aging rooms—some of them smack in the costly middle of Manhattan or Chicago. So, beef becomes increasingly expensive as it ages. Generally, it keeps getting better and better, in flavor and in texture, until it becomes "high," and takes on an unpleasantly sweet and fermented aroma and flavor. At least that's been my experience.

Wet-aging was developed in the seventies and is now by far

the most common method. A primal cut of beef is Cryovac'd (vacuum-sealed in a shroud of airtight plastic) and refrigerated. When the aging time is over, rarely more than three weeks, and the plastic is cut away, the hunk of beef is nearly all usable. There is no shrinkage or mold. Except for the cost of simple refrigeration and the cost of money, wet-aged beef is no more expensive than when it began.

The problem with wet-aging is that it tenderizes meat without developing its flavor. If you search through the food science and technology journals you find little agreement about how aging works. But there is strong consensus on its effect. This quotation from the *Journal of Muscle Foods* (please don't laugh—I have an entire book entitled *Muscle Foods*) is typical: "Dry-aged lean had a beefier flavor and a more brown/roasted flavor than vacuum-aged [wet-aged] or unaged samples. Vacuum-aged samples had a more intense sour note and a more bloody/serumy flavor. . . ." Wet-aging became endemic when the meat industry convinced itself in the early eighties that tenderness alone—not flavor or juiciness or marbling—was what the consumer wanted. (Cattlemen and meat retailers had consumer surveys to prove it; now, the same types of research show that flavor is just as important as tenderness.) Even worse, wet-aging often softens the beef way beyond lusciously tender to repulsively mushy. Its only virtue is cheapness. Any claims to the contrary are made solely to lull the public into believing that they are eating the best.

Forty years ago, it was taken for granted that the better grades of beef would be dry-aged for at least six weeks. And even then, writers such as James Beard complained that true aging, for six to eight weeks or longer, even to the moment when the beef was covered with a fuzzy layer of white or greenish mold, was becoming a thing of the past. My own butcher at Balducci's in Greenwich Village will age a piece of beef for as long as you want it, as will the more expensive Lobel's on upper Madison Avenue. Research shows that the maximum increase in tenderness is achieved at three weeks of dry-aging. But the flavor keeps developing from the initial fresh, iron-meaty taste to a round, buttery, complex, and mouthwatering savor. Eight weeks seems just right to me, though some might find the taste a little gamy or high. Because of its cost, true and proper dry-aging is becoming even rarer than USDA Prime. Yet it is indispensable to perfection.

Joseph Mitchell, writing in the *New Yorker* in 1939, described an old New York City institution known as the "beefsteak," a large and noisy banquet held in a rented hall where 100 to 200 guests consumed gluttonous quantities of sliced steak and beer. (Lamb chops and kidneys might be served on the side.) This was our local version of the Texas barbecue, the clambake, or the fish fry—communal meals held annually by social or political clubs, or organized specially to commemorate an election, an achievement, or perhaps nothing at all. The thick steaks were rolled in salt and pepper; grilled rare, often over hickory wood; sliced and dipped into a sauce composed of butter, steak juice, beef drippings, and a dash of Worcestershire sauce; laid onto slices of toast or day-old bread; and eaten with the hands. Mitchell visited a butcher who had supplied a multitude of "beefsteaks." That these were working-class celebrations makes the high quality of the beef the more revealing:

"Mr. Wertheimer took [an entire short loin] off a hook in his icebox and laid it on a big, maple block. It had been hung [dry-aged] for eight weeks and was blanketed with blue mold. The mold was an inch thick. He cut off the mold. Then he boned the shell and cut it into six chunks. . . . When he finished with the shell, six huge steaks, boneless and fatless, averaging three inches thick and ten inches long, lay on the block. They made a beautiful still life." Now we know what a New York strip is meant to be.

I imposed upon Stanley Lobel to take me into the bowels of the New York City meat market. Stanley, 64, may be the most knowledgeable and dedicated butcher in the country. He and his brother Leon, sons David and Mark, and nephew Evan run the legendary Lobel's butcher shop on Madison Avenue. Stanley reluctantly agreed and made me pay for the tour by insisting that I awaken at 3:45 a.m. It turns out that the New York City meat market has a multitude of bowels scattered around the city, and I was to visit only three of them. We first drove to a low-rise, industrial part of Brooklyn, to a famous company called AVA Beef Products, and donned white smocks and embarrassing hair nets. Here were room after room—each one breezier and colder than the last—filled with primal cuts of USDA Prime beef being aged on racks. Stanley tried to teach me the difference between mediocre Prime grade marbling and the finer, more homogeneous pattern. Lobel's sends a good part of the meat it buys down to AVA for between six and eight weeks of dry-aging.

As the sun rose, we drove back to Manhattan to the vestiges of the old meat market on West 14th Street and Gansevoort Street, near the Hudson River. Though the market has been nearly gentrified out of existence, there are holdouts, some of them quite famous and well established, such as Gachot & Gachot, which supplies several of the top steak houses in the city, including Peter Luger. Unlike most wholesale meat distributors who receive primal cuts of beef in cardboard boxes from the large meatpackers, at Gachot & Gachot whole beef carcasses hang from long hooks attached to tracks in the ceiling. The company buys directly from two small slaughterhouses whose agents roam the Midwest for the best grain-fed cattle they can find. (Controversially, some meat buyers still prefer steers raised or finished in the corn belt.) Stanley revealed at last that he buys most of Lobel's USDA Prime beef in the Bronx, at the Hunts Point market, which he visits several times a week at six in the morning on the way down from his house in Westchester. He has not yet agreed to take me along.

How many times have I read that USDA Prime beef is incredibly scarce, and that dry-aging is nearly nonexistent? Not in Brooklyn they aren't, or on 14th Street, or at 11 retail butcher shops around Manhattan alone. Stanley continually hears restaurants and butchers complain they can't find this quality of beef. They just don't want to pay for it, he says. How much USDA Prime are America's ranches and feedlots producing? In the 1970s, 6 percent to 7 percent of graded cattle were Prime. This dropped to between 1 percent and 2 percent throughout most of the eighties and nineties. And now, for the first time in memory, Prime is on the rise, the USDA tells me. In the past three years, it has moved from 2 percent to 3 percent. While the increase may seem modest, 1 percent of all the graded beef in America is a vast, nearly unimaginable quantity. The magic of the marketplace is happily at work!

Prong Three—Searching the Nation. Name a major steak house in the United States, and the odds are that it has bitterly disappointed me at some point in the past ten years. My assistant Gail and I undertook an extensive telephone survey. We made a list of the 78 steak houses in the United States with the highest ratings from several reliable sources. We began with William Rice's excellent *Steak Lover's Cookbook* (Workman, 1997), a sheaf of magazine articles, and the steak-house list in *Zagat Survey: America's Top Restaurants, 2001*. Then we added some personal favorites and several generally admired establishments in Chicago, Kansas City, and New York City (all towns with leading reputations for steaks) that had somehow slipped past our other sources' discerning palates. (Even so, it is likely that we missed a few promising candidates.) And we confined ourselves to "fine dining" steak houses, as the industry calls them, giving only a cursory glance at the "casual" category.

Gail and I split the work straight down the middle: I telephoned 3 steak houses, and she telephoned the other 75. First we revealed our purpose and then asked the restaurants' managers or head chefs what grade of beef they buy, how long it's been aged, and by what method. We eliminated eight places that had recently shifted their food theme away from steak, or were identical to others on the list within the same small high-end chain, or were secretive. Only New York's Sparks Steak House totally refused to talk. I assume they had nothing to hide.

Then we made a chart. At first the results looked good. Half the restaurants buy USDA Prime for every cut of steak, more than half if you count those who feel, incorrectly, that the less expensive USDA Choice filet mignon is just as good as Prime— because filet is inherently tender. Twenty-one steak houses dry-age their beef, as they should, compared with thirty-four places using the dreaded wet-aging method, with the rest employing some combination of the two. But this is all not as benign as it sounds. On average, the dry-agers stopped after 23 days, not long enough for true beefy excellence. And how many of these 78 greatest steak houses in America do all three things completely right—dry-aging their USDA Prime beef for five weeks or longer?

The answer is . . . two. Only two steak houses passed our stringent test! *Two steak houses in a nation of 270 million eaters are worth patronizing for their steaks alone.* They are Peter Luger in Brooklyn and Bern's Steak House in Tampa. Can this possibly be true?

If we loosen our criteria just a notch and include steak houses that serve USDA Prime dry-aged for just four weeks, no more, we would have to consider The Precinct, in Cincinnati; Pierpont's, Hereford House, and Plaza III, in Kansas City; and, in New York City, the Post House, Smith & Wollensky, and the Palm. But only the original Palm serves dry-aged beef—the one founded in 1926 on Second Avenue by two Italian immigrants who, according to legend, had intended to name it The Parma, after their native city, until a New York licensing clerk misspelled it. Other members of what is now the Palm chain use the wet-aging method, a sort of bait-and-switch, and their meat is vastly inferior. The other two upscale chains—Morton's and Ruth's Chris—serve wet-aged steaks, and in the latter's New York City location, the steaks were, on one visit, so mushy as to be nearly inedible. The original Ruth's Chris in New Orleans is a delightful and satisfying place in which to eat.

I was happily familiar with Peter Luger, but had only read about Bern's Steak House, where the beef was said to be USDA Prime, dry-aged for between five and ten weeks. Could it be that they, too, are in possession of the secret truth? I took a three-hour flight to Tampa, checked into a hotel, took a taxi to Bern's, ignored Ricardo's itchy palm at the podium, was kept languishing at the bar while customers who had not ignored Ricardo's itchy palm were seated before me, was finally allowed to eat and drink my dinner, slept for a few hours back at the hotel, and returned to the airport in the early morning. I'm still not sure where Tampa is situated, except that it's in Florida, though it looked to be a very nice place.

Bern's is like no restaurant I have ever seen. It is huge, capable of serving 320 people at one time, plus another 250 who have gone upstairs for dessert. I will not describe the many rooms and their corny decoration, the incredibly rigorous training of the waiters and waitresses, my lukewarm feelings about several side dishes, the 26 types of caviar, the pride of the staff and their reverence for founder Bern Laxer (now sadly incapacitated) and his family. I had flown to Tampa for the beef. Incidentally, the wine list is the largest in the world, offering more than 7,000 choices backed up by a half-million bottles. There are 385 dessert wines alone and, to my delight, 160 wines by the glass. *Wine Spectator* loves Bern's.

The three innermost pages of the menu concern steaks, all grilled over lump charcoal. You choose how many inches or how many ounces you wish to eat. After I informed my excellent waitress, Vanessa Villarroel, of my preference for very well-aged beef, for which Bern's is famous, she asked some questions in the kitchen and returned with the happy news that I could have a ten-week porterhouse or an eight-week rib steak. I ordered both—a porterhouse cut three inches thick and a rib steak slightly thinner, with the bone still attached—plus lots of side dishes. You can choose from among eight degrees of doneness. At most places, if you try to order your steak somewhere between rare and medium-rare, you are met with an uncomprehending stare. But this is exactly how I prefer my steak—no longer jellylike but with only the first signs of grain—for reasons I will elaborately explain later. Bern's has solved this lifelong problem by offering its steaks very rare with no crust, very rare with a crust, rare with a cold center, rare with a warm center, and medium-rare. Even then I had to fudge it, asking for rare with a *very* warm center.

Bern's porterhouse was the best steak I have had in many years, very crusty on the outside, just between rare and medium-rare on the inside, juicy, rich, and full of the powerful and satisfying flavor of real dry-aged beef—nearly ten weeks in the aging room, according to the man in the kitchen who cuts the steaks just when you order them. I ate with a broad smile on my face, which is not the easiest way to chew, first out of sensory delight and then out of spiritual satisfaction. For the first time since the start of my five-prong steakhouse project, I knew for certain that I was not operating under the sway of paranoid delusions or psychotic fantasies. The rib steak was mighty fine as well.

After I had eaten my fill, I revealed my profession, was shown into the kitchen, and watched the amazing head grill chef, a woman named Essie Emanuel (addressed as Miss Essie and an employee of Bern's for 38 years), cook some steaks on the huge charcoal grill. Her method is easily adaptable to your backyard charcoal grill, and I'll describe it to you later. A few days later, I persuaded a reluctant Dave Laxer (Bern's son, now in charge) to sell me a raw three-inch porterhouse, aged for six and a half weeks, and send it to California, where I grilled it up. Yes, the beef at Bern's is exceptional. Yes, they possess the secret truth.

Prong Four—Loosening Up. This was a completely unexpected prong. I was dining at Nick & Stef's Steakhouse in Madison Square Garden in New York City, one of a chain established by Joachin Splichal which grants its individual restaurants autonomy in buying beef. There is a huge glassed-in dry-aging locker in the restaurant window, but nobody in the dining room knew with any certainty the age or USDA grade of the steaks we ordered—which were quite good, if slightly young-tasting, especially the tender and beefy New York strip. Suddenly, the chef appeared, and it turned out to be an old friend, Alexandra Guarnaschelli, who had cooked at Guy Savoy in Paris, where she rose to the post of *chef poissonière* (not easy for either a girl or for an American). Alexandra had just taken over the kitchen and had not yet formulated her own beef policies. That excellent New York strip was USDA Prime and had come from Marc Sarrazin at Debragga and Spitler on Washington Street in the old meat market, where it had been wet-aged for one week and dry-aged for three weeks, transported to the restaurant's aging locker, and kept another week or so.

My taste buds forced me to admit that the combination of wet- and dry-aging for five or more weeks might be a promising idea. The only place in our steak-house survey that combined wet- and dry-aging for six weeks or more is Emeril Lagasse's Delmonico Steakhouse in Las Vegas. After a long telephone conversation, the restaurant agreed to send me one of each model of steak they offer. The New York strip especially was tender, beefy, and savory; I would love to have tasted it after another week of ripening.

Alex's inquiring mind made her an easy mark for my suggestion that we conduct an informal tasting at the restaurant with some friends. We visited Marc Sarrazin at Debragga and made elaborate plans to procure additional primal cuts on a schedule that would allow Alex to dry-age some of them several weeks longer than usual.

Several months passed. Then we met for the tasting, fortified by several good California merlots and large bowls of the best French fries I can remember. The long-aged filet was dark and tough, but pared down to its much diminished core, was very good to eat. We sampled three huge rib steaks, probably the higher end of USDA Choice, with their long bones still attached—one fresh and two dry-aged, one for three weeks and the other for ten. The fresh rib was tough, lacking a beefy flavor and tasting bloody and sour. The three-week rib was still too young, and the ten-week was over the hill, tasting high and fermented. Unluckily, its thick protective layers of fat had been mistakenly removed before dry aging, and so predictably its outer portions tasted unpleasant. Aged correctly for 10 weeks, it would have seemed only slightly too advanced in age. Our reactions to the USDA Prime shell steaks, dry-aged for zero, three, and seven weeks, were similar, except that the seven-week model was just fine, after we had cut off some of the outer crust. Alexandra was so excited about the effects of dry-aging on flavor that in the fall she may offer some of her steaks in long-aged premium versions, at a higher price, of course. The ancient knowledge slowly spreads.

Prong Five—Bringing It All Home. At last the cow in my kitchen had come to term—seven weeks of dry-aging in the refrigerator plus one at Balducci's. I will admit that I was eager to be rid of it so that I could restock with the many pounds of other treats that normally occupy the space. At the same time, I could barely control my excitement at butchering and eating a huge rib steak that I had perfected myself.

The experts are nearly unanimous in warning you not to try dry-aging at home. You will never be able to maintain the precise conditions required, they say. One false step and the beef will become an incubator for dangerous bacteria. You may die. This is a job for professionals.

In order to avoid a wrongful-death action from any of my readers or their survivors, legatees, heirs, or assigns, I guess I'd also better warn you not to try this at home. Under any circumstances whatsoever.

The conditions inside my refrigerator were far from what they should have been. I know that my humidity was way too low—between 50 and 60 percent. The temperature often rose past 40°F, as I am accustomed to opening the refrigerator door several times an hour for snacks and the like. I cannot even imagine how to measure the airspeed of my fan; I destroyed one fan early on, when its motor froze up in the cold, and bought a bigger one, with a power cord that snakes out between the gray rubber padding on the inside of the refrigerator door. But my primal cut of beef seemed to be doing just fine. Its appearance and aroma betrayed no signs of bacterial spoilage. Yet I still feared it was possible that deep inside the meat, the microbial equivalent of an ant farm was thriving. The meat on both exposed ends had turned a dark red, nearly black, and had shriveled excessively because of the low humidity, with thin, pale patches of white mold. I weighed the entire rib section on my bathroom scale. It was six pounds slimmer than before, a loss of 20 percent.

The time had come for the shriveled, moldy ends to be cut off, along with layers of fat, and the beef to be sliced into steaks and grilled.

And so they were, though with more difficulty than I had anticipated. My plan was to take my hacksaw and slice the beef—what amounted to an entire, seven-rib rib roast—crosswise right through the bone into six or seven steaks, each one 2¼ inches thick. I began by trying to saw lengthwise to eliminate the long bone on the bottom to which all the rib bones are attached. Failing at that, I shifted to other stratagems. But my old hacksaw seemed daunted by these young bones, and I confirmed the general principle that when both your hands and the handle of your saw are covered with molten fat, your ability to aim and operate it first deteriorates and then completely vanishes. After a half hour, I threw up my hands and with a sharp, strong knife, simply removed all the meat in one piece, reserving the bones for a fantastically delicious bone roast the next day (salt, pepper, and seven hours in a 250°F oven.) Then, standing before this rough-hewn, 18-inch, proteinaceous cylinder of red flesh, I cut off both ends, losing another 18 percent of the meat, and sliced the rest into six three-inch steaks—beautiful, bright-red, marbled, aromatic steaks. Except that, several weeks before, when the meat on one end had shrunk away from its fat (which had been immobilized by the cold and could not keep close to the contracting meat), an airspace had opened up, penetrating four inches into the meat and, it now appeared, bringing a brownish discoloration and an unpleasant, fermented odor to one end of two of the steaks. I discarded them.

Now my four remaining USDA Prime, eight-week-dry-aged, boneless rib-eye steaks were another 30 percent more expensive than a few minutes ago. But no matter. I grilled them over a deep and generous fire, let them rest on a rack for about ten minutes, and sliced them up. They were close to ideal—nicely crusted on the outside with no tough and dry stripes of gray beneath the crust, just a beautiful, juicy, smooth core of deep and vivid red—what you might call . . . rare with a very warm center. The texture was tender without the slightest hint of mushiness; the meat offered resistance at first and then happily yielded. And the flavor was complete: There were the meaty tastes of minerals, iron, and blood; there were the rounded beefy tastes of butter, nuts, and broth; there was the savor of dry-aging, especially around the periphery, not yet fermented but very sophisticated; and there were the crisp, browned, toasty, mouthwatering flavors of the crust.

My steaks were unreasonably costly and for two months had completely immobilized my refrigerator. But there was a moment last night at the dining-room table when nothing in the world could possibly have mattered but the taste, texture, and juice of my handmade steak.

Once I had had my fill of *spinalis dorsi* and the nearby musculature, while the deep crimson juices still trickled down my chin and onto the front of my shirt, I brought my magnifying glass close to the oozing red cut edge of the meat, squinted, and refocused my eyes on the narrow columns and bundles of muscle running vertically through the steak, and the horizontal stripes running across the meat at each level of doneness, from the deeply browned and crusted surface at the top, through the narrow, dry gray-brown stripe just beneath, and then layers of gray-pink, dusty rose, scarlet, and finally, across the very middle, a purplish crimson. I had sucessfully aimed for the nameless zone between rare and medium-rare, but the truth is that even a perfectly grilled steak is composed of layers at every degree of doneness. And so each slab of beef becomes an edible laboratory for exploring the most crucial of questions: How much of each color do you want, and how can you attain them?

There are those who view the world in an easygoing manner, thinking that some people prefer their steak rare, and others well done, and that it's simply a matter of taste. But it is not a matter of taste. Harsh and fascistic as it may sound, there is in truth only one perfect degree of doneness. All others are error, at least in those who, like us, agree that steak should be tasty, tender, and juicy.

Consider the purplish crimson stripe in the very center. This part of the meat is raised to a temperature of only 90°F by the time it comes off the grill; it is in essence raw—without much flavor and without any juice. Some diners may prefer their entire steak to taste and feel like beef sashimi, perhaps seared on the outside. Cooking does not really start until meat is heated beyond 100°F; before this point, meat will be gel-like and hard to chew. Little of the marbling fat will have melted, and the bland proteins will not have broken down into beefy-tasting free amino acids. This is called *"bleu"* by the French or very rare by us.

Starting at 100°F, the protein molecules start to uncoil and bond with one another, and the connective tissue shrinks. Now both the moisture trapped among the protein molecules in the muscle fibers and the liquefied fat begin to emerge. By about 120 degrees, the water and fat are flowing freely as delicious juice. So the deepest interior of a thick, mouthwatering steak must be brought to 105 degrees on the grill; it will rise to a juicy 120 degrees after it has rested awhile, as the juices disperse more evenly and the temperatures even out a bit. This is perfection: The meat is no longer jellylike but has taken on only the first signs of grain and has been brought to that narrowest of ranges where the juices have started to flow, the marbling fat is melting, and the protein is breaking down into its incredibly flavorful constituent amino acids, but before the bundles of muscle fibers tighten.

Over 130°F, the proteins coagulate to the point of toughness, as the vertical grain of the meat becomes first distinct and then tight, and more of the moisture between protein molecules is squeezed out, either to evaporate from the surface of the steak or to drip into the fire. This is what is usually meant by medium-rare, and while the meat is still pretty good to eat, it has just passed perfection.

It follows that the outer stripes of light pink, gray-pink, gray-tan, and tan-brown have no gastronomic attraction compared with the deep red and lighter rose layers of meat, and many disadvantages—until we get to the well-done outer crust, which is the most flavorful and deeply savory part of a steak, the lucky product of concentrated meat juices, decomposed fats, free amino acids, sugars, and the famous Maillard reactions, chemical processes that make well-browned meats among the most indelible tastes in all of cooking. So an ideal grilled steak should consist mainly of two colors: the savory and mouthwatering, crisp, deeply reddish-brown surface, and the just-opaque, juicy, red or rosy inner meat on which the heat of the grill has begun its transformation. All other layers should be minimized.

This can be best achieved with a nice thick steak, two to three inches, and, for most cooks, an instant meat thermometer. While a good crust requires quick high heat, a tender interior comes from slower cooking, which is difficult to accomplish entirely on the grill. But as Miss Essie's gigantic porterhouse proved to me, it is far from impossible, and I'll describe in detail just below how she does it. The method I have used for years—grilling, cooking in the oven, and grilling again—is also guaranteed to achieve a sort of greatness.

Harold McGee (On Food and Cooking, The Curious Cook) and two colleagues have devised a mathematical model of the grilling or griddling of meat. One of their conclusions is that to cut down on those undesirable pink to gray layers, you should see that the initial temperature of the meat is as high as practical—probably room temperature or just above—that you should flip the meat often, even very often, and that the cooking temperature should be relatively low. Searing the meat to produce a tasty crust would be done before or afterward at a high temperature.

I have not tested these three findings, which will require many thick steaks and truckloads of charcoal. But I will, believe me. In any event, all three are consistent with the second and third recipes below, except for the flipping part, which, I am sure, can be seamlessly integrated. All three are challenged by Miss Essie's method, which starts with cold meat, prohibits flipping, and uses essentially one grilling temperature to cook the inside and produce a good crust simultaneously.

BERN'S STEAK-HOUSE STEAK

(Adapted from Miss Essie)

Scrape and scrub your charcoal grill. Light a deep and very generous fire of lump charcoal using much more fuel at one end than at the other. As the grill heats up, grease it with steak fat. Choose a fine, 3-inch-thick steak, maybe a porterhouse, USDA Prime grade dry-aged as near to eight weeks as you can find it. Remove all separable fat—to prevent flareups. Brush it on both sides with room-temperature butter mixed with a little black pepper. Wait until the calmest part of the fire has piped down to moderate. (Place your palm over the coals at the exact height of the grill on which the steak will sit; you should be able to hold it nearly 4 seconds, or a millisecond less. At this temperature, the inside and surface of a 3-inch steak with lots of marbling (fat is an insulator) should reach perfection at the same moment.

Put the steak, still pretty cold from the fridge, over the area of the fire you have tested. Move it around when flareups occur; these would simply burn the surface instead of crusting it. If you are grilling a porterhouse, remember that the filet mignon side needs less cooking than the strip-steak side; so be sure to keep the filet more toward the cooler part of the fire, or at its edge. When you turn over the steak in 7 or 8 minutes, it should have a beautiful crust on the underside. Again brush both sides with peppered butter and place the steak over whatever section of the charcoal is now at the proper temperature. After 5 more minutes, lift the steak with tongs and take its internal temperature with an instant-read meat thermometer, *which you should insert through the side of the steak into the center of the largest muscle.* Throw out all existing temperature charts. When the thermometer reads 105 to 110°F, remove the steak and let it rest on a rack over a plate for ten minutes. Its internal

- - - - -

temperature should have reached 120°F. When you slice it, the steak should be precisely . . . rare with a very warm center. Miss Essie does not need a meat thermometer.

GRILLED RIB STEAK
The Long Way

Have your butcher cut one or more USDA Prime rib steaks, with the bone attached, from the center of the rib section (say, ribs 8, 9, or 10, counting from the front). The meat should have been dry-aged for at least 6 weeks and as many as 8, or even more. The steak(s) should be 2¼ inches thick all around and weigh about 2 pounds each.

Three hours before you plan to grill the steaks, trim most of the external fat and scrape both meaty surfaces with the edge of a knife. Rub a generous teaspoon of salt into every surface of each steak. Then wrap the steaks in waxed paper or glazed butcher's paper and let them come to room temperature on a rack.

About ½ hour before grilling time, preheat your oven to 300°F. Make a fire in your grill, using enough fuel so that the fire will remain very hot for about 20 minutes. When the fire is ready, set the spotlessly clean, oiled rack 3 to 5 inches from the source of heat and leave it for about 5 minutes. Then grill the steak on one side for about 3 minutes, until the underside is dark brown but not blackened, except perhaps on the large chunks of fat. Dry the upper side with a paper towel, turn, and

- - - - -

grill for about 2 minutes. Insert an instant-read meat thermometer midway into the edge of the steak and slide it into
the center of the largest muscle. The temperature should read
about 85°F to 90°F. Remove the thermometer.

Set the steak on a rack over a skillet or baking pan and into
the oven for 5 to 8 minutes. The meat's internal temperature
should read about 100°F when it comes out of the oven. Let it
rest on its rack for up to 15 minutes, if this is convenient, or finish cooking immediately.

Now return the steaks to the grill and cook for about a
minute and a half on each side, wiping dry the side to be
grilled with a paper towel before grilling it, and sprinkling
each side amply with salt and freshly ground black pepper
when it's finished. The internal temperature at the heart of the
largest muscle should be about 110°F.

Let the steak rest for 5 to 10 minutes before serving. The
internal temperature will rise to 120°F as the juices circulate,
even into the dried-out proteins just beneath the steak's surface, which will grow less tight and can now reabsorb them.

NOTE ON FUEL

Wood burns too hot for most home grills, but a brick fireplace, indoors or out, with an adjustable rack and a fire of oak plus a little hickory or mesquite, is capable of wonderful things. Just burn a large quantity of wood (say, 6 fat logs) down to coals, then add a few smaller pieces for perfumed smoke and a searing flame right before grilling. Wood burns very quickly. The solution is to start a second wood fire right next to the first.

Charcoal is second best. Hardwood lump charcoal is much better than briquettes. Let the charcoal burn for about a ½ hour until it is covered with white ash. Then, right before grilling, sprinkle amply with wood chips that have been soaked for ½ hour in water. The meat will take on a nice wood flavor.

Most gas grills are simply not hot enough to do the job well. If you do use a gas grill, you can introduce a bit of woodsy aroma by wrapping some wood chips or sawdust in a square of aluminum foil, piercing a few holes in the foil, and placing the packet on the hot lava rocks.

GRILLED RIB STEAK
The Shorter Way

The twice-grilled recipe just above answers the vexed question, "Should we sear the steak at the beginning or at the end?" with the reply, "Both." Done carefully, I believe it creates the most savory crust without burning the meat. Done with the slightest negligence, you will end up with a way overdone steak, a ruined meal, and a reputation in tatters. An easier alternative is to skip the final grilling. Achieve a good crust in the first grilling; the meat should measure about 95°F. Put it in the oven, until the temperature rises to about 110°F. Let the steak rest outside the oven, on the rack, for ten minutes as the juices reposition themselves and the internal temperature rises to 120°F or a little higher.

A PERFECTLY FINE UNGRILLED STEAK

I do all my grilling in California, where I have an embarrassment of grills. The last time I lit up a charcoal grill on my fire escape in Manhattan, the fire department arrived, with a shiny red ladder truck, a pumper truck, and a red officer's car. They always come in battalion strength in Manhattan, because we live so close to one another here. The firemen were very large, and they came up the back stairs in full uniform, carrying oxygen tanks and huge axes, looking for a fire or a fight.

- - - - -

The next time, instead of grilling, I used a method I had learned in France: Remove the 2½- to 3-inch steak(s) from the refrigerator, cut off most of the external fat, rub it with a little olive oil and then with ample salt and pepper, and bring to room temperature for 2 hours or more. In a cast-iron pan or large heavy-bottomed sauté pan, heat 6 tablespoons of butter (¾ stick, most of which remains in the pan) over medium-high heat, add the steak and, moving it from time to time, sauté until a firm, dark brown crust forms on the bottom, about 7 minutes; turn and repeat on the other side, spooning some of the cooking butter over the steak from time to time. Keep the heat high enough so that the butter sizzles nicely; it should brown but not blacken. After 5 minutes, start taking the meat's temperature. If the steak is thick enough, you should follow the temperatures in the recipe above and finish the steak in a preheated 325°F oven. Thus, with little effort, you can achieve a beautifully crisp, reddish-brown, and extremely savory crust and a perfectly rare-to-medium-rare interior.

AUGUST 1997 AND SEPTEMBER 2001

Author's notes: Tasting steak: For the first steak tasting we conducted, Tom Colicchio, the celebrated chef at Gramercy Tavern and at Craft, and I visited his beef supplier, J. T. Jobbagy Inc., on Washington Street in the old meat market, and asked him to age several of Craft's rib steaks for 33 days (standard), 47 days, and 65 days. In the end, most of us would have preferred dry-aging somewhere in the middle. In order to taste the beef itself, we experimentally eliminated the butter with which Tom and many other chefs, including those at Peter Luger and Bern's, flavor their steaks just before serving; and we cut off the crust.

We saw immediately that a good crust and a bath of butter can overwhelm the taste buds with immediate and shallow pleasure—and hide a host of inadequacies in the meat itself.

Buying steak: If your own butcher or favorite steak house can't supply well-aged USDA Prime beef, you might consider ordering your steaks through the mail. Both Lobel's and Peter Luger Steakhouse have gone into the mail-order steak business, selling unfrozen USDA Prime dry-aged beef from their Web sites (www.lobels.com and www.peterluger.com). Though not perfect, they both blew away Omaha Steaks and Livingston Meats, and are my baseline for judging other brands. Both charge prices that make you wish you were a vegetarian. Niman Ranch's nearly organic beef is also excellent. They concentrate on what they feed and how they handle their cattle; their steaks are regularly cut too thin for me; but once I ordered the entire shell and sliced it into six three-inch steaks myself.

An act of mercy: When parts of this chapter first appeared in *Vogue,* Raymond Sokolov of the *Wall Street Journal* read of my longing for *spinalis dorsi,* with mounting pity. He offered to fund a complete *spinalis* dinner. We met at Lobel's, bought an entire well-aged rib section, all seven ribs, and asked them to remove the *spinalis dorsi* in one piece and cut the rest into steaks for another day. The *spinalis* measured about seven by 11 inches and as thick as 1½ inches in the center.

At Sokolov's place in Greenwich Village, we built a huge wood fire on a very warm evening, let it burn down to coals, and simply grilled the *spinalis.* So maybe it was thirty seconds overdone. Mistakes are made. Nonetheless, the great succulence of the meat and the generosity of the *Journal* will not be soon forgotten in the annals of steak.

STANDARDS AND PRACTICES

How many trees have died in vain, how many pots of ink have been spilled to no purpose, how many heaps of wheat might have been spared," I grumbled as our hired car crawled its way through lower Manhattan. We circled round and round the narrow one-way streets, trying to reach a short stretch of Duane Street that I am now convinced is logically inaccessible. At last, we abandoned the car and proceeded on foot. Our purpose was to buy another tart. It would be our eighth. Although we had not yet tasted our trophies in the tranquility of my kitchen, they appeared unlikely to taste as good as the tart I had baked the night before from a widely published recipe. And that should be a crime.

Twice before, I had had the same dazzling flash of insight as today. On the first occasion, it was chocolate-chip cookies. I have tried hundreds of variations, both store-bought and homemade. For me, there is no mood so foul or dark that cannot be brightened by a major chocolate-chip cookie or two. The problem is that most of them are barely more than edible. And yet the dilemma is so easily solved that it hardly deserves the name of dilemma. All you need do is go to the supermarket, wheel your cart to the Nestlé Toll House Semi-Sweet Morsels aisle, grab hold of a happy yellow bag of Nestlé Toll House Semi-Sweet Morsels, and let the recipe printed on the back—nearly unchanged for the past 68 years—guide the rest of your shopping and baking experience. *Et voilà*—a perfectly nice chocolate-chip cookie, especially if you go light on the flour. Then how is it possible for anybody to bake an inferior specimen? That's my point.

But even perfectly nice is not enough. As of this writing and according to my own taste, the finest chocolate-chip cookies are made by two companies, Kathleen's and Tate's. They are both thinner, crisper, lighter, less cakelike, and more delicious than the original Toll House version. Neither company has published its true recipe. Through a remarkable feat of reverse engineering I have come pretty close.

BEST SO FAR CHOCOLATE-CHIP COOKIES

2 cups all-purpose flour

1 tsp. salt

1 tsp. baking soda

½ lb. unsalted butter (two sticks, 1 cup)

¾ cup light brown sugar, firmly packed

¼ cup dark brown sugar, firmly packed

¾ cup granulated white sugar

1 tsp. vanilla extract

2 Tbs. water

1 egg

9 oz. (¾ package or 1½ cup)
Nestlé's Toll House Semi-Sweet Morsels

Preheat the oven to 375°F. In a bowl, combine the flour, salt, and baking soda. In a mixer, cream the butter and stir in the three types of sugar. Add the vanilla extract, water, and egg, and beat together. Beat in the flour mixture. Stir in the chocolate morsels. Drop onto nonstick baking sheets by rounded teaspoons. Bake for about 10 minutes. Remove to a rack to cool.

Now, I am not saying that an even better chocolate-chip cookie cannot be created. Indeed, given my belief in the perfectability of man (generically speaking), I am sure one will soon emerge. But for now, nobody, especially no professional baker, has the slightest excuse for making a chocolate-chip cookie substantially inferior to this Best So Far version, and anybody who does should be judged harshly.

(Uh-oh! I have just noticed that Nestlé uses vanillin in its morsels—the disagreeable, chemically synthesized vanilla substitute; with every year that passes, vanillin tastes more repulsive to me. Nobody prefers it to real vanilla. The only reason for using it is that it's cheaper. How much does Nestlé save? Probably less than a penny on each 12-ounce bag. Henceforth, I will personally cut up a better sort of dark chocolate.)

"And the same goes for *tuiles*," I groused as, still on Duane Street, we trudged back to the car with our purchased tart. Its flabby pastry was filled with a lemon curd that had a rubbery, unnatural-looking glaze on top. We headed north to West 14th Street, where, among the remains of New York's once-proud wholesale meat market, a fancy bakery has found its place amidst the refrigerator trucks and bloody carcasses. Soon tart number nine was safely nestled next to us in the backseat, and we could head back to my home office–test kitchen.

Tuiles, of course, are those large, round, curved, wafer-thin cookies often served with coffee at French and modern American restaurants. I have eaten them in every corner, every hill and dale, every nook and cranny of the United States and France. The best are lacy, low in flour, and full of a wonderful toasted-almond flavor. The worst are nearly tasteless, crumbly, dry, and starchy. A banal *tuile* can ruin the meal that preceded it.

My favorites are served at Alain Ducasse's Louis XV restaurant in Monaco, and once I had tasted them, I could not get their combination of orange zest and caramelized almonds out of my head. Of the thousands of *tuiles* I had sampled before and since, none have made me so glad to be an active eater, though some versions with almonds alone have come close. My urgent attempts to duplicate them at home through guesswork were humiliating failures.

Then Ducasse published his first cookbook, *La Riviera d'Alain Ducasse* (Albin Michel, 1992), and there they were again, the perfect *tuiles*. As of that very moment, nobody in the world had any excuse for baking awful *tuiles*. Now, you may not go quite as crazy over the combination of orange zest, almonds, and caramelized sugar as I do, and that, I suppose, is your privilege. So you may want to fiddle here and there with the ingredients. But here's the point again: Alain Ducasse's transcendent *tuiles*— the most perfect *tuiles* so far—are now a minimum standard, a floor below which a baker may sink only at his or her peril.

THE MOST PERFECT *TUILES* SO FAR
(Adapted from *La Riviera d'Alain Ducasse*)

1 orange

1 cup (scant) superfine sugar

9 Tbs. melted unsalted butter, cooled to room temperature

1½ cups almonds, without skins, finely chopped

⅓ cup all-purpose flour

¼ cup Grand Marnier

1 tsp. pure vanilla extract

Wash the orange in hot water to remove pesticides and wax, and dry it. Zest the surface of the orange on the fine holes of a grater; be careful to remove only the orange-colored outer layer of the skin and none of the bitter white. Set the zest aside. Cut the orange in half and juice it. You will need just under ½ cup of orange juice. In a medium-sized bowl, stir thoroughly together the sugar and the melted butter, then stir in, in this order, the grated zest, the almonds,

- - - - -

the flour, the orange juice, the Grand Marnier, and the vanilla extract.

Refrigerate the batter for at least an hour as you preheat your oven to 350°F. Drop the batter by tablespoonsful onto a nonstick cookie sheet (or ovenproof nonstick frying pan, for that matter), spacing them three inches apart. With the back of a spoon, press the little mounds into disks about 3 inches across. Bake for 5 to 6 minutes, or until the *tuiles* are dark golden and lacy. Let them cool and firm up for 30 seconds, then loosen them with a thin, flexible knife held almost flat to the cookie sheet. This part takes a bit of practice and timing. Press the *tuiles* over a narrow rolling pin or a wine bottle and leave for 30 seconds or until they hold their shape. Remove and let cool entirely.

Note: In a delicious alternative suggested by Ducasse, you can begin an hour or two in advance by removing the zest from another orange in wide strips with a vegetable peeler, simmering it in equal parts of sugar and water until nearly translucent, about an hour, and cutting them crosswise into the thinnest strips. Add these to the batter along with the grated zest.

Tarts are more complex than *tuiles* and cookies and come with an endless variety of fillings, but the principle is just the same. In 1990, a new shop opened up a block from my home office–test kitchen, and it is called the City Bakery. As it stands directly on my way to the Union Square Greenmarket, sampling the perfect little four-inch tarts and the hot chocolate at City Bakery became a biweekly activity, an amusing little quarter-hour restorative after the rustic rigors of vegetable shopping were over but lunch was still two hours away. From the start, these tarts and hot chocolate were among the best in town, and over the years they have only gotten better.

The word *tart* can mean many things. As a culinary term, it once included all kinds of dishes in which a savory or sweet pastry crust enclosed anything from meat and fish to cheese and fruit. Today we use *pie* for filled pastries with a top crust and *tart* for open, usually round, disks of pastry having low sides and filled with fruit or sweet custard or cream. When applied to a girl or woman, its original sense was one of endearment, a term that a guy might affectionately apply to his own sister, daughter, or girlfriend. Only later did *tart* come to mean a prostitute or catamite. A *torte* is an elaborate sweet cake.

The tart pastry at City Bakery is crisp and sweet and so tender that it disappears in your mouth as your teeth close down on it— leaving only the flavor of browned butter, like the delicious golden edges of the best butter cookies you have ever eaten. The pastry is rolled a good eighth-inch thick, pressed into a metal hoop called a flan ring, and filled either before or after baking with dark chocolate custard, or sliced fruit in a toasted almond cream, or a sweetly acidic lemon custard, or a crackling crème brûlée. The possibilities are limitless: every kind of fruit filling, the entire universe of custards and flans, even something as simple as whipped cream sweetened and scented and topped with ripe berries, like a shortcake.

How many times have you watched somebody (including yourself) scraping off the filling from a tart and leaving the pastry? Nobody has ever done that in the entire history of City Bakery, at least when I've been there. The pastry recipe was created by Maury Rubin, who owns and runs the place. His ingredients follow the general lines of French *sablée* dough—*sablée* means "sandy"—though the method Maury uses for mixing the dough is more typical of the standard French tart pastry—*pâte brisée* or *pâte sucrée,* which is less sweet, less cookielike, less crumbly, and much less good to eat.

Maury Rubin grew up in the seventies in Baltimore as a sports fanatic, and a few years out of college became a television producer in the ABC sports department in New York City, winning two Emmys for segments on social issues for Howard Cosell's *Sportsbeat* program. After the show ended and Cosell retired from television, Maury traveled to France for the first time, enrolled in a pastry school an hour from Lyons, then underwent a series of apprenticeships in Paris patisseries, spending the longest time at a well-regarded neighborhood place, Pâtisserie Rousseau-Seurre. His grandfather had been a Jewish bread baker in Baltimore, and when Maury returned to New York, he thought it would be perfectly fitting to establish his own pastry shop. After weeks of grazing around Manhattan, he was not at all happy with the state of pastry here and thought he could do better. Which in most departments he did.

Maury says that his tart dough is nothing more than the *pâte sucrée* from Rousseau-Seurre with a little cream added, but anybody familiar with standard French recipes for *pâte sucrée* and with Maury's own pastry formula would know that this is an unusual example of extreme modesty on his part. Just kidding. Maury published his recipe in a beautiful little volume called *Book of Tarts* (Morrow, 1995). He designed the book himself and won a James Beard award for its design. As you can see in the book, Maury's minimalist dots and lines have advanced the modern art of pastry decoration. At City Bakery, Maury insists on organic flour and fruits only when they are in season at the Greenmarket.

And the moment his book was published, nobody in America had any excuse for baking a tart with pastry any less terrific than Maury's. Now, unlike me, you may prefer a dough that is less buttery and less sweet than City Bakery's. It is a free country, and you have every right to try and make better tart pastry. But you no longer have a right to make a worse one.

And thus it was that my assistant, Kathryn, and I spent the afternoon ranging about lower Manhattan in search of tarts. (Our hunt was simplified by Ed Levine's recently published *New York Eats (More)* [St. Martin's Press, 1997], a complete revision and update of his earlier *New York Eats*.) At last our car pulled up to the entrance of my home office, and while I, by division of labor, made certain that Levine's book had been rescued from the backseat, Kathryn carried our tottering tower of tart and cake boxes upstairs, groaning under the weight. We set about evaluating them in a loosely constructed double-blind test, with Kathryn unpacking and numbering the various candidates, and me coming in for the chewing part.

The results gratifyingly fulfilled my most terrible fears. One tart shell was hard as a rock. Another could barely be penetrated with household implements and had no taste. One was cakelike and mealy. Another was cakelike and spongy. Three were soggy and truly distasteful.

One admirable tart emerged: the delicious Fruit-Noisette Tart from the Balthazar Bakery (which tragically is not available in the restaurant itself). Its pastry was the equal of City Bakery's, and the inclusion of ground almonds—also a stated alternative when you follow Maury's recipe—made it rich and fragile and ecstatically delicious. I detect the hand of Paula Oland in this masterpiece, though Paula is known to be Balthazar's master bread baker, not its confectioner. Balthazar's other tarts are made with more ordinary dough and are unremarkable.

In a day or two, we will hire a car and sally forth to the pastry palaces of the ritzy Upper East Side of Manhattan. But if current trends continue, only one out of nine of them, or 11 percent, will offer tart pastry as good as City Bakery's. There is, as I trust I have demonstrated, no excuse for this.

As a public service, I have modified Maury Rubin's pastry recipe so that it is even easier and quicker to make—in a food processor. Maury's book contains a wonderful range of tart fillings, from lemon cream and chocolate custard to apricots on a simple bed of honeyed whipped cream, and a very approximate home version of City Bakery's plum tart with toasted almond cream. Here, I will give you a featherlight lemon soufflé filling from Paula Oland of Balthazar Bakery. The combination may be the best you have ever eaten. The only special equipment you need is four-inch, straight-sided flan rings (though you can successfully use four-and-a-half-inch, metal, fluted tart molds). The only tricky part is getting the pastry dough to line the rings in a beautifully neat manner.

If a baker, at home or in commerce, cannot make better pastry than Maury's, he or she should simply follow Maury's recipe or throw in the towel and find other work. As a leftover sixties liberal, I believe that the long arm and beady eyes of the government have no place in our bedrooms, our kitchens, or the backseats of our parked cars. But I also feel that the immediate appointment of a Special Pastry Prosecutor would do much more good than harm. We know the free market has totally failed when 89 percent of all the tart pastry, chocolate-chip cookies, and *tuiles* in America are far less delicious than they would be if bakers simply followed a few readily available recipes. What we need is a system of graduated fines and perhaps short jail sentences to discourage the production of totally depressing baked goods. Maybe a period of unpleasant and tedious community service could be substituted for jail time. Of course, the government would first have to post the ideal recipes and give everybody a week to learn them. Starting now.

THE GOLD STANDARD FOR TART PASTRY

13 Tbs. cold unsalted butter (1½ sticks plus 1 Tbs., or 6½ oz.),
cut into about a dozen slices
1 egg yolk from a large egg
⅓ cup confectioner's sugar, very firmly packed (¾ oz.)
1 Tbs. plus 1 tsp. heavy cream
1½ cups unbleached, all-purpose flour (8 oz.), measured
by the scoop-and-level method
Special equipment: 8 flan rings, 4 inches wide and ⅞ inches high,
available from Bridge Kitchenware (212-688-4220) and
Sur La Table (800-243-0852).

In a food processor, blend all the ingredients except the flour for about 30 seconds, until smooth, scraping down halfway through and at the end. Add the flour, and blend just until the dough forms a ball, about 5 seconds more. Scrape the dough out of the work bowl, pat and roll into a rough cylinder, cut crosswise into 6 approximately equal pieces, flatten the pieces into little hamburger shapes, wrap each in plastic, and refrigerate until firm, about 1 hour.

When you are ready to form the tarts, remove 1 patty from the refrigerator, roll it out on a lightly floured surface with a floured rolling pin to an even ⅛-inch thickness, or even a little thicker, about 6 inches across. Cut out a circle about 5½ inches across. Set 1 flan ring on your countertop. With a metal dough scraper or spatula or a large knife, lift the circle of dough and drape it over the flan ring.

Maury uses a 3-step procedure to fit the pastry tightly and evenly into the ring. First lift the edges of the pastry circle and coax the dough down into the ring without stretching it—the dough should remain an even ⅛-inch thick. Now, rotating the ring as you go, push straight down along the sides of the

— — — — —

ring so that the dough closely lines the bottom and sides. Finally, rotating the ring again, press forward with your thumbs against the dough on the inside bottom edge of the ring so that the pastry will form a sharp right angle when it is baked and unmolded. With the help of a spatula, lift the tart shell in its flan ring, turn it over, and check that the bottom is smooth and fits tightly against the ring all the way around.

Turn right side up and trim the edges of the pastry against the rim with a paring knife; the top edge should be square and ⅛-inch thick, not tapered. If the dough becomes soft and fragile, refrigerate it. Maury's pastry is extremely forgiving: You can easily mold and patch it with your fingers.

Continue with the other 5 flan rings. Gather the excess dough into 2 balls. Press each into a patty, refrigerate them, roll them out, and line the remaining 2 flan rings.

As each tart shell is formed, set it on 1 or more cookie sheets lined with parchment paper. Freeze for at least ½ hour before baking; you can leave the tart shells in their rings in the freezer for several months, closed tightly in plastic, and bake them directly from the freezer. Depending on their filling, each tart makes a lavish dessert for one or can be cut neatly in half and served with ice cream or sugared berries.

To bake, preheat your oven to 375°F. Bake the shells in their flan rings on cookie sheets lined with parchment paper for 15 to 18 minutes, or until they are a deep golden brown, rotating the baking sheet after 10 minutes. With a wide spatula, transfer the shells to a rack and remove the rings with tongs. The shells can be left for a day or two at room temperature.

For recipes in which the tart shells and filling will be baked together, prebake the shells for 12 minutes in their rings to prevent burning the outside of the tarts in the final baking.

Yield: 6 4-inch tart shells (or 2 9-inch shells)

LEMON SOUFFLÉ TARTS
(Adapted from Paula Oland, Balthazar Bakery)

6 eggs

1 cup (scant) sugar

3 Tbs. cake flour or all-purpose flour

2 Tbs. heavy cream

1 cup lemon juice

Grated zest of 4 to 6 lemons, according to taste

¼ tsp. baking soda

¼ cup superfine sugar

6 to 8 4-inch tart shells, fully but lightly baked

Confectioner's sugar

Separate the eggs, placing all 6 yolks in one bowl and 3 whites in another; reserve or discard the remaining 3 whites. In the metal bowl of a mixer, beat the yolks at medium-high speed, gradually adding the sugar and continuing to beat the mixture until it becomes light yellow and thick. Beat in the flour, lower the speed to medium, and gradually beat in the cream, the lemon juice, and the zest.

Place the mixer bowl directly over medium heat on the stovetop. Using a rubber spatula, continuously stir the mixture. As it becomes hot and then steamy, stir more vigorously, scraping the bottom of the bowl several times a minute. The filling will thicken fairly suddenly (at about 180°F on a thermometer) and then begin to bubble. Remove from the heat, stir in the baking soda, and watch the mixture foam. Stir and let cool to room temperature. Use immediately or refrigerate, covered, for up to two days in a nonmetallic bowl.

In a mixer or by hand, whisk the 3 egg whites at high speed until foamy, sprinkle with the superfine sugar, and continue whisking until soft peaks form. Stir about ¼ of the egg whites into the lemon-yolk mixture to lighten it, then gently fold in the remaining egg whites. Fill each of 6 to 8 fully prebaked tart shells with ½ cup of the mixture and bake at 350°F for 18 to 20 minutes until set but still slightly wobbly and lightly colored on the surface. As they cool, the lemon soufflé tarts will deflate. Dust with a little confectioner's sugar sprinkled through a sieve and decorate, if you like, with a strip of candied lemon rind or a few berries. Serve at room temperature.

Yield: 4 individual tarts.

APRIL 1998

Index

Note: Page numbers for recipes are in **bold** type.